God's Church-Community

T&T Clark Studies in Systematic Theology

Edited by
Ivor Davidson
Ian McFarland
Philip G. Ziegler
John Webster†

Volume 36

God's Church-Community

The Ecclesiology of Dietrich Bonhoeffer

David Emerton

LONDON • NEW YORK • OXFORD • NEW DELHI • SYDNEY

T&T CLARK
Bloomsbury Publishing Plc
50 Bedford Square, London, WC1B 3DP, UK
1385 Broadway, New York, NY 10018, USA
29 Earlsfort Terrace, Dublin 2, Ireland

BLOOMSBURY, T&T CLARK and the T&T Clark logo are trademarks of
Bloomsbury Publishing Plc

First published in Great Britain 2020
This paperback edition published in 2022

Copyright © David Emerton, 2020

David Emerton has asserted his right under the Copyright, Designs and Patents Act, 1988, to be identified as Author of this work.

For legal purposes the Acknowledgements on p. ix–x constitute an extension of this copyright page.

All rights reserved. No part of this publication may be reproduced or transmitted in any form or by any means, electronic or mechanical, including photocopying, recording, or any information storage or retrieval system, without prior permission in writing from the publishers.

Bloomsbury Publishing Plc does not have any control over, or responsibility for, any third-party websites referred to or in this book. All internet addresses given in this book were correct at the time of going to press. The author and publisher regret any inconvenience caused if addresses have changed or sites have ceased to exist, but can accept no responsibility for any such changes.

A catalogue record for this book is available from the British Library.

Library of Congress Control Number: 2020932390

ISBN: HB: 978-0-5676-9313-6
PB: 978-0-5676-9773-8
ePDF: 978-0-5676-9314-3
eBook: 978-0-5676-9316-7

Series: T&T Clark Studies in Systematic Theology, volume 36

Typeset by Deanta Global Publishing Services, Chennai, India

To find out more about our authors and books visit www.bloomsbury.com and sign up for our newsletters.

*For my girls
present and absent*

Contents

Acknowledgements	ix
List of abbreviations	xi
Introduction	1
1 Ecclesiological topography	13
I. Introduction	13
II. The problematic articulated	13
III. The problematic explicated	16
i. 'Hard' dogmatic ecclesiology	17
ii. 'Hard' ethnographic ecclesiology	29
iii. 'Soft' ethnographic ecclesiology	37
iv. 'Soft' dogmatic ecclesiology	45
IV. Conclusion	52
2 The theological foundations of Bonhoeffer's ecclesiological methodology	53
I. Introduction	53
II. Theological foundations: Eschatology	55
III. Theological foundations: Pneumatology	63
IV. Theological foundations: Theology *against* sociology?	68
V. Conclusion	72
3 God's church-community: Bonhoeffer's 'both/and' ecclesiological methodology	75
I. Introduction	75
II. Socio-historical *human* community: A threefold typology	77
i. *Gemeinschaft, Gesellschaft* and *Herrschaftsverband*	78
a. Bonhoeffer's theological ontology of human personhood	83
III. *God's* church-community: A sociological structure sui generis	95
i. The eschatological tension of God's church-community	96
ii. The pneumatological actualization of God's church-community	100
IV. Conclusion	109
4 The pneumatological space of God's church-community	113
I. Introduction	113
II. Pentecost: The event of the foundation of God's church-community	115

	III. God's church-community: Confessional aspects	127
	i. The 'space' of proclamation	128
	ii. The 'space' of spiritual care	133
	IV. Conclusion	137
5	The eschatological time of God's church-community	139
	I. Introduction	139
	II. The last things and things before the last	142
	i. The way of radicalism or compromise?	144
	ii. The patience of God: A motif for eschatological time	148
	III. Preparing the way: Ecclesiological implications	155
	IV. Conclusion	162
Conclusion		165
Bibliography		171
Index		181

Acknowledgements

Although born of many solitudinous hours reading and writing, a book only comes kicking and screaming into life with the help of many other people, and so it is right to acknowledge my gratitude to them.

To this end, I would like to thank: Professor Tom Greggs, for his constant encouragement and support, ever-critical and constructive feedback and humble willingness 'to become a Christ' to me during my PhD at the University of Aberdeen, upon which this book is based; Professor Paul Janz, for nurturing my nascent interest in the life and work of Dietrich Bonhoeffer at Kings College London; and the Right Revd Dr Graham Tomlin, Dr Jane Williams and Dr Chris Tilling for helping me take my first theological steps at St Mellitus College, London.

I am deeply grateful for the financial support I received from St Luke's College Foundation, The Foundation of St Matthias and The College of Arts and Social Sciences at the University of Aberdeen, which helped fund my doctoral research. My deepest gratitude in this regard, however, is reserved for the people of St Stephen's Church, Twickenham, who not only sent me and my family out and up to Aberdeen covered in prayer but with extraordinary financial provision: I will be forever humbled by such selfless support that enabled me to follow-after God's call. Without the generosity of St Stephen's my doctoral research and thus this book would not have been possible.

For personal support a number of other people must be thanked: Jerry Booker, for his empathetic listening and gentle and prayerful support during a difficult transition from one context to another; Byron and Elaine McKibben, for being true pastors; and Kenny Primrose, for his willingness to become a confidant, encourager and constant source of edifying conversation about faith, theology and the world, not least during dreich Aberdonian evenings spent sampling the finer offerings of French vineyards.

My greatest thanks, however, must go to my family. My dad's support has never been anything but loving and generous, and his being is to me a gracious reminder that in the kingdom of God death and life are inextricably, painfully and gloriously interconnected. My parents-in-law, Roland and Jacqui, suffered their eldest daughter moving back home sixteen years after she first left, yet now with a husband, daughter and an imminent new daughter in tow: for allowing us to live out in their home three months of Emerton family life en route to Aberdeen (and for many hours of childcare since), I owe much. My daughters – Lois and Sophie-Joan – have enabled me to know evermore deeply God's overabounding love and have without doubt proven their credentials as adequate (and much needed) distractions from the intricacies of theological thinking. Lastly, but most importantly, my wife, Naomi, in ways which undoubtedly have tested our marriage vows, has been ever-steadfast and patient in her love and support of me, not least in her bearing and keeping me during many years of study and the period of writing this book. Of the many blessings God has graciously bestowed upon me, Naomi is the most precious and beloved, and my thanks to her can only ever be inadequate.

Part of n.89 in Chapter 2 appeared in David Emerton, Review of Michael Mawson, *Christ Existing as Community: Bonhoeffer's Ecclesiology* (Oxford: Oxford University Press, 2018). *Ecclesiology* 15 (2019): 233–6. © Koninklijke Brill NV, Leiden, 2019. DOI:10.1163/17455316-01502008. Reprinted by permission of BRILL.

Scripture quotations are from New Revised Standard Version Bible, copyright © 1989 National Council of the Churches of Christ in the United States of America. Used by permission. All rights reserved worldwide.

Abbreviations

DBW 1   *Sanctorum Communio: Eine dogmatische Untersuchung zur Soziologie der Kirche.* In *Dietrich Bonhoeffer Werke.* Edited by Joachim von Soosten. München: Chr. Kaiser Verlag, 1986.

DBW 2   *Akt und Sein: Transzendentalphilosophie und Ontologie in der systematischen Theologie.* In *Dietrich Bonhoeffer Werke.* Edited by Hans-Richard Reuter. München: Chr. Kaiser Verlag, 1988.

DBW 3   *Schöpfung und Fall: Theologische Auslegung von Genesis 1-3.* In *Dietrich Bonhoeffer Werke.* Edited by Martin Rüter and Ilse Tödt. München: Chr. Kaiser Verlag, 1989.

DBW 4   *Nachfolge.* In *Dietrich Bonhoeffer Werke.* Edited by Martin Kuske and Ilse Tödt. München: Chr. Kaiser Verlag, 1989.

DBW 5   *Gemeinsames Leben Das Gebetbuch der Bibel.* In *Dietrich Bonhoeffer Werke.* Edited by Gerhard Ludwig Müller and Albrecht Schönherr. München: Chr. Kaiser Verlag, 1987.

DBW 6   *Ethik.* In *Dietrich Bonhoeffer Werke.* Edited by Ilse Tödt, Heinz Eduard Tödt, Ernst Feil and Clifford Green. München: Chr. Kaiser Verlag, 1992.

DBW 8   *Widerstand und Ergebung: Briefe und Aufzeichnungen aus der Haft.* In *Dietrich Bonhoeffer Werke.* Edited by Christian Gremmels, Eberhard Bethge and Renate Bethge. München: Chr. Kaiser Verlag, 1998.

DBW 9   *Jugend und Studium: 1918-1927.* In *Dietrich Bonhoeffer Werke.* Edited by Hans Pfeifer. München: Chr. Kaiser Verlag, 1986.

DBW 10 *Barcelona, Berlin, Amerika: 1928-1931.* In *Dietrich Bonhoeffer Werke.* Edited by Reinhart Staats and Hans Christoph von Hase. München: Chr. Kaiser Verlag, 1992.

DBW 11 *Ökumene, Universität, Pfarramt: 1931-1932.* In *Dietrich Bonhoeffer Werke.* Edited by Eberhard Amelung and Christoph Strohm. München: Chr. Kaiser Verlag, 1994.

DBW 12 *Berlin: 1932-1933.* In *Dietrich Bonhoeffer Werke.* Edited by Carsten Nicolaisen and Ernst-Albert Scharffenorth. München: Chr. Kaiser Verlag, 1997.

DBW 14 *Illegale Theologen-Ausbildung: Finkenwalde 1935-1937.* In *Dietrich Bonhoeffer Werke.* Edited by Otto Dudzus and Jürgen Henkys. München: Chr. Kaiser Verlag, 1996.

DBW 15   *Illegale Theologen-Ausbildung: Sammelvikariate 1937-1940*. In *Dietrich Bonhoeffer Werke*. Edited by Dirk Schulz. München: Chr. Kaiser Verlag, 1998.

DBW 16   *Konspiration und Haft 1940-1945*. In *Dietrich Bonhoeffer Werke*. Edited by Jørgen Glenthøj, Ulrich Kabitz and Wolf Krötke. München: Chr. Kaiser Verlag, 1996.

DBWE 1   *Sanctorum Communio: Theological Study of the Sociology of the Church*. In *Dietrich Bonhoeffer Works*. Edited by Clifford J. Green, trans. Reinhard Krauss and Nancy Lukens. Minneapolis: Fortress Press, 1998.

DBWE 2   *Act and Being: Transcendental Philosophy and Ontology in Systematic Theology*. In *Dietrich Bonhoeffer Works*. Edited by Wayne Whitson Floyd Jr., trans. H. Martin Rumscheidt. Minneapolis: Fortress Press, 1996.

DBWE 3   *Creation and Fall: A Theological Exposition of Genesis 1-3*. In *Dietrich Bonhoeffer Works*. Edited by John W. de Gruchy, trans. Douglas Stephen Bax. Minneapolis: Fortress Press, 2004.

DBWE 4   *Discipleship*. In *Dietrich Bonhoeffer Works*. Edited by Geffrey B. Kelly and John D. Godsey, trans. Barbara Green and Reinhard Krauss. Minneapolis: Fortress Press, 2001.

DBWE 5   *Life Together* and *Prayerbook of the Bible*. In *Dietrich Bonhoeffer Works*. Edited by Geffrey B. Kelly, trans. Daniel W. Bloesch and James H. Burtness. Minneapolis: Fortress Press, 1996.

DBWE 6   *Ethics*. In *Dietrich Bonhoeffer Works*. Edited by Clifford J. Green, trans. Reinhard Krauss, Charles C. West and Douglas W. Stott. Minneapolis: Fortress Press, 2006.

DBWE 8   *Letters and Papers from Prison*. In *Dietrich Bonhoeffer Works*. Edited by John W. de Gruchy, trans. Isabel Best, Lisa E. Dahill, Reinhard Krauss, Nancy Lukens, Barbara and Martin Rumscheidt, and Douglas W. Stott. Minneapolis: Fortress Press, 2010.

DBWE 9   *The Young Bonhoeffer: 1918-1927*. In *Dietrich Bonhoeffer Works*. Edited by Paul Duane Matheny, Clifford J. Green and Marshall D. Johnson, trans. Mary C. Nebelsick and Douglas W. Stott. Minneapolis: Fortress Press, 2003.

DBWE 10   *Barcelona, Berlin, New York: 1928-1931*. In *Dietrich Bonhoeffer Works*. Edited by Clifford J. Green, trans. Douglas W. Stott. Minneapolis: Fortress Press, 2007.

DBWE 11   *Ecumenical, Academic, and Pastoral Work: 1931-1932*. In *Dietrich Bonhoeffer Works*. Edited by Victoria J. Barnett, Mark S. Brocker and Michael B. Lukens, trans. Anne Schmidt-Lange, Isabel Best, Nicolas Humphrey, Marion Pauck and Douglas W. Stott. Minneapolis: Fortress Press, 2012.

DBWE 12   *Berlin: 1932-1933*. In *Dietrich Bonhoeffer Works*. Edited by Larry L. Rasmussen, trans. Isabel Best, David Higgins and Douglas W. Stott. Minneapolis: Fortress Press, 2009.

DBWE 14   *Theological Education at Finkenwalde: 1935-1937*. In *Dietrich Bonhoeffer Works*. Edited by H. Gaylon Barker and Mark S. Brocker, trans. Douglas W. Stott. Minneapolis: Fortress Press, 2013.

DBWE 15   *Theological Education Underground: 1937-1940*. In *Dietrich Bonhoeffer Works*. Edited by Victoria J. Barnett, trans. Victoria J. Barnett, Claudia D. Bergmann, Peter Frick, Scott A. Moore and Douglas W. Stott. Minneapolis: Fortress Press, 2015.

DBWE 16   *Conspiracy and Imprisonment: 1940-1945*. In *Dietrich Bonhoeffer Works*. Edited by Mark S. Brocker, trans. Lisa E. Dahill and Douglas W. Stott. Minneapolis: Fortress Press, 2006.

Introduction

There is a word that evokes tremendous feelings of love and bliss among Catholics who hear it, a word that stirs in them the most profound depths of religious feeling ranging from the awe and dread of judgment to the bliss of God's presence, but a word that assuredly also evokes feelings of home for them, feelings of the sort only a child feels in gratitude, reverence, and self-surrendering love toward its mother, the feelings that come over us when after a long time away we once again enter our parents' home, our own childhood home. And there is also a word that to Protestants has the sound of something infinitely banal, something more or less indifferent and superfluous, a word that does not make a person's heart beat faster, a word often associated with feelings of boredom, a word that in any event does not lend wings to our religious feelings – and yet a word that will seal our fate if we are unable to find in this word a new, or rather the original meaning. Woe to us if this word … does not soon acquire significance for us again, indeed if it does not become a matter with which our very lives are concerned. Yes, the word whose glory and greatness we want to examine today is 'church'.[1]

With these words began Dietrich Bonhoeffer's sermon on the eighth Sunday after Trinity, 1928 – words which drew his listeners to a theological theme that runs like a scarlet thread through his life and thought, and that acts to tie together his theological oeuvre from first to last as its most central dogmatic *res*.[2] What is further significant is the way in which these words are suggestive of a dichotomous understanding of the church against which Bonhoeffer's ecclesial thought is persistently and resolutely set. The church is described as either the locus of 'God's presence' or 'something infinitely banal'; the church is experienced and understood from the perspective of either a 'Catholic' extraordinariness or a 'Protestant' ordinariness, pitting – suggestively – divine and human action against each other in ecclesiological description. It is this 'either/or' dichotomy that spurs in Bonhoeffer the desire to find in the word 'church' 'a new, or rather the original meaning' by seeking in his ecclesial thought to give voice instead to the agential relation in the church's being of what might be described – in light of the sermon's opening words – as divine extraordinariness and human ordinariness.

This book concerns this agential relation as Bonhoeffer seeks to articulate it in his ecclesiology.[3] More specifically, the book advocates that Bonhoeffer understands the

---

[1] *DBWE* 10, 505.
[2] On this latter claim, see Chapter 2 of this book for a detailed discussion.
[3] While it is possible to speak of Bonhoeffer's 'ecclesiology' per se, there is no conventional systematic presentation of the doctrinal locus within the corpus of his writings. To speak thus is therefore to be dependent, constructively, on the whole corpus, and to assume and to apply to those writings a

church as a pneumatological and eschatological community in space and time: in the time between the ascension of Christ and the *eschaton*, the church exists as the event of the divine act of *convocatio* which takes place in and through the Holy Spirit of God to create in spatio-temporality the particular and contingent socio-historical human community that the church as *congregatio* is in its orientation to the eschatological telos. In this thick theological description of the church's existence, the asymmetrical yet interconnected relation of divine and human togetherness, and the derivative and necessary articulation of both divine and human agency, is critical. For Bonhoeffer, the church exists as *God's* church-community: the church is a sociological structure sui generis distinct from all other socio-historical forms of human community, and it is so as God the Holy Spirit creates it thus. If, then, ecclesiological description is not to succumb to presenting in an account of the church what Bonhoeffer describes as a 'materialistic-secular'[4] ecclesiology in consequence of a disproportionate or wholly exclusive emphasis on the church's socio-historical human form, then ecclesiological description must begin by describing the operative and gracious act of God the Holy Spirit who is the church's efficient, sustaining and perfecting cause. At once, however, the church also exists, for Bonhoeffer, as God's *church*-community: the church is a socio-historical form of (fallible and sinful) human community. If, then, ecclesiological description is not equally to succumb to presenting in an account of the church what Bonhoeffer describes as an 'idealistic-docetic'[5] ecclesiology in consequence of a disproportionate or wholly exclusive emphasis on the *ad intra* or *ad extra* life of God, then ecclesiological description, having secured the sheer gratuitous nature of the church's being in space and time, must account (derivatively) for the church's socio-historical human form.

The ecclesiologist performs this task (according to Bonhoeffer) by attending to the work of God the Holy Spirit: the Holy Spirit of God who actualizes and animates the being of God's church-community as a particular and contingent socio-historical human community *in* spatio-temporality by acting operatively within space and time, through space and time, and outwith space and time, in order to draw space and time to its consummation in new creation, of which God's church-community is a proleptic manifestation. By attending to this eschatological and teleological movement of God the Holy Spirit, the ecclesiologist, moreover, takes spatio-temporality seriously as a *theological* category. She understands spatio-temporality first and foremost not as an anthropological or sociological category but as a theological, or, more precisely, a pneumatological and eschatological one, which ontologically, epistemically and morally has been 'apocalypsed' by the advent in space and time of God in Christ by the Holy Spirit, and by the coming of God the Holy Spirit at Pentecost.[6] In understanding

---

definition of systematicity that trades not on conventionality (or regularity) but on relationality (or irregularity). On 'conventional' and 'relational' systematicity, see A. N. Williams, *The Architecture of Theology: Structure, System, and Ratio* (Oxford: Oxford University Press, 2011), 1–22; and on 'regular' and 'irregular' dogmatics, see Karl Barth, *Church Dogmatics* [hereafter *CD*] 4 vols in 13 pts, ed. and trans. G. W. Bromiley, T. F. Torrance et al. (Edinburgh: T&T Clark, 1956–1975), I/1, 275–87.
[4] *DBW* 14, 423.
[5] Ibid.
[6] On these themes, see Chapter 2, Chapter 4 and Chapter 5 of this book for a detailed discussion.

space and time thus, the ecclesiologist thereby understands and speaks of the being of God's church-community as a particular and contingent socio-historical human community which is oriented in space and time to the eschatological telos properly – that is, theologically – as '*both* a historical community *and* one established by God'.[7] Or, put alternatively, with appropriate dogmatic ordering and proportionality in ecclesiological speech, the ecclesiologist must address both divine and human agency in her ecclesiological description, with the latter being relativized but not minimalized by the former.[8] This the ecclesiologist does (according to Bonhoeffer) by understanding and speaking of the relation of divine and human agency in the church's being as held together by God the Holy Spirit.

Given this perspective, which this book categorizes as the 'both/and' ecclesiological methodology of Bonhoeffer's ecclesial thought,[9] and which (as it will be demonstrated) is a consequence of the strictly theological, and more specifically pneumatological and apocalyptically eschatological foundations upon which Bonhoeffer builds his thought,[10] it is the argument of this book that Bonhoeffer proffers a unique methodological approach to ecclesiological description. This approach is one which not only makes a significant contribution over against other contributions to ecclesiology per se but more emphatically is one which the book contends is therapeutic to – and offers material content that is fruitful for a constructive and critical analysis of – an endemic problematic present in approaches to contemporary ecclesiological discourse.[11] Put simply, this problematic is the tendency to attend in ecclesiological description *either* 'ethnographically' to the church's socio-historical human form *or* 'dogmatically' to God's *ad intra* or *ad extra* life (and to either one at the expense of the other).[12] The

---

[7] *DBW* 1, 79 (emphasis added). The book discusses this theme in Chapter 3.
[8] On these themes, see Chapter 1 of this book for a detailed discussion. The language of 'ordering' and 'proportionality' is taken from John Webster and Tom Greggs, and has to do with the arrangement, locating and (thereby) relationality of doctrinal *loci* in theological inquiry, and with the construal of those relations in respect of the quotient of the doctrines represented, both in terms of their material dogmatic content and formal presentation. See John Webster, 'Introduction: Systematic Theology', in John Webster, Kathryn Tanner and Iain Torrance, ed. *The Oxford Handbook of Systematic Theology* (New York: Oxford University Press, 2007), 12–13; Tom Greggs, 'Proportion and Topography in Ecclesiology: A Working Paper on the Dogmatic Location of the Doctrine of the Church', in R. David Nelson, Darren Sarisky and Justin Stratis, ed. *Theological Theology: Essays in Honour of John B. Webster* (London: Bloomsbury T&T Clark, 2015), 89–106; and Tom Greggs, *Dogmatic Ecclesiology Volume One: The Priestly Catholicity of the Church* (Grand Rapids: Baker Academic, 2019), xxx–xl.
[9] To categorize Bonhoeffer's ecclesial thought thus is not simply to assert that Bonhoeffer understands and describes the church as both creature of the Holy Spirit of God and socio-historical human community, but rather, and additionally, that he understands and describes the 'how' of the unity prescribed by the word 'and'. In Bonhoeffer's 'both/and' ecclesiological methodology the word 'and' designates *not* 'the paradox, the inconceivability, the miracle, beyond which we cannot and must not try to go' (Claude Welch, *The Reality of the Church* (New York: Charles Scribner's Sons, 1958), 38), but instead is understood and parsed in reference to the person and work of God the Holy Spirit.
[10] The book discusses this theme in Chapter 2.
[11] On this theme, see Chapter 1 of this book for a detailed discussion.
[12] On the meaning and use of the alternative designations 'dogmatic' and 'ethnographic' as descriptors for two 'types' of approach to contemporary ecclesiological discourse, see Chapter 1. The assumption that a distinction between the dogmatic and ethnographic in ecclesiological description necessitates their strict separation is countered by Nicholas Adams and Charles Elliot,

result of this tendency is that ecclesiological speech is torn, and the doctrinal locus of ecclesiology problematized, ultimately, with respect to the relationality of divine and human agency and the concomitant concern of appropriate dogmatic ordering and proportionality in ecclesiological description. By making plausible the claim that Bonhoeffer's pneumatological and eschatological 'both/and' ecclesiological methodology is therapeutic to this endemic 'either/or' problematic, the book thus contends that Bonhoeffer's ecclesial thought breaks open a necessary 'third way' in ecclesiological description between the Scylla of 'ethnographic' ecclesiology and the Charybdis of 'dogmatic' ecclesiology. Methodologically, therefore, the book proceeds as a diagnostic problematization and suggested reparative resolution in thinking ecclesiologically 'beyond but with Bonhoeffer'.[13] The book does this precisely by its making plausible the claim that Bonhoeffer's 'both/and' ecclesiological methodology proffers material content by which to analyse critically and constructively not only an endemic 'either/or' problematic in contemporary ecclesiological discourse but also, and in relation thereto, a unique methodological therapy. In this lies the significance of Bonhoeffer's ecclesial thought for today, setting as it does – what the book will argue to be – a programmatic theological grammar for ecclesiology per se,[14] as it seeks to account for the glory and greatness of the word 'church'.

To substantiate the argument of this book, Chapter 1 operates diagnostically in first articulating and then second explicating an endemic problematic present in approaches to contemporary ecclesiological discourse. The problematic is articulated in reference to the asymmetrical yet interconnected relation of divine and human togetherness in the church's being expressed *in nuce* in God's covenantal promise as appropriated to the church in Corinth: 'I will be their God, and they shall be my people.'[15] The Corinthian church is at once *both* the *people* of God *and God's* people –

'Ethnography Is Dogmatics: Making Description Central to Systematic Theology', *Scottish Journal of Theology* 53 (2000), 339–64. Adams and Elliot suggest that dogmatic theology is best practised through the work of detailed practical description of God's world because dogmatic presuppositions 'are *already* at work in the descriptions themselves' (Adams and Elliot, 'Ethnography Is Dogmatics', 346). In this way, explicit clarification of dogmatic presuppositions adds little or nothing to what Adams and Elliot see as the inherently dogmatic work of description. To re-describe dogmatics thus would seem, however, to negate, problematically, a constitutive element of the dogmatic task itself as *Wissenschaftlich*: its critical and corrective function in relation to its enquiring into the actual content of that which is described, and thereby the agreement or otherwise of the *fides quae creditur* with the witness of scripture – a witness which itself stands external to any such description. Dogmatics is not *just* a work of description. Rather, as Karl Barth states: 'Dogmatics is the self-examination of the Christian church in respect of the *content* of its distinctive talk about God' (*CD* I/1, 11). On the scientific nature of dogmatics, see *CD* I/1, 280–7. The emphasis on descriptive dogmatics is prefigured in the work of, for example, George A. Lindbeck, *The Nature of Doctrine: Religion and Theology in a Postliberal Age* (Louisville: Westminster John Knox Press, 1984); William T. Cavanaugh, *Torture and Eucharist: Theology, Politics, and the Body of Christ* (Oxford: Blackwell, 1998); and Stanley Hauerwas, *Christian Existence Today: Essays on Church, World, and Living In Between* (Eugene: Wipf & Stock, 2010).

[13] John W. de Gruchy, 'A Concrete Ethic of the Cross: Interpreting Bonhoeffer's Ethics in North America's Backyard', *Union Seminary Quarterly Review* 58.1–2 (2004), 43.

[14] On understanding theology as grammatical, see Lindbeck, *The Nature of Doctrine*, esp. pp. 79–84; cf., Ludwig Wittgenstein, *Philosophical Investigations*, trans. G. E. M. Anscombe, P. M. S. Hacker and Joachim Schulte rev. 4th edn (Oxford: Wiley-Blackwell, 2009), 123e: 'Grammar tells what kind of object anything is.'

[15] 2 Cor. 6.16.

a covenantal relation which in its *divine* origin and ongoing existence is unilateral, but intrinsic to which is *human* response. On this basis, it is suggested that in 2 Cor. 6.16 the ecclesiologist is confronted by the most basic ecclesiological task. This task is that of holding together in an account of the church *both* divine *and* human agency, thereby ensuring that both the being of God and God's operative and gracious acts and the being of the church's socio-historical human form – that human form being derivative of and dependent upon those divine acts (hence the preceding of 'they shall be my people' by 'I will be their God') – are spoken of appropriately and with due concern for the ordered covenant relation in which divine and human togetherness exists in the church's being, and thus in a genuinely theological manner. By successfully prosecuting this most basic ecclesiological task, the ecclesiologist, therefore, heeds the Pauline καὶ in 2 Cor. 6.16, and in doing so refuses to succumb to an endemic problematic present in approaches to contemporary ecclesiological discourse – that of attending in ecclesiological description, with disregard for the Pauline καὶ, *either* to God's *ad intra* or *ad extra* life (to 'I will be your God') *or* to the church's socio-historical human form (to 'they shall be my people'), and of presenting in an account of the church, concomitantly, either a purely 'dogmatic' or purely 'ethnographic' approach to ecclesiology. The chapter proceeds, therefore, to explicate this endemic problematic in relation to contemporary ecclesiological literature. It does so by bringing each 'type' of ecclesiological approach into constructive and critical dialogue – a dialogue which is facilitated and indeed complexified by each 'type' being troped with respect to 'hard' and 'soft' versions. The purpose of this distinction is to delineate ecclesiological accounts in which the endemic problematic functions explicitly as a normative and necessary methodological foundation, and those in which the endemic problematic can be seen to be displayed implicitly. By presenting the material content of the chapter in this way, the helpful and mutually corrective nature of each 'type' of ecclesiological approach will be seen. However, it will be demonstrated that in both 'dogmatic' and 'ethnographic' ecclesiology – be it the 'hard' or 'soft' version of each ecclesiological 'type' – there is at work *dis*ordered and *dis*proportionate ecclesiological speech which limits the ability of either approach to prosecute successfully the most basic ecclesiological task of holding together in an account of the church both divine and human agency. The chapter thus seeks to construct a pathway for presenting Bonhoeffer's own ecclesial thought as a necessary 'third way' in ecclesiological description, and more acutely his 'both/and' ecclesiological methodology as therapeutic precisely to the endemic problematic which is present in approaches to contemporary ecclesiological discourse.

Having diagnosed in Chapter 1 an endemic problematic present in approaches to contemporary ecclesiological discourse, Chapter 2 begins the consideration of Bonhoeffer's own ecclesiological description that treats, in consequence of its 'both/and' ecclesiological methodology, this endemic 'either/or' problematic therapeutically. To this end, Chapter 2 is concerned to construct the theological foundations upon which Bonhoeffer's ecclesial thought and its 'both/and' ecclesiological methodology is built. By drawing principally on both the beginning of his lectures, *Creation and Fall*, and his doctoral dissertation, *Sanctorum Communio*, it is demonstrated that these foundations are strictly theological (rather than sociological), and more specifically apocalyptically eschatological and pneumatological, such that the church's being in space and time is understood by Bonhoeffer, in the time between the ascension of Christ and the *eschaton*, as being oriented to the eschatological telos in virtue of the person and work of God the Holy Spirit.

Critically, it is these pneumatological and apocalyptically eschatological foundations and the concomitant understanding of the being of the church in its orientation in space and time to the eschatological telos, which enable Bonhoeffer's ecclesial thought to operate therapeutically in its treatment of the endemic problematic present in approaches to contemporary ecclesiological discourse. Indeed, not only do these pneumatological and apocalyptically eschatological foundations serve to fund Bonhoeffer's 'both/and' ecclesiological methodology – in which both divine and human agency are held together in an account of the church that gives voice to the asymmetrical yet interconnected relation of divine and human togetherness in the church's being, and affords appropriate space in that account to both God's own being and the being of the church's socio-historical human form – but also determinatively distinguish for Bonhoeffer the sui generis sociological structure of the being of God's church-community from all other forms of socio-historical human community. Thus, having established the theological foundations of Bonhoeffer's ecclesial thought in Chapter 2, Chapter 3 proceeds to explicate, with reference to Bonhoeffer's own historic construction of the endemic problematic, precisely how he builds the structure of his 'both/and' ecclesiological methodology on those pneumatological and apocalyptically eschatological foundations. In order to do this, the chapter begins by articulating Bonhoeffer's threefold typology of socio-historical human community as constructed in *Sanctorum Communio*. The chapter does this because Bonhoeffer proceeds to establish in dialogue with that typology his pneumatologically and apocalyptically eschatologically founded 'both/and' ecclesiological methodology. This methodology, in turn, enables Bonhoeffer to conceive the church's being as established by *God the Holy Spirit* as the particular and contingent socio-historical (and sinful) *human* community that the church in space and time is. In consequence of this perspective the distinctive sociological structure of God's church-community is brought into view. The chapter contends specifically that, for Bonhoeffer, a threefold actualizing work of the Holy Spirit of God is thus determinative of the church's being in space and time and its unique ontic-social relations. Indeed, it is an account of God the Holy Spirit which can hold together in the being of God's church-community an account of *both* divine *and* human agency, such that Bonhoeffer's pneumatologically and apocalyptically eschatologically founded ecclesiological description can be said to break through the endemic 'either/or' problematic present in approaches to contemporary ecclesiological discourse. It is concluded, therefore, that the ecclesiologist today, if she is to give voice in her ecclesiological description to the asymmetrical yet interconnected relation of divine and human togetherness in the church's being appropriately, must parse the Pauline καὶ in 2 Cor. 6.16 in reference to the Holy Spirit of God.

Having explicated Bonhoeffer's pneumatologically and apocalyptically eschatologically founded 'both/and' ecclesiological methodology, Chapters 4 and 5 together seek to outline the way in which this methodology further enables Bonhoeffer to account for the particular and contingent socio-historical human community that the church in space and time is in a genuinely theological way. Here, Bonhoeffer's theological, and more precisely pneumatological and apocalyptically eschatological, conceptualization of spatio-temporality as grounded *extra se* in God and God's operative and gracious acts is engaged to demonstrate how, in order to account for the being of God's church-community in space and time, it is necessary to speak theologically about empirical phenomenology, both in accordance with, and as a further exemplification of, the logic inherent to Bonhoeffer's 'both/and' ecclesiological methodology. Accordingly, and drawing primarily on Bonhoeffer's New Testament lectures delivered at Finkenwalde, together with *Discipleship* and *Life Together*, Chapter 4 argues that the 'space' which Bonhoeffer understands God's church-community to occupy in spatio-temporality is best identified as a *pneumatological* space set apart and against the space of the world within the world so as to be with and for the world. In this construction, it is suggested that Bonhoeffer recapitulates in vivid spatial language his argument from *Sanctorum Communio* that the being of God's church-community is actualized in space and time as a sui generis sociological structure by a threefold work of God the Holy Spirit. Furthermore, the chapter argues that this pneumatological space, actualized in the time between the ascension of Christ and the *eschaton* by the coming of God the Holy Spirit, can be specified more acutely as a *confessional* space. This coming of God the Holy Spirit is the event of the church's foundation in which the church is given its own human empirical form and associated vocational function(s) by the Holy Spirit of God. This confessional space that God's church-community occupies in spatio-temporality as a socio-historical human community, in turn, is understood by Bonhoeffer to be 'filled' definitively by what is described, in the context of the chapter, as the spaces of proclamation and spiritual care. Moreover, because these two spaces have their genesis in the event of the church's foundation at Pentecost, and functionally speaking are operative for Bonhoeffer only by the Holy Spirit of God, they can be seen as two particular and contingent events of the pneumatological and confessional space of God's church-community, which, in and through God the Holy Spirit, hold together both divine and human agency in consequence of Bonhoeffer's 'both/and' ecclesiological methodology.

With Chapter 4 being concerned to outline the pneumatological space of God's church-community, Chapter 5 turns to account for the being of God's church-community in time. Here, Bonhoeffer's pneumatological and apocalyptically eschatological conceptualization of spatio-temporality is again engaged, but now in reference to his *Ethics* fragment, *Die letzten und die vorletzten Dinge*, and its categories of 'last things' and 'things before the last'. On the basis of this conceptualization, the chapter contends that the time within which God's church-community has its being is best identified as *eschatological* time, and that definitive of this time is an existent dynamic relationality between God and temporal-historical reality, in which temporal-historical reality – and thereby the being of God's church-community in this reality – is both conditioned by and preserved for the final reality of God in new creation. On the basis of this conditionality and preservation, it is thus suggested that the dynamic relationality that exists in Bonhoeffer's thought between God and temporal-historical reality in eschatological time might best be accounted for by reference to the category of divine *patience*, such that eschatological time can be specified more acutely as the time of God's patience. Taking its cue from the trajectory of Bonhoeffer's own thought, the chapter then moves to establish the critical significance of eschatological time as the time of God's patience for Bonhoeffer's theological account of the particular and contingent socio-historical human community that the church in space and time is. The chapter does this by deploying Bonhoeffer's motif of 'preparing the way' (*Wegbereitung*) to articulate, in light of the dynamic relationality which exists between God and temporal-historical reality in the time of God's patience, a specific ecclesial commission which is fulfilled by God's church-community in responsible ecclesial action that, in and through the Holy Spirit of God, works towards establishing in both the church and the world two concrete conditions: 'being human' (*Menschseins*) and 'being good' (*Gutseins*).[16] Moreover, because such action is possible for Bonhoeffer only from within the pneumatological space of God's church-community, it is action which, functionally speaking, not only is operative by God the Holy Spirit but also, and thereby, upholds the existent dynamic relationality between the final reality of God (or last things) and temporal-historical reality (or things before the last) in the time of God's patience. In this way, responsible ecclesial action which fulfils the specific ecclesial commission of God's church-community in this time can be seen to hold together both divine and human agency in accordance with, and as further exemplification of, Bonhoeffer's pneumatological and eschatological 'both/and' ecclesiological methodology.

Given the concerns and argument which animate this book, this book seeks to contribute both to the ongoing task of interpreting Bonhoeffer's ecclesiology evermore responsibly on the basis of his complete theological oeuvre and to wider ecclesiological discourse concerning the church's self-understanding. The manner of this contribution is threefold. First, by identifying the pneumatological and apocalyptically eschatological foundations upon which Bonhoeffer builds his ecclesial thought, and by establishing, derivatively, his ecclesiological methodology as a pneumatological and eschatological 'both/and' ecclesiological methodology in which an account of God the Holy Spirit holds together in the being of God's church-community an account of both divine and human agency with appropriate dogmatic ordering and proportionality, the book is distinct in relation to extant material on Bonhoeffer's ecclesiology. While a fuller description of this distinction is located in Chapter 2 (and outworked, subsequently, in Chapter 3, 4 and 5), it is sufficient to say here that in this extant material Bonhoeffer's ecclesiology is indexed almost exclusively to the person and work of Jesus Christ, or else to a theological anthropology, and with little or no material attention being given therein to *how* the church for Bonhoeffer *is* 'both a historical community and one established by God'.[17] Such indexations fail to appreciate, then, not only the more properly pneumatological and apocalyptically eschatological foundations of Bonhoeffer's ecclesial thought, but also his pneumatological and eschatological 'both/and' ecclesiological methodology which is built on those foundations and by which his ecclesial thought is subsequently structured. Moreover, in doing so, these indexations risk positioning Bonhoeffer's understanding of the church in such a way that threatens to dissolve the church's pneumatologically constituted and eschatologically oriented sui

---

[16] *DBW* 6, 153 and 157.
[17] *DBW* 1, 79.

generis sociological structure, which, for Bonhoeffer – and precisely in consequence of the work of God the Holy Spirit – distinguishes the being of God's church-community as a particular and contingent socio-historical human community from all other socio-historical forms *of* human community.[18] The one clear exception to these indexations of Bonhoeffer's ecclesiology in extant Bonhoeffer scholarship is the work of Tom Greggs.[19] Yet even here, the pneumatological tone – at least presentationally – is downstream of a Christological one,[20] and in part is cautionary: 'There are questions to be asked', writes Greggs, 'about the role of the Spirit in [Bonhoeffer's] account [of the church]. Recognizing that ... Bonhoeffer does talk about the Spirit' he nevertheless locates the church 'so closely with the person of Christ' that 'contemporary theology, drawing from Bonhoeffer, [may] wish to deepen an account of the Spirit to unpack the way in which the church is Christ existing as community – a church which is such as the Spirit enables it'.[21] In light of the argument of this book, however, Bonhoeffer's

---

[18] It is such a dissolution that notwithstanding his desire (articulated in words which emphasize the most basic ecclesiological task of holding together in an account of the church both divine and human agency) to 'attend to the church as a concrete, social entity, much like any other, while still maintaining that *this* community has been established in Christ and is a work of the Holy Spirit', is evident, seemingly, in the work of Michael Mawson: see Michael Mawson, *Christ Existing as Community: Bonhoeffer's Ecclesiology* (New York: Oxford University Press, 2018), 1–2; Michael Mawson, 'Theology and Social Theory – Reevaluating Bonhoeffer's Approach', *Theology Today* 71.1 (2014), 69–80; and Michael Mawson, 'The Spirit and the Community: Pneumatology and Ecclesiology in Jenson, Hütter and Bonhoeffer', *International Journal of Systematic Theology* 15 (2013), 453–68. Pace Mawson, the church is not 'a concrete, social entity, *much like any other*' (Mawson, *Christ Existing as Community*, 1–2, emphasis added) and cannot be attended to in ecclesiological description as if it is. For Bonhoeffer (*contra* Mawson), there *is* a 'final basis for distinguishing the Christian community from other human polities' (Mawson, 'The Spirit and the Community', 468), and this final basis is the work of God the Holy Spirit. By this work God's church-community does in fact embody 'an alternative "counter ontology"' to all other socio-historical forms of human community (see Mawson, 'Theology and Social Theory', 77; cf., Mawson, *Christ Existing as Community*, 51 and 181–3). In making this argument this book is distinct, therefore, from – and might be seen as a supplement to, and indeed a deepening of – Mawson's own vital contribution, articulating as the book does the sui generis nature of the church as a sociological structure in space and time, and concomitantly Bonhoeffer's ecclesiology as deriving neither from his Christology nor even from his pneumatologically indexed Christology, as Mawson, seemingly, suggests (see Mawson, *Christ Existing as Community*, 121–49), but rather from his apocalyptically and eschatologically indexed pneumatology. The book thus also stands *contra* Clifford Green and his positioning of Bonhoeffer's ecclesiology within the context of an *a priori* theology of human sociality. See Clifford J. Green, *Bonhoeffer: A Theology of Sociality*, rev. edn (Grand Rapids: Eerdmans, 1999). For further discussion of Green's position, see Chapter 2, Section IV of this book, and for further discussion and a possible mitigation of Mawson's position, see Chapter 2, Section IV and Chapter 3, Section III.ii, respectively.

[19] See Tom Greggs, 'Bearing Sin in the Church: The Ecclesial Hamartiology of Bonhoeffer', in Michael Mawson and Philip G. Ziegler, ed. *Christ, Church and World: New Studies in Bonhoeffer's Theology and Ethics* (London: Bloomsbury T&T Clark, 2016), 77–99; and Tom Greggs, 'Ecclesiology', in Michael Mawson and Philip G. Ziegler, ed. *The Oxford Handbook of Dietrich Bonhoeffer* (Oxford: Oxford University Press, 2019), 225–40.

[20] Thus Greggs: 'To understand Bonhoeffer's ecclesiology through a singular focus on its relation to Christology would be to neglect the operation of God the Holy Spirit in Bonhoeffer's account' (Greggs, 'Ecclesiology', 232) – an operation which Greggs moves to consider only *after* his discussion of the church as the body of Christ, which itself is derivative (presentationally speaking) of his Christologically indexed discussion of Bonhoeffer's concept of 'vicarious representative action' (*Stellvertretung*). On Bonhoeffer's concept of *Stellvertretung*, see Chapter 3, Section III.ii of this book.

[21] Greggs, 'Bearing Sin in the Church', 95.

ecclesial thought must already be said to include within itself the 'deep' pneumatology that Greggs calls for – and indeed begins to work out[22] – proffering as it does an apocalyptically eschatologically indexed pneumatology as the most foundational dogmatic *res* of Bonhoeffer's ecclesiology.

In arguing thus, the book, second, and derivatively, develops constructively what at present, within the wider corpus of Bonhoeffer scholarship, is a much understudied yet critically significant theme of Bonhoeffer's theological oeuvre: his pneumatology and concomitant apocalyptic eschatology.[23] In doing so, the book contributes to the work called for by Mark Lindsay 'to illuminate more precisely the nature and extent of the presence of eschatological thinking in Bonhoeffer's overall theology'.[24] The book provides the most thoroughgoing constructive account of Bonhoeffer's eschatology to date,[25] as well as the first book-length exposition of Bonhoeffer's understanding of the Holy Spirit.[26] This the book does – albeit within the delimited context of Bonhoeffer's ecclesiology – by proposing that the structure of Bonhoeffer's ecclesial thought cannot be understood without the strictly pneumatological and apocalyptically eschatological foundations upon which it is built.

Third, and finally, the book positions Bonhoeffer's pneumatological and eschatological 'both/and' ecclesiological methodology as a therapeutic response to an endemic 'either/or' problematic present in approaches to contemporary ecclesiological discourse. As noted earlier, the book thus outlines a programmatic theological grammar to which the ecclesiologist must be faithful if her ecclesiological description is to give a genuinely theological account of the church's being in space and time. As a result, it is hoped that the ongoing ecclesiological task of accounting for the church as *the church* may be better understood, and the critical significance of Bonhoeffer's ecclesial thought for this task illuminated. It is also hoped that the book augments the craft of ecclesiology per se and that it may stir ecclesiologists and church practitioners alike to ask afresh what perhaps is the most decisive ecclesiological question: *What is the church?* And more acutely, *what constitutes* the church *as* the church?[27] And

---

[22] See Greggs, 'Ecclesiology', 232–4.

[23] The use of 'theme' in the singular here is intentional. Pneumatology and eschatology belong inseparably together as doctrinal *loci*. The third article of the Nicene-Constantinopolitan creed witnesses definitively to this fact as does the testimony of scripture: the Holy Spirit is ἀρραβών and ἀπαρχή of the future coming of Christ in glory (see 2 Cor. 1.22, 5.5; Eph. 1.13-14; and Rom. 8.23), and is thus, as an end-time gift, the proleptic manifestation of new creation in present space and time, and the agent by which (both individual and universal) eschatological consummation takes place (see Rom. 8.11, 19-21 and 23).

[24] Mark R. Lindsay, 'Bonhoeffer's eschatology in a world "come of age"', *Theology Today* 68.3 (2011), 292.

[25] Cf., David H. Manrodt, 'The Role of Eschatology in the Theology of Dietrich Bonhoeffer' (PhD diss., The Ecumenical Institute, St. Mary's Seminary and University, 1978), who offers a comprehensive but largely *descriptive* survey of eschatological motifs in the Bonhoeffer oeuvre and prior to the publication of *Dietrich Bonhoeffer Werke*; and Mark R. Lindsay, 'Eschatology', in Mawson and Ziegler, ed. *The Oxford Handbook of Dietrich Bonhoeffer*, 257–69, who identifies and traces, briefly, the eschatological horizon to Bonhoeffer's theological corpus.

[26] Cf., Christopher R. J. Holmes, 'The Holy Spirit', in Mawson and Ziegler, ed. *The Oxford Handbook of Dietrich Bonhoeffer*, 168–78.

[27] It is precisely this question which animates the recent, rigorous and rich ecclesiology of Tom Greggs. See Greggs, *Dogmatic Ecclesiology Volume One*.

this question is most decisive because not only does one's answer to it ultimately drive the fundamental form of church that one seeks to nurture and develop through one's participation in or leadership of the church[28] but also the way in which one approaches the study of the church itself, and therefore, concomitantly, one's proffered ecclesiological description, both in terms of its material dogmatic content and formal presentation. For the ecclesiologist and church practitioner alike, the book hopes to act, therefore, as something of a clarion call towards genuinely theological ecclesiological speech which is allied to genuinely theological ecclesial action.

---

[28] That is, treatment of the question of *what* the church is should always precede, in any and all ecclesiological discourse, the question of what the church is called to *be* and/or the question of what the church *does*.

1

Ecclesiological topography

I. Introduction

This chapter is concerned with the diagnosis of a problematic which is endemic to contemporary ecclesiological discourse and to which Dietrich Bonhoeffer's ecclesial thought, and in particular his account of the church as a pneumatological and eschatological community in space and time, is considered to be therapeutic. The chapter, therefore, functions diagnostically – a function prosecuted herein, first, by an articulation of the problematic and, then, second, by way of a detailed explication of this problematic in relation to contemporary ecclesiological literature. This explication proceeds by way of analysis of two 'types' of ecclesiological approach. These types, in light of the problematic, are designated 'dogmatic' and 'ethnographic', and in the course of the analysis are brought into constructive and critical dialogue.[1] Moreover, to facilitate this dialogue, each ecclesiological 'type' is troped with respect to 'hard' and 'soft' versions. By presenting the material content of the chapter in this way, the chapter seeks intentionally to construct a pathway for presenting what it will be argued is a necessary 'third way' in ecclesiological description – one, which, in its treatment of the endemic problematic, thinks beyond but with Bonhoeffer's ecclesial thought.

II. The problematic articulated

'I will be their God, and they shall be my people.'[2] In this Pauline appropriation of God's covenantal promise to the church in Corinth, it is not too great an exaggeration to say that the theologian is confronted by the central problematic of ecclesiological discourse: that of the asymmetrical yet interconnected relation of divine and human togetherness in the church's being, and the concomitant issue of holding together in an account of the church both divine and human agency. Indeed, such covenant

---

[1] The alternative designations 'dogmatic' and 'ethnographic' are adopted for typological analysis of ecclesiological discourse only; they are not an exhaustive description of the work of the individual theologians upon which this chapter draws to illustrate two typological approaches to ecclesiological description which unhelpfully are often set against each other. Indeed, space does not allow as thorough going an analysis of the work of individual theologians as the author would like, but principal points are made through exemplification.
[2] 2 Cor. 6.16.

togetherness of God and his people to which Paul indexes the being of the Corinthian church, while certainly a real togetherness in which divine commitment and human obligation is intrinsic, is nonetheless unilateral in origin: the covenant comes into being and is sustained in being by God alone, on the basis of both what God has done and on what God will do. Thus, it is *God* and *God's* acts, past, present and future, which determine God's covenant togetherness with God's people: 'I will look with favour upon you and make you fruitful and multiply you, and I will maintain my covenant with you … I will place my dwelling in your midst … I will walk among you, and will be your God, and you shall be my people.'[3] This *divine* determination of Israel to be the people of God, while conditioned not by Israel's response to God but only by God himself, nevertheless requires a *human* response as an indivisible aspect of it. As God's people, Israel is to be – both for God's sake and the world's sake – a kingdom of priests and a holy nation: a people, who, as a particular and contingent socio-historical reality, define God as their God and thereby are oriented towards God such that they obey God and faithfully keep and observe God's commandments.[4]

It is this vocation which subsequently the church has come to participate in by virtue of its sharing in that self-same determination of Israel to be God's people – a point, which, by his quotation from Lev. 26.12, Paul now sets before the church in Corinth precisely to remind the church of God's commitment to his people and his people's obligation to God as intrinsic to the covenant togetherness in which the church exists and is to exist as God's people. In parallel with the whole people of Israel, Paul identifies the Corinthian church in their origin and continued existence as a people determined by *God*, and yet, notwithstanding this divine determination, as a people who, in their socio-historical existence, are by *human* response to define God as their God and be oriented in space and time to God. The church in Corinth is God's *people* ('they shall be my people'), but these people are not just any people. Rather, they are a people who, in their response to God, are already at once determined by God as *God's* people ('I will be their God'). In indexing the being of the Corinthian church in this way, Paul's ecclesiological description not only stresses an asymmetrical yet interconnected relation of divine and human togetherness but raises by this fact the question of how, in her account of the church, the ecclesiologist gives voice appropriately to *both* divine *and* human agency.

Indeed, to hold together these two aspects of the church's being, both by a precise parsing of the Pauline καὶ in 2 Cor. 6.16 and by a careful consideration of the given order to the relation of divine and human togetherness therein – that is, to the preceding of 'they shall be my people' by 'I will be their God' – is the most basic ecclesiological task. If the ecclesiologist wishes to speak about the being of the church and to speak of it in accordance with scripture and the Christian tradition – one might say to speak of it in a genuinely theological manner – then she must speak of it *first* as an operative and gracious act of God, which *second* takes place in space and time to create a particular and contingent socio-historical human community. In other words, when speaking both descriptively and critically about the being of the church, the

---

[3] Lev. 26.9-13.
[4] See Exod. 19.5-6 and Lev. 26.1-3.

ecclesiologist must ensure that she affords in her ecclesiology appropriate space for an account of *both* divine *and* human agency – with the former relativizing but not minimalizing the latter – and gives due attention both to the being and form of the socio-historical human community that the church is and to the being of God and God's operative and gracious acts which are the efficient, sustaining and perfecting cause of that community.

Put formally, the issue at stake here in ecclesiological description is one of systematicity: of the arrangement and locating of doctrinal *loci* in theological inquiry, and more specifically of where one doctrinal locus is placed in relation to other doctrinal *loci*; how the relation between these different *loci* is subsequently construed (regarding especially the proportionality of the doctrines represented); and thus ultimately of which doctrine (if any) is considered most basic or foundational.[5] The importance of this for the task of systematic theological inquiry cannot be overstated: it is the case not only that any one doctrinal locus is untreatable solipsistically and thus must be exposited always in reference to the way it interconnects (coherently) with other doctrinal *loci* but also that the doctrine placed beneath or deriving from the doctrine that is considered in that interconnection most (or even more) basic or foundational will be materially affected in terms of its content by what goes before it – that is, by its ultimate (or more immediate) dogmatic *res*.[6] All of this is to say that 'dogmatic topography'[7] in ecclesiological description (and theological inquiry) matters. Indeed, the ecclesiologist must ensure that her account of the church is always appropriately dogmatically ordered with due proportion, such that any ecclesiological discussion is dependently informed by other doctrinal *loci* – most basically or foundationally a doctrine of God – yet in that dependent formation always resists any move to either sublate or exclude (duly proportionate) ecclesiological speech about the socio-historical human community that the church is.

To the extent the ecclesiologist successfully prosecutes this most basic ecclesiological task, her ecclesiology will hold together an account of *both* divine *and* human agency, and in doing so give voice appropriately to the asymmetrical yet interconnected relation of divine and human togetherness in the church's being and afford appropriate space in that account to both the operative and gracious acts of God and the being and form of the socio-historical human community that the church is. Furthermore, in terms of the material dogmatic content and formal presentation of the doctrine of the church thereby offered, both a doctrine of God ('I will be their God') and a doctrine of the human person ('they shall be my people') will be spoken of together, but with due concern for how these doctrinal *loci* relate, topographically, one to another in and

---

[5] This is to assume a definition of systematicity (following Anna Williams) that trades not on conventionality – the concept here being used to refer to a coherent and comprehensive account of (multiple) Christian doctrine(s) ordered locus by locus – but on relationality: on the tracing of links between doctrinal *loci* and on the indicating of how any one specific locus (as the single subject of theological inquiry) is informed by or determines another, and thereby exhibits 'an impetus towards coherence and comprehensiveness'. See Williams, *The Architecture of Theology*, 1–22 [1].

[6] See Greggs, 'Bearing Sin in the Church', 77–8; cf., Sarah Coakley, *God, Sexuality, and the Self: An Essay 'On the Trinity'* (Cambridge: Cambridge University Press, 2013), 41: '*Wherever one chooses to start* [one's systematic theology] *has implications for the whole, and the parts must fit together.*'

[7] Greggs, 'Bearing Sin in the Church', 78; cf., Greggs, *Dogmatic Ecclesiology Volume One*, xxxiv–xl.

through the καὶ of 2 Cor. 6.16. In doing so, and in consequence of such due concern for appropriate dogmatic ordering and proportionality in ecclesiological description, the ecclesiologist, moreover, will eschew what is an erroneous but endemic problematic present in approaches to contemporary ecclesiological discourse: the tendency to attend in ecclesiological description, with disregard for the Pauline καὶ, *either* to 'I will be their God' *or* to 'they shall be my people', and thus to present in an account of the church *either* a 'dogmatic' *or* 'ethnographic' ecclesiology. The former prioritizes a more properly or narrowly 'theological' description of God's *ad intra* or *ad extra* life at the expense of a socio-historical account of the church particularly and contingently conceived – in 'dogmatic' ecclesiology the church is, essentially, what *God* does. The latter prioritizes a 'socio-historical' description of the church's human empirical form at the expense of a theological account of God's own life – in 'ethnographic' ecclesiology the church is, essentially, what *humans* do. Ecclesiological speech is rent asunder, and the doctrinal locus of ecclesiology problematized with respect to the relation of divine and human agency and the concomitant question of dogmatic ordering and proportionality in ecclesiological description. Thus, it is this endemic problematic of describing in an account of the church either 'dogmatically' the *ad intra* or *ad extra* life of God, or 'ethnographically' the particular and contingent socio-historical church-community, which this chapter now turns to explicate in relation to contemporary ecclesiological literature.

III. The problematic explicated

While recognizing the helpful and mutually corrective nature of each typological approach to ecclesiological description, the explication that follows is concerned to demonstrate – through bringing each ecclesiological 'type' into constructive and critical dialogue – what in both 'types' is *dis*ordered and *dis*proportionate ecclesiological speech, which thus works to limit their ability to prosecute successfully the most basic ecclesiological task of holding together in an account of the church both divine and human agency. Furthermore, to facilitate the dialogue between each 'type' of ecclesiological approach, the explication proceeds by way of a presentation of both 'hard' and 'soft' versions of each ecclesiological 'type'. In troping each ecclesiological 'type' in this way, the chapter is concerned, moreover, to distinguish between those theologians for whom the endemic problematic is an *explicit* (or 'hard') methodological *claim* – and thus who make it a normative and necessary foundation of both their own ecclesiological description and indeed ecclesiology per se – and those for whom (it might be said) the endemic problematic is an *implicit* (or 'soft') logical *consequence* – and thus who make it not a normative or necessary foundation of their own ecclesiological description, but nevertheless display it therein. Put differently, while the 'hard' ecclesiologist *states* the endemic problematic explicitly, the 'soft' ecclesiologist *shows* it implicitly. The typological analysis begins, therefore, with an explication of the 'hard' versions of 'dogmatic' and 'ethnographic' ecclesiology respectively, before turning to explicate the 'soft' versions of each ecclesiological 'type'. In presenting the two typological approaches to contemporary ecclesiological discourse in this dialogical way, a pathway will necessarily be cleared in which to situate Bonhoeffer's therapeutic methodological treatment of the endemic problematic and its attendant disorder and disproportion in ecclesiological speech.

i. 'Hard' dogmatic ecclesiology

For the 'hard' dogmatic ecclesiologist the endemic problematic is considered an explicit methodological claim which necessarily norms *theologically* ecclesiological discourse. The being of the church is spoken of properly in ecclesiological discussion *only* if the ecclesiologist attends *first* to the *ad intra* or *ad extra* life of *God*, and thereby sets her doctrine of the church under a doctrine of God and God's operative and gracious acts. Thus, for the 'hard' dogmatic ecclesiologist what is methodologically paramount in ecclesiological description is an account of divine agency. That account (as will be demonstrated) orders the resultant ecclesiological description so exclusively to God's own life, that that description is set categorically not only against the prevailing tide of contemporary ecclesiological accounts in which attention to the socio-historical phenomena of the church is seen as the normative and necessary foundation of ecclesiological discussion[8] but also by the sheer density of its own dogmatic content is insufficiently transparent towards – and thus at risk of marginalizing the significance of – the church's socio-historical human form. This 'dogmatic' ecclesiological stance (perhaps) finds its 'hardest' expression in the ecclesial thought of John Webster.

Invoking Calvin's imagery of the church as the society which exists in 'the society of God'[9] it is not the empirical but the theological that for Webster constitutes what is foundationally normative and necessary in ecclesiological discussion: 'A theology of the church is not simply a phenomenology of ecclesial social history but an inquiry into that history's ontological ground in the being and works of the church's God.'[10] The doctrine of the church is an 'extension' of the doctrine of God,[11] and is thus arrived

---

[8] In mind here are those accounts that emphasize ecclesial human reality, social-scientific (or 'thick') description, modelling, church polity, function and governance, and/or anthropological concepts of habit, practice and virtue. Some (varied) examples include: Avery Dulles, *Models of the Church* (New York: Image Books, 2002); Stanley Hauerwas, *A Community of Character: Toward a Constructive Christian Social Ethic* (Notre Dame: University of Notre Dame Press, 1981); Edward Schillebeeckx, *Church: The Human Story of God*, trans. John Bowden (New York: The Crossroad Publishing Company, 1996); Johannes A. van der Ven, *Ecclesiology in Context* (Grand Rapids: Eerdmans, 1996); Nicholas M. Healy, *Church, World, and the Christian Life: Practical-Prophetic Ecclesiology* (Cambridge: Cambridge University Press, 2000); Reinhard Hütter, *Suffering Divine Things: Theology as Church Practice*, trans. Douglas Stott (Grand Rapids: Eerdmans, 2000); Mary McClintock Fulkerson, *Places of Redemption: Theology for a Worldly Church* (Oxford: Oxford University Press, 2007); and (with the exception of John Webster's contribution) the collection of essays in Pete Ward, ed. *Perspectives on Ecclesiology and Ethnography* (Grand Rapids: Eerdmans, 2012) together with its partner volume Christian B. Scharen, ed. *Explorations in Ecclesiology and Ethnography* (Grand Rapids: Eerdmans, 2012). For further discussion of these ecclesiological accounts, see Section III.ii and III.iii of this chapter.
[9] John Calvin, *Institutes of the Christian Religion*, ed. John T. McNeill, trans. Ford Lewis Battles, 2 vols (Louisville: Westminster John Knox Press, 2011), IV.i.3 (2:1015); cf., John Webster, '"In the Society of God": Some Principles of Ecclesiology', in Ward, ed. *Perspectives*, 200–22.
[10] Webster, 'In the Society of God', 200.
[11] See ibid., 201; and John Webster, *Word and Church: Essays in Christian Dogmatics* (Edinburgh: T&T Clark, 2001), 195.

at not by virtue of inductive social-scientific description of the church's phenomenal surface but (only) through 'Trinitarian deduction'.[12] This deduction Webster locates in a threefold movement in the 'self-moved' movement of the immanent divine life of one or another divine person, before tracing that movement through the economic work of the undivided Godhead, and then (and *only* then) explicating it finally in ecclesiological terms.[13] In this way, Webster seeks to secure that ecclesiology 'has its place in the flow of Christian doctrine from teaching about God to teaching about everything else in God'.[14] Indeed, only after securing the primacy of this dogmatic ordering and content does Webster move to consider the 'kinds' of socio-historical phenomena that characterize the church as the society which exists in God's society, and then also to posit the fundamental 'forms' of the church by which that society is structurally identified in its socio-historical existence.[15]

While careful to distinguish his position from the deductive methodology of social trinitarianism,[16] and alive to the ever present danger of dogmatic idealism,[17] Webster constructs this 'dogmatic' ecclesiology both to warn against the conviction that 'the real' in ecclesiological discussion 'is the social-historical' and to deny the associated ecclesiological sequencing that 'the church is the people of God because certain events occur within a group of human beings'.[18] Such degenerate causal ordering is precisely the product of what Webster sees as a prior and more fundamental concern: the conflation of ecclesiology's proximate *res* (the socio-historical form of the church) with its principal *res* (the theological reality of the immanent and (suspended) economic work of the triune God).[19] For Webster, such conflation is characteristic of a wider 'dogmatic dysfunctionality' of Christian theology and doctrinal *loci* which are 'seriously under-determined' by 'concrete material reference' to the doctrine of God.[20] This dysfunctionality, moreover, is traced by Webster to the contemporary theological propensity to 'deregionalize' the theological task by pressing theological disciplines to give an account of themselves in terms drawn largely from non-theological fields of enquiry[21] or to warrant this task by appealing to certain doctrinal *loci* which all too often are 'randomly chosen, abstractly conceived, and without much sense of their systematic linkages'.[22] Either way, the fundamental concern is the same: the *res* of Christian theology and the conflation of its proximate and principal aspects which gives

---

[12] Webster, 'In the Society of God', 205.
[13] See ibid., 206ff.
[14] Ibid., 205.
[15] See ibid., 214–20.
[16] Webster has in mind the analogy drawn by Colin Gunton in which the church is an 'echo' of the personal relations of the immanent Trinity. See Webster, 'In the Society of God', 206; cf., Colin E. Gunton, 'The Church on Earth: The Roots of Community', in Colin E. Gunton and Daniel W. Hardy, ed. *On Being the Church* (Edinburgh: T&T Clark, 1989), 48–80. For further discussion of Gunton's analogy, see Section III.iv of this chapter.
[17] See Webster, 'In the Society of God', 201–2; cf., Webster, *Word and Church*, 196.
[18] Webster, 'In the Society of God', 202.
[19] Ibid., 201–2.
[20] See John Webster, *Holy Scripture: A Dogmatic Sketch* (Cambridge: Cambridge University Press, 2003), 11 and 17.
[21] See John Webster, *Confessing God: Essays on Christian Dogmatics II* (London: T&T Clark, 2005), 7 and 22.
[22] Webster, 'In the Society of God', 202.

rise to the typical but mistaken conviction upon which theology and contemporary ecclesiology subsequently trade. In Webster's words: 'Since the object of Christian theology is the economy of God's works as creator and reconciler of humankind, then theology should naturally direct its attention to the temporal and social as the sphere of God's presence and activity.'[23] For Webster, however, 'the temporal economy, including the social reality of the church in time, has its being not *in se* but by virtue of God who alone is *in se*. Time and society are derivative realities, and that derivation is not simply a matter of their origination; it is a permanent mark of their historical condition.'[24] As such, 'the real' in ecclesiological description is located not in the socio-historical but in God as the ontological ground of all derivative or creaturely reality – including the reality of the church.[25] The ecclesiologist is thus required 'to invest a great deal of theological energy in the depiction of the person and work of … God.'[26] Webster continues: 'Most of all, what will be required will be a rich description of divine aseity as it is manifest in the work of redemption.'[27] All of this is to say that the church's being is 'ectopic', and both protologically and teleologically so; at every moment of its existence the church is neither *self*-generated nor *self*-sustaining, but *is* only 'because God is and acts *thus*'.[28] Out of God's own immanent perfection and in a movement or turning *ad extra*, God determines *ex nihilo* to establish, preserve and perfect a reality 'outside' of his own Trinitarian life.[29]

To speak about the creature of God's grace that the church is, the ecclesiologist, then, must speak first about God's *ad intra* life and his gracious *ad extra* action, such that ecclesiology is always 'set under the metaphysics of grace', and the socio-historical human form of the church understood as 'one long reference to its origin in God's goodness'.[30] Indeed, without such dogmatic order and its concomitant prioritizing of a theology of divine aseity and divine agency in ecclesiological description, an account of the church 'does not attain its object, misperceiving the motion to which its attention is to be directed, and so inhibited in understanding the creaturely movements of the communion of saints'.[31] For Webster, there is, then – or there should be – a proper 'hierarchical arrangement' between types of ecclesiological investigation: the first-order dogmatic task of investigating ecclesiology's principal *res* must always precede and govern the second-order phenomenological task of investigating ecclesiology's proximate *res*.[32] Moreover, by respecting this hierarchy the ecclesiologist resists presenting a 'naturalized ecclesiology' in which the second-order phenomenological task interrupts or overtakes the first-order dogmatic task, or the results of the first-order dogmatic task are assumed to correlate directly with those of the second-order

---

[23] Ibid., 202–3.
[24] Ibid., 203.
[25] See Webster, *Word and Church*, 214–15.
[26] Ibid., 215.
[27] Ibid.
[28] John Webster, 'On Evangelical Ecclesiology', *Ecclesiology* 1.1 (2004), 10.
[29] See ibid., 17.
[30] Webster, 'In the Society of God', 203 and 205.
[31] Ibid., 221.
[32] Ibid.

phenomenological task.[33] In either case, a 'naturalized ecclesiology' not only obfuscates its proper object – God and God's operative and gracious acts – but also reductively collapses what it should otherwise properly and particularly articulate: the fundamental asymmetry of divine and human agency in the church's being.[34]

This forcefully dogmatic concept of the church and the underlying ecclesiological principles it enunciates is without doubt expressed by others in ecclesiological discussion – not least the desire to set that discussion under a metaphysics of grace, either out of concern for appropriate dogmatic ordering and proportionality in ecclesiological description or to *re*regionalize the theological task against what John Milbank describes as the tendency of non-theological disciplines to 'police' the 'sublime'.[35] For Milbank, in whose work Webster's own clarion-call in this direction finds something of a manifesto, the pathos of modern theology is precisely its self-assumed 'false humility' before socio-scientific fields of inquiry – a humility which positions theology in reference to secular reason and thereby surrenders theology's (rightful) claim to be the metadiscourse that positions all other discourse.[36] In Milbank's move 'beyond secular reason', there is, then, no reality more basic than the theological. Theology alone is 'the discourse of non-mastery'[37] and thus to submit that non-theological disciplines somehow permit yet more fundamental access to ecclesial (and non-ecclesial) reality is tantamount to an idolatrous denial of theological truth. Indeed, such a submission surrenders any critical sense that theological speech about ecclesial (and non-ecclesial) reality is *ir*reducible to social-scientific description of socio-historical phenomena. Such speech is – or should always be – speech that speaks of God and God's gracious acts *tout court*.[38] With respect to the reality of the church per se, this speech, moreover, is (according to Milbank) a consequence of the fact that the church exists finitely not as a 'place' or 'identifiable site' within socio-historical existence, that is, 'not *in* time, but *as* time, taken in the mode of gift and promise'.[39] As gift and promise, the church, significantly, is given – and superabundantly so in the eucharist – but not already realized, 'for the body and blood of Christ only exist in the mode of gift, and they can be gift (like any gift) only as traces of the giver and promise of future provision from the same source'.[40] For Milbank, the church, then, *is* only *in* the eucharist or 'on the site of the eucharist', which itself, however, is not a site because it 'suspends presence in favour of memory and expectation'.[41] In this way, the church exists not as 'an ideal *presence* real or imagined' but rather 'as an enacted, serious fiction' – something like 'an "ideal" happening' or 'transmission' through time,

---

[33] See Webster, 'In the Society of God', 221.
[34] See Webster, *Word and Church*, 195–6; cf., Christoph Schwöbel, 'The Creature of the Word: Recovering the Ecclesiology of the Reformers', in Gunton and Hardy, ed. *On Being the Church*, 110–55.
[35] See John Milbank, *Theology and Social Theory: Beyond Secular Reason* (Oxford: Basil Blackwell, 1990), 101–43.
[36] See ibid., 1.
[37] Ibid., 6.
[38] See ibid., 276.
[39] John Milbank, 'Enclaves, Or Where Is the Church?', *New Blackfriars* 73 (1992), 341 and 343 (emphasis added).
[40] Ibid., 342.
[41] Ibid.

which consequently involves the ecclesiologist in offering 'critical narratives of the (endless) genesis of the Church' always in reference to the prior (sacramental) action of God, which alone is determinative of the church's being.[42]

As T. F. Torrance conceives it (and in terms which prefigure the concerns of both Milbank and Webster), the church's being in space and time, grounded as it is in the being and action of God, is such that the church 'lives a life from beyond itself', and thus 'points beyond itself' (somewhat paradoxically) to its own 'inner dogmatic form'[43] – that is, to the divine election of God the Father, which has been actualized in the body and blood of the Son, Jesus Christ, and from whom the being of the church is derived and maintained.[44] It follows that only in the Eucharist – where 'Christ is fully present, present bodily' – does the church (as Christ's body) become the church in its truest sense, 'as it engages in the communion of the Body and Blood of Christ, as it carries out the ordinance of the Lord, the Head of the Body'.[45] Torrance continues: 'Thus in the Eucharist the Church assumes true form and order in obedience to the Word, but as such that order is not static, but dynamic, not a state but an action.'[46]

In Emil Brunner's words, the church 'is precisely no "thing", no "it", but a "he", Christ and His Holy Spirit. It is just in this that resides the miraculous, the unique, the once-for-all nature of the Church'[47] as Christ's body. This nature, moreover, is determined not by the church's socio-historical human form but by its transcendent origin in God's eternal loving will.[48] And again, this will is said to come to expression most intensively in the Eucharist, where in consequence of Christ's presence mediated through the Holy Spirit, the church becomes (ever again) the body of Christ.[49] Precisely in this way is the church 'miraculous'; it participates 'in the special character of the holy, the

---

[42] See ibid., 342–4.
[43] See Thomas F. Torrance, *Royal Priesthood*, Scottish Journal of Theology Occasional Papers No. 3 (Edinburgh: Oliver and Boyd, 1955), 56, 97 and 71; cf., idem, Thomas F. Torrance, *Theology in Reconstruction* (Eugene: Wipf & Stock, 1996), 192–3.
[44] See Torrance, *Royal Priesthood*, 29 and 64; cf., Anders Nygren, *Christ and His Church*, trans. Alan Carlsten (Philadelphia: The Westminster Press, 1956), 100 and 14: 'The Church is nothing in itself' and 'what the Church is, in the deepest sense, emerges only as the Church is seen in its indissoluble relationship with Christ: it is as the "Body of Christ".'
[45] Torrance, *Royal Priesthood*, 72.
[46] Ibid. The fullness of Christ's bodily presence in the Eucharist and the associated co-inherence between Christ and the church as Christ's body is, however, mitigated by Torrance through reference to Christ's atonement and (primarily) his ascension. Indeed, the church as Christ's body is still 'other than Christ' – who despite his eucharistic presence is still absent and yet to come – and lives in the time between his first and final advents. Ultimately, the relation between Christ and the church as Christ's body is an eschatological one, conceived by Torrance in terms of both immediacy and reserve (see Torrance, *Royal Priesthood*, 29–35, 45–50 [46], 56–62 and 72–3). This distinction demarcates Torrance's position from that of Nygren, who, without due concern for Christ's ascension, problematically collapses the self-same relation: as the body of Christ 'the church *is* Christ as he is present among and meets us upon earth after his resurrection'. See Nygren, *Christ and His Church*, 89–115 [32] (emphasis altered). On the significance of Christ's ascension for a doctrine of the church, see Douglas Farrow, *Ascension & Ecclesia: On the Significance of the Doctrine of the Ascension for Ecclesiology and Christian Cosmology* (Edinburgh: T&T Clark, 1999).
[47] Emil Brunner, *The Misunderstanding of the Church*, trans. Harold Knight (London: Lutterworth Press, 1952), 10–11.
[48] See Emil Brunner, *The Christian Doctrine of the Church, Faith, and the Consummation: Dogmatics Volume III*, trans. David Cairns (London: Lutterworth Press, 1962), 23–4.
[49] See Brunner, *The Misunderstanding of the Church*, 65.

numinous, the supernatural', and as such is 'in point of fact unintelligible from a purely sociological standpoint'.[50]

This eucharistic referent, and associated 'eschatological reserve'[51] in ecclesiological description, demands what Douglas Farrow terms an 'epistemological rebound' in ecclesiology, precisely because there is always 'something more' to the church than the socio-historical phenomena of its human empirical form.[52] The church exists (ontologically) in distinction to the world,[53] and 'all [ecclesiological] labours are in vain if they are not grounded beyond themselves in the mystery of the kingdom of God … the moment they propose to be self-sufficient, to deal only with what is publicly accessible, they cease to be churchly and hence to be Christian'.[54] For Farrow, 'It is not *vis-à-vis* the world's own social, religious or scientific communities that the truth of the Christian communion is ultimately to be uncovered', but (only) in the Eucharist itself, in which the church has, and is ever-renewed-in, its being.[55]

As Henri de Lubac observes, while the church's socio-historical human form offers itself up to social-scientific investigation, for that investigation to assume a critical role in ecclesiological description would be to negate the fact that this socio-historical human form is itself 'divine in its foundation'.[56] This foundation, which de Lubac traces to the divine processions,[57] effectively constitutes the church as 'a mysterious extension in time of the Trinity', from which the church comes, and of which the church is 'full'.[58] Consequently, the church originates and exists neither by or for itself nor by human decision or intention, but only as a divine *convocatio*.[59] And this divine call, which summons the church as *congregatio* into reality – a reality which Christ and the Holy Spirit animate, and which (again) comes to perfect expression in the Eucharist – significantly renders the church 'always anterior and superior to anything which can be enumerated and distinguished in her'.[60] In other words, the church 'transcends the limits of her visibility',[61] and thus is a mystery. De Lubac writes: 'The church is a mystery because, coming from God and entirely at the service of his plan, she is an organism of salvation, precisely because she relates wholly to Christ and apart from him has no existence, value or efficacy'.[62] For this reason, the church qua church is

---

[50] Brunner, *The Misunderstanding of the Church*, 12.
[51] Torrance, *Royal Priesthood*, 45.
[52] See Farrow, *Ascension and Ecclesia*, 6, 3 and 264–5: this 'something more' is (according to Farrow) the consequence of 'the christological enigma' of the *Christus praesens* and the *Christus absens* introduced in the Eucharist, and through which the church as Christ's body becomes the church.
[53] See Farrow, *Ascension and Ecclesia*, 3.
[54] Ibid., 6–7.
[55] See ibid., 2.
[56] See Henri de Lubac, *The Splendour of the Church*, trans. Michael Mason (London: Sheed and Ward, 1956), 68–71 [69].
[57] See ibid., 71.
[58] See Henri de Lubac, *The Church: Paradox and Mystery*, trans. James R. Dunne (Shannon: Ecclesia Press, 1969), 24.
[59] See de Lubac, *The Splendour of the Church*, 70; cf., Karl Barth, *Dogmatics in Outline*, trans. G. T. Thompson (London: SCM Press, 1949), 142.
[60] See de Lubac, *The Splendour of the Church*, 76.
[61] de Lubac, *The Church*, 27.
[62] Ibid., 15. In a fashion similar to Nygren, de Lubac (problematically) over-identifies the church (as '*the* body of Christ') with Christ himself. The relation between Christ and the church (as Christ's

totally removed from the epistemological realm of objectivity, and is thus inaccessible to cognitive process; the church cannot be known or interpreted out of itself and this notwithstanding the church's socio-historical human form.[63] In ecclesiological discussion there is, then, an urgent need for the ecclesiologist to beware the illusion of 'an over-naturalistic type of thinking', in light of which 'the Church appears as if founded on human principles and directed to human ends or is explained by human analogies that have been insufficiently scrutinized'.[64] It is for the ecclesiologist to resist, therefore, an anthropological determination of ecclesial reality, and, in Joseph Ratzinger's words, the concomitant reduction of this reality 'to the level of the makeable'.[65]

For Ratzinger, the ecclesiologist as 'maker' must be set negatively against the ecclesiologist as 'wonderer', and while the latter refuses to confine the mystery that the church is to empirical, this-worldly reality, the former loses sight of that mystery and 'values his own activity above all'.[66] Ratzinger continues: '[The maker] thereby restricts his horizon to the realm of things that he can grasp and that can become the object of his making.'[67] However, as a mystery the church is not something that is 'makeable'; what truly 'makes' the church is neither human decision nor intention, but the sacramental action of Christ himself.[68] Ratzinger writes: 'Church cannot be made but only received, that is to say, received from a source where she already exists and really exists: from the sacramental communion of [Christ's] Body as it makes its way through history.'[69] Thus, it is this perpetual eucharistic moment of giving and receiving, in which the being of the church truly *is*, that the ecclesiologist must persistently turn to if her account of the church is not to be determined by overly naturalistic thinking which concomitantly presents a 'makeable' ecclesiology. Indeed, a sacramental ecclesiology furnishes 'a completely theocentric understanding of the Church' in which the foreground is occupied not by the lived social or empirical reality of the church's history but by the gift of God explicated in strictly theological terms.[70] In this way, the ecclesiologist has concern for appropriate dogmatic ordering and proportionality in ecclesiological description: what is needed in this description is 'not a more human,

---

body) is collapsed so sufficiently by de Lubac that (on occasion) he can conceive of the church as 'the incarnation continued'. See de Lubac, *The Splendour of the Church*, 112; and de Lubac, *The Church*, 24.

[63] See de Lubac, *The Church*, 14.
[64] See de Lubac, *The Splendour of the Church*, 9.
[65] Joseph Cardinal Ratzinger, *Called to Communion: Understanding the Church Today*, trans. Adrian Walker (San Francisco: Ignatius Press, 1996), 139.
[66] See ibid., 140 and 143.
[67] Ibid., 143.
[68] See ibid., 161–2.
[69] Joseph Cardinal Ratzinger (Pope Benedict XVI), *Church, Ecumenism, and Politics: New Endeavors in Ecclesiology*, trans. Michael J. Miller et al. (San Francisco: Ignatius Press, 2008), 20. In consequence of this communion with Christ, the Eucharist is forever 'the place where the Church is generated, where the Lord never ceases to found her anew; in the Eucharist the Church is most compactly herself', such that 'the Church *is* Eucharist', 'the presence of Christ, our contemporaneity with him, his simultaneousness with us'. See Ratzinger, *Called to Communion*, 37 and 75 (emphasis added); and Ratzinger (Pope Benedict XVI), *Church, Ecumenism, and Politics*, 14.
[70] See Joseph Ratzinger, *Introduction to Christianity*, trans. J. R. Foster (London: Burns & Oates, 1969), 259.

but a more divine Church.'[71] Here, Ratzinger issues the self-same dogmatic corrective to ecclesiological description as offered paradigmatically by Webster – albeit one, which, while maintaining the fundamental asymmetry of divine and human agency in the church's being, is indexed less to divine aseity traced (in more Protestant terms) through a doctrine of reconciliation, and more to divine aseity traced (in more Catholic terms) through a eucharistic doctrine of the mysterious union of Christ as head to the church as his body. This is a corrective which, nevertheless, is made to attend to ecclesiological speech with due proportion and with an appropriate sense of dogmatic order therein, and to say (along with Torrance) that 'the Church is nothing without God':[72] as a creature of God's operative and gracious action, the church exists only in the mode of gift and is thus *ir*reducible to its socio-historical human form.

In this sense, many of the foregoing arguments can be seen also in relation (though not a relation of dependence) to the ecclesial thought of Karl Barth. While seeking to affirm the socio-historical (or visible) existence of the church against any kind of 'ecclesiastical Docetism', and thus wanting to treat the church always as 'a definite human phenomenon' which like any other worldly phenomenon is graspable in historic or social-scientific terms,[73] what the church most essentially *is* is, for Barth, nevertheless irreducible to its phenomenal surface. In contrast to the 'apparent' church, the 'actual' church is, in a sense, invisible.[74] The invisibility of the 'actual' church results from what Barth sees as the 'third dimension' of the church's existence,[75] in which the church is what it truly is only in consequence of divine action:

> What is this being of the community, this spiritual character, this secret, which is hidden in its earthly and historical form and therefore invisible, or visible only to the special perception of faith? The answer – which does indeed point to a third dimension – can only be this: The community *is* the earthly-historical form of existence of Jesus Christ Himself ... His body, created and continually renewed by the awakening power of the Holy Spirit.[76]

As the Spirit-awakened body of Christ, and precisely in its socio-historical existence which it has thereby, the church has no 'purely natural vitality'[77] – that is, no reality apart from Jesus Christ.[78] In other words, even as a human construction the church cannot be considered in relation to human agency.[79] For Barth, 'although we are in the

---

[71] Ratzinger, *Called to Communion*, 146.
[72] Torrance, *Theology in Reconstruction*, 192.
[73] See *CD*, IV/1, 652ff. [652 and 653].
[74] For Barth's elaboration of his doctrine of the church under the rubric of the 'actual' and 'apparent' church, see *CD*, IV/2, 614–726; Karl Barth, 'The Real Church', *Scottish Journal of Theology* 3 (1950), 337–51; and Karl Barth, *God Here and Now*, trans. Paul M. van Buren (London: Routledge and Kegan Paul, 1964), 61–85.
[75] See *CD*, IV/1, 655.
[76] Ibid., 660–1 (emphasis added).
[77] *CD*, I/2, 689.
[78] The church as Christ's body is a 'repetition' of the incarnate Word of God, such that 'the being of Jesus Christ is the being of the Church'. See *CD*, I/2, 215 and *CD*, IV/2, 655, respectively; cf., *CD*, I/2, 214–221 and *CD*, IV/1, 662–8.
[79] See *CD* I/2, 221.

Church, are indeed ourselves the Church', the church cannot be thought the outcome of free human undertaking, as if it was 'created, formed and introduced by individual men on their own initiative, authority and insight'.[80] Rather, the church is 'God's own act'.[81] Indeed, the church *is* only 'because and as God is at work it in by His Holy Spirit' – both in its original founding and in its continual preservation.[82] The 'actual' church arises and is by 'the divine *creatio continua*'[83] – that is, as God in Godself works in the church in the person of the Holy Spirit as 'the quickening power of the living Lord Jesus Christ'.[84] For Barth, the 'actual' church exists only in the divine 'event' of its constitution and up-building to be the church: 'Gathered together, as an act coming down from heaven, from God's eternal throne and out of the secret of the triune God, and coming forth upon earth … the Church exists by *happening*. The Church exists as the *event* of this *gathering together*.'[85] In other words, the being of the church is in the event of the divine act of *convocatio*,[86] such that the church as *congregatio* is only 'from above, from God', and 'not from below … from the side of its human members'.[87] Thus, only as and when this divine act of the triune God takes place does the church 'actually' exist. While what the 'actual' church is in its spiritual character is not without manifestation or analogy in its socio-historical existence, 'it is not unequivocally represented' therein: 'The gathering and maintaining and completing of the [church] community, as the mystery of what its visible form is on this [its spiritual] level, is in the hand of God, and as His own work, a spiritual reality, its third dimension, it is invisible, it cannot be perceived but only believed.'[88]

In this way Barth articulates the concern shared in 'hard' dogmatic ecclesiology that 'the real' in ecclesiological discussion is not the socio-historical but the theological, and with it the concomitant need to set such discussion under a metaphysics of grace by maintaining the fundamental asymmetry of divine and human agency in the church's being and thus the primacy of dogmatic content in ecclesiological description. Indeed, this 'backward reference'[89] of all ecclesial being and action to the action and being of

---

[80] Ibid., 221 and 213.
[81] Ibid., 221.
[82] See *CD*, IV/2, 616.
[83] *CD*, I/2, 688.
[84] *CD*, IV/2, 61.
[85] Barth, *God Here and Now*, 62.
[86] At work here is Barth's theological ontology, or more precisely, as Paul T. Nimmo construes it, the 'actualistic ontology' with which Barth theologically operates (see Paul T. Nimmo, *Being in Action: The Theological Shape of Barth's Ethical Vision* (London: T&T Clark, 2007), 4ff.). For Barth, the being of God is 'God's being in act' and God in Godself is 'the event of His action' – paradigmatically in his action of revelation, as well as in his action of election, creation, reconciliation and redemption. Thus, 'with regard to the being of God, the word "event" or "act" is *final*, and cannot be surpassed or compromised'. See *CD*, II/1, 262 and 263.
[87] Barth, *God Here and Now*, 68.
[88] *CD*, IV/1, 657. This is not to say, however, that what the 'actual' church *is* is de facto invisible. Barth writes: 'The Real Church is truly not invisible, but visible.' However, the 'actual' (or 'real') church is visible 'at that point, and only there, where she is *made* visible by an act of God and the witness of the Holy Ghost'. Barth argues that 'in this visibleness [the church] will be seen in faith'. Thus, what the 'actual' church is in its socio-historical form is not *generally* visible, but visible only to the 'special visibility' of Christian faith. See Barth, 'The Real Church', 338 (emphasis added); and *CD*, IV/1, 654–6.
[89] Webster, *Word and Church*, 225.

God – to which one should add, in light of the church existing in the time between the first and final advents of Jesus Christ,[90] a *forward* reference – simply serves to remind the ecclesiologist of the need to guard against 'the over-inflation of ecclesiology' into a 'quasi-independent' theological theme.[91] This is precisely the concern of the 'hard' dogmatic ecclesiologist: that 'ecclesiological hypertrophy'[92] in effect results in accounts of the church which are 'too dense, too humanly solid, and therefore insufficiently transparent towards – ostensive of – the self-presentation of God'.[93] Put differently, ecclesiology 'can so fill the [dogmatic] horizon that it obscures the miracle of grace which is fundamental to the church's life and activity'.[94] It is thus the task of 'hard' dogmatic ecclesiology, with its inherent commitment to due order and proportionality in ecclesiological speech, to resist such a move 'by keeping alive the distinction between, and due order of, uncreated and created being; by indicating that phenomena of the church are not irreducible but significative; and by introducing into each ecclesiological description and passage of ecclesiological argument direct language about God, Christ, and the Spirit'.[95] In doing so, the 'hard' dogmatic ecclesiologist works not only to explicate (what she considers) the true object of ecclesiological discussion but also to guard against the reductive metamorphosis of that object into a naturalized phenomenological imposter.

In this way is the doctrine of the church accorded its proper place within dogmatic topography and the ecclesiologist enabled to speak about the church's being in a genuinely theological manner – that is, by speaking of it *first* as an operative and gracious act of God, and not as a community created and sustained in its socio-historical existence by human agency. In the words of Greggs: 'In discussing divine aseity in ecclesiology, one establishes the foundational principle of the non-necessity of creation in order to be reminded of the divine gracious creation of the church external to the human society.'[96] However, at the point at which this reminder or dogmatic corrective against human agency is heard, and appropriate space for an *a priori* account of divine agency made, it then becomes necessary – if the ecclesiologist wishes to speak about the being of the church in a genuinely theological manner – to move on to describe the particular and contingent socio-historical church-community that the operative and gracious act of God creates *in space and time*. For example, what is the nature of that community? What are its habits, practices or virtues? How does God's act relate to ecclesial human reality and lived ecclesial life? How is that life ordered? And why does God choose to create this particular form of spatio-temporal and socio-historical community as the locus of divine and human togetherness? As Torrance puts it: 'The Church is a divine creation, but in the divine economy … The Church was formed in history as God called and entered into communion with his people.'[97] Or in Ratzinger's

---

[90] See *CD*, IV/1, 725–39.
[91] See Webster, *Word and Church*, 213.
[92] Webster, 'On Evangelical Ecclesiology', 11.
[93] Webster, *Word and Church*, 225.
[94] Webster, 'On Evangelical Ecclesiology', 11.
[95] Webster, 'In the Society of God', 221.
[96] Greggs, 'Proportion and Topography in Ecclesiology', 95.
[97] Torrance, *Theology in Reconstruction*, 192.

words: 'Precisely this theocentric image of the Church is entirely human, entirely real.'[98] There is, then, as Brunner describes, a 'clamant need' for the ecclesiologist to attend sufficiently to the human empirical reality of the church's lived socio-historical existence.[99] Thus, as Webster himself states: 'It is clearly important that this emphasis on the priority of divine action over the church as an act of human association should not be allowed to eclipse the "visibility" of the church.'[100] Not least, because divine action, as Ratzinger observes, 'is always theandric, that is, divine-human action'[101] – a point not lost on the later Barth, for whom the meaning and power of God in Godself is found only in his togetherness with humanity: 'God shows and reveals who He is and what He is in His Godness, not in the vacuum of a divine self-sufficiency but genuinely just in this fact that He exists, speaks, and acts as *partner* (without doubt the absolutely superior partner) of man.'[102] For Barth, there is in theological discussion a dogmatic need to say 'yes' to human existence with as much force as he had once said 'no'.[103] Likewise, the ecclesiologist, having heard the 'no' of 'hard' dogmatic ecclesiology and so guarded her account of the church against any tendency to 'forget God' by way of a disproportionate emphasis on human agency in ecclesiological speech, is at once required – and so as to not 'forget human existence' in that self-same speech – to say an apposite 'yes'.[104]

It is precisely this 'yes', however, which, while acknowledged and indeed called for in 'hard' dogmatic ecclesiology, is, in the resultant ecclesial accounts, given insufficient (or no) space, which, in one sense, is to say that even in the *Church Dogmatics* there is in fact little 'church'.[105] Indeed, when confronted by 'hard' dogmatic ecclesiology one is left wondering *what* church the ecclesiologist is actually speaking about, or *where* her church actually is. In fact (seemingly) it appears that the ecclesiologist is not actually speaking about *the church* particularly and contingently conceived. Whether it be through an account of divine agency indexed to a doctrine of God's *ad intra* life as manifest in the work of reconciliation, or to a eucharistic doctrine of the mysterious union of Christ as head to the church as his body, 'hard' dogmatic

---

[98] Ratzinger, *Introduction*, 259.
[99] See Brunner, *Dogmatics Volume III*, 35; cf., Milbank, 'Enclaves', 344; and Milbank, *Theology and Social Theory*, 380: the ecclesiologist must supplement her 'critical narratives of the (endless) genesis of the Church' with 'judicious narratives of ecclesial happenings' so as to be 'rigorously concerned with the actual genesis of real historical churches'. In response to Milbank's call, see Christian B. Scharen, '"Judicious Narratives", or Ethnography as Ecclesiology', *Scottish Journal of Theology* 58 (2005), 125–42.
[100] Webster, *Word and Church*, 196.
[101] Ratzinger (Pope Benedict XVI), *Church, Ecumenism, and Politics*, 125.
[102] Karl Barth, *God, Grace and Gospel*, Scottish Journal of Theology Occasional Papers No. 8, trans. James Strathearn McNab (Edinburgh: Oliver and Boyd, 1959), 37 (emphasis in original); cf., *CD*, I/2, 787: 'If the eternal being [God], with which doctrine has to do, is not implicated in its realisation in actual life, what kind of a being is it? What has it to do with the God of biblical revelation?' While the relationship of God to human existence (as that between creator and creature) cannot be equalized in any sense, in the Word of God, God has, for Barth, eternally elected to be God with and for his people, and eternally elected his people to be with and for God. See *CD*, I/2, 793–94; and *CD*, II/2, 509–51.
[103] See Barth, *God, Grace and Gospel*, 32–7.
[104] See *CD*, I/2, 794.
[105] I am indebted to Tom Greggs for this turn of phrase.

ecclesiology simply renders too great a distinction between God's immanent divine life and both the life of the church in its human empirical form and the economic work of the undivided Godhead in creating and sustaining the church precisely in that form. It is this distinction which thus lays 'hard' dogmatic ecclesiology open to the critique of presenting in somewhat theoretical or abstract terms an idealistic or overly 'spiritualized' account of the church – one which (in doing so) tends towards dissolving the church's being in spatio-temporality as *congregatio* into the event of the divine act of *convocatio*. Indeed, such is the force of the latter that the former is not because it *is* in spatio-temporality, but only as it comes to *be*, in time, and time again, in the *event*ful act of God. In other words, the emphasis in 'hard' dogmatic ecclesiology is placed so strongly on what the operative and gracious act of God endlessly creates out of the socio-historical human form of the church, that that form per se (seemingly) has no *actual* but only *possible* being. Or else, one might say that in 'hard' dogmatic ecclesiology the ontology of the church is construed in 'occasionalist'[106] or more precisely actualistic terms – an actualism, which, in the resultant ecclesiological description, has a tendency, moreover, to deny (ontologically speaking) the actuality or reality of the human empirical form of the church as being dependently distinct from the action of the triune God.[107] Consequently, and despite its own inherent commitment to due order and proportionality in ecclesiological description, 'hard' dogmatic ecclesiology is itself in danger of dogmatically *dis*proportionate and (conceivably) *dis*ordered ecclesiological speech, only in the direction opposite to that which it seeks to guard against. Here, divine aseity and divine agency (to quote Webster back at himself) 'so fill the horizon'[108] of ecclesiology that they obscure – and so lead to the neglect of – the socio-historical phenomena of the church in its particular and contingent reality. To trace the doctrinal locus of ecclesiology so exclusively as 'hard' dogmatic ecclesiology does to God's own life, then runs the risk not only of positing God behind or outside of God's revelation and economy of grace but also of marginalizing the significance of the church's socio-historical human form for ecclesiological discussion. It is this concern which is symptomatic of the second 'type' of approach to ecclesiological description which this chapter is concerned to explicate in relation to contemporary ecclesiological literature in light of the endemic problematic. Thus, having explicated the endemic

---

[106] The term is Welch's and one which he applies (critically) to Barth. See Welch, *The Reality of the Church*, 66–7.

[107] A point which is made (albeit more narrowly) by Colm O'Grady in the context of his critique of Barth's understanding of the church as Christ's body, which (according to O'Grady) has the tendency in part 'to absorb the mystery of the church into the mystery of Jesus Christ' thereby denying the church's existence 'as a mysterious reality in its own right – from Christ, yes, *but also distinct from him and over against him* [as his Spouse]'. See Colm O'Grady, 'The Church the Body of Christ in the Theology of Karl Barth and in Catholic Theology', *Irish Theological Quarterly* 35.1 (1968), 11–21 [20–21 and 21]. Implicitly, the point also raises the question of whether the ontology of the church as construed in 'hard' dogmatic ecclesiology is in fact actualistic enough (so as to sound Barth's dogmatic 'yes' to the particular and contingent socio-historical church-community), and concomitantly the question of where the being of the church (*in se* and per se) is actually held. For further discussion of these questions (including a therapeutic critique of the *in*sufficient actualism of 'hard' dogmatic ecclesiology), see Chapter 3, Section III and IV of this book.

[108] Webster, 'On Evangelical Ecclesiology', 11.

problematic in relation to 'hard' dogmatic ecclesiology, the chapter now turns to do so in relation to 'hard' *ethnographic* ecclesiology.

ii. 'Hard' ethnographic ecclesiology

The 'hard' ethnographic ecclesiologist (like her dogmatic counterpart) considers the endemic problematic an explicit methodological claim that necessarily norms any and all ecclesiological discourse, albeit *ethnographically* not theologically. Accordingly, the being of the church is spoken of properly in ecclesiological discussion only if the ecclesiologist *first* attends – says 'yes' (to establish 'plausibility' in ecclesiological description) – *not* to an account of God's own *ad intra* or *ad extra* life but to the church's particular and contingent socio-historical reality.[109] Thus, for the 'hard' ethnographic ecclesiologist, what is methodologically paramount in ecclesiological discussion is an account of *human* agency. That account (as will be demonstrated) orders the resultant ecclesiological description so exclusively to an investigation of the church's socio-historical human form that that description (problematically) not only rends the doctrinal locus of ecclesiology from a doctrine of God and God's operative and gracious acts but also obfuscates the fundamental asymmetry of divine and human action in the church's being – both through a reductive collapsing of divine agency into human subjectivity, and a folding of ecclesiological speech about divine action into language about ecclesial human reality.

This 'ethnographic turn' in contemporary ecclesiological discourse, which itself is derivative of a prior convergence on 'culture' in theological inquiry,[110] has as its object then the making of ecclesiological description 'more recognisably real'.[111] Such reality is sought by the 'hard' ethnographic ecclesiologist through an articulation of a

---

[109] See Pete Ward, 'Introduction', in Ward, ed. *Perspectives*, 4–5. The concern (as articulated therein) is with the apparent disconnection between what is said doctrinally or theologically about the church and the lived social or empirical reality of its history, and hence with the credibility or ultimate authenticity of ecclesiological speech.

[110] This convergence is most frequently traced to the seminal work of George Lindbeck, *The Nature of Doctrine*, and his argument therein for a cultural-linguistic approach to the task of theology. More recently, this paradigmatic shift towards culture as a categorical hermeneutic for theological inquiry has been taken up by Kathryn Tanner, *Theories of Culture: A New Agenda for Theology* (Minneapolis: Fortress Press, 1997). For Tanner, a postmodern anthropological notion of culture serves to explicate the theological task more fully. Given that religious beliefs and the concrete social practices in which they are inextricably implicated are a form of culture, the task of theology is the exploration of the 'meaning dimension' of those beliefs and practices. Not only is the (proper) subject matter of theology 'Christian social practices' expressed in 'explicitly cultural terms', but (according to Tanner) theology itself, as a 'culture-specific' (human) activity, is one type of 'material social practice among others' (see Tanner, *Theories of Culture*, x, 64 and 72). Theology, then, as it seeks to explore everyday Christian beliefs and practices, which, in Sheila Greeve Davaney's words, are situated in 'the thick matrices of culture', cannot help but draw upon cultural analysis and criticism to prosecute its proper work (see Sheila Greeve Davaney, 'Theology and the Turn to Cultural Analysis', in Delwin Brown, Sheila Greeve Davaney and Kathryn Tanner, ed. *Converging on Culture: Theologians in Dialogue with Cultural Analysis and Criticism* (Oxford: AAR/Oxford University Press, 2001), 9). As Pete Ward writes: 'What is required is a way of working theologically which recognizes theology's own cultural contingency and deals with the theological as culture and culture as theological.' See Pete Ward, *Participation and Mediation: A Practical Theology for the Liquid Church* (London: SCM Press, 2008), 67.

[111] Scharen, 'Judicious Narratives', 125.

reparative ecclesiological method. This method considers ecclesiological speech to be normatively a matter of practical rather than theoretical reasoning, and thus orients such speech away from abstract dogmatic content to ecclesial human reality and church praxis. At the heart of 'hard' ethnographic ecclesiology is the methodological conviction that the being of the church is understood best not through dogmatic (or Trinitarian) deduction but in its 'situatedness' as church,[112] as the church is constituted and sustained in spatio-temporality by the concrete coming together of its human members and by the practices and beliefs enacted therein. Thus, in her account of the church the ecclesiologist must treat *most of all* the church as a human empirical reality, which is wholly accessible to – and which must be inductively investigated in terms of – social-scientific (and historic-cultural) tools of analysis.[113] In other words, and against the abstract, idealist, asocial and ahistorical tendencies of 'hard' dogmatic ecclesiology, it is for the ecclesiologist to present a 'concrete, realist, and historically conscious' ecclesiological account;[114] and only in such an account does the ecclesiologist have 'proper' concern for due order and proportionality in ecclesiological description.

As Roger Haight states: 'The principle object of ecclesiology consists in the empirical organization or collectivity or communion called church', and 'this empirical, human church is the starting point for the study of the church and the basic referent for the word "church".'[115] The reason for this is, in Johannes van der Ven's words, 'God gives to the people to form the church themselves, to do the church themselves.'[116] Or as Joseph Komonchak puts it: 'The Church is an event within human consciousness' – that is, the church comes to be (and does so precisely as Christ's body) only if and because 'certain events occur within the mutually related consciousness of a group of human beings'.[117] For Komonchak, the proper 'object' of ecclesiological discussion is thus those precise events – 'the set (or sets) of experiences, understandings, symbols, words, judgments, decisions, actions, relationships, and institutions which distinguish the group of people called "the Church".'[118] If the ecclesiologist, then, is to discern in her account of the church the 'true nature' of the church, her ecclesiological discourse, as Christopher Brittain puts it, 'cannot remain at the level of ideal and abstract theorizing'.[119]

Indeed, for Brittain, the contradictions and conflicts that arise necessarily in the context of 'lived human existence *as such*' (and out of which theology and ecclesiology emerge) are themselves 'too complicated and painful for the church to be transparent to

---

[112] See Ward, 'Introduction', 2.
[113] See Harald Hegstad, *The Real Church: An Ecclesiology of the Visible* (Cambridge: James Clarke & Co., 2013).
[114] See Roger Haight, S.J., *Christian Community in History*, vol. 1 (New York: Continuum, 2004), 4–5.
[115] Ibid., 5 and 37.
[116] van der Ven, *Ecclesiology in Context*, xiv.
[117] Joseph Komonchak, 'Ecclesiology and Social Theory: A Methodological Essay', *The Thomist* 45 (1981), 269; cf., H. Richard Niebuhr, 'The Churches and the Body of Christ', in H. Richard Niebuhr, *'The Responsibility of the Church for Society' and Other Essays*, ed. Kristine A. Culp (Louisville: Westminster John Knox Press, 2008), 126: as the community of Christ, the church 'exist[s] in the minds, in the personalities and in the interpersonal relations of men'.
[118] Komonchak, 'Ecclesiology and Social Theory', 262.
[119] Christopher C. Brittain, 'Ethnography as Ecclesial Attentiveness and Critical Reflexivity: Fieldwork and the Dispute over Homosexuality in the Episcopal Church', in Scharen, ed. *Explorations*, 132.

itself, or to the theologian'.[120] Consequently, social-scientific description of the church's phenomenal surface serves to enhance both the 'self-reflexivity' of ecclesiology per se, and the ecclesiologist's own (required) capacity to attend to the church's particular and contingent socio-historical reality.[121] Thus, for the 'hard' ethnographic ecclesiologist, ecclesiological description must be articulated, necessarily, as 'the ethnography of religious belief [and practice]',[122] which, against 'hard' dogmatic ecclesiology, is to posit that a doctrine of the church is properly arrived at only by virtue of inductive social-scientific description of the church's phenomenal surface, to which the church's being is reducible.

Edward Schillebeeckx writes: 'The church community as mystery cannot be found behind or above concrete, visible reality. The church community is to be found *in* this reality.'[123] As he puts it elsewhere: 'There is no "surplus of revelation" behind or above the socio-historical forms of [the church and its] ministry.'[124] This is precisely the concern of the 'hard' ethnographic ecclesiologist – that 'the real' in ecclesiological description *is* the socio-historical and thus the concomitant denial that the church's being in space and time has a character sui generis which is grounded in and points towards a reality which in its divinity escapes the critical gaze of historic-cultural and social-scientific fields of inquiry.[125]

In James Gustafson's words: 'There may be an irreducible uniqueness, a differentium that distinguishes the Church from all other historical communities but this does not make it absolutely different in kind.'[126] As such, the church is subject to the same

---

[120] See ibid., 137.
[121] See ibid., 133; and not least in relation to the reality of ecclesial sin, which 'hard' dogmatic ecclesiology tends either to ignore or to limit its material treatment of to an empirical distortion of the church's true theological identity. Webster writes: ecclesial acts are 'movements moved by God' (Webster, 'In the Society of God', 215) – a statement which either renders all sinful ecclesial acts as moved by God or views them (and this would seem the more appropriate inference) as being attributable not to God or to the church as such but only to sinful human beings whose sinful acts somehow remain detached from the reality of the (holy) church and from the being and action of God in which that reality is itself grounded. Such a position, moreover, and notwithstanding Webster's affirmation that 'there is no greater sinner than the Christian Church' (John Webster, *Holiness* (London: SCM Press, 2003), 60), would seem to coalesce with the Catholic concept of the sinlessness of the church as Christ's body. de Lubac writes: 'At one and the same time the Church is without sin in herself and never without sin in her members' (de Lubac, *The Splendour of the Church*, 80). It is precisely this disjuncture, and the concomitant inability of 'hard' dogmatic ecclesiology to address adequately the reality of ecclesial sin that (according to Brittain) the 'ethnographic turn' helps the ecclesiologist to overcome, furnishing as it does a 'thick' description of actual and sinful ecclesial life. See Christopher C. Brittain, 'Why Ecclesiology Cannot Live By Doctrine Alone: A Reply to John Webster's "In the Society of God"', *Ecclesial Practices* 1 (2014), esp. 20–5.
[122] Delwin Brown, 'Refashioning Self and Other: Theology, Academy, and the New Ethnography', in Brown, Greeve and Tanner, ed. *Converging on Culture*, 51.
[123] Schillebeeckx, *Church*, 213.
[124] Edward Schillebeeckx, *The Church with a Human Face: A New and Expanded Theology of Ministry*, trans. John Bowden (New York: The Crossroad Publishing Company, 1988), 5.
[125] See Davaney, 'Theology and the Turn to Cultural Analysis', 7.
[126] James M. Gustafson, *Treasure in Earthen Vessels: The Church as a Human Community* (New York: Harper & Brothers, 1961), 5. This 'differentium' or 'irreducible uniqueness' of the church per se is instead said to be derived from the object of the church's faith: Jesus Christ. See Gustafson, *Treasure in Earthen Vessels*, 88 and 13. The point is made also by Welch, *The Reality of the Church*, 69–70; and H. Richard Niebuhr, *The Purpose of the Church and Its Ministry* (New York: Harper & Brothers, 1956), 19–21.

socio-historical processes as other human empirical communities and is thus open to analysis by the social sciences and humanities.[127] Those fields of inquiry are in turn then elevated over against 'the so-called subject-matter of theology (God)' as the determinative criterion in ecclesiological description.[128] 'Hard' ethnographic ecclesiology is concerned in its account of the church not with dogmatic (or Trinitarian) deduction but with what Kathryn Tanner describes as the theological creativity of 'postmodern "bricoleur"' – that is, 'a creativity expressed through the modification and extension of materials already [existing] on the ground'.[129] In Victor Anderson's words, 'hard' ethnographic ecclesiology is concerned, therefore, with a 'worldly theology'[130] constructed internal to, and out of, the worldly processes of socio-historical existence, and of which the ecclesial thought of Mary McClintock Fulkerson (perhaps) stands as the 'hardest' ethnographic expression.

Confronted with the 'worldly' reality of the church and in order to make 'full theological sense' of it,[131] Fulkerson appropriates the resources of cultural anthropology and in particular the tools of social-scientific analysis to fund a 'thick' description of the 'situational' character of lived ecclesial life.[132] Indeed, only by doing so does the ecclesiologist in her account of the church not overlook 'the worldly way' in which the church lives out the Christian faith and in which God *as God* is 'God-with-us'.[133] Hence, 'to do theological justice to this [church] community will be to write about its people, about its habits and idiosyncrasies, its mistakes and its blindness, as well as its moments of honesty and grace'.[134] For Fulkerson, dogmatic theological inquiry is, however, unable to do this because of the 'purely ideational'[135] terms in which it is

---

[127] See Gustafson, *Treasure in Earthen Vessels*, 5.
[128] See Mark Chapman, 'On Sociological Theology', *Journal for the History of Modern Theology* 15 (2008), 8.
[129] Tanner, *Theories of Culture*, 166.
[130] See Victor Anderson, 'Secularization and the Worldliness of Theology', in Brown, Davaney and Tanner, ed. *Converging on Culture*, 71–85.
[131] See Fulkerson, *Places of Redemption*, 7.
[132] See ibid., 7–12. To seek to establish the primacy of 'situation' in ecclesiological description is to acknowledge what liberationists have long maintained – that is, that action or praxis must always precede thinking and understanding. For Leonardo Boff, 'true ecclesiology' comes about not through the positing of 'theological hypotheses' but only because of 'ecclesial practices' already at work within the church. The ecclesiologist 'must analyse the various practices in effect and from there arrive at the theoretical premises and formulations behind these practices' (see Leonardo Boff, *Church: Charism and Power: Liberation Theology and the Institutional Church*, trans. John W. Diercksmeier (London: SCM Press, 1985), 1). Only to the extent that the ecclesiologist begins her ecclesiology with an analysis of such praxis is that ecclesiology (inductively) true. The call of liberation theology is thus for '[a] true "ecclesiogenesis"' (Boff, *Church*, 9), in which the church is not 'thought of from the top down, but from the bottom up' (Leonardo Boff, *Ecclesiogenesis: The Base Communities Reinvent the Church*, trans. Robert R. Barr (Maryknoll: Orbis Books, 1986), 15). However, for the liberationist, while ecclesiology must begin with church praxis and ecclesial human reality, that reality, although 'already deciphered with socioanalytical tools', must still be 'read [subsequently] with the eyes of faith and theology' to ensure the resultant ecclesiology goes 'beyond mere phenomenological analysis' (see Boff, *Church*, 20 and 1). Whether such a move in fact 'ensures' the outcome claimed by Boff is, however, disputable on grounds similar to those set out below in relation to 'hard' ethnographic ecclesiology's detheologization of ecclesiology per se.
[133] Fulkerson, *Places of Redemption*, 6.
[134] Ibid., 9.
[135] Ibid., 233.

conceived. This 'ideational' framework problematically bypasses and, moreover, seeks to impose 'correct' Christian doctrine upon 'the complex configuration of the lived situation' of faith, and does so without regard for, and thus in implicit suppression of, the way in which 'lived or everyday theologizing' arises organically out of both theological and non-theological convictions.[136] In the ordinary practice of faith, '"belief and value commitments" are usually left underdeveloped and "ambiguous"', and thus by its very nature 'the pattern of a dogmatic system will occlude the contradictory way commitments occur'.[137] Consequently, the task of ecclesiological description – *if* the ecclesiologist is to attend to 'the "primary analytic" object'[138] of theological discussion – is most 'properly' the task of practical theological inquiry.

What is most basic or foundational in ecclesiological description is, then, not a doctrine of God or even a doctrine of the church per se but rather the fruits of empirical study which alone are capable of displaying the ambiguity and implication of the church in its socio-historical existence.[139] The reason for this is located by Fulkerson not simply in dogmatic theology's tendency to bypass and suppress the lived situation of faith but more acutely in dogmatic theology's 'ideational' methodology, which is ignorant of how theological inquiry is in fact initiated.[140] For Fulkerson, 'the generative process of theological understanding is a process *provoked*', and more specifically provoked by a 'wound' – a disjunction, that is, which compels theological creativity in response to the sense 'that something [wrong] must be addressed', that harm in fact must be redressed.[141] Ultimately, the process of theological inquiry 'is defined by an a priori logic of transformation',[142] and precisely in consequence of this logic – its 'theo-logic' – does Fulkerson consider her ecclesiology per se 'theological'.[143]

Notwithstanding the concern of 'hard' ethnographic ecclesiology to say 'yes' to ecclesial human reality and church praxis, and to do so by way of social-scientific and historic-cultural description of the church's lived socio-historical existence in reaction against the theological idealization of that existence by 'hard' dogmatic ecclesiology, Fulkerson's point here should not be lost. For in the move against what Gustafson describes as 'theological reductionism',[144] the 'hard' ethnographic ecclesiologist nonetheless seeks to guard her ecclesiological speech from collapsing into 'social reductionism'[145] and denying thereby that the church *is* a theological reality.[146] Indeed,

---

[136] See ibid., 8 and 233–4.
[137] Ibid., 8.
[138] Mary McClintock Fulkerson, 'Interpreting a Situation: When Is "Empirical" Also "Theological"?', in Ward, ed. *Perspectives*, 129.
[139] See Fulkerson, *Places of Redemption*, 13 and 7.
[140] Ibid., 13.
[141] See ibid., 12–18 [13 and 14] (emphases altered).
[142] Ibid., 14.
[143] Ibid., 238. The logic is *theo*logical because a 'wound' (and the situations of harm which give rise to it), while not read by Fulkerson explicitly as 'sin', is theo*logically* suggestive of sin, and the concomitant notion of 'redress' theo*logically* suggestive of redemption of that 'sin'. See Fulkerson, *Places of Redemption*, 235ff.
[144] Gustafson, *Treasure in Earthen Vessels*, 100.
[145] Ibid., 107.
[146] This move may in part be motivated by a theological concern 'to warn', as Brittain writes, 'against taking the existing empirical church *as* the church itself, thereby losing any critical capacity for

as expressed in 'hard' ethnographic ecclesiology, the 'ethnographic turn' and prior convergence on 'culture' in theological inquiry seeks neither the reduction of the theological to the empirical[147] nor the 'detheologization' of ecclesiological description per se,[148] such that the church is understood as the product of human agency alone,[149] but rather an empirical – and thus genuinely theological – prosecution of the ecclesiological task: an account of the church which at once is located empirically but committed theologically,[150] and which, moreover, can (according to Pete Ward) be expressed Christologically.

On the basis of Paul's Christological hymn in Col. 1.15-20, Ward avers: 'We want to speak simultaneously about the theological and the social/cultural reality of the church because of Christ who is at once the one in whom "all things" hold together and "head of the church."'[151] On this Christological basis, Ward proceeds to note the methodological fallacy of a correlational distinction between the empirical and the theological, for 'if all things are "in Christ", then this must relate to social and cultural expressions, and this is also true of the means that might be used to research it.'[152] Concomitantly, theology is said, therefore, to have no innate disciplinary superiority over (or particularity from) the social sciences, and interdisciplinary conversation in ecclesiological discourse arises precisely because of 'the possibility of analogy and dialogue from social and cultural realities that are in Christ.'[153] However, for such a contention to hold good, and for the 'hard' ethnographic ecclesiologist not to be found here doing precisely what she seeks to guard her ecclesiological speech against – that is, from reducing the theological to the empirical and thus denying the theological reality of the church per se – Ward has to perform what (seemingly) is a subtle act of exegetical misdirection; Paul does not say to the Colossians that 'all things' are '*in* Christ', but that 'in' (or 'by') Christ 'all things' hold together or are sustained continually. And to say the latter is not to say the former as Ward does to read the empirical *as* the theological. Put otherwise, what is 'in Adam' is not yet 'in Christ', and consequently an ontological distinction between creator and (fallen) creation must be maintained – a distinction which Ward's exegetical misdirection problematically lets slip.[154]

---

ecclesiology to call the church's into question'. See Brittain, 'Ethnography as Ecclesial Attentiveness and Critical Reflexivity', 137.

[147] See Ward, *Participation and Mediation*, 43.
[148] See Harald Hegstad, 'Ecclesiology and Empirical Research on the Church', in Scharen, ed. *Explorations*, 40.
[149] See James Nieman and Roger Haight, S.J., 'On the Dynamic Relation between Ecclesiology and Congregational Studies', in Scharen, ed. *Explorations*, 13.
[150] See Ward, *Participation and Mediation*, 18; cf., Gustafson, *Treasure in Earthen Vessels*, 111: the task is to seek a 'theological interpretation of the social character of the Church.'
[151] Ward, 'Introduction', 2-3.
[152] Ibid., 3.
[153] Ibid.
[154] Cf., Marianne Meye Thompson, *Colossians and Philemon: The Two Horizons New Testament Commentary* (Grand Rapids: Eerdmans, 2005), 30 and 31: 'The world is not part of God nor is God part of the world, but neither does the world exist independently of the sustaining power of God.' To state that 'all things' were created 'through' and 'for' Christ and 'hold together' 'in' Christ is to express the agency of Christ in God's work of creating, sustaining and redeeming the world, and to assert that as the agent of God's work 'Christ has supremacy over all that is created'. This supremacy,

That slip, ultimately, thus does lay 'hard' ethnographic ecclesiology open to the critique of presenting in its account of the church both a reduction of the theological to the empirical and a 'detheologization' of ecclesiological description per se, or to recall, respectively, Webster's and Ratzinger's terminology, of presenting a 'naturalized' or 'makeable' ecclesiology without an appropriate and proportionate sense of dogmatic order therein. The consequence of this is not only to conflate in an account of the church the proximate *res* of ecclesiology with its principal *res* but also to run the risk in that account of collapsing divine agency into human subjectivity, and of folding ecclesiological speech about divine action into language about ecclesial human reality – a point demonstrated not least by Fulkerson's *theo*logical ecclesiology and its theo*logical* suggestiveness.

Indeed, for Fulkerson this theo*logical* suggestiveness posits at once that reference to divine agency in ecclesiological description can be proffered not as direct speech of the operative and gracious acts of God, but as indirect '*testimony to transformations that are attributable to God*'.[155] In determining what is 'theological', primacy is given by Fulkerson to the socio-historical experience of 'redemptive alteration', or to 'ecclesial redemptive sociality as mediator or as *appresentor* of transcendence'.[156] As defined by Fulkerson, the 'proper' subject matter of theology (and ecclesiology) is not, then, God and God's acts, but the human experience of 'transformation in the direction of an ultimate good: redemption'.[157] Moreover, for Fulkerson, redemption is an ultimate good itself mediated through intersubjective and sociopolitical realities.[158] Consequently, in the words of Harold Hegstad, 'theological statements regarding the church are statements about the empirical church'.[159] While such a radical collapse of divine agency into human subjectivity in ecclesiological description is not replicated so intensely by others in contemporary ecclesiological discourse, the risk of folding speech about divine action into language about ecclesial human reality most certainly is.

Haight, for example, argues that the church as a human community has 'a certain' and 'constitutive relationship' to God.[160] This relationship renders ecclesiology a 'theological' discipline and concomitantly irreducible to the conclusions of social-scientific tools of analysis because 'the church is experienced religiously or theologically, because in it and through it people recognize the presence and activity of God'.[161] However, that 'the church is *experienced*' theologically, and 'in it and through it *people* recognize' God puts the ultimate emphasis in ecclesiological speech not on divine action but on human agency, and does so by way of folding speech about the former into language about the latter.[162] Similarly, for Komonchak, to say that the church is a human social reality is 'not [to] intend a "reduction" of the Church to simply another social reality in the

---

moreover, is ontological in nature; Christ is 'the firstborn of all creation' (Col. 1.15) and 'was before all things' (Col. 1.17).
[155] Fulkerson, *Places of Redemption*, 237.
[156] Fulkerson, 'Interpreting a Situation', 140.
[157] Ibid.
[158] See ibid.
[159] Hegstad, 'Ecclesiology and Empirical Research on the Church', 40.
[160] See Haight, *Christian Community in History*, vol. 1, 36.
[161] Ibid., 5.
[162] See ibid (emphasis added).

world', for 'the Church remains the creation of the mysterious God's self-gift in Word and Spirit'.[163] However, Komonchak continues: 'It is not God but Christian men and women who constitute the Church ... the Church is constructed when divine favor transforms and promotes conscious acts of *human* intentionality and intersubjectivity.'[164] This transformation and promotion takes place such that 'the Church is not the divine initiative itself, but the human-social response to God's grace and word'.[165] Or, as Gustafson argues, the church cannot be satisfactorily understood apart from its 'relation to' God as 'the gift and work of God', but God in that work uses 'that which can be interpreted without reference to him' – that is, the realm (and processes) of the natural and social – as the agency by which to effect the church as 'an historically continuous body of persons known as Christians'.[166] Not only does Gustafson risk denying the non-necessity of creation and creation's ontological ground in God and in God's operative and gracious acts, but he also (along with Komonchak) ultimately folds ecclesiological speech about divine action into language about ecclesial human reality. He thus tends towards collapsing divine agency into human subjectivity in his account of the church, here understood in terms of common Christian faith and the gathering together of Christian people. As Claude Welch argues, the being of the church, first of all, is 'a human community responding' – albeit one which responds to the activity of God – and concomitantly the ontology of the church is, in the first instance, 'the humanly subjective pole' of the relationship between God and human beings.[167]

In rendering the church's ontology thus, 'hard' ethnographic ecclesiology folds ecclesiological speech about divine action into language about ecclesial human reality to such an extent that the being of God and God's operative and gracious acts are evacuated as the church's efficient and sustaining cause. What remains in ecclesiological discussion is a disproportionate description – albeit a 'thick' one – of the phenomenal surface of a human community, which while standing in a certain (responsive) relationship to God, is nevertheless created and sustained in its social-historical existence by human agency. 'Hard' ethnographic ecclesiology is thereby guilty of disordered and disproportionate ecclesiological speech. As a doctrinal locus, ecclesiology – beginning and ending as it does with the contingency and particularity of the church's (observable) human empirical form – is treated independently from the doctrine of God, and the ecclesiologist stands liable to undergirding her account of the church (at worst) by a capitulation to methodological atheism, or (at best) by making the empirical (and anthropological) the foundational dogmatic *res* of ecclesiology. Either way, when confronted by 'hard' ethnographic ecclesiology, one is left wondering if the ecclesiologist, in attempting to ensure (through her recourse to the tools of social-scientific analysis) that her account

---

[163] Joseph A. Komonchak, *Foundations in Ecclesiology*, Supplementary Issue of the *Lonergan Workshop Journal*, vol. 11 (Boston: Boston College, 1995), 56.
[164] Ibid. Cf., van der Ven, *Ecclesiology in Context*, 40: 'God brings people together by the fact that people come together themselves. God inspires them to togetherness by the fact that they inspire themselves to togetherness. God motivates them to a community through the fact that they motivate themselves to a community.'
[165] Komonchak, *Foundations in Ecclesiology*, 151.
[166] See Gustafson, *Treasure in Earthen Vessels*, 104, 105, 108 and 6 (emphasis altered).
[167] See Welch, *The Reality of the Church*, 46 and 48; cf., Niebuhr, *The Purpose of the Church and Its Ministry*, 17–27.

of the church sounds an appropriately proportionate 'yes' to the church's lived socio-historical existence, has in fact not failed to hear the 'no' of 'hard' dogmatic ecclesiology, and so succumbed (as the early Barth feared) to 'forget God' in the process of doing so. It is precisely this concern which is symptomatic of the '*soft*' form of this second 'type' of approach to ecclesiological description which this chapter is concerned to explicate in relation to contemporary ecclesiological literature in light of the endemic problematic. Thus, having explicated the endemic problematic in relation to both 'hard' dogmatic and 'hard' ethnographic ecclesiology, the chapter now turns to do so in relation to the 'soft' version of this latter ecclesiological 'type'.

iii. 'Soft' ethnographic ecclesiology

For the 'soft' ethnographic ecclesiologist, the endemic problematic (in contrast to her 'hard' ethnographic colleague) is not considered an explicit methodological claim to be stated in order necessarily to norm ethnographically any and all ecclesiological discourse, but rather can be seen as an implicit logical consequence of her own ecclesiological description. In other words, while that description is not built upon a necessary and normative claim about the foundation of ecclesiology per se, it nevertheless displays certain presumptions and thus continues to exemplify the logic of attending in an account of the church *either* to the life of God 'dogmatically' *or* to the particular and contingent socio-historical church-community 'ethnographically'. While the 'soft' ethnographic ecclesiologist (*along with* her 'hard' ethnographic colleague, but *contra* the 'hard' dogmatic ecclesiologist) considers the 'proper' object of ecclesiological discussion to be the church's lived socio-historical existence, she nevertheless sees the associated and explicit methodological claim of 'hard' ethnographic ecclesiology as problematic in absolute terms. Methodologically, the 'soft' ethnographic ecclesiologist seeks to warrant her ecclesiological discussion, ultimately, by an appeal to a theological account – however variously conceived – of God's *ad intra* or *ad extra* life. Notwithstanding that theological account, the resultant ecclesiological description (as will be demonstrated), in consequence of its disproportionate emphasis on ecclesial human reality and church praxis still, however, problematically rends the doctrinal locus of ecclesiology from a doctrine of God, and thus forgets – to one extent or another – the church's irreducible uniqueness in its being constituted and sustained in space and time by God and God's operative and gracious acts. In other words, there is in 'soft' ethnographic ecclesiology an inadequate demarcation of the sui generis nature of the church in distinction from all other socio-historical forms of human community. This 'ethnographic' ecclesiological stance is (perhaps) displayed most obviously in the ecclesial thought of Stanley Hauerwas, and in his emphatic and tireless description of the church as an alternative human *polis* that embodies a particular set of human practices configured in response to the story of God, and which make the reality of that story visibly manifest.[168]

---

[168] See, for example, Hauerwas, *A Community of Character*; Stanley Hauerwas, *In Good Company: The Church as Polis* (Notre Dame: University of Notre Dame Press, 1995); and Stanley Hauerwas, *The Peaceable Kingdom: A Primer in Christian Ethics* (Notre Dame: University of Notre Dame Press, 1983).

Hauerwas's claim that 'the church is a social ethic'[169] and thus constituted and sustained by people of theological virtue who witness to the triune God as 'creator of all that is'[170] is symptomatic of the way in which the ecclesiologist (according to Hauerwas) is to conceive ecclesiological (and theological) inquiry per se. For Hauerwas, such inquiry is 'a performative discipline' in which 'the "what" of what we believe' is inseparable 'from the "how"'.[171] This is not only to underscore an indispensable link in ecclesiological inquiry between doctrine and life but also (and intentionally) to conflate positively what David Kelsey describes as the 'logic of belief' – that is, the meaning and interconnection of dogmatic statements about God and God's relation to all that is not God – with the 'logic of the life of belief' – that is, the way in which that belief is lived out in practice.[172] Theology (and ecclesiology) must, then, always be done 'in a way that does not abstract doctrine from ways of life in which doctrine does work'.[173] Indeed, for Hauerwas, 'the grammar of "belief" invites a far too rationalistic account of what it means to be a Christian. "Belief" implies propositions about which you get to make up your mind before you know the work they are meant to do.'[174] This is not to say, however, that the '"what" of what we believe' is unimportant, but simply that questions about belief must have purchase on 'how' one's life is lived if ecclesiological inquiry is to guard against presenting (in a fashion after the 'hard' dogmatic ecclesiologist) an overly abstract or 'spiritualized' account of the church. There is thus a need not only for the church to recover what Hauerwas describes as 'peasant Catholicism'[175] – whereby Christianity is understood not as 'a set of beliefs or doctrines you believe in order to be a Christian', but about becoming part of and participating in the community of the

---

[169] See Hauerwas, *The Peaceable Kingdom*, 99.

[170] Stanley Hauerwas, *Sanctify Them in the Truth: Holiness Exemplified* (Edinburgh: T&T Clark, 1998), 38; and Stanley Hauerwas, *With the Grain of the Universe: The Church's Witness and Natural Theology* (Grand Rapids: Brazos Press, 2001), 215. The argumentative force of this assertion should not be lost in the overall construction of the church that Hauerwas offers. What 'is' is, for Hauerwas, contingent in character and 'can be properly displayed only as God's free gift.' As creator, God is the beginning and end of all creaturely existence; creatures are 'constituted by a *telos* not of [their] own making' and the church is a creation of God (see Hauerwas, *Sanctify Them in the Truth*, 38–9 and 45). Ecclesial life is possible only because God makes it so, and so while not wanting to deny the value of social-scientific tools of analysis for investigating the creaturely reality of the church, Hauerwas is concerned to dismiss in ecclesiological description 'the uncritical use of social-scientific paradigms which often, if applied rigorously and consistently, methodologically preclude the theological claims necessary for the church's intelligibility' (Hauerwas, *Christian Existence Today*, 130 n.15).

[171] Stanley Hauerwas, *The Work of Theology* (Grand Rapids: Eerdmans, 2015), 271 and 269; cf., James J. Buckley and David S. Yeago, 'Introduction: A Catholic Evangelical Theology', in James J. Buckley and David S. Yeago, ed. *Knowing the Triune God: The Work of the Spirit in the Practices of the Church* (Grand Rapids: Eerdmans, 2001), 9: 'What Christians *say* about the triune God cannot be adequately explicated without reference to what Christians most characteristically *do* in worship and obedience to that God.' See also the collection of essays in Miroslav Volf and Dorothy C. Bass, ed. *Practising Theology: Beliefs and Practices in Christian Life* (Grand Rapids: Eerdmans, 2002) all of which explicate – in one way or another – the conviction that thinking and belief about God must go hand-in-hand with the way in which lives are lived practically.

[172] See Hauerwas, *The Work of Theology*, 266–78; cf., David H. Kelsey, *Eccentric Existence: A Theological Anthropology*, 2 vols (Louisville: Westminster John Knox Press, 2009), 1:15, 1:80–119 and 2:683–9.

[173] Hauerwas, *The Work of Theology*, 271.

[174] Stanley Hauerwas, *Hannah's Child: A Theologian's Memoir* (London: SCM Press, 2010), x.

[175] See Hauerwas, *Sanctify Them in the Truth*, 77–80.

church and its practices by which 'one's body [is] shaped, [and] one's habits determined, in a manner that the worship of God is unavoidable'[176] – but also for the ecclesiologist to recover ecclesiological speech, which, 'if it is to be truthful', is 'embedded in the practices of actual lived [church] communities'.[177] For Hauerwas, it is observable social practices which are the content of description of the church.

It is this forcefully 'performative' concept of the church and the underlying construction of theological (and ecclesiological) method upon which it trades, which, despite his own critical analysis of Hauerwas' ecclesiological description,[178] is echoed by Nicholas Healy in his critique of 'blueprint ecclesiologies',[179] and in consequence of which Healy identifies with Hauerwas's fundamental methodological claim that to treat ecclesiological inquiry as a system of 'belief' is necessarily to distort that inquiry.[180] In Healy's view (and hence his critique) 'blueprint ecclesiologies' give the impression that only after the ecclesiologist has *first* got her '*thinking* about the church right' can she then proceed to attend to its lived socio-historical existence. It is, as Healy puts it, 'as if good ecclesial practices can be described only after a prior and quite abstract consideration of true ecclesial doctrine'.[181] The problem Healy locates is not only in the obvious absence of any theological agreement over a definitive or denotative (theoretical) 'model' in ecclesiological description on the basis of which the normative force of 'blueprint ecclesiologies' hang[182] but also in the attendant preference for reflecting on the church's essential and theoretical identity in abstraction from its empirical and actual reality, not least from the reality of ecclesial sin.[183] Healy writes: 'Blueprint ecclesiologies thus foster a disjunction not only between normative theory and normative accounts of ecclesial practice, but between ideal ecclesiology and the realities of the concrete church.... As a consequence, blueprint ecclesiologies frequently display a curious inability to acknowledge the complexities of ecclesial life in its pilgrim state.'[184] So as to acknowledge this state, Healy (in a fashion similar to Hauerwas) asserts the need to reorder ecclesiological discussion per se to that which arises out of, and is directed necessarily towards, 'contextual ecclesial praxis'.[185] Healy makes this move by appropriating the theodramatic horizon of Hans Urs von Balthasar.[186] This 'dramatic' horizon, in which theological discourse is articulated best from the perspective of a participant living entirely within the ongoing, tensile and conflictual movement of the drama that is Christian existence prior to final eschatological completion, stands (in von Balthasar's thought) in direct contrast to an 'epic' horizon in which theological discourse steps out of that drama to assume a spectator's standpoint external and

---

[176] Ibid., 79.
[177] Ibid., 157.
[178] See Nicholas M. Healy, *Hauerwas: A (Very) Critical Introduction* (Grand Rapids: Eerdmans, 2014).
[179] See Healy, *Church, World, and the Christian Life*, 25–51.
[180] See Hauerwas, *The Work of Theology*, 277.
[181] Healy, *Church, World, and the Christian Life*, 36.
[182] See ibid., 30–5.
[183] See ibid., 10.
[184] Ibid., 37.
[185] Ibid., 46
[186] See ibid., 52–76; cf., Hans Urs von Balthasar, *Theo-Drama: Theological Dramatic Theory*, 5 vols trans. Graham Harrison (San Francisco: Ignatius Press, 1988–1998).

distant to it, and from which a 'smooth' account of Christian doctrine is developed absent of the tensions inherent in ongoing Christian existence.[187] For Healy, the parallels between the methodological characteristics of 'blueprint ecclesiologies' and von Balthasar's 'epic' horizon are obvious;[188] hence his appropriation of the 'dramatic' counterweight, which not only negates 'any closure for Christian [and ecclesial] existence to the other side of the eschaton'[189] but also illuminates the very tensile nature of this existence. This tensile nature of ecclesial existence determines that ecclesiology must be duly ordered to 'include *explicit* analysis of the ecclesiological context as an integral part of *theological* reflection upon the church'.[190] Thus, it is axiomatic – and indeed necessary – that in her account of the church the ecclesiologist should deploy social-scientific tools of analysis to attend appropriately to the socio-historical human form of the church in its pilgrim state.[191]

That said, and notwithstanding Healy's concern for the ecclesiologist to establish in her account of the church the centrality of ecclesial human reality and church praxis, that account must nevertheless be authorized (according to Healy) by a 'robust' doctrine of God and have as its 'initially independent' 'starting-point' a thoroughgoing statement of the economic work of the immanent Trinity.[192] Moreover, that account must describe, subsequently, lived ecclesial life from *within* this 'dogmatic' perspective, and maintain God's freedom and in particular that of the Holy Spirit to act independently or apart from the church and its practices.[193] Indeed, without such an account, the ecclesiologist

---

[187] See von Balthasar, *Theo-Drama*, vol. 2, 54–62; cf., Ben Quash, *Theology and the Drama of History* (New York: Cambridge University Press, 2005).
[188] See Healy, *Church, World, and the Christian Life*, 76.
[189] Ibid., 72.
[190] Ibid., 39. It is significant for the argumentative force of this assertion that Healy conceives the ecclesiological context as being in no way separable from the church itself, such that 'church' and 'context' could be regarded as two independently describable and (subsequently) correlatable entities. Instead, 'the concrete church lives within and is formed by its context', and thus the identity of the church is constituted by theological, non-theological and even anti-theological elements. See Healy, *Church, World, and the Christian Life*, 38–9 [39] and 167.
[191] See Healy, *Church, World, and the Christian Life*, 154–85. This perspective also guides the work of Paul Avis, for whom the church's nature – and indeed the truth of God and thus doctrine per se – cannot be known *a priori* in abstraction from the particular and contingent socio-historical reality in which the church is inescapably embedded. In language echoing that of Healy, Avis writes: 'It will not do to start with a paper blueprint of the Church … The Church is known in ecclesial praxis – practical experience of being the church, shaped by theology, but not by theology alone' (Paul Avis, *Reshaping Ecumenical Theology: The Church Made Whole?* (London: T&T Clark, 2010), 60). Ecclesiological description 'demands an empirical earthing for its statements' and thus recourse to the disciplines and methods of social science (see Paul Avis, *Ecumenical Theology and the Elusiveness of Doctrine* (London: SPCK, 1986), 43). On the need for ecclesiology to reflect more explicitly at the level of lived or actual faith and to include in its purview social-scientific tools of analysis to account appropriately for the worldly being of the church, cf., Karl Rahner, *Theological Investigations* [hereafter *TI*], 23 vols trans. Karl-H. Kruger, David Bourke et al. (London: Darton, Longman & Todd, 1961–1992), XVII, 197–207; and XII, 218–28 and 230–3.
[192] See Nicholas M. Healy, 'Practices and the New Ecclesiology: Misplaced Concreteness?', *International Journal of Systematic Theology* 5 (2003), 287–308 [301 and 302] (which stands as a significant corrective, in part, to his argument in *Church, World, and the Christian Life*).
[193] See Healy, 'Practices and the New Ecclesiology', 302. This latter point is made *contra* Reinhard Hütter. Hütter sees the church as constituted and defined by a nexus of its (own) teaching and practices indexed exclusively to the work of the Holy Spirit. Hütter argues that the church is 'the soteriological locus of God's actions' – a 'space' or 'public' that is 'constituted by specific core

threatens (in a fashion similar to the 'hard' ethnographic ecclesiologist) to collapse in her account of the church divine agency into human subjectivity, or to fold speech about divine action into language about ecclesial human reality. Or in Healy's words: 'to collapse the object of faith into ourselves'.[194] While Healy is adamant, therefore, that ecclesiological description must necessarily arise out of and be directed towards ecclesial human reality (and in that be attentive to human agency), such description must itself always begin and end in reference to God's action.[195] The task of ecclesiology, then, is to be prosecuted not simply by way of *non*-theological social-scientific tools of analysis but by specific *theological* forms of those tools – that is, by way of a 'theological history', a 'Christian sociology' and/or an 'ecclesiological ethnography'.[196] Not only does this approach remain, however, somewhat tentative or undefined in Healy's own ecclesiological work,[197] but it is one which is *still* focused *most of all* on lived ecclesial life and church praxis. The resultant ecclesiological description is disproportionate in its attention to human agency, affording thereby insufficient space to divine agency in its account of the church, which thus continues to exemplify the logic of the endemic 'either/or' problematic. This approach, moreover, finds something of a manifesto, and in fact greater and wider definition, in the earlier work of Daniel Hardy.

For Hardy, the need to think theology and non-theological disciplines together in this way arises not only in critique of the inability of 'hard' dogmatic ecclesiology to treat adequately the complexity of ecclesial life lived in situ but also (and more fundamentally) on account of the ways and activity of God which are said to be *with* and *in* the world.[198] Hardy writes: 'The truth and purposes of God are "refracted"

---

practices and church doctrine' (Hütter, *Suffering Divine Things*, 27). He continues: 'These practices are understood pneumatologically as acts to be interpreted enhypostatically as "works" of the Spirit' (Hütter, *Suffering Divine Things*, 132). For Hütter, the real subject of the church's core practices is not the human agent but the Holy Spirit. Indeed, while human activity is always actively present in such practices, it does not constitute them. The reason for this is that the relation of the church (and its members) to the Holy Spirit, modally, is always receptive, and thus the church's action strictly pathic as the Holy Spirit acts upon it. The church's core practices, then, are distinct human activities whose point is their *passivum* as they subsist enhypostatically *in*, and thus gain their binding authoritative status from, the poiesis of the Holy Spirit (see Hütter, *Suffering Divine Things*, 158). For Healy, Hütter's construction not only binds the Holy Spirit to the church in a way which makes it hard to see how the Holy Spirit might work outwith or even prophetically over against the church and its practices but also (somewhat idealistically) renders those practices impervious to sin, and thus (problematically) limits in an account of the church the effect of human agency (see Healy, 'Practices and the New Ecclesiology', 297–9). Ultimately, Hütter's ecclesiological description, notwithstanding its concern to attend to ecclesial praxis, fails (in a fashion similar to the 'hard' dogmatic ecclesiologist) to sound an appropriately proportionate 'yes' to the church's lived socio-historical existence.

[194] Healy, 'Practices and the New Ecclesiology', 302.
[195] See Nicholas M. Healy, 'Karl Barth's Ecclesiology Reconsidered', *Scottish Journal of Theology* 57 (2004), 298.
[196] See Healy, *Church, World, and the Christian Life*, 151–85 [161, 167 and 169]; cf., Milbank, *Theology and Social Theory*, 380ff.
[197] Here 'tentative or undefined' in terms of *how* the ecclesiologist in her ecclesiological description goes about prosecuting in practice a theological form of historical, sociological and/or cultural analysis. That said, a model form of 'ecclesiological ethnography' can be seen (according to Healy) in the thick theological analysis of William Cavanaugh's *Torture and Eucharist*. See Healy, *Church, World, and the Christian Life*, 183–4.
[198] See Daniel W. Hardy, *God's Ways with the World: Thinking and Practising Christian Faith* (Edinburgh: T&T Clark, 1996).

– as it were spread like a band of colour – in other forms of life and thought', and thus theological (and ecclesiological) inquiry – if it is to resist abstractness – must 'rediscover the dynamic of God's life and work in this "band of colour" and from it.'[199] In the first instance, such a rediscovery necessitates that theological (and ecclesiological) inquiry proceeds upon the basis of a 'symbiotic relation' between theology and multiple disciplinary convictions – a relation in which those disciplines 'are allowed to "pass through"' or interpenetrate each other in such a way so as to integrate the truth of theological and non-theological forms of inquiry,[200] '*unfolding* the former into the latter and *enfolding* the latter into the former'.[201] Significantly, this is not to say that the former and the latter are identical – only that they should interact with or more precisely 'refract' each other in order to (re)discover 'a fuller way' to account in theological (and ecclesiological) description for the rich diversity of ways in which the presence and activity of God in the world is mediated.[202] There is thus a need in ecclesiology for the ecclesiologist 'to move off one's chair', to 'wander first and then think theologically and practically in response to what they have found.'[203] Indeed, the ecclesiologist must energetically oppose any 'dogmatic' tendency towards 'ahistorical completeness'[204] that would presume ecclesiology (or theology) to be a fixed set of doctrinal propositions from which all necessary implications for Christian belief and church praxis could normatively be deduced, and concern herself instead with lived ecclesial life: to theologize only in relation to what the church in socio-historical actuality is and by giving acute theological attention to the materiality of that actuality and the sciences which study it. Thus, the ecclesiologist must not (abstractly or idealistically) 'construct' the church, but 'find' it in its socio-historical existence.

This 'finding', in view of the potential danger for 'found theology' to collapse (in a fashion similar to 'hard' ethnographic ecclesiology) the 'theological' into the empirical, is, however, underwritten for Hardy by an application of the doctrine of the Trinity.[205] In the second instance, therefore, the rediscovery that Hardy calls for in theological (and ecclesiological) inquiry necessitates a certain Trinitarian, and specifically pneumatological account of the way in which the dynamic relationality of

---

[199] Hardy, *God's Ways with the World*, 1–2.
[200] See ibid., 319 and 323; cf., Daniel W. Hardy, *Finding the Church: The Dynamic Truth of Anglicanism* (London: SCM Press, 2001), 106.
[201] Daniel W. Hardy, 'A Magnificent Complexity', in David F. Ford and Dennis L. Stamps, ed. *Essentials of Christian Community: Essays for Daniel W. Hardy* (Edinburgh: T&T Clark, 1996), 348 (emphasis in original).
[202] See Hardy, *God's Ways with the World*, 71, 323–4 and 326.
[203] Daniel W. Hardy (with Deborah Hardy Ford, Peter Ochs and David F. Ford), *Wording a Radiance: Parting Conversations on God and the Church* (London: SCM Press, 2010), 86. It is this emphasis in Hardy's theological thought that has led Peter Ochs to describe it as an exercise in 'found theology' – that is, a theology which begins with and is constructed out of what is found already within the world (see Peter Ochs, *Another Reformation: Postliberal Christianity and the Jews* (Grand Rapids: Baker Academic, 2011), 167–75). Found theology, as Ben Quash argues, makes a theological virtue of ongoing history and serves to remind the theologian that theology itself is 'historically discovered ("found"), and will always be so'. See Ben Quash, *Found Theology: History, Imagination and the Holy Spirit* (London: Bloomsbury T&T Clark, 2013), 1 and 279.
[204] Quash, *Found Theology*, 1.
[205] See Hardy, *Finding the Church*, 33; Hardy, *God's Ways with the World*, 324–5; and Hardy, *Wording a Radiance*, 45–54.

Father, Son and Holy Spirit is self-structured 'in an ongoing "relation" with human life *in* the world.'[206] This 'relation' not only identifies God as one whose being is directed being – directed towards the creature, that is – but also directs the creature (and indeed creation itself) (to move) towards the creator; 'Everything *is* toward God, *attracted* to God,'[207] and the creature, by way of their being created, 'attracted' to other creatures thereby. In this way, 'attraction' names for Hardy a creaturely (and divine) ontology of 'towardness', which not only informs the 'inherent sociality of all creation'[208] but also creates an intensive and dynamic form of abductive socio-poiesis in which the Holy Spirit – working in and through history, and by the generation and shaping of ever-expanding orders of relation (hence the attraction's socio-poiesitic nature) – draws all of creation transformatively beyond itself (hence the attraction's abductive nature) and into (fulfilment in) God's kingdom.[209] This 'attraction', moreover, is 'distributed' in three interpenetrating and mutually implicated 'socio-poietic modalities',[210] and in light of which ecclesiology must be addressed not only 'to "the Church" in a self-limited sense, but also to sociopoiesis through-out all of God's creation'[211] as creation is implicated in the historical-pneumatological movement towards true or redeemed sociality.

Notwithstanding its certain Trinitarian and pneumatological basis, Hardy's move here renders the church 'not altogether distinguished from those forms of society that do not explicitly embody God's purposes'.[212] Indeed, for Hardy, the church is but one form among many societal forms by which people live and seek to (best) structure (and thus restructure) their relations through which society as a whole transcends itself socio-poiesitically.[213] In other words, the church is but one subspecies of created sociality among others, and significantly one whose distinctiveness is located by 'soft' ethnographic ecclesiology not in the act and activity of God per se but ultimately in an account of human thought and action indexed to ecclesial practice. Hardy writes: 'The distinctive character of a *church* is that it finds the meaning of society in God, and seeks to bring society into closer and closer approximation of the truth that also frees people to be fully themselves, that is to the truth of God.'[214] The church, as a societal form, is thus distinguished from all other forms of society (religious or otherwise) 'on the basis of its beliefs about God'.[215] Or more precisely, as Healy continues, on the basis of what

---

[206] Daniel W. Hardy, 'God and the Form of Society', in D. W. Hardy and P. H. Sedgwick, ed. *The Weight of Glory: A Vision and Practice for Christian Faith: The Future of Liberal Theology* (Edinburgh: T&T Clark, 1991), 143 (emphasis added).
[207] Hardy, *Wording a Radiance*, 48.
[208] Ibid., 49; cf., Hardy, 'Created and Redeemed Sociality', in Gunton and Hardy, ed. *On Being the Church*, 21–47.
[209] See Hardy, *Wording a Radiance*, 45–54; cf., Daniel W. Hardy, 'Receptive Ecumenism – Learning by Engagement', in Paul D. Murray, ed. *Receptive Ecumenism and the Call to Catholic Learning: Exploring a Way for Contemporary Ecumenism* (Oxford: Oxford University Press, 2008), 428–40.
[210] Hardy, 'Receptive Ecumenism', 434: the three modalities being 'nation', 'global civilization' and 'church'.
[211] Hardy, *Wording a Radiance*, 53.
[212] Hardy, *Finding the Church*, 40.
[213] See ibid., 238–41.
[214] Ibid., 240.
[215] Nicholas M. Healy, 'What Is Systematic Theology?', *International Journal of Systematic Theology* 11 (2009), 37.

the church believes to be 'its unique relation'[216] or 'Spirit-empowered *orientation*'[217] to God through Jesus Christ, and concomitantly 'its mediating function'[218] to witness to that relation through ecclesial praxis and the quest of its members to live authentic Christian lives in the world.[219] Healy's argument here thus echoes that of Hauerwas, for in Hauerwas' words, what distinguishes the church qua church is 'the *kind* of narrative that determines its life'.[220] While the church is distinctive to other human communities as a 'theological politics',[221] that distinctiveness is, for Hauerwas, not an ontological but ethical designation: 'The only difference between church and world is the difference between agents' – that is, the difference between the basic personal postures of those who do and do not confess the story of God as their story.[222]

As one variance of the genus of created sociality among others, there is, then, for the 'soft' ethnographic ecclesiologist (seemingly) nothing ontologically distinct about the being of the church in spatio-temporality, such that the church as a human community might be considered sui generis in nature. The difference between church and world, construed as it is in terms of Christian belief and action, does not (as Hauerwas hopes the case to be) 'go all the way down'.[223] Therefore, and notwithstanding the concern of the 'soft' ethnographic ecclesiologist to warrant her ecclesiological description of lived ecclesial life and church praxis theologically by reference to the action of God, 'soft' ethnographic ecclesiology (in a fashion similar to 'hard' ethnographic ecclesiology) is laid open to the critique of collapsing in its account of the church divine agency into human subjectivity, of folding speech about divine action into language about ecclesial human reality or of locating the church in the 'natural' creating work of God and not in God's redeeming work. While her ecclesiological description (in distinction to her 'hard' ethnographic colleague) *is* undergirded by an account of God's *ad intra* or *ad extra* life, and is thus *not* open to the critique of collapsing the theological into the empirical without remainder, the church's distinctiveness for the 'soft' ethnographic ecclesiologist nevertheless lies – ultimately – not in a theological account of God's own life but in a particular kind of human life embodied in a particular set of human practices configured in response to God. For all it may seem, therefore, that the 'soft' ethnographic ecclesiologist in warranting her account of the church's lived socio-historical existence by a theological account of God's own life proffers a 'both/and' ecclesiological methodology, or, as Hauerwas puts it, a view of the church as both a 'natural' and 'graced' community,[224] her ecclesiological description nevertheless emerges in the context of lived ecclesial life and church practice – about which she *subsequently* theologizes – and concomitantly is inadequately attentive to

---

[216] Healy, 'What is Systematic Theology?', 37.
[217] Healy, *Church, World, and the Christian Life*, 17.
[218] Healy, 'Ecclesiology, Ethnography, and God', 193.
[219] See ibid., 197–8.
[220] Hauerwas, *A Community of Character*, 4.
[221] Arne Rasmusson, *The Church as Polis: From Practical Theology to Theological Politics as Exemplified by Jürgen Moltmann and Stanley Hauerwas* (Notre Dame: University of Notre Dame Press, 1995), 188.
[222] See Hauerwas, *The Peaceable Kingdom*, 101.
[223] Hauerwas, *The Work of Theology*, 5.
[224] See Hauerwas, *The Peaceable Kingdom*, 103.

the sui generis nature of the church as a human community. In other words, 'soft' ethnographic ecclesiology presents – in consequence of a disproportionate emphasis on human agency – an account of the church which, again to recall Webster's and Ratzinger's terminology, is overly 'naturalized' or 'makeable', and which is absent of an appropriate sense of dogmatic order. Here, not only is it forgotten that the church qua church *is* uniquely constituted in spatio-temporality by *divine* agency – and so is not just one creaturely entity in creation among others – but ecclesiology is rendered too independent as a doctrinal locus from the doctrine of God. As the 'no' of 'hard' dogmatic ecclesiology serves to remind the ecclesiologist, ecclesiology is not, however, an independent locus. Yes, the church is God's *people*, but the church is so only because *God* has first determined to be his people's God. It is precisely this divine determination and the concomitant dogmatic order which it necessitates in ecclesiological description that the 'soft' ethnographic approach to ecclesiology problematically forgets and thus obfuscates. While the 'soft' ethnographic ecclesiologist does indeed speak about God's own *ad intra* or *ad extra* life, such speech remains proportionately but something of a remote (or presupposed) ecclesiological backdrop against which more dense and critical speech about lived ecclesial life and church practice is set, and in consequence of which the church's being in spatio-temporality is rendered distinct not in any sense ontologically in consequence of the being of God and God's operative and gracious acts but only ethically in responsive human action thereto.[225] When confronted by the 'soft' ethnographic approach to ecclesiology, one is left wondering, therefore, if God is *still* not (in some ways) missing from the resultant ecclesiological description, in which the church's being (and ecclesiology per se) is problematically rent once more from its dogmatic connections. It is precisely this concern that stands, moreover, at the forefront of the '*soft*' form of the *first* 'type' of approach to ecclesiological description which this chapter is concerned to explicate in relation to contemporary ecclesiological literature. Thus, having first explicated the endemic problematic in relation to 'hard' dogmatic ecclesiology, and subsequently in relation to both 'hard' and 'soft' ethnographic ecclesiology, the chapter now turns to do so, finally, in relation to 'soft' 'dogmatic' ecclesiology.

iv. 'Soft' dogmatic ecclesiology

For the 'soft' dogmatic ecclesiologist the endemic problematic (in contrast to her 'hard' dogmatic colleague but echoing her 'soft' ethnographic counterpart) is not stated as an explicit and programmatic methodological claim in order necessarily to norm ecclesiology theologically. The problematic is rather an implicit logical consequence of her own ecclesiological description, which continues to display certain assumptions. In the case of 'soft' dogmatic ecclesiology (as per 'hard' dogmatic ecclesiology, but *contra* ethnographic ecclesiology) the 'proper' object of ecclesiological discussion is not the

---

[225] In relation to the work of Hardy speech about God is, arguably, *more* than something of a remote (or presupposed) backdrop to his ecclesiology, especially in his application of the doctrine of the Trinity within his explication of created and redeemed sociality. That said, it remains the case for Hardy that redeemed sociality is not a distinctive of the church but rather of creation per se.

church's lived socio-historical existence but God's own life, albeit often specifically a 'social' understanding of that Trinitarian life. In ecclesiological description, a theology of divine aseity and divine agency is thus methodologically paramount for the 'soft' dogmatic ecclesiologist. However, the 'soft' dogmatic ecclesiologist seeks to retain in her ecclesiological account – to one extent or another – the 'ineradicable materiality' of theological and ecclesiological propositions.[226] What makes a 'soft' dogmatic ecclesiological account stand in distinction to that proffered by her 'hard' dogmatic colleague, therefore, is not only the *mode* of accounting for the doctrine of the church subsequent to a doctrine of God's *ad intra* life – a mode which (as will be seen) might itself be theologically precarious – but also the *economic* emphasis on the particularity and finitude of 'the church as it is' upon which God acts.[227] This economic emphasis thereby renders the 'hard' dogmatic ecclesiologist's thoroughgoing dissolution of the church's being in space and time into the act and activity of God problematic. Notwithstanding the concern of 'soft' dogmatic ecclesiology to treat, therefore, the church theologically as the church exists concretely in spatio-temporality, the resultant ecclesiological description – in consequence of its disproportionate emphasis on God's own life – risks (in a fashion similar to 'hard' dogmatic ecclesiology) construing the being of the church without full reference to its spatio-temporal reality. In doing so, the 'soft' dogmatic ecclesiologist not only marginalizes in her ecclesiological description the church's lived social-historical existence but also renders too close a connection between God's immanent divine life and the life of the church in its human empirical form. This 'dogmatic' ecclesiological stance is (perhaps) best expressed in the ecclesial thought of Colin Gunton.

Working (in Barth's wake) against what he sees as an over-determination of ecclesiological description on docetically tending Christological grounds, and thus in critique of 'dogmatically flawed' ecclesiological speech which makes 'too much' of the church's divinity and 'too little' of its humanity, Gunton seeks (ironically perhaps) an account of the church rooted in God, and 'even as such' (and thereby in display of the endemic problematic) belonging finitely and fallibly to the created world.[228] In his ecclesiological description, Gunton thus proceeds to affirm the church's existence in spatio-temporality as it is constituted pneumatologically in the economic action of the Holy Spirit and grounded ontologically in the immanent life of God as triune.[229] For Gunton, the being of the church is seen (analogously and indirectly) as an 'echo' or 'bodying forth' in space and time of the kind of being-in-relation that God is in the personal relations of the immanent Trinity in eternity.[230] Moreover, it is precisely

---

[226] See Robert W. Jenson, *Systematic Theology*, vol. 1 [hereafter *ST1*] (New York: Oxford University Press, 1997), 19.

[227] See Hans Küng, *The Church* (London: Burns & Oates, 1967), 1; cf., *TI*, XII, 142.

[228] See Gunton, 'The Church on Earth', 48–80 [62 and 74].

[229] See ibid., 57–77; and Colin Gunton, *The Actuality of Atonement: A Study of Metaphor, Rationality and the Christian Tradition* (Edinburgh: T&T Clark, 1988), 173–205.

[230] See Gunton, 'The Church on Earth', 69; cf., Colin Gunton, *Theology through the Theologians: Selected Essays, 1972-1995* (Edinburgh: T&T Clark, 1996), 194. Gunton sees this move as needing to proceed with great dogmatic care – hence its *indirect* nature – if it is to neither collapse 'the utter ontological otherness of God and the world' nor lose 'the dynamic of what is the essence of the economy as theologically construed: a structured open embracing of time by eternity' (see Colin Gunton, *The One, The Three and the Many: God, Creation and the Culture of Modernity* (Cambridge: Cambridge University Press, 1993), 228 and 161). Theological (and ecclesiological) inquiry must

the economic (and eschatological) work of the Holy Spirit which realizes *now* this 'echo' of that which belongs to the age to come, and does so, significantly, by way of 'earthly, this-worldly means' located within the socio-historical human form of the church itself.[231] In this way, the Holy Spirit is seen by Gunton as the divine agent that 'particularizes' the church's human empirical form, in the sense of enabling that form to be concretely what it truly *is*:[232] a distinctive communal way of being in the world, whose life – as an 'echo' or social extension in space and time of the immanent Trinity – is oriented towards God by the action of the Holy Spirit in virtue of its own enacted relation to the life, death and resurrection of Jesus Christ. The church's 'true' being is thus qualified by Gunton both pneumatologically and eschatologically, being oriented as it is beyond itself to its eschatological telos, and being wholly dependent in (and for) that orientation on the action of the Holy Spirit. For Gunton, the church comes about and consequently 'must, ever and again, take place'[233] in the eschatological action of the Holy Spirit.[234] In the words of Hans Küng: 'The Spirit of God in his freedom *creates* the Church, and constantly creates it anew from those who believe. ... Through the operation of the Spirit the Church is created and created afresh each day.'[235] This is

---

affirm, therefore, 'in *relative* distinction' a doctrine of the immanent Trinity from the economic, so as 'to allow for personal space between God and the world' (Colin Gunton, *Intellect and Action: Elucidations on Christian Theology and the Life of Faith* (Edinburgh: T&T Clark, 2000), 103) and to maintain securely that creation *is* only 'by virtue of its continuing dynamic dependence upon its creator'. See Gunton, 'The Church on Earth', 67.

[231] See Gunton, *The Actuality of Atonement*, 179. These 'earthly' ecclesial means include proclamation of the Word of God; celebration of the sacraments; living truthfully (and responsibly) in light of Jesus's way of being in the world; and living as a community of praise. See Gunton, *The Actuality of Atonement*, 178–203. On the last two of these earthly ecclesial 'means', see Hauerwas, *A Community of Character*, 36–52; and Daniel W. Hardy and David F. Ford, *Praising and Knowing God* (Philadelphia: The Westminster Press, 1985), respectively.

[232] See Gunton, *Theology through the Theologians*, 114.

[233] Ibid., 202.

[234] Cf., Jürgen Moltmann, *The Church in the Power of the Spirit: A Contribution to Messianic Ecclesiology*, trans. Margaret Kohl (London: SCM Press, 1977), wherein the church is said to be what it truly is – 'the community and fellowship of Christ' – only 'in the Holy Spirit' (Moltmann, *The Church in the Power of the Spirit*, 33). Thus, the church is present wherever and only *as* the Holy Spirit 'mediate[s] the presence of the history of Christ and the future of the new creation'. Moltmann continues: 'What is called "the church" is this mediation' (Moltmann, *The Church in the Power of the Spirit*, 35). Consequently, the ecclesiologist cannot say '*what* the church is', but only '*where* the church happens', precisely because in the eschatological action of the Holy Spirit 'the church is a *happening* which is not totally absorbed by its definition' (Moltmann, *The Church in the Power of the Spirit*, 65 and 122). Furthermore, to 'find' the church, the ecclesiologist must begin her ecclesiology not with abstract or idealistic concepts of the church but from 'the happening of Christ's presence' (Moltmann, *The Church in the Power of the Spirit*, 122) as it is mediated in history. For Moltmann, the yardstick of a dogmatic ecclesiology is thus the eschatological person of Jesus Christ, and against his 'interest' (Moltmann, *The Church in the Power of the Spirit*, 14) in the church must all other possible tools of analysis be tested and ultimately limited. It is noteworthy that Moltmann's statement about 'the community and fellowship of Christ' which the church truly is 'in the Holy Spirit', is followed directly by his saying (problematically), 'the Spirit is this fellowship' (Moltmann, *The Church in the Power of the Spirit*, 33) – a conflation of the Spirit with the church which (seemingly) would include the church in the Godhead per se.

[235] Küng, *The Church*, 175–6. That the church receives its being from the Holy Spirit, moreover, constitutes for Küng what distinguishes the church from all other forms of human community. Only the church is in receipt of the Holy Spirit, and only the church can make demonstration of the Holy Spirit in power. However, the Holy Spirit is not – and must never be identified with – the church. See Küng, *The Church*, 168–9, 173 and 179.

all to say (in a fashion after the 'hard' dogmatic ecclesiologist) that the church exists 'exocentrically'[236] – receiving its own (true) being passively in the mode of gift, as the Holy Spirit makes real in the temporal and historical-visible church-community 'anticipations' of the eternal community that God is, and that in the age to come will be.[237]

Robert Jenson writes: 'The church is what she is just and only as anticipation of what she is to be.'[238] What the church anticipates is her inclusion in the community of Trinitarian persons of which the church's own communal way of being is 'sheer *arrabon*'.[239] In its socio-historical existence, the church is 'an event *within the event* of the new age's advent', and as such is neither 'a phenomenon of this age, patient of the concepts and hypotheses of secular social history' nor 'simply heaven, describable in this age only in the imagery of apocalyptic',[240] but rather is a 'divine-humanity'.[241] In other words, for Jenson, while the being of the church is grounded in the *ad intra* life of God and so linked ontologically as Christ's body to the second person of the Trinity, and thereby is considered *prior* to (and *distinct* from) creation, the church nevertheless is a work of God *ad extra in* creation. The unmediated and wholly antecedent will of God dictates (according to Jenson) that the church chosen in God's divine intention as being other than the world is exactly the church that exists in the world by the (economic) action of the Holy Spirit.[242] Jenson argues: '"It is the proper work of the Holy Spirit, to make the church." And we must add: the Spirit does this by giving himself to be the spirit of this community, by bestowing his own eschatological power to be her liveliness.'[243] The Holy Spirit releases the church-community from the determinisms of its socio-historical existence, so that an actual human community can

---

[236] Gunton, *Intellect and Action*, 199.
[237] See Colin E. Gunton, *The Christian Faith: An Introduction to Christian Doctrine* (Oxford: Blackwell Publishing, 2002), 122.
[238] Robert W. Jenson, 'The Church and the Sacraments', in Colin E. Gunton, ed. *The Cambridge Companion to Christian Doctrine* (New York: Cambridge University Press, 1997), 216.
[239] See Robert W. Jenson, *Systematic Theology*, vol. 2 [hereafter *ST2*] (New York: Oxford University Press, 1999), 222.
[240] See ibid., 171 and 172. It is for this reason that Jenson (in a fashion similar to Moltmann and Hauerwas), while not wanting to deny that social-scientific tools of analysis 'may sometimes be convenient' for ecclesiological investigation, is concerned to establish that any such 'borrowings' be 'strictly ad hoc' and done 'with great circumspection' and 'considerable bending of the recruited concepts' (*ST2*, 172). This must be so not only because of the church's anticipatory being but because of the nature of theological inquiry per se. Theology, Jenson writes, 'claims to know elements of reality that are not directly available to the empirical sciences ... but that yet must be known ... if such lower-level cognitive enterprises are to flourish. ... Theology, with whatever sophistication or lack thereof ... claims to know the one God of all and so to know the one decisive fact about all things, so that theology must be either a universal and founding discipline or a delusion.' See *ST1*, 20.
[241] Simon Chan, 'The Church and Development of Doctrine', *Journal of Pentecostal Theology* 13.1 (2004), 64 (commenting directly on Jenson's point here).
[242] See *ST2*, 173.
[243] Ibid., 197. Jenson's problematic conflation of the Holy Spirit with (the spirit of) the church-community should be noted here: the Holy Spirit *is* – gives 'himself *to be*' – the spirit of the church-community. Or as Jenson writes elsewhere: 'It is the church's founding miracle that her communal spirit is identically the Spirit that the personal God is and has' (*ST2*, 181). This correspondence means that 'the spirit of the church *is* the Holy Spirit himself'. See *ST2*, 196 (emphasis added).

be united with Christ and can thus act as mediator of creation's translation into God.[244] The *communio* that the church is, therefore, results primarily not from the self-same communion that its human members have with Christ in common but instead from the communion of God with his people in Christ.[245] Jenson states: '*We* do not create our communion, moved by our – in itself very real – affinity. We receive one another with Christ and Christ with one another; we at once receive Christ and the church in which we receive him.'[246] Thus, at every step of the ecclesiological way the ecclesiologist must insist on divine agency and specifically on the agency of the Holy Spirit, by which the *communio* of God is animated in the church's life and the church becomes Christ's body in its being epicletically and anamnetically united to the Son's created body.[247] Ultimately, the economic action of the Holy Spirit in constituting the socio-historical existence of the church is thus indexed (properly according to Jenson) eucharistically. Only in the Eucharist does the church realize what it is truly, for in the Eucharist the Holy Spirit makes the church Christ's body and thus at once – ontologically speaking and in relation to Christ – *signa et res*: the presence of the remembered Jesus as the sign of the One who is to come.[248]

For Jenson, this eucharistic paradox which forms the church's 'ontological heart', by which the church is understood as the sacramental coincidence of future and past,[249]

---

[244] See *ST2*, 179.

[245] See ibid., 222.

[246] Ibid. Contra 'hard' ethnographic ecclesiology, the church (according to Jenson) is not constituted by the autonomous association of individual human wills. Yes, there can be no church without the concrete coming together of faithful and obedient believers, but such faith and obedience is preceded by, and is completely dependent upon, the antecedent will of God and action of the Holy Spirit.

[247] See *ST2*, 211–27. Notwithstanding a passing reference to its spousal relation and, therefore, distinction to Christ, the church is united so completely to Christ that, for Jenson, 'the church is ontologically the risen Christ's human body' (*ST2*, 213). In a fashion similar to Nygren and de Lubac, Jenson thus (problematically) over-identifies the church as Christ's body with Christ himself, and threatens to collapse the transcendence of the risen and ascended bodily Christ into sheer immanence. On the point of critique, see Colin E. Gunton, '"Until He Comes": Towards an Eschatology of Church Membership', *International Journal of Systematic Theology* 3 (2001), 187–200.

[248] See *ST2*, 259–60.

[249] See ibid., 260. The point is made similarly by Küng in his constructed relation of neither separation nor identification between the church's '*real essence*' and its '*historical form*' (see Küng, *The Church*, 3–6 [5]). For Küng, between identity and difference there is an event of eschatological co-inherence, such that through Christ and in the Holy Spirit the coming reign of God is already 'evident and effective … in the Church' (Küng, *The Church*, 95). Moreover, that '*the real essence of the real Church is expressed in historical form*' means that the 'starting-point' of ecclesiological discussion must be not 'an ideal Church situated in the abstract celestial spheres of theological theory', but 'the *real* Church as it exists in our world' (Küng, *The Church*, 5). Ecclesiological description is conditioned historically precisely because the eschatological action of God through Christ and in the Holy Spirit convokes an historical people as God's people (see Küng, *The Church*, 130). The church is constitutively '*the great concilium of the faithful, convoked in the Spirit by God Himself through Christ*' (Hans Küng, *Structures of the Church* (London: Burns & Oates, 1965), 12). Thus, the ecclesiologist must neither 'retreat into harmless theologumena, remote from real life, about the "essence" of the Church' (in a fashion after the 'hard' dogmatic ecclesiologist) nor 'disregard the essence of the Church which is dictated by its origins', and so (in a fashion after the 'hard' ethnographic ecclesiologist) 'concern [herself] simply with the present form of the Church, becoming absorbed with ecclesiastical activity' (Küng, *The Church*, 5).

and acquires what John Zizioulas describes as 'the *memory of the future*',[250] thus works to resist a complete historicization of the church qua church. In other words, in the Eucharist the linearity of history is transcended eschatologically.[251] Indeed, as Zizioulas argues, the economic action of the Holy Spirit by which the *eschata* are brought (paradigmatically) into history (in the Eucharist) confronts history per se 'with its consumation, with its transformation and transfiguration'.[252] Zizioulas writes: 'By bringing the *eschata* into history, the Spirit does not vivify a pre-existing structure; He *creates* one; He changes linear historicity into a *presence*'.[253] This action dilates the historical sequence of past, present and future to the infinite dimensions of the *eschaton*, and the Holy Spirit transcends linear historicity as 'the Lord' thereby.[254] In the eucharistic synaxis, the work of the Holy Spirit thus makes of the church's socio-historical human form an eschatological (or ecclesial) being – what Zizioulas calls 'a *eucharistic hypostasis*'[255] or '"mode of existence", *a way of being*'[256] as communion bound to God's own communal way of being – which frees the church from the causality and determinisms of historicity, and gives it a foretaste of eternal life as the image of the triune God.[257] Consequently, the church's being in the Eucharist is manifested as that which is 'instituted, that is, historically *given*' in the event of the socio-historical communion of God's people gathered to celebrate the Eucharist itself, and as that which is pneumatologically '*con-stituted*, that is, constantly realized as an event of free communion, prefiguring the divine life and the Kingdom to come'.[258] For Zizioulas, the church receives her 'biological' being from the human social response to Christ in history. This 'biological' being only becomes true 'ecclesial' being, however, as (and each time) the Holy Spirit constitutes the church qua church in the actual eucharistic synaxis.[259] The Eucharist is *not* the liturgical act of an already existing or ontologically prior church, but it is itself the event that constitutes (epicletically) the church's being, 'enabling the Church to *be*',[260] according to God's own Trinitarian way of being. Thus, for Zizioulas (and in a fashion similar to both Jenson and Gunton), the church, ultimately, 'is an event which takes place unceasingly afresh' in space and time, existing

---

[250] John D. Zizioulas, *Being as Communion: Studies in Personhood and the Church* (London: Darton, Longman & Todd, 1985), 180.

[251] A parallel might be drawn here to the thought of Hardy. For Hardy, the 'extensities' of social life – the dimensions of past, present and future – are 'layered' (eschatologically) and thus conjoined by the action of the Holy Spirit in the Eucharist. The Eucharist as such is the 'practical activity which founds church society'. See respectively Hardy, *Finding the Church*, 242–52; and Hardy, *Wording a Radiance*, 65.

[252] Zizioulas, *Being as Communion*, 180.

[253] Ibid.

[254] Ibid.

[255] Ibid., 59.

[256] Ibid., 15.

[257] See ibid., 22; cf., Miroslav Volf, *After Our Likeness: The Church as the Image of the Trinity* (Grand Rapids: Eerdmans, 1998), 129 and 197: 'The Spirit unites the gathered congregation with the triune God and integrates it into a history extending from Christ, indeed, from the Old Testament saints, to the eschatological new creation. This Spirit-mediated relationship with the triune God and with the entire history of God's people … constitutes an assembly into a church' as 'an εἰκών ("image") of the Trinity'.

[258] See Zizioulas, *Being as Communion*, 22.

[259] See ibid., 25.

[260] Ibid., 21.

not as a human community instituted in any *permanent* socio-historical sense[261] but rather and only insofar as the eucharistic communion of the gathered people of God *ever again* becomes the church – that is, the body of Christ – as the *eschaton* is realized in the repeated action of the Eucharist.[262]

Given this emphasis in her ecclesiological description, the 'soft' dogmatic ecclesiologist (in a fashion similar to her 'hard' dogmatic colleague) is thus at risk of marginalizing the socio-historical reality of the church as it exists particularly and contingently. The risk is such that what remains in her ecclesiological description of the particular and contingent socio-historical church-community is nothing but a *Hohlraum* to be 'filled' occasionally and thereby actualized and animated as 'church' by the pneumatologically and eucharistically mediated *communio* of the triune God. Indeed, in the economic emphasis on the particularity and finitude of 'the church as it is' (to recall Küng's terminology), there is in fact proportionately very little speech about the concrete life and form of the church. In 'soft' dogmatic ecclesiology, the human empirical form of the church is thus somewhat 'swallowed up' by a description of God's own divine life and divine agency in relation to divine activity. This disproportionate description thereby negates the ability of 'soft' dogmatic ecclesiology to account for the church in terms of a genuine 'both/and' ecclesiological methodology in which divine agency relativizes but does *not* minimalize human agency. Furthermore, in the related and ensuing deployment of the social trinitarian terms 'relation' and 'relationality' in her description of the life of God, the 'soft' dogmatic ecclesiologist (at least from the perspective of her 'hard' dogmatic colleague) is permitted ironically both to move all too easily and freely from the being of God to the being of the church without first safeguarding *adequately* either the sheer gratuitous character of the church's created existence or its unqualified difference from the life of God which brings the church into being. In other words, in its emphasis on the correspondence and even co-inherence of ecclesial and Trinitarian *communio*, 'soft' dogmatic ecclesiology fails to hear *sufficiently* the 'no' of 'hard' dogmatic ecclesiology, and in doing so – and irrespective of its indirect (eschatological) nature – betrays in ecclesiological description 'a drift into divine immanence'.[263] It is this 'drift' that threatens, moreover, to collapse the utter ontological distinction between uncreated and created, and to deny thereby the non-necessity of creation precisely in the over-identification of the church's being with the being of God. 'Soft' dogmatic ecclesiology also fails to speak of creaturely life in its integrity as creation with the associated human agential forms and practices that attend to them. Thus, where the 'soft' ethnographic ecclesiologist is open to the critique of rendering ecclesiology too *independent* as a doctrinal locus from the doctrine of God, her 'soft' dogmatic counterpart is exposed to the critique run contrariwise. Here, ecclesiology is associated too *closely* with a doctrine

---

[261] See John D. Zizioulas, 'Le Mystère de l'Église dans la tradition orthodoxe', *Irénikon* 60 (1987), 333.
[262] In the Eucharist, church and Christ are said (by Zizioulas) to become 'completely' identified such that 'all separation between Christology and ecclesiology vanishes in the Spirit' (see respectively, Zizioulas, 'La Mystère de l'Église', 328; and Zizioulas, *Being as Communion*, 111). In a fashion similar to Nygren, de Lubac and Jenson, Zizioulas thus threatens to absorb (problematically) the particularity of the church into the person of Christ and to over-identify the church as Christ's body with Christ himself.
[263] Webster, *Holiness*, 55.

of God, and ecclesiological speech about divine agency proportionately quashes all such speech about lived ecclesial life and human agency.

IV. Conclusion

This chapter has been concerned to articulate and explicate subsequently in relation to contemporary ecclesiological literature an endemic problematic present in approaches to contemporary ecclesiological discourse. The chapter has done so by parsing in reference to ecclesiological topography the Pauline appropriation of God's promise to be *God* as God of a *people* and by way of a related and detailed dialogical analysis of two typological approaches to ecclesiological description. As troped herein, these approaches either state explicitly as a 'hard' methodological claim or show implicitly as a 'soft' logical consequence the endemic problematic and the binarized tendency therein of presenting in an account of the church *either* a 'dogmatic' description of God's own *ad intra* or *ad extra* life, *or* an 'ethnographic' description of the particular and contingent socio-historical church-community. While recognizing the helpful and mutually corrective nature of each typological approach, the above analysis has raised concerns with what in each 'type' is disordered and disproportionate ecclesiological speech. On the one 'dogmatic' hand, this speech is open to the critique of theoretical abstraction or over-spiritualization; of ecclesiological actualism or of dissolving the church as *congregatio* into the event of the divine act of *convocatio*; of marginalizing the significance of the church's socio-historical human form (not least in relation to the reality of ecclesial sin); and of focusing disproportionately on the doctrine of God either by rendering too great a distinction (so the 'hard' dogmatic ecclesiologist) or too close a connection (so the 'soft' dogmatic ecclesiologist) between God's own *ad intra* and *ad extra* life and the life of the church particularly and contingently conceived. On the other 'ethnographic' hand, such speech is open to the critique of ecclesiological 'naturalization'; of conflating the proximate dogmatic *res* of ecclesiology with its principal *res*; of collapsing divine agency into human subjectivity or of folding speech about divine action into language about ecclesial human reality; of failing to attend to the sui generis nature of the church as community; and of rendering ecclesiology (too) independent as a doctrinal locus from the doctrine of God and God's operative and gracious acts. All of this, to one extent or another, limits the ability of the ecclesiologist – be they 'dogmatic' or 'ethnographic' – to proffer a genuinely theological account of the church in which *both* divine *and* human agency are spoken of together with due proportion, and with an appropriate sense of dogmatic order therein. It is here that the ecclesial thought of Dietrich Bonhoeffer is prescient. Bonhoeffer offers (as will be seen) material content by which to analyse critically and constructively this exact limitation of contemporary ecclesiological discourse, and also a distinctive and helpful methodological approach – one which is therapeutic to the endemic problematic and its attendant disorder and disproportion in ecclesiological speech. Such an approach presents what might be seen as a necessary 'third way' in ecclesiological description. Thus, it is to Bonhoeffer's ecclesial thought to which the book now turns.

2

The theological foundations of Bonhoeffer's ecclesiological methodology

I. Introduction

The previous chapter diagnosed an endemic problematic present in approaches to contemporary ecclesiological discourse and proposed that the ecclesial thought of Dietrich Bonhoeffer is therapeutic to it. It is thus now necessary to turn in this chapter (and in the chapters that follow) to consider Bonhoeffer's own ecclesiological description. This description, it will be argued, is one that offers not only material content by which to analyse critically and constructively the endemic problematic but also a distinctive, helpful and, in light of the diagnosis proffered in Chapter 1, vital contribution to questions of ecclesiological method.

In its concern for appropriate dogmatic ordering and proportionality in ecclesiological description (the preceding of 'they shall be my people' by 'I will be your God' and the intervening καὶ), Bonhoeffer's ecclesial thought breaks through the endemic problematic and serves to treat therapeutically the binarized tendency of presenting in an account of the church (be it as an explicit methodological claim or as an implicit logical consequence) *either* a 'dogmatic' description of God's own *ad intra* or *ad extra* life *or* an 'ethnographic' description of the particular and contingent socio-historical church-community. Bonhoeffer's ecclesial thought proposes what this book categorizes as a 'both/and' ecclesiological methodology in which the being of the church is conceived from *both* a 'dogmatic' *and* an 'ethnographic' perspective simultaneously, such that in critique of 'hard' and 'soft' versions of each ecclesiological 'type' both divine and human agency are held together in an account of the church which concomitantly gives voice to the asymmetrical yet interconnected relation of divine and human togetherness in the church's being, and affords appropriate space in that account for *both* the being of God and God's operative and gracious acts *and* the being of the church's socio-historical human form.

The implications of Bonhoeffer's 'both/and' ecclesiological methodology for ecclesiological method (as will be demonstrated) are thus far-reaching, not least in terms of Bonhoeffer's articulation of the sui generis sociological structure of the being of *God's* church-community in distinction from all other forms of socio-historical *human* community. However, discussion of this distinction and Bonhoeffer's 'both/and' ecclesiological methodology which determines it is reserved for Chapter 3: the discussion is reserved because Bonhoeffer's 'both/and' ecclesiological methodology is a *consequence* of a prior set of theological assumptions which are unidentified in extant material on Bonhoeffer's ecclesiology and out of which his 'both/and' ecclesiological methodology arises. Indeed, independent of these assumptions Bonhoeffer's ecclesial thought cannot be properly understood.

This chapter seeks to identify those theological assumptions and thereby lay the theological foundations upon which the 'both/and' ecclesiological methodology of Bonhoeffer's ecclesial thought is subsequently built. Given this derivative and dependent relation between Bonhoeffer's ecclesiological methodology and its theological foundations, it is necessary, therefore, that those foundations are laid before and in order that Chapter 3 can then proceed to explicate how Bonhoeffer builds the structure of his 'both/and' ecclesiological methodology upon them. In laying these theological foundations, the chapter, moreover, is concerned to establish – in 'relational' terms – the systematic nature of Bonhoeffer's ecclesiology, and in doing so to reidentify its foundational dogmatic *res* in order to issue a corrective to the well-trodden path in extant Bonhoeffer scholarship of identifying that dogmatic *res* as a doctrine of the person and work of Jesus Christ or (less commonly) as a doctrine of the human person.[1] Problematically, these identifications – because they identify the foundational dogmatic *res* of Bonhoeffer's ecclesiology improperly – not only fail to appreciate the 'both/and' ecclesiological methodology of Bonhoeffer's ecclesial thought but also risk positioning Bonhoeffer (to use the language of Chapter 1) either as a 'soft' dogmatic ecclesiologist by their over-identifying the connection between the church and Christ in Bonhoeffer's ecclesiology or as a 'soft' (or even 'hard') ethnographic ecclesiologist in consequence of their dissolving by their reading of Bonhoeffer's ecclesiology his understanding of the sui generis nature of the church as a human community. In light of the argument of this book, however, Bonhoeffer cannot be considered either a 'dogmatic' or 'ethnographic' ecclesiologist, for it is the argument of this book that Bonhoeffer's 'both/and' ecclesiological methodology breaks through the endemic 'either/or' problematic.

To this end, and with respect to its task of laying the theological foundations upon which Bonhoeffer subsequently builds his 'both/and' ecclesiological methodology, this chapter argues, firstly, that any engagement with Bonhoeffer's ecclesial thought must be founded on his understanding of the being of the church as oriented to the eschatological telos. In this respect, the chapter will demonstrate that for Bonhoeffer the doctrine of eschatology is concerned primarily and uncompromisingly with *this* world, and as such is to be conceived in a properly apocalyptic register. Furthermore, it will be demonstrated that this orientation of the church's being to the eschatological telos is derivative of the person and work of God the Holy Spirit. Thus the chapter argues, secondly, that (according to Bonhoeffer) to speak about the being of the church as oriented to the eschatological telos is to speak, most proximately, pneumatologically. In this respect – and in terms of relational systematicity – the chapter will demonstrate (as a corrective to extant material on Bonhoeffer's ecclesiology) that the foundational dogmatic *res* of Bonhoeffer's ecclesial thought is an apocalyptically eschatologically

---

[1] On these identifications, see Section III and Section IV, respectively.

indexed pneumatology. The theological foundations upon which Bonhoeffer builds his 'both/and' ecclesiological methodology and which the chapter seeks to lay, therefore, perhaps somewhat surprisingly – given the Lutheran theological traditions at play in shaping Bonhoeffer's theology, and especially against the backdrop of the all-important Lutheran ecclesiological point that the church is *creatura verbi divini* – are *pneumatological* and apocalyptically *eschatological* in dimension.[2] To buttress the chapter's argument that the foundations of Bonhoeffer's 'both/and' ecclesiological methodology are strictly theological, the third and final section of the chapter comprises an examination of Bonhoeffer's own stated methodological starting point of his doctoral dissertation. Here, the chapter will demonstrate that the articulated given relation in *Sanctorum Communio* between the categories of the theological and the sociological establishes in Bonhoeffer's ecclesial thought a *theological* interpretative paradigm in which Bonhoeffer's 'both/and' ecclesiological methodology is subsequently and resolutely set, and which, therefore, must be considered programmatic for any consideration of Bonhoeffer's ecclesiological description.

II. Theological foundations: Eschatology

One of the reasons that extant material on Bonhoeffer's ecclesiology fails to appreciate the 'both/and' ecclesiological methodology of his ecclesial thought and identifies the foundational dogmatic *res* of that thought improperly is that it is inattentive to the dogmatic locus of eschatology as the proximate dogmatic *res* of his ecclesiology. It is, therefore, necessary to outline herein the eschatological assumptions at work in Bonhoeffer's ecclesial (and theological) thought, so as to be able to consider in the chapters that follow how this eschatological foundation serves to fund his 'both/and' ecclesiological methodology.

Bonhoeffer's interest in the doctrine of eschatology and in particular its presence, nature and role in the corpus of his writings is contested.[3] This contest (in its longevity) has seen Bonhoeffer's eschatological interests understood variously as altogether or largely absent;[4] strictly or intentionally limited to certain periods of his life or to parts

---

[2] For Luther, of course, Word and Spirit can never be separated. On the presence of Luther in Bonhoeffer's theological thought, see Michael P. DeJonge, *Bonhoeffer's Reception of Luther* (Oxford: Oxford University Press, 2017). For discussion of the Reformer's conception of the church as *creatura verbi divini*, see Schwöbel, 'The Creature of the Word'; and Paul Avis, *The Church in the Theology of the Reformers* (London: Marshall, Morgan & Scott, 1981). The 'all-important' ecclesiological point is summarized helpfully by Edmund Schlink, *The Coming Christ and the Coming Church* (Edinburgh: Oliver & Boyd, 1967), 116: 'The Church is, because Jesus Christ constantly is acting upon her. She was not before this action; and she is not for an instant without this action.'

[3] See Philip G. Ziegler, 'Eschatology and Secularity in the Late Writings of Dietrich Bonhoeffer', in John W. de Gruchy, Stephen Plant and Christiane Tietz, ed. *Dietrich Bonhoeffer's Theology Today: A Way between Fundamentalism and Secularism?* (München: Gütersloher Verlagshaus, 2009), 129.

[4] See, for example, Gerhard Sauter, *Die Theologie des Reiches Gottes beim älteren und jüngeren Blumhardt* (Zürich-Stuttgart: Zwingli Verlag, 1962), 297; Martin Honecker, *Kirche als Gestalt und Ereignis: Die sichtbare Gestalt der Kirche als dogmatisches Problem* (München: Chr. Kaiser Verlag, 1963), 156; Rainer Mayer, *Christuswirklichkeit: Grundlagen, Entwicklung und Konsequenzen der Theologie Dietrich Bonhoeffers* (Stuttgart: Calwer Verlag, 1969), 52 and 101–2; Heinrich Ott, *Reality*

of particular works;[5] and in fact elevated, either to having a decisive role in particular works and in the development of particular theological themes[6] or to being essential and integral to Bonhoeffer's whole theological thought,[7] such that one might parse his theology in reference to it.[8] It is this suggestion of parsing Bonhoeffer's theology in reference to eschatology which this book seeks to implement and indeed develop constructively, albeit in a more strictly delimited ecclesiological way. That one is not wrong to insist on the necessity of an eschatological reading of Bonhoeffer's ecclesiology – that is, of his understanding of the being of the church as a being which is oriented and thus determinatively defined in its relation to the eschatological telos – is itself suggested by his own concern to (re-)establish the proper place of eschatology in dogmatic theology. As Bonhoeffer puts it at the beginning of his 1926 paper, *Kirche und Eschatologie*:

> It is always a sign of religious strength and true seriousness when in theology eschatology is its own field of study, concerning which one does not fill up, in accordance with one's duty and a little modestly, just a few pages as an appendage to dogmatics – as we so often observe in the theology of the nineteenth-century – but on the contrary, when, after the example of the Reformers, one truly recognizes eschatology as the end and goal, to which everything else [in dogmatics] is related.[9]

That this 'everything else' most decisively includes for Bonhoeffer the doctrine of the church is made explicit by the opening words of his lectures *Creation and Fall*, words

---

and Faith: The Theological Legacy of Dietrich Bonhoeffer, trans. Alex A. Morrison (Philadelphia: Fortress Press, 1972), 178 and 311; and Larry Rasmussen, *Dietrich Bonhoeffer: His Significance for North Americans* (Minneapolis: Fortress Press, 1990), 75–6.

[5] See, for example, Eberhard Bethge, *Dietrich Bonhoeffer, A Biography: Theologian, Christian, Man for His Times*, rev. and ed. Victoria J. Barnett (Minneapolis: Fortress Press, 2000), 87 and 842; William Hamilton, '"The Letters Are a Particular Thorn": Some Themes in Bonhoeffer's Prison Writings', in Ronald Gregor Smith, ed. *World Come of Age: A Symposium on Dietrich Bonhoeffer* (London: Collins, 1967), 160; James W. Woelfel, *Bonhoeffer's Theology: Classical and Revolutionary* (Nashville: Abingdon Press, 1970), 225 and 251–2; and Ernst Feil, *The Theology of Dietrich Bonhoeffer*, trans. Martin Rumscheidt (Minneapolis: Fortress Press, 1985), 89 and 152.

[6] On the decisive role that eschatology plays, for example, in Bonhoeffer's lectures *Creation and Fall*, *Discipleship*, his *Ethics* and (*contra* Bethge, Hamilton and Feil) his prison letters, see respectively, Lindsay, 'Bonhoeffer's Eschatology in a World "Come of Age"', 290–302; Jonathan D. Sorum, 'The Eschatological Boundary in Dietrich Bonhoeffer's *Nachfolge*' (PhD diss., Luther Northwestern Theological Seminary, 1994); Barry Harvey, *Taking Hold of the Real: Dietrich Bonhoeffer and the Profound Worldliness of Christianity* (Eugene: Cascade Books, 2015), 34–46; John Panteleimon Manoussakis, '"At the Recurrent End of the Unending": Bonhoeffer's Eschatology of the Penultimate', in Brian Gregor and Jens Zimmermann, ed. *Bonhoeffer and Continental Philosophy: Cruciform Philosophy* (Bloomington: Indiana University Press, 2009), 226–44; Ziegler, 'Eschatology and Secularity in the Late Writings of Dietrich Bonhoeffer', 124–38; Phillip Ziegler, 'Dietrich Bonhoeffer – An Ethics of God's Apocalypse?', *Modern Theology* 23.4 (2007), 579–94; Phillip Ziegler, '"Voices in the Night": Human Solidarity and Eschatological Hope', in Bernd Wannenwetsch, ed. *Who Am I? Bonhoeffer's Theology Through His Poetry* (London: T&T Clark, 2009), 115–45; and Robert Holyer, 'Toward an Eschatology of the Past', *Theology* 89 (1986), 209–18.

[7] See Manrodt, *The Role of Eschatology in the Theology of Dietrich Bonhoeffer*; Harvey, *Taking Hold of the Real*, 34–5; and Lindsay, 'Eschatology'.

[8] See Lindsay, 'Bonhoeffer's Eschatology in a World "Come of Age"'; and Lindsay, 'Eschatology'.

[9] DBW 9, 336.

which irrevocably define the being of the church in relation to 'the end'. Bonhoeffer writes: 'The church of Christ witnesses to the end of all things. It lives from the end, it thinks from the end, it acts from the end, it proclaims its message from the end.'[10] That end – the end of all things, or, as Bonhoeffer subsequently puts it, 'the end of our whole world' – is Jesus Christ:[11] Jesus Christ, who, in judgement and in hope, is the 'end' of all that is 'old' – an 'end', however, which does not *issue from* the 'old', and thus is related to the 'old' neither continuously nor purposively, but instead as 'the real end of the old' and so at once as the *beginning* of the 'new'.[12] This is the world of new creation. In this way, the being of the church, therefore, begins, is moving towards and ends with Jesus Christ. The being of the church *is* and so properly understands itself only *in* its coming forth from God and in its returning to God.[13]

To speak about the being of the church is thus to speak teleologically and more specifically *eschatologically*, for the telos towards which the church's being is oriented (and so intended) is precisely its own eschatological end. In other words, there is, in the being of the church a continuous and purposive direction of travel, in the sense, that is, of the church being *in via*.[14] Hence the church, for Bonhoeffer, is the 'orphaned church'.[15] It lives in the time between the ascension of Christ and the *eschaton*,[16] and so it lives as an alien people sojourning to their heavenly home.[17] This sojourn reaches its terminus only at the point when God, in and through Christ's own self in his future *parousia*, is all in all.[18] Accordingly, the church lives and exists 'not from itself, but

---

[10] DBWE 3, 21.
[11] Ibid., 22.
[12] See ibid., 21 and 22.
[13] See *DBWE 1*, 95 and 101; cf., Reinhold Seeberg, *Christliche Dogmatik*, Erster Bd. (Leipzig: A. Deichertiche Verlagsbuchhandlung, 1924), 140; and Thomas Aquinas, *Summa Theologica*, trans. Fathers of the English Dominican Province (Westminster: Christian Classics, 1981), 1.1.3 and 1.90.3.
[14] Contra Honecker, *Kirche als Gestalt und Ereignis*, 156: 'The body of Christ exists in the world and is not on the way to its future.'
[15] *DBWE* 12, 469.
[16] See ibid.
[17] See *DBWE* 10, 507. Bonhoeffer understands not only the church's being from within this eschatological and dynamic perspective but also his own being and indeed life itself. This is evident both from the closing words of his farewell sermon to the German Evangelical congregation in Barcelona, and his meditation on Ps. 119.19. See *DBWE* 10, 546-51; and *DBWE* 15, 496-528.
[18] See 1 Cor. 15.21-28. The being of the church is thus directed being – being which is directed *towards* the future that is God. That God himself *is* the future is made clear in scripture, not least in the name ('ehyer 'äšher 'ehyer) with which God reveals himself to Moses (see Exod. 3.14). This name is not static but ever-active and dynamic: 'I am who I am' after all is equally well translated 'I will be who I will be', or 'I am the One who always is' (see John I. Durham, *Word Biblical Commentary, Volume 3: Exodus* (Mexico City: Thomas Nelson, Inc., 1987), 38). The God who reveals himself to Moses is the God of the future (just as he is also the God of the past and the God of the present). As such, God, who 'was and is and is to come' (Rev. 4.8), is forever ahead of us, and by the futurity of his being is always pulling his people (in eschatological movement) forwards, into and towards the future that God is. Moreover, the futurity of God's being is the reason why, for Bonhoeffer, not only the being of the church but Christian faith itself must be said to be *of* the future. As Bonhoeffer understands it, faith (at bottom) is the result of the 'direct act' of God on the human being in faith. This divine 'act' establishes *as faith* intentional and immediate God-directed 'being'. As *actus directus* (direct consciousness), faith is *fides directa* (direct faith) and thus is directionally prospective or forwards in orientation, and thereby is said to be evasive of the 'reflexive act' of human reason. Consequently, *actus directus* is differentiated from *actus reflexus* (the consciousness of reflection) in which the

rather receives its life from outside itself'[19] – that is, from an external (and forwards) orientation which is said to determine wholly the spatio-temporal and historical present. Bonhoeffer writes: '*The present (time) is determined from outside* and not from within … by that which approaches, by the future that is coming [*die Zukunft*] … and this future (that is coming) is Christ, is the Holy Spirit.'[20] Not only is the gospel 'in a decisive manner fundamentally eschatological',[21] but the present being of the church in space and time is itself (and most fully) not a temporal but a supra-temporal (*überzeitlicher*) and thus *eschatological* reality,[22] which as such bears past and future in itself.[23] The church is that precisely because 'the authentic present',[24] which is Christ himself, itself resides external to the present, but comes – by the Holy Spirit of God – decisively into and recapitulates itself in the present. More specifically, 'the authentic present' resides in the 'future' or better still in the advent of Jesus Christ, and thus ultimately in the Holy Spirit of God, who, as an end-time gift, is active decisively not only in the raising of Jesus Christ from the dead (itself the quintessence of the world of new creation)[25]

human being's cognitive capacities of rational apprehension or sensible perception seek to mediate faith by their own reflection such that faith is *fides reflexa* (reflexive faith), and thus is directionally retrospective or backwards in orientation (see *DBWE* 2, 28–9 and 158–60). Bonhoeffer writes, *fides directa* is 'the act of faith which, even though completed within a person's consciousness, could not be reflected in it' (*DBWE* 2, 158). Here, 'consciousness is purely "outwardly directed"' towards God. In *fides reflexa*, however, 'consciousness has the power to become its own object of attention', becoming conscious, that is, of its own self in reflection (see *DBWE* 2, 28). In other words, the difference between *fides directa* and *fides reflexa* is that of between the immediacy of Levi's following-after Jesus Christ and his eschatological movement forwards (out of his tax booth) into and towards the future that God (in Christ) is, and the mediated response of a certain would-be disciple and his movement backwards (to first bury his father) into and towards the past and himself. See Mk 2.14 and Lk. 9.57-62; cf., *DBWE* 4, 57–62. On the eschatological nature and direction of faith, see also Chapter 3, Section III.i of this book.

[19] *DBW* 14, 398.
[20] Ibid., 404–5; cf., *DBW* 11, 209. It is important to note that *Zukunft* does not translate the Latin word *futurum* (i.e. what 'will be', in the sense of that which will develop *out* of the past and present), but rather the Latin word *adventus* (i.e. what 'is coming'), which itself renders the Greek word *parousia*, and which in the context of the New Testament (being the subject of Bonhoeffer's lecture here) refers exclusively to the future coming of Christ in glory, of which the Holy Spirit is ἀρραβών and ἀπαρχή (see Jürgen Moltmann, *The Coming of God: Christian Eschatology*, trans. Margaret Kohl (Minneapolis: Fortress Press, 1996), 25; cf., 2 Cor. 1.22, 5.5; and Rom. 8.23). Thus, as Bonhoeffer defines it in his postdoctoral dissertation: 'Future [*Zukunft*] means: the determination of being from outside by that which is (yet) "to come"' (*DBW* 2, 157). Consequently, as Rachel Muers observes, 'life "out of the future" (paradigmatically the life of the *child*) is [for Bonhoeffer] life in dependence on what comes from beyond oneself'. See Rachel Muers, *Keeping God's Silence: Towards a Theological Ethics of Communication* (Oxford: Blackwell Publishing, 2004), 83.
[21] *DBW* 11, 209; cf., Karl Barth, *The Epistle to the Romans*, trans. Edwyn C. Hoskyns (Oxford: Oxford University Press, 1968), 314; and *CD*, II/1, 634.
[22] See *DBW* 9, 340.
[23] See *DBW* 10, 189; cf., *DBW* 8, 186–93, 232–8, 241–51 and 466–71, and Bonhoeffer's persistent emphasis therein on the remembrance and expectation for an eschatological future of the past. On the importance of the past in Bonhoeffer's understanding of the present as an eschatological reality, see Holyer, 'Toward an Eschatology of the Past', 209–18.
[24] *DBWE* 14, 418.
[25] The eschatological event of Christ's resurrection is thus 'the most profound yes of God to the world' (*DBWE* 12, 290–1) precisely because, and as the free pneumatological act of God, the resurrection (and with it God's kingdom) breaks into the midst of the 'old' (fallen) world as 'the final sign of its end and its future' (*DBW* 6, 150), and thereby is *the* mark of God's willing and calling into existence the world of new creation.

but also, and at once, in the proleptic manifestation of that eschatological advent *in* (present) space and time. Bonhoeffer asserts that 'the Holy Spirit is the pledge of our inheritance towards our salvation as God's possession' on the day of Christ's future *parousia*,[26] and as such 'the Holy Spirit is real *presently*'.[27] Bonhoeffer continues: 'But … the consummation is as yet not present; after this our world there is yet another world which already here and there breaks through and becomes visible [in this world].'[28] The Holy Spirit, then, 'always drives beyond itself towards an eschatology',[29] unfolding the *eschaton* in present space and time and ensuring thereby that the world of new creation resides *already* in what is the *in*authentic present. This 'already' is dependent, first, on the event of Christ's own pneumatological filled-ness as the καινὸς ἄνθρωπος or, in other words, as the eschatological person par excellence,[30] in whose resurrection 'fulfilled reality' is realized and the world of new creation announced and begun.[31] The 'already' is dependent, however, second, on the founding of the church at Pentecost in the coming of 'the historic [*geschichtliche*] reality of the Holy Spirit',[32] and also, and at once, is an 'already' that refers to its own *not yet* complete and thereby future fulfilment. Bonhoeffer is clear that the kingdom of God while active *in* history is only consummated at the *end of* or *beyond* history, and is thus to be conceived as both temporally present yet still to come and (in consequence thereof) as also developing – in the sense of growing – in space and time.[33] That the church exists and lives precisely in and from its external orientation to this its (tensile) future end – to a future, however, which is already made present, and to an end which has already begun or itself is a beginning[34] – thus transposes Bonhoeffer's understanding of eschatology out of an exclusively 'last-

---

[26] See *DBW* 4, 276–7; cf., *DBWE* 14, 810; Rom. 8.11 and 23; and 2 Cor. 1.22, 5.5.
[27] *DBW* 14, 722.
[28] Ibid.
[29] *DBW* 9, 390.
[30] See *DBWE* 14, 446; cf., the action of the Holy Spirit on and towards Jesus Christ not only in his resurrection but also at his biological conception (Lk. 1.30-35), baptism (Lk. 2.21-22) and in the commencement and carrying out of his public ministry (Lk. 4.1-2, 14-15, 18 and 10.21).
[31] See Eva Harasta, 'Bonhoeffer's Lutheran Ecclesiology and Inter-Religious Dialogue: A Dogmatic Reading of Bonhoeffer', in Peter Frick, ed. *Bonhoeffer and Interpretative Theory: Essays on Methods and Understanding* (Frankfurt am Main: Peter Lang, 2013), 245.
[32] *DBWE* 14, 438.
[33] See *DBW* 9, 312–13 and 324. On 'futurist' and 'presentative' eschatology, and the inherent tension in conceiving the kingdom of God as either a future reality, present state or as both a future reality and a present state, see respectively, Johannes Weiss, *Jesus' Proclamation of the Kingdom of God*, trans. Richard H. Hiers and David L. Holland (London: SCM Press, 1971), Albert Schweitzer, *The Quest of the Historical Jesus*, trans. W. Montgomery (London: Adam and Charles Black, 1910), and E. P. Sanders, *The Historical Figure of Jesus* (London: Allen Lane/The Penguin Press, 1993); C. H. Dodd, *The Parables of the Kingdom* (London: Nisbet & Co., 1935), Marcus J. Borg, *Jesus: A New Vision: Spirit, Culture, and the Life of Discipleship* (San Francisco: Harper & Row, 1987), and John Dominic Crossan, *The Historical Jesus: The Life of a Mediterranean Jewish Peasant* (Edinburgh: T&T Clark, 1991); and Norman Perrin, *The Kingdom of God in the Teaching of Jesus* (London: SCM Press, 1963), N. T. Wright, *Jesus and the Victory of God* (London: SPCK, 1996), and James D. G. Dunn, *Christianity in the Making Volume 1: Jesus Remembered* (Grand Rapids: Eerdmans, 2003).
[34] Moltmann writes: 'In the end *is* the beginning' (Moltmann, *The Coming of God*, x (emphasis altered)) – an eschatological perspective of existence as 'tensed existence' (Sabine Dramm, *Dietrich Bonhoeffer and the Resistance*, trans. Margaret Kohl (Minneapolis: Fortress Press, 2009), 210) with which Bonhoeffer not only lived but purportedly went to his death: 'This is the end, for me, the beginning of life.' See Ferdinand Schlingensiepen, *Dietrich Bonhoeffer 1906-1945: Martyr, Thinker, Man of Resistance*, trans. Isabel Best (London: T&T Clark, 2012), 378. For an alternative perspective

things' or 'apocalyptic' register and into a (present) spatio-temporal and historical one, albeit one which itself is fundamentally and most fully eschatological.

Indeed, as the world of new creation comes decisively into and proleptically manifests itself in present space and time in the advent of Jesus Christ by God the Holy Spirit, spatio-temporality is not just eschatologically qualified, but rather is 'decisively re-made'[35] *as eschatological* reality. This reality of the world of new creation, which is the future of the world, is at once – in the work of the Holy Spirit of God raising Jesus Christ from the dead, and in the coming of God the Holy Spirit at Pentecost and thus in the being of the church itself – 'inalienably present to the world'.[36] To talk 'as if the present were intelligible *in se* and *per se*' is, then, as Christopher Holmes states, 'deeply mistaken'.[37] Holmes argues: 'The present, in the truest sense of the term, is pneumatologically determined'.[38] This determination is such that spatio-temporality is, in dimension, eschatological.[39] In this sense, Bonhoeffer's eschatology is, as David Manrodt notes, 'a profoundly this-worldly concept',[40] to the extent that 'eschatology and living fully and completely in this world' cannot be considered to 'constitute a zero-sum game'.[41] Indeed, for Bonhoeffer, eschatology is concerned primarily and uncompromisingly not with an ahistorical last-things utopia, nor, in Bonhoeffer's words, with a 'fantasy-filled enthusiasm and apocalyptic curiosity',[42] but rather – and because of the advent in present space and time of new creation – with 'life on earth'.[43] More specifically, eschatology is concerned (according to Bonhoeffer) with the way in which (the hope of) that advent now 'refers' the church and its members not to an eternal realm of the hereafter – to a better world beyond or behind this world (*Hinterwelt*) – but to *this* life 'in a wholly new way'.[44] This way, precisely because the world of new creation breaks into the world to affirm the world,[45] is the way of a profound 'this-worldliness' (*Diesseitigkeit*)[46] which Bonhoeffer considers the defining

---

on Bonhoeffer's last words, see Charles Marsh, *Strange Glory: A Life of Dietrich Bonhoeffer* (London: SPCK, 2014), 388.

[35] See Ziegler, 'Dietrich Bonhoeffer – An Ethics of God's Apocalypse?', 580.
[36] Muers, *Keeping God's Silence*, 82.
[37] Holmes, 'The Holy Spirit', 175.
[38] Ibid.
[39] This suggestion that Bonhoeffer develops a pneumatologically determined eschatology as the foundational ontology of reality is thus *contra* André Dumas, *Dietrich Bonhoeffer: Theologian of Reality*, trans. Robert McAfee Brown (London: SCM Press, 1971), and Ott, *Reality and Faith*, who both suggest that Bonhoeffer's foundational ontology of reality is Christological.
[40] Manrodt, *The Role of Eschatology in the Theology of Dietrich Bonhoeffer*, 155.
[41] Harvey, *Taking Hold of the Real*, 35.
[42] DBWE 9, 311.
[43] DBWE 8, 447.
[44] Ibid.
[45] See DBW 12, 267; DBWE 8, 373: 'What matters is not the beyond but *this* world ... What is beyond this world is meant, in the gospel, to be there *for* this world'; and Bonhoeffer's consideration of eschatology in terms of his categories of 'last things' and 'things before the last'. On Bonhoeffer's categories of 'last things' and 'things before the last', see Chapter 5 of this book for a detailed discussion.
[46] Literally, 'this-sidedness', and thus a polemic against the 'otherworldliness' (*Hinterwelten*) of an eternal realm of the hereafter. See *DBW* 8, 541–2; and *DBW* 12, 264, 265 and 267; cf., Clifford J. Green, 'Sociality, Discipleship, and Worldly Theology in Bonhoeffer's Christian Humanism', in Jens Zimmermann and Brian Gregor, ed. *Being Human, Becoming Human: Dietrich Bonhoeffer and Social Thought* (Cambridge: James Clark & Co., 2010), 83–5.

mark of the eschatologically new human being who has been overwhelmed by the advent in present space and time of new creation, and who lives, therefore, wholly from that coming and in the shadow of that which is to come.[47] Bonhoeffer writes: 'Only when one loves life and the earth so much that with their loss all else seems to be lost and at its end may one believe in the resurrection of the dead and a new world.'[48] To live from the resurrection in this way, one thereby participates, through the Holy Spirit of God, in the unfolding of new creation with*in* present space and time in the time between the first and final advents of Jesus Christ.[49]

Thus, it is in this properly apocalyptic register that Bonhoeffer's eschatological thought and his concomitant understanding of the being of the church as a being which is oriented to the eschatological telos is to be read.[50] Bonhoeffer's eschatology is *properly* apocalyptic, because, as recent studies in Pauline apocalyptic have discerned, the apocalypse of God's gospel is not just an unveiling or disclosing of a previously hidden and heavenly future state but is an invasive and redemptive event *in* space and time.[51] This event is one whereby God in Christ through the agency of the Holy Spirit acts, and continues to act, to destroy decisively the 'old' or present (fallen) world by his incursion into it from the future – an incursion which *is* the beginning in this world of the world of new creation. Douglas Harink writes: 'God's *apokalypsis* is not only a showing but also a doing which effects what is shown.'[52] For Philip Ziegler, the apocalypse of God's gospel in Bonhoeffer is 'an event that *initiates*, even as it *discloses*,

---

[47] See *DBW* 11, 386, 388 and 392.
[48] *DBW* 8, 226.
[49] See *DBWE* 8, 333. It is this foregoing emphasis in Bonhoeffer's eschatological thought that not only serves to render any attempt to treat Bonhoeffer's understanding of eschatology exclusively in futurist terms as wholly inappropriate but also suggests that one might identify Bonhoeffer as a missing link between Barth and the so-called 'theologians of hope'. Cf., Jürgen Moltmann, *Theology of Hope: On the Ground and the Implications of a Christian Eschatology*, trans. James W. Leitch (London: SCM Press, 1967), 16: 'From first to last, and not merely in the epilogue, Christianity is eschatology ... The eschatological is not one element *of* Christianity, but it is ... the key in which everything in it is set'; Johannes B. Metz, *Theology of the World*, trans. William Glen-Doepel (New York: Herder and Herder, 1969), 90: 'Eschatology is not a [dogmatic] discipline besides other [dogmatic] disciplines, but that basic discipline which determines, forms, and shapes every theological statement'; Gerhard Sauter, 'The Concept and Task of Eschatology – Theological and Philosophical Reflections', *Scottish Journal of Theology* 41.4 (1988), 507: '[Eschatology cannot be described] simply as one component of dogmatics among others ... *theology as such is eschatology*'; and Wolfhart Pannenberg, *Systematic Theology*, vol. 3, trans. G. W. Bromiley (Grand Rapids: Eerdmans, 1998), 531: 'Eschatology is not just the subject of a single chapter in dogmatics; it determines the perspective of Christian doctrine as a whole.' Pointedly, all of these statements echo the words of Bonhoeffer in 1926 (see p. 56, above).
[50] Barry Harvey's words are thus appropriate: 'Bonhoeffer's theology thrusts us into the middle of an ongoing apocalyptic drama', such that 'the notion of apocalyptic ... is altogether appropriate as a description of his fundamental theological imaginary'. See Harvey, *Taking Hold of the Real*, 3.
[51] See, for example, J. Christiaan Beker, *Paul's Apocalyptic Gospel: The Coming Triumph of God* (Philadelphia: Fortress Press, 1982), 29–53; J. Louis Martyn, *Galatians: A New Translation with Introduction and Commentary* (New York: Doubleday, 1997), 97–105; Martinus C. de Boer, 'Paul, Theologian of God's Apocalypse', *Interpretation* 56.1 (2002), 21–33; Douglas Harink, *Paul Among the Postliberals: Pauline Theology Beyond Christendom and Modernity* (Grand Rapids: Brazos Press, 2003), 68–73; and Douglas A. Campbell, *The Deliverance of God: An Apocalyptic Reading of Justification in Paul* (Grand Rapids: Eerdmans, 2009).
[52] Harink, *Paul Among the Postliberals*, 69.

a new state of affairs'.[53] Most critically, this new state of affairs is marked by an active warfare between the opposite 'apocalyptic pair'[54] of the 'old' or present (fallen) world and the world of new creation – albeit a war in which the redemptive power of the latter is already victorious, but nonetheless one which necessitates the former 'be seen *only* in the bifocal vision of apocalyptic'[55] – and is universal in its scope. There is 'no reserve of space or time or concept or aspect of creation outside of, beyond or undetermined by [this] critical, decisive and final action of God'.[56] In other words, the 'old' or present (fallen) world *is* 'apocalypsed' (*apokalyphtēnai*) – that is, located (ontologically, epistemically and morally) by the apocalypse of God's gospel, such that the 'old' or present (fallen) world in its entirety, including every moment within it, is in immediate relationship to God.[57] The world (according to Bonhoeffer) is thus understood better than it understands itself from its future end.[58] It is in this sense that spatio-temporality (to recall Ziegler's terminology) is 'decisively re-made' as an eschatological or properly apocalyptic reality.[59] This is a 're-making' in the wake of which present earthly circumstance, and indeed concrete day-to-day life in that circumstance is seen and lived from an eschatological or properly apocalyptic perspective – from the perspective, that is, that spatio-temporality (and life in this reality, including lived ecclesial life and church practice) is *between* apocalypse and (future) *parousia*. In this eschatological or properly apocalyptic perspective, spatio-temporality is thus taken seriously as a theological reality in light of the future of God that has and is to come.[60]

It is precisely this eschatological or properly apocalyptic perspective – derivative of the 're-making' of spatio-temporality in the event of God's advent in space and time in the person of Jesus Christ and thus ultimately in the Holy Spirit of God – that works in Bonhoeffer's ecclesial thought (as will be demonstrated in Chapters 4 and 5) to resist, in distinction to 'dogmatic' ecclesiology, the presentation of an overly abstract or 'spiritualized' account of the church in which the church's particular and contingent socio-historical form is either marginalized or 'swallowed up' by an account of God's own life. Furthermore, it is this eschatological or properly apocalyptic perspective that for Bonhoeffer determinatively now 'refers' the being of the church and its members (indeed, in one sense, the being of all people) 'to their life on earth

---

[53] Ziegler, 'Dietrich Bonhoeffer – An Ethics of God's Apocalypse?', 581.
[54] Martyn, *Galatians*, 100.
[55] Ibid., 105.
[56] Harink, *Paul Among the Postliberals*, 69.
[57] See *DBW* 1, 193; *DBW* 8, 354; and *DBW* 10, 513; cf., Leopold von Ranke, *The Theory and Practice of History*, ed. Georg G. Iggers (Abingdon: Routledge, 2011), 21.
[58] See *DBWE* 8, 428 and 431.
[59] It is this properly apocalyptic and eschatological reality, and the active warfare between the 'old' or present (fallen) world and the world of new creation by which it is marked, that makes Jennifer McBride's assertion that 'the world's new ontology' – derivative of the 'cosmic accomplishment' of God's *apokalypsis* – is such that 'the grain of the universe is now patterned after the life, death and resurrection of Jesus', problematic (see Jennifer M. McBride, *The Church for the World: A Theology of Public Witness* (New York: Oxford University Press, 2012), 87). It does not follow, necessarily, that that which is located and 're-made' by God's *apokalypsis* is 'patterned after' it: ontologically, epistemically or morally.
[60] See *DBW* 11, 386.

in a wholly new way'.⁶¹ The being of the church and its members is a being that is overwhelmed by the coming of new creation, and more acutely is a being that 'hears the Apocalypse'⁶² and thus is oriented to the eschatological telos. This orientation works in Bonhoeffer's ecclesiological description (as will be seen in Chapter 3) to determinatively distinguish the being of *God's* church-community (precisely as a socio-historical *human* community) from all other socio-historical forms *of* human community, and thereby to guard that description against succumbing, in distinction to 'ethnographic' ecclesiology, either to ecclesiological 'naturalization' or to a dissolution of the sui generis nature of the church as a human community. Moreover, that the being of the church is determinatively referred to the eschatological telos means that to speak teleologically and eschatologically about the church's being is also and most foundationally to speak *pneumatologically*: as the foregoing discussion has made clear the eschatological assumptions at work in Bonhoeffer's ecclesial (and theological) thought rest on an understanding of the person and work of God the Holy Spirit.

III. Theological foundations: Pneumatology

Given the foregoing discussion, the dogmatic locus of eschatology can be said to be the proximate dogmatic *res* of Bonhoeffer's ecclesiology, but at once the proximate dogmatic *res* of Bonhoeffer's apocalyptic eschatology must be said to be the dogmatic locus of pneumatology.⁶³ One might say, therefore, that the foundational dogmatic

---

⁶¹ DBWE 8, 447; and 'all people' in the sense that it is precisely this eschatological or properly apocalyptic perspective which is operative in shaping Bonhoeffer's theological ontology of human personhood. For discussion of this ontology, see Chapter 3, Section II.i.a of this book.

⁶² DBW 14, 420.

⁶³ Pneumatology is often understood as being absent or significantly underdeveloped in Bonhoeffer's theology. For example, Bethge discusses Bonhoeffer's understanding of the church in *Sanctorum Communio* without a single reference to the Holy Spirit (see Bethge, *Dietrich Bonhoeffer*, 81–4); Frits de Lange asks why Bonhoeffer could 'not discuss ecclesiology in the more flexible language of pneumatology instead of invoking the very demanding concept of *Christus praesens*' (Frits de Lange, 'Waiting for the Word: The Churches' Embarrassment in Speaking about God', in John W. de Gruchy, ed. *Bonhoeffer for a New Day: Theology in a Time of Transition* (Grand Rapids: Eerdmans, 1997), 109); Farrow makes reference to Bonhoeffer's 'glaring pneumatological deficiency' (Farrow, *Ascension and Ecclesia*, 177); Ann L. Nickson writes of 'the pneumatological inadequacies of Bonhoeffer's theology', most notably in *Sanctorum Communio* (Ann L. Nickson, *Bonhoeffer on Freedom: Courageously Grasping Reality* (Aldershot: Ashgate, 2002), 59); Muers notes 'the lack of a developed pneumatology in Bonhoeffer's work' (Muers, *Keeping God's Silence*, 91); Gary D. Badcock notes that while Bonhoeffer 'took recourse in pneumatological ideas', he 'seldom mentions the Holy Spirit in his overall theology and does little to develop it as a separate theological theme' (Gary D. Badcock, *The House Where God Lives: Renewing the Doctrine of the Church for Today* (Grand Rapids: Eerdmans, 2009), 80 and 183); McBride writes that 'the absence of a developed pneumatology … in Bonhoeffer's thought is noteworthy' (McBride, *The Church for the World*, 57); Michael Welker charges Bonhoeffer of articulating (in his early writings) 'a clearly discernible Hegelianizing pneumatology', which fails to '[distinguish] clearly between the objective spirit [of the church-community] and the Holy Spirit' (Michael Welker, *God the Revealed: Christology*, trans. Douglas W. Stott (Grand Rapids: Eerdmans, 2014), 170); and David Höhne states that in Bonhoeffer's theology 'there is a noted absence of the [Holy] Spirit' (David A. Höhne, *Spirit and Sonship: Colin Gunton's Theology of Particularity and the Holy Spirit* (Farnham: Routledge, 2016), 23). The understanding that pneumatology is absent or underdeveloped in Bonhoeffer's theology

res of Bonhoeffer's ecclesiology is an apocalyptically eschatologically indexed pneumatology. How Bonhoeffer builds his 'both/and' ecclesiological methodology on this pneumatological foundation will be seen in Chapters 3, 4 and 5. However, what is critical for the argument of this book (as it is developed in those chapters) is that, as doctrinal *loci*, pneumatology, ecclesiology and eschatology belong together in an inseparable but strictly derived (ordered) relation. It is necessary, therefore, to be clear about what this relation is so as to be able to consider in the chapters that follow how it serves to fund the 'both/and' ecclesiological methodology of Bonhoeffer's ecclesial thought.

As doctrinal *loci*, the relation between pneumatology, ecclesiology and eschatology in Bonhoeffer's theological thought is evidenced most clearly by reference to the third article of the Nicene-Constantinopolitan creed, according to which both the doctrine of the church and the doctrine of 'last things' are located (derivatively) 'under' the doctrine of the Holy Spirit. In terms of creedal sequencing, the creedal subclause on eschatology follows after the creedal subclause on ecclesiology, and these both *emerge from* and 'under' the creedal clause on the person and work of the Holy Spirit. They do *not* arise from the creedal clause on the person and work of Jesus Christ, which would be to condition ecclesiology by Christology,[64] and thereby, creedally speaking, *mis*locate the doctrine of the church 'under' the creed's second article instead of properly 'under' its third. All of this is clear from the Latin rendering of the creed's third article: *Et in Spiritum Sanctum ... Et unam, sanctam, catholicam et apostolicam Ecclesiam ... Et expecto resurrectionem mortuorem, et vitam venturi saeculi.*[65] Significantly, the point of creedal sequencing is not lost on Bonhoeffer himself, whose own concern with the creeds' third article, and indeed with the 'relationality' of the doctrines of pneumatology, ecclesiology and eschatology, came to dominate his theological studies in (and from) the winter semester of 1925/6.[66] This preoccupation is so much the case that Hans Pfeifer states, 'One would not be wrong in placing [Bonhoeffer's] [doctoral] dissertation in this context [of the third article].'[67] Pfeifer's claim might be said to apply equally well, however, not only to Bonhoeffer's postdoctoral dissertation but also to his

---

is challenged (in one way or another) by Geffrey B. Kelly and F. Burton Nelson, *The Cost of Moral Leadership: The Spirituality of Dietrich Bonhoeffer* (Grand Rapids: Eerdmans, 2003), 51–82; Mawson, *Christ Existing as Community*, esp. 126ff.; Myles Werntz, *Bodies of Peace: Ecclesiology, Non-Violence, Witness* (Minneapolis: Fortress Press, 2014), 47–54 and 262–4; Holmes, 'The Holy Spirit'; and Greggs, 'Ecclesiology', esp. 232–4.

[64] As Bonhoeffer himself states, Jesus is *'the foundation* of the church', but he is *'not the founder* of the church'. See *DBW* 11, 271.

[65] Here, the differentiation between belief *in* the Holy Spirit, and the church which emerges from and 'under' the third article is clear. Indeed, there is no preposition 'in' before *ecclesiam* in the creed and there is thus, as Calvin writes, 'no good reason why many insert the preposition "in"', for as Calvin continues: 'We testify that we believe *in* God' (Calvin, *Institutes*, IV.i.2 (2:1013)). Or as Yves Congar puts it: 'It is ... possible to believe *in* God, to accept him as the end of one's life, but it is not possible to believe in the same way *in* the Church' (Yves Congar, *I Believe in the Holy Spirit*, trans. David Smith (New York: The Crossroad Publishing Company, 2015), vol. 2, 5). Instead, *we believe the church*. Not only is there no 'in' preceding *ecclesiam* in the creed, but by this creedal preposition the triune God is affirmed as uncreated from all that is created and thus as the One *in* whom we believe.

[66] See, for example, *DBWE* 9, 285–300, 310–94, and 502–9.

[67] Hans Pfeifer, 'Editor's Afterword', *DBWE* 9, 574.

theology as a whole.⁶⁸ Indeed, according to Bonhoeffer himself, the connection between 'the essence' and 'factual content' of *Act and Being* and *Sanctorum Communio* lies in his understanding both works as being 'basically about nothing other than the church'.⁶⁹

Moreover, it is precisely the church, which, for Bonhoeffer, is at the same time both the prerequisite or precondition (*Voraussetzung*) for, and object (*Gegenstand*) of, dogmatic theology itself, such that the church is said to stand '*before* the brackets' in which dogmatic theology is done.⁷⁰ That the church stands thus is not, however, to say that in dogmatic theology there is, therefore, a lacuna, but rather that the church qualifies all other dogmatic content which stands '*within* the brackets'.⁷¹ Accordingly, the doctrine of the church is not only to be treated as 'the first point of doctrine of dogmatics',⁷² but in fact it is the doctrinal locus which pervades dogmatic theology as a whole and thereby all other doctrinal *loci*. Bonhoeffer writes: 'Every individual theological problem not only points back to the reality of the church ... but theological thought in its entirety also recognizes itself as something that belongs solely to the church.'⁷³ Thus, for Bonhoeffer, and precisely 'in order to establish clarity about the inner logic of theological construction', the theologian should 'start' her theology 'not with the doctrine of God but with the doctrine of the church'.⁷⁴ To do so, is *not*, however, to suggest that 'the church, as an object of doctrine, might be "more important" than God',⁷⁵ or that ecclesiology should thus be rendered in theology (in a fashion after 'ethnographic' ecclesiology) as an independent doctrinal locus – that is as 'a separate fourth article' of the creed,⁷⁶ independent so-to-speak of the divine life in the sense of having its own dogmatic *res*. Bonhoeffer does not treat the doctrine of the church in any sense as if it is. Bonhoeffer (as will be demonstrated in Chapter 3 in critique of 'ethnographic' ecclesiology) is clear: the church *is* only in and through God the Holy Spirit. That the theologian should 'start' her theology with the doctrine of the church in the order of presentational knowing *is*, however, to suggest that in terms of presentational systematicity the most central dogmatic *res* of Bonhoeffer's theology might be best identified as *ecclesiology*.⁷⁷ This identification would itself seem

---

⁶⁸ It is notable in this respect that Sabine Dramm suggests that perhaps the most appropriate way to approximate 'the content and goal' of Bonhoeffer's theology and its distinct 'innermost core' is with reference to the articles of the Apostles Creed. However, in Dramm's discussion of the third article that follows this suggestion, there is, astonishingly, only *one* explicit reference to the person and work of the Holy Spirit – a reference which seemingly serves to collapse pneumatology into ecclesiology without remainder: 'What is commonly called the Holy Spirit ... manifests itself ... in the existence of the church.' See Sabine Dramm, *Dietrich Bonhoeffer: An Introduction to His Thought*, trans. Thomas Rice (Peabody: Hendrickson Publishers, 2007), 31ff. [31 and 32] and 56–66.
⁶⁹ *DBWE* 11, 45.
⁷⁰ See *DBW* 11, 255 and 252 (emphasis added).
⁷¹ Ibid., 252–3.
⁷² Ibid., 260.
⁷³ *DBWE* 10, 408.
⁷⁴ *DBWE* 1, 134.
⁷⁵ Eva Harasta, 'The Responsibility of Doctrine: Bonhoeffer's Ecclesiological Hermeneutics of Dogmatic Theology', *Theology Today* 71.1 (2014), 16.
⁷⁶ See Greggs, 'Proportion and Topography in Ecclesiology', 98.
⁷⁷ Within the wider corpus of Bonhoeffer scholarship a number of different hermeneutical keys for reading him have been suggested. For example, Christology has been accorded ultimacy by (among others) John D. Godsey, *The Theology of Dietrich Bonhoeffer* (London: SCM Press, 1960); John A. Phillips, *Christ for Us in the Theology of Dietrich Bonhoeffer* (New York: Harper & Row,

to be authorized by Bonhoeffer himself. Indeed, from his confident and passionate declaration at the age of fourteen of his intention to reform the church,[78] through his first encounter with its beatific glory in Rome,[79] and his submission of ecclesiologically concentrated academic writings and active concern (pre-eminently at Finkenwalde)

1967); Feil, *The Theology of Dietrich Bonhoeffer*; Woelfel, *Bonhoeffer's Theology*; and H. Gaylon Barker, *The Cross of Reality: Luther's Theologia Crucis and Bonhoeffer's Christology* (Minneapolis: Fortress Press, 2015); 'reality' (understood on the basis of a Christological ontology) has been proposed by Dumas, *Dietrich Bonhoeffer*, and Ott, *Reality and Faith*; 'sociality' has been offered by Green, *Bonhoeffer*; divine and human 'identity' (circumscribed Christologically) by Charles Marsh, *Reclaiming Dietrich Bonhoeffer: The Promise of His Theology* (New York: Oxford University Press, 1994); 'life' (interpreted Christologically) as a key by Ralf K. Wüstenberg, *A Theology of Life: Dietrich Bonhoeffer's Religionless Christianity*, trans. Doug Stott (Grand Rapids: Eerdmans 1998); 'freedom' (notably a Christologically defined freedom) by Nickson, *Bonhoeffer on Freedom*; 'silence' (again, notably, a Christologically interpreted silence) by Muers, *Keeping God's Silence*; 'guilt' and its 'acceptance' (mandated Christologically) by Christine Schließer, *Everyone Who Acts Responsibly Becomes Guilty: The Concept of Accepting Guilt in Dietrich Bonhoeffer: Reconstruction and Critical Assessment* (Neukirchen-Vluyn: Neukirchener Verlag, 2006); the concept of 'person' (understood on a Christological basis) by Michael P. DeJonge, *Bonhoeffer's Theological Formation: Berlin, Barth, and Protestant Theology* (Oxford: Oxford University Press, 2012); 'confession unto repentance' (patterned after the person and work of Christ) by McBride, *The Church for the World*; and 'Luther and Lutheranism' by DeJonge, *Bonhoeffer's Reception of Luther*. Within these different hermeneutical keys, 'if there is one consensus in Bonhoeffer studies it is' then, as Christiane Tietz states (following a well-trodden path), 'that Bonhoeffer's theology is essentially Christ-oriented' (Christiane Tietz, 'The Role of Jesus Christ for Christian Theology', in Mawson and Ziegler, ed. *Christ, Church and World*, 9). This orientation is such that 'Christology is the *cantus firmus* of all his thinking' (Christiane Tietz, 'Bonhoeffer's Strong Christology in the Context of Religious Pluralism', in Clifford J. Green and Guy Carter, ed. *Interpreting Bonhoeffer: Historical Perspectives, Emerging Issues* (Minneapolis: Fortress Press, 2013), 188). Or as Woelfel puts it: Christology 'is the golden thread which ties together his works from first to last' (Woelfel, *Bonhoeffer's Theology*, 134). On a meta (or systematic) level such a conclusion is, however, challenged by Wayne Whitson Floyd, *Theology and the Dialectics of Otherness: On Reading Bonhoeffer and Adorno* (Lanham: University Press of America, 1988). Given the kaleidoscopic legacy of Bonhoeffer's theological thought, Floyd draws attention to the need to dispel any illusion as to the systematic unity or '*coherence* of Bonhoeffer's theology' (see Floyd, *Theology and the Dialectics of Otherness*, 6; cf., Dumas, *Dietrich Bonhoeffer*, 276). Floyd's point is rehearsed provocatively in the dissent thesis of David H. Hopper, *A Dissent on Bonhoeffer* (Philadelphia: The Westminster Press, 1975). Hopper sees an inherent and paradoxical tension in successive Bonhoeffer interpreters who identify a basic or systematic unity in Bonhoeffer's thought but do so by appealing to different hermeneutical keys or aspects of his thought, thus neglecting (or minimizing) the work of others in establishing their own thesis. Hopper suggests instead that there is in fact no systematic unity – Christological or otherwise – to Bonhoeffer's thought; or if there is any such unity then it is to be found not in a theological or dogmatic unity but rather in anthropological motifs drawn from Bonhoeffer's own aristocratic life and quest for spiritual identity. Thus, to identify, on a macro level, Bonhoeffer's theological thought as systematic, and (more pertinently) on a micro (or doctrinal, locus-specific) level, the central dogmatic *res* of Bonhoeffer's theology as ecclesiology, is contentious, especially if one recalls Phillips's words that 'ecclesiology simply has no usefulness as a basic interpretative principle for understanding the *whole* of [Bonhoeffer's] theology' (Phillips, *Christ for Us in the Theology of Dietrich Bonhoeffer*, 27). Nevertheless, it is a suggestion that can be and (with respect to that micro-level) has been made: see William Kuhns, *In Pursuit of Dietrich Bonhoeffer* (Dayton: Pflaum Press, 1967); Brendan Leahy, '"Christ Existing as Community": Dietrich Bonhoeffer's Notion of Church', *Irish Theological Quarterly* 73 (2008), 32–59; Barry Harvey, 'The Narrow Path: Sociality, Ecclesiology, and the Polyphony of Life in the Thought of Dietrich Bonhoeffer', in Zimmermann and Gregor, ed. *Being Human, Becoming Human*, 102–23; Harasta, 'Bonhoeffer's Lutheran Ecclesiology and Inter-Religious Dialogue', 239–50; and Greggs, 'Ecclesiology'.

[78] See Bethge, *Dietrich Bonhoeffer*, 36.
[79] See *DBWE* 9, 82–109.

for the church's preservation and renewal in the midst of National Socialism and Hitler's *Gleichschaltung*, to final theological thoughts and prescient questions from prison on what it might mean for the church to be 'church' in a post-Christian era, not only is Bonhoeffer's theology ecclesiologically founded, but, together with his own life, it is so consistently centred upon and oriented to the church that ecclesiology *can* be seen as the central dogmatic *res*, or *cantus firmus*,[80] of *all* Bonhoeffer's writings and of his elucidation of Christian doctrine therein. Moreover, given both Bonhoeffer's expressed concern for the third article of the Nicene-Constantinopolitan creed and, indeed, the beginning of his lectures *Creation and Fall*,[81] the central dogmatic *res* of Bonhoeffer's theology is an ecclesiology of which the foundational dogmatic *res* is not Christology or theological anthropology but an apocalyptically eschatologically indexed pneumatology.[82]

Consequently, if the theologian is to speak about the being of the church in her ecclesiological description in a genuinely theological manner, then according to

---

[80] See *DBWE* 8, 393–5.

[81] See Section II of this chapter.

[82] It is precisely this suggestion, and its reidentification of the foundational dogmatic *res* of Bonhoeffer's ecclesiology, that demarcates the argument of this book from extant Bonhoeffer scholarship, for even those who claim that ecclesiology is central to Bonhoeffer's theology nevertheless index his ecclesiology (to one extent or another) to Christology. Thus Kuhns, *In Pursuit of Dietrich Bonhoeffer*, 260: Bonhoeffer's 'ecclesiology can in no way be separated from his … Christology; indeed, the two constantly lead into one another'; Leahy, 'Christ Existing as Community', 34: 'Christo-centric ecclesial reform and renewal' is the *cantus firmus* of Bonhoeffer's writings; Harvey, 'The Narrow Path', 103: 'a proper understanding of church' in Bonhoeffer's writings is delivered 'in relation to Christological and eschatological concerns'; and Harasta, 'Bonhoeffer's Lutheran Ecclesiology and Inter-Religious Dialogue', 239: while 'Christology does not contradict or rival his [primary] ecclesiological focus', the two doctrines are 'interrelated foci of Bonhoeffer's theology'. This tendency to coordinate ecclesiology with Christology, and in doing so – creedally speaking – *mis*locate Bonhoeffer's ecclesiology 'under' Christology, such that the connection between the doctrine of the church and a doctrine of God (indexed to the person and work of Jesus Christ) is overidentified in Bonhoeffer's ecclesial thought at the risk of positioning Bonhoeffer (to use the language of Chapter 1) as a 'soft' dogmatic ecclesiologist, is also seen in, for example, Godsey, *The Theology of Dietrich Bonhoeffer*, 264: 'Christology includes ecclesiology within itself'; Feil, *The Theology of Dietrich Bonhoeffer*, 60: 'Ecclesiology [in Bonhoeffer's theology] becomes more profound when shaped by Christology'; Bethge, *Bonhoeffer*, 62: Bonhoeffer 'found[s] ecclesiology on Christology'; Joel Lawrence, *Bonhoeffer: A Guide for the Perplexed* (London: T&T Clark, 2010), 37: 'Bonhoeffer's ecclesiology can only be grasped from the perspective of his Christology'; Jeff Nowers, 'Hegel, Bonhoeffer, and Objective *Geist*: An Architectonic Exegesis of Sanctorum Communio', in Adam C. Clark and Michael Mawson, ed. *Ontology and Ethics: Bonhoeffer and Contemporary Scholarship* (Eugene: Pickwick Publications, 2013), 48: 'Christology and ecclesiology, [are] two dogmatic *loci* that Bonhoeffer weaves tightly together (he is a "Christo-ecclesiologist")'; and Mawson, *Christ Existing as Community*, 121–49, who therein, seemingly, derives Bonhoeffer's ecclesiology from a pneumatologically indexed Christology. The one clear exception to this tendency is the work of Tom Greggs, but even here, as noted in the introduction to this book, the pneumatological tone – at least presentationally – is downstream of a Christological one and in part is cautionary. As Greggs writes: 'The foundational *res* of ecclesiology requires being founded upon the divine person who creates and sustains the church, and either a more foundational *res* of pneumatology is needed or an intermediate *res* of pneumatology should be offered in relation to how the church is "in Christ"' (Greggs, 'Bearing Sin in the Church', 95). It is the argument of this book, however, that Bonhoeffer's understanding of the church in fact does offer an apocalyptically eschatologically indexed pneumatology as its most foundational dogmatic *res*. On Bonhoeffer's deeply pneumatological understanding of the way in which the church as Christ's body is 'Christ existing as church-community', see Chapter 3, Section III of this book.

Bonhoeffer – perhaps somewhat surprisingly and despite (scholarly) caricatures to the contrary – she must understand it, first and foremost, as being oriented to the eschatological telos in virtue of the work of God the Holy Spirit. Indeed, that the foundations of Bonhoeffer's ecclesial thought are to be constructed in this theological and more specifically pneumatological and apocalyptically eschatological way is the fundamental premise of all that follows in this book – a premise, which, while explicitly stated at the beginning of *Creation and Fall*, can be seen to have its genesis in Bonhoeffer's doctoral dissertation, *Sanctorum Communio*.

IV. Theological foundations: Theology *against* sociology?

The argument of this chapter that the foundations of Bonhoeffer's 'both/and' ecclesiological methodology are strictly theological can be buttressed and indeed demonstrated by an examination of Bonhoeffer's own stated methodological starting point of his doctoral dissertation, and in particular the articulated given relation therein between the categories of the theological and the sociological. This relation establishes in Bonhoeffer's ecclesial thought a *theological* interpretative paradigm within which his 'both/and' ecclesiological methodology is subsequently built, and which must be considered, therefore, to set a programmatic (interpretative) directive for any reading of Bonhoeffer's ecclesiological description.

Seeking to ground such a contention in *Sanctorum Communio* may at first sight seem, however, somewhat spurious, especially given Bonhoeffer's own stated methodological starting point to his dissertation – that is, to understand the nature and structure of the church 'as revealed in Christ, from the perspective of social philosophy and sociology'.[83] Methodologically, this starting point is itself derivative of, and parasitic upon, the prior (and indeed programmatic) statement contained in the work's *Preface*: that all 'basic Christian concepts' – 'person', 'primal state', 'sin' and 'revelation' (to which one could, and indeed should, add 'church') – are 'social' in intent, and can be understood 'fully' only in reference to 'sociality'.[84] Categorically speaking, Bonhoeffer's ecclesial thought might appear, therefore, to be constructed not on pneumatological and apocalyptically eschatological foundations – not even (perhaps) on theological foundations – but rather on sociological foundations. To draw such a conclusion would, however, be to misconstrue and misread Bonhoeffer at this categorical and foundational level. Or, at the very least, such a reading would be to propose a hermeneutic that synoptically fails to treat Bonhoeffer first and foremost (as he himself understood himself) as a theologian, and more acutely, as a dogmatician (*Dogmatiker*).[85] Bonhoeffer worked methodologically and intentionally with theological categories for the purpose of prosecuting the primary theological task of elucidating Christian doctrine as a function and in service of the church.[86] Such a reading (at worst) also fails to recognize

---

[83] *DBWE* 1, 33.
[84] See ibid., 21.
[85] See *DBW* 1, 172; cf., *DBWE* 10, 198–9.
[86] Cf., Dietrich Bonhoeffer, *Zettelnotizen für eine "Ethik"*, Ergänzungsband zu *DBW* 6 [hereafter ZE], ed. Ilse Tödt (München: Chr. Kaiser Verlag), 32: 'Today we find "Christian ethics" freed from

Bonhoeffer's apocalyptically eschatologically indexed pneumatology as the most foundational dogmatic *res* of his ecclesiology, or (at best) intentionally limits his interest in the doctrinal *loci* of eschatology and pneumatology so as to treat those *loci* as subordinate in his ecclesial thought to Christology or theological anthropology.

Notwithstanding Bonhoeffer's methodological deployment of the categories of social philosophy and sociology to understand the nature and structure of the church, to read Bonhoeffer aright at this categorical and foundational level one must pay heed, however, to the specific ordering that Bonhoeffer himself gives to the constituent parts of his own stated methodological and programmatic starting points. It is the nature and structure of the church 'as revealed in Christ' that Bonhoeffer sets out to understand, but he does so 'from the perspective of social philosophy and sociology'.[87] Bonhoeffer writes, 'In the present ecclesiological work the attempt is made to make a dogmatic-theological reflection on the concept of the church from the point of view of socio-philosophical and sociological insights.'[88] Order and proportion here are key. The sociological categories of social philosophy and sociology are rendered by Bonhoeffer subservient – and necessarily so – to the theological category of the object of his study: the *church*, as it is revealed in Christ.[89] Similarly, all 'basic Christian concepts' can be

---

Christian doctrine, Christian behaviour that is not at all aware of its Christianness [*Christlichkeit*]. Only recently have people again come to ask after the foundation of their behaviour and thus come back to doctrine and to the church. The issue is this: the unification of the two, to lead-back to faith.' On the proposal for reading Bonhoeffer with a dogmatic hermeneutic, see also Harasta, 'Bonhoeffer's Lutheran Ecclesiology and Inter-Religious Dialogue', 239–40.

[87] See *DBWE* 1, 33. On Bonhoeffer's understanding of the sociological categories of social philosophy and sociology, and his engagement with social theory in *Sanctorum Communio*, see the excellent work of Mawson, *Christ Existing as Community*, 39–55; cf., Chapter 3, Section II of this book.

[88] *DBW* 1, 200.

[89] Mawson's recent re-evaluation and indeed rehabilitation of Bonhoeffer's engagement with social theory from a theological perspective in *Sanctorum Communio* is thus persuasive (see Mawson, *Christ Existing as Community*). As Mawson writes – in critique of Peter Berger and others (notably Marsh, Dumas, Green and Hegstad) – Bonhoeffer 'had little, if any, interest in … a dialogue [between theology and the social sciences]', and instead was interested only and 'more narrowly in that kind of sociology that might be of service to theology, and in how such service might be rendered' (Mawson, *Christ Existing as Community*, 45; cf., Peter Berger, 'Sociology and Ecclesiology', in Martin E. Marty, ed. *The Place of Bonhoeffer: Problems and Possibilities in His Thought* (London: SCM Press, 1963), 53–80; Marsh, *Reclaiming Dietrich Bonhoeffer*, 68; Dumas, *Dietrich Bonhoeffer*, 218; Green, *Bonhoeffer*, 27; and Hegstad, *The Real Church*, 60–1). That said, Mawson's articulation of the theological perspective or 'dialectic' on the basis of which he sees Bonhoeffer rehabilitating the concepts and insights of social theory to understand and thus explain the nature and structure of the church, and indeed (seemingly) human existence per se, ultimately, however, is problematic. According to Mawson this 'dialectic of creation, sin, and reconciliation' means that 'we can only approach and conceptualize the church in its concrete sociality *as* created, sinful, and reconciled' (Mawson, *Christ Existing as Community*, 40 and 53). Yes, indeed. But as Mawson goes on to state problematically: 'The decisive insight from theology, then, is that there is only ever the human being and community in their standing before God, that is, as at once created, sinful, and reconciled' (Mawson, *Christ Existing as Community*, 54). Yes and *no*, however. The move that Mawson (seemingly) makes here is one which appears to generalize the ontological status of being in Christ (in the church) – that is, of the one who is created as a creature, fallen as a sinner and reconciled in Christ *simul iustus et peccator* – to being in Adam – that is, to the one who is created as a creature, fallen as a sinner, but is *not yet* reconciled in Christ. So *yes*, 'there is only ever the human being and the community in their standing before God' (Mawson, *Christ Existing as Community*, 54); but *no*, there is not '*only* ever the one who has been created, has fallen into sin, and is reconciled in Christ' (Mawson, *Christ Existing as Community*, 50, emphasis added); and *no*, the human being cannot

fully understood but 'only in reference to sociality'.[90] Again, the sociological category of sociality is rendered subservient to the theological category of the object of study: basic *Christian* concepts. Thus, programmatically and methodologically, Bonhoeffer deploys and utilizes the non-theological category to make it always serve and be fruitful for the theological category,[91] which itself is considered *a priori*.[92] As Bonhoeffer asserts: 'In this inquiry social philosophy and sociology are placed in the service of dogmatics.'[93] The work's subtitle makes the matter clear that Bonhoeffer's primary task in *Sanctorum Communio* is to prosecute '*a dogmatic inquiry* into the sociology of the church'.[94] The work, then, 'does not belong in the discipline of sociology of religion, but in dogmatics',[95] and as such is one which presupposes the doctrinal locus of ecclesiology – indexed foundationally to an apocalyptically eschatological pneumatology – as its dogmatic hermeneutic.[96] Moreover, that the object of Bonhoeffer's study (the

> '*only* be properly conceived of in this threefold manner' (Mawson, *Christ Existing as Community*, 50, emphasis added). Rather, before God – and as Bonhoeffer's theological ontology of 'being in' makes clear – there is *only* ever the one who is created as a creature, has fallen into sin and is reconciled in Christ (in the church), *and* the one who is created as a creature, has fallen into sin, but remains unreconciled in Adam. It would seem, therefore, that Mawson's threefold theological 'dialectic' is *fully* accurate only as an ontological description of being in Christ (in the church), and consequently, his application (and reading) of it (in)to Bonhoeffer's understanding of human being and social reality per se, and indeed to social theoretical concepts and insights in order that they themselves might be considered 'Christian' or 'theological', is problematic. It is also noteworthy that Mawson sees his reading of Bonhoeffer's theological disruption and reworking of social theory as enabling him to subsequently demarcate the approach of Bonhoeffer (as Mawson reads it) from that of Milbank. According to Mawson, Milbank's understanding of 'theology as a social science' (see Milbank, *Theology and Social Theory*, 380ff.) is derivative of an account of ecclesial existence as itself embodying 'an alternative "counter ontology"' to that of secular social theory (see Mawson, 'Theology and Social Theory', 77), whereas Bonhoeffer's threefold theological 'dialectic' and his concomitant emphasis on the 'disrupted and disrupting nature' of ecclesial existence (seemingly) precludes such an ontology (see Mawson, *Christ Existing as Community*, 181–3). However, as it will be demonstrated in Chapter 3 of this book, it is precisely Bonhoeffer's argument in *Sanctorum Communio* that the church as *God's* church-community does indeed embody 'an alternative "counter ontology"', and not just to that of secular social theory but to all other socio-historical forms of *human* community such that the being of the church *is* a sociological structure sui generis. It is the church's sui generis sociological structure – which Mawson (in a fashion after the 'soft' ethnographic ecclesiologist) problematically dissolves in his reading of Bonhoeffer – that demands the *necessary* subservient relation of the sociological category to the theological category when the object of study is the church. On the church's sui generis sociological structure, see Chapter 3, Section III.ii of this book.

[90] See *DBWE* 1, 21.
[91] See *DBW* 1, 200: 'Since in the current time the interest of the field of science is directed towards sociological problems, occasion will thus be given to think about the fruitfulness of insights flowing from there to our dogmatic subject and (also) to demonstrate the limits that here exist.'
[92] While not wanting to deny the value of non-theological categories of analysis for investigating the structure and nature of the church and other basic Christian concepts, Bonhoeffer is concerned, ultimately, to delimit the explanatory power of such categories vis-à-vis the theological category within which is set God's own act – the beginning 'back behind' which one cannot go (see *DBWE* 11, 231). In order to prosecute the primary theological task of elucidating Christian doctrine, the theologian (according to Bonhoeffer) must work first and foremost with the category of the theological.
[93] *DBW* 1, 13.
[94] Ibid., 12 (emphasis added).
[95] Ibid., 12.
[96] It is precisely for this reason that Green's assertion that Bonhoeffer sets ecclesiology 'in the midst of a "theology of sociality"' is problematic (see Green, 'Editors Introduction', *DBWE* 1, 1; cf., Green,

church) is a dogmatic category determines precisely that, for Bonhoeffer, 'there is no sociological concept of the church, which is not theologically founded'.[97] The nature and structure of the church can be understood only 'from within' – only, that is, 'from the standpoint of the gospel' and with the eyes of (Christian) faith.[98] Bonhoeffer writes: 'It is only *within* the church-community that one can pass judgment *on* the church community. By nature the church-community cannot be judged from the outside.'[99] This is not to say, however (as will be demonstrated in the chapters that follow), that Bonhoeffer denies that the church *is* an 'empirical phenomenon', or that the church as such – when 'looked at from outside' – is impervious to becoming the object of 'a sociological morphology' (*eine soziologische Morphologie*), but rather to say that so to render the church is to make 'all theological reflection ... superfluous', and to fail to take seriously 'the claim of the church to be the church of God'.[100] Indeed, only 'when one steps *into* [the church], bowing in faith to its claim', does one find 'an adequate criterion for legitimating the claim of the church to be *God's* church-community'.[101] Only from within this theological approach, and its concomitant construction of the necessary subservient relation of the category of the sociological to that of the theological, is the theologian, then, able (according to Bonhoeffer) to develop adequately 'a systematic understanding of the community-structure of the Christian church'.[102] Thus does the articulated given relation in *Sanctorum Communio* between the categories of the theological and the sociological establish in Bonhoeffer's ecclesial thought a theological interpretative paradigm within which his 'both/and' ecclesiological methodology is

---

Bonhoeffer, esp. 13 and 21–4). Not only do Green's words suggest that Bonhoeffer views the church (in a fashion similar to 'hard' ethnographic ecclesiology) as the *a posteriori* embodiment of an *a priori* concept of human sociality, but (seemingly) ignore (thereby) Bonhoeffer's theological ontology, according to which the concept of sociality is understandable neither *in se* nor per se but only in reference to being in Adam or Christ. As Harvey states:

> [Green's] way of putting the matter is not so much incorrect as it is misleading, for it can leave the impression that ecclesiology is properly a function of a more basic conception of sociality and thus leaves it in jeopardy of being positioned by secular social science and social theory, or at least by conceptions of humankind's social nature that see the church as one particular species of a more generic conception of human community. (Harvey, 'The Narrow Path', 104)

To position the church in the way Green does – or at least to leave the church at risk of being so-positioned – fails, therefore, to appreciate properly the centrality of ecclesiology to Bonhoeffer's whole theological thought as its most central dogmatic *res*, and the very fact that God's church-community, in virtue of its pneumatological and apocalyptically eschatological foundations, *is* (as will be demonstrated in Chapter 3 of this book) a sociological structure sui generis. Green's positioning of Bonhoeffer's ecclesiology thus, ultimately, is 'theologically unsound, reflecting', as Harvey writes, 'the recurring temptation in modern theology to "naturalize the supernatural," or as Bonhoeffer might put it, to erase the distinction between the penultimate and the ultimate' (Harvey, 'The Narrow Path', 103). On Bonhoeffer's theological ontology of human personhood, see Chapter 3, Section II.i.a of this book; and on Bonhoeffer's 'ultimate'/'penultimate' distinction, see Chapter 5, esp. Section II.

[97] *DBW* 9, 477.
[98] See *DBWE* 1, 33.
[99] *DBWE* 12, 516.
[100] See *DBW* 1, 79–80.
[101] See ibid., 80 (emphasis added).
[102] See *DBWE* 1, 21.

subsequently set, and in accordance with which any consideration of Bonhoeffer's ecclesiological description must be developed.

V. Conclusion

This chapter has sought to identify and thereby lay the theological foundations upon which Bonhoeffer's ecclesial thought and its 'both/and' ecclesiological methodology is subsequently built. The chapter stands as a corrective to extant material on Bonhoeffer's ecclesiology in that those foundations have been demonstrated to be apocalyptically eschatological and pneumatological in dimension, such that the foundational dogmatic *res* of Bonhoeffer's ecclesiology must be considered, most properly, an apocalyptically eschatologically indexed pneumatology. This conclusion has been reached by articulating, firstly, Bonhoeffer's understanding of the church's being in space and time as being oriented to the eschatological telos, and by demonstrating, secondly, that, for Bonhoeffer, this orientation of the church's being is derivative of the person and work of God the Holy Spirit. The chapter's argument that the foundations of Bonhoeffer's ecclesial thought and its 'both/and' ecclesiological methodology are (in this way) strictly theological has been buttressed, furthermore, by considering, thirdly, the specific ordering of Bonhoeffer's own stated methodological starting point of his doctoral dissertation, and in particular the articulated given relation between the categories of the theological and the sociological therein in which the category of the theological is established as the interpretative paradigm of Bonhoeffer's ecclesiological description.

That Bonhoeffer's understanding of the being of the church must be described *theologically* as teleological and apocalyptically eschatological, and thus most foundationally as pnuematological arises, moreover, because its dogmatic subject matter (the being of the church itself) exists in spatio-temporality as a socio-historical human community *only* in its relation to the 'end' – that is, the eschatological person of Jesus Christ, who, as the 'end' and by the work of the Holy Spirit of God is the 'beginning' of the world of new creation – and *only*, and more acutely, as the church's being is created, sustained and perfected thus in virtue of the eschatological action of the Holy Spirit in the time between the ascension of Christ and the *eschaton*. That said, it is important to state that while this conclusion may suggest that Bonhoeffer presents in his account of the church a purely 'dogmatic' approach to ecclesiology and should, therefore, be considered – in light of the analysis proffered in Chapter 1 – as either a 'hard' or 'soft' dogmatic ecclesiologist, it will be demonstrated in Chapter 3 that this would in fact be to misunderstand Bonhoeffer's methodological approach to ecclesiological description. Indeed, it will be seen that Bonhoeffer's understanding of the being of the church in its orientation to the eschatological telos and his concomitant attention to the work of God the Holy Spirit in and upon and outwith the church enables Bonhoeffer (perhaps paradoxically, but in critique of both 'hard' and 'soft' dogmatic ecclesiology) to attend with due proportion to the particular and contingent socio-historical human community that the church as *congregatio* is in space and time, such that in Bonhoeffer's ecclesiological speech divine agency appropriately relativizes human agency but critically does not minimize it. The concrete life and form of the church in Bonhoeffer's ecclesiological description (as will be demonstrated) is neither marginalized in an overly abstract or 'spiritualized' account of the church as it is in 'hard' dogmatic ecclesiology, nor 'swallowed up' by a disproportionate emphasis on God's own life as it is in 'soft' dogmatic ecclesiology. Instead, the being of the church is construed by Bonhoeffer with full reference to the church's spatio-temporal reality precisely because of his understanding of the work of God the Holy Spirit. However, because of Bonhoeffer's concern to norm ecclesiology *theologically* by attending to the work of the Holy Spirit of God, Bonhoeffer's ecclesiological description (as will be demonstrated) is also able to safeguard adequately – unlike 'soft' dogmatic ecclesiology – the sheer gratuitous nature of the church's created spatio-temporal reality as the event of the divine act of *convocatio*, and thus the church's unqualified difference from the life of God which brings the church into being. It will be seen that this emphasis on the operative and gracious act of God the Holy Spirit to create in spatio-temporality the particular and contingent socio-historical human community that the church is in its orientation to the eschatological telos *also* works, therefore, to determinatively distinguish Bonhoeffer's account of the church from 'hard' and 'soft' ethnographic ecclesiology. Bonhoeffer's ecclesiological description (as will be demonstrated) neither renders the doctrinal locus of ecclesiology independent from a doctrine of God and God's operative and gracious acts as per 'hard' ethnographic ecclesiology, nor does Bonhoeffer's ecclesiological description emerge first and foremost in the context of lived ecclesial life and church practice such that he presents a 'naturalized' ecclesiology which is inattentive to the sui generis nature of the church as a human community as per 'soft' ethnographic ecclesiology. For Bonhoeffer, the being of *God's* church-community *as* a socio-historical *human* community is distinct from all other socio-historical forms *of* human community. All this is to say that it will be seen that Bonhoeffer's ecclesial thought and its 'both/and' ecclesiological methodology, in which the being of the church is conceived from *both* a 'dogmatic' *and* an 'ethnographic' perspective simultaneously, is built on the pneumatological and apocalyptically eschatological foundations that have been identified in this chapter. The following chapter, then, proceeds to explicate how Bonhoeffer builds the structure of his 'both/and' ecclesiological methodology precisely on these theological foundations.

3

God's church-community

Bonhoeffer's 'both/and' ecclesiological methodology

I. Introduction

Having established the theological and more specifically pneumatological and apocalyptically eschatological foundations upon which Bonhoeffer's ecclesial thought and its 'both/and' ecclesiological methodology is built, this chapter will explicate how Bonhoeffer proceeds to build the structure of his 'both/and' ecclesiological methodology upon them. This methodology, in which the being of the church is conceived from *both* a 'dogmatic' *and* an 'ethnographic' perspective simultaneously in consequence of the pneumatological and apocalyptically eschatological foundations upon which it is built, will be seen to treat therapeutically the endemic 'either/or' problematic present in approaches to contemporary ecclesiological discourse that was diagnosed in Chapter 1.

Indeed, to attend in ecclesiological description *either* 'dogmatically' to God's *ad intra* or *ad extra* life, *or* 'ethnographically' to the church's socio-historical human form (and to either one at the expense of the other) – or, as Bonhoeffer puts it, *either* to the 'essential' *or* 'empirical' aspects of the church – is to misunderstand the being of the church itself.[1] On the one hand, an '*historicizing*' and 'sociological' – or in the language of this book (and its designated ecclesiological 'types') 'ethnographic' – approach to ecclesiological description reductively conflates the church with a '*religious community*' or human society, albeit a religious one, and, in pointing to 'the "religious motives"' of its human members as the fundamental impulse for their concrete coming together as *congregatio*, overlooks the fact that it is God in Christ by the agency of the Holy Spirit who realizes and actualizes God's church-community and its unique ontic-social relations.[2] On the other hand, a '*religious*' and 'theological' – or in the language of this book (and its designated ecclesiological 'types') 'dogmatic' – approach to ecclesiological description expansively conflates the church as *convocatio* with '*the Realm of God*' and,

---

[1] See *DBWE* 1, 125.
[2] See ibid., 125–6. Bonhoeffer has in mind here the ecclesial thought of Ernst Troeltsch and the (perceived) problem therein of accounting for the church in terms of a purely sociological historicism. On this, see Mawson, *Christ Existing as Community*, 15–23; cf., Ernst Troeltsch, *The Social Teaching of the Christian Churches*, 2 vols, trans. Olive Wyon (London: George Allen & Unwin, 1931).

in doing so, refuses to take seriously both the historicity of human beings and the antecedent will of God 'that all God's revelation, both in Christ and in the church, be concealed under the form of historical life'.[3]

For Bonhoeffer, neither approach understands nor speaks properly about the being of the church precisely because the church is 'both a historical community and one established by God'.[4] Moreover, in its dual nature the 'church "is" always both things simultaneously', but it is that only because the church is determined by God in the simultaneity of its being: 'God, not we, makes the church into that which it is'.[5] As a divine act, therefore, the church is fundamentally prior to any and all human action.[6] Only through the act of God is the church 'there',[7] but critically the church is 'there' as a socio-historical human community – as the place where God's divine will to be God as God of a people (*his* people) is concretized in space and time.[8] The church, then, comes into being (according to Bonhoeffer) only because of the operative and gracious act of God. But that the church *is* because of God's *act* is at once to say that the church has *being* in space and time as a particular and contingent socio-historical human community. In other words, the church as *congregatio* occupies a certain physical 'space' (*Ort*) or 'place' (*Raum*) *in* space and time,[9] but it does so only in consequence of the event of the divine act of *convocatio*. For Bonhoeffer, 'One must speak of the being and act of the church together.'[10] Consequently, the need arises – if the theologian is to speak in her ecclesiological discussion both descriptively and critically about the being of the church in a genuinely theological manner – to treat methodologically (and therapeutically) the binarized tendency in evidence in approaches to contemporary ecclesiological discourse (as Bonhoeffer here articulates it) of describing in an account of the church either the *ad intra* or *ad extra* life of God 'dogmatically', *or* the particular and contingent socio-historical church-community 'ethnographically'. A 'third way' in ecclesiological description is thus required. This way will be one with due concern for the asymmetrical yet interconnected relation of divine and human togetherness in the church's being and for appropriate dogmatic ordering and proportionality in ecclesiological speech. This 'third way' will thereby eschew the endemic 'either/or' problematic present in approaches to contemporary ecclesiological discourse in order to think beyond but with the 'both/and' ecclesiological methodology of Bonhoeffer's ecclesial thought.

The task of this chapter, then, is to explicate how Bonhoeffer builds the structure of his 'both/and' ecclesiological methodology on the pneumatological and apocalyptically eschatological foundations of his ecclesial thought laid in Chapter 2. In order to do

---

[3] See *DBWE* 1, 125–6. Here Bonhoeffer has in mind the ecclesial thought of the early Barth and the (perceived) problem therein of accounting for the church theologically in a way that threatens its particular and contingent socio-historical reality. On this, see Mawson, *Christ Existing as Community*, 23–30; cf., Chapter 1, Section III.i of this book.
[4] *DBW* 1, 79.
[5] See *DBWE* 12, 264; cf., *DBWE* 11, 306.
[6] See *DBWE* 1, 277.
[7] See *DBW* 11, 298.
[8] See *DBWE* 1, 141; and *DBWE* 10, 506.
[9] See *DBW* 14, 422–66. On the 'space' of God's church-community, see Chapter 4 of this book.
[10] *DBWE* 11, 274.

this, the chapter begins by articulating Bonhoeffer's threefold typology of socio-historical human community that he constructs in *Sanctorum Communio*. This is done because it is in dialogue with this threefold typology that Bonhoeffer proceeds to build his pneumatologically and apocalyptically eschatologically founded 'both/and' ecclesiological methodology. The second section of this chapter then demonstrates how Bonhoeffer does this. Here, it will be seen that the apocalyptically eschatological and pneumatological foundations of Bonhoeffer's ecclesial thought enable Bonhoeffer to conceive and speak of the church's being as established and sustained by God the Holy Spirit as a particular and contingent human community that combines and surmounts simultaneously all three 'types' of socio-historical human community. For Bonhoeffer, the church exists in space and time as a socio-historical form of (fallible and sinful) human community, but it does so *as* a sociological structure sui generis distinct from all other socio-historical forms *of* human community. As it will be demonstrated, the church exists in this way as God the Holy Spirit creates it thus: in the time between the ascension of Christ and the *eschaton*, the church exists as the event of the divine act of *convocatio* which takes place in and through the Holy Spirit of God to create in spatio-temporality the particular and contingent socio-historical human community that the church as *congregatio* is in its orientation to the eschatological telos. More specifically, the chapter argues (in its second section) that, for Bonhoeffer, the church's pneumatological and eschatological being in space and time and its unique ontic-social relations are the consequence of a threefold actualizing work of God the Holy Spirit. In articulating this threefold work, it will be seen that it is precisely Bonhoeffer's account of the Holy Spirit of God that holds together in the being of God's church-community an account of *both* divine *and* human agency. This account is such that Bonhoeffer's pneumatologically and apocalyptically eschatologically founded 'both/and' ecclesiological methodology can be said to be therapeutic to the endemic 'either/or' problematic present in approaches to contemporary ecclesiological discourse, and to thus break open the necessary 'third way' in ecclesiological description between the Scylla of 'ethnographic' ecclesiology and the Charybdis of 'dogmatic' ecclesiology.

II. Socio-historical *human* community: A threefold typology

In the process of constructing in *Sanctorum Communio* his threefold typology of socio-historical human community, Bonhoeffer – through a utilization of concepts and insights drawn from 'formal-analytic' sociology,[11] and in particular the work

---

[11] In Bonhoeffer's usage sociology is said to deal in 'the study of the structures of empirical communities' and is thus concerned to trace 'the many complex interactions [of human sociality] back to certain constitutive acts of spirit that comprise the distinctive characteristic of the structure' (see *DBWE* 1, 30). In other words, sociology is the attempt to classify (empirically) the social structures that the being together – sociality – of human beings gives rise to. Within the category of sociology itself, Bonhoeffer, moreover (following Ernst Troeltsch), distinguishes between two schools of thought, both of which he finds deficient *theologically*. First, the 'historical-philosophical' school of sociology is deficient because its claim to establish a philosophy of history as the normative foundation for accounting for the whole history of human sociality (including its social structures and formations) (see *DBWE* 1, 25–6) simply renders the school unfit to understand and thus explain the nature

of Ferdinand Tönnies – locates the constitutive element of that community in phenomenological acts of human willing.[12] Only where human spirit is consciously and purposefully at work is social human community – sociality – said to be actually present or formed per se.[13] Moreover, those acts of the willing human spirit, depending on the existent form of relational or social bond between the wills themselves, result in the construction of one of three types of socio-historical human community: *Gemeinschaft*, *Gesellschaft* or *Herrschaftsverband*.[14]

i. *Gemeinschaft*, *Gesellschaft* and *Herrschaftsverband*

In consequence of a directional relation (or determination) of human wills, human wills willing together and with one another in sociality can will one of two things.[15] On the one hand, if the acts of human willing are 'reciprocal'[16] – that is, if persons mutually will and intend each other – then being-with (and for) one another is said to be willed as an *end in itself*.[17] Such willing (a '*will to meaning*') gives rise to a 'structure of meaning', or, following Tönnies's terminology, the *first* type of empirical social formation – *Gemeinschaft*.[18] On the other hand, if the acts of human willing are

and structure of the church – and indeed human existence per se – as a theological category. For Bonhoeffer, theology must proceed 'from its own basis' and thus must begin with 'the act of God', and not with the (universally) interpretative capacity of human subjectivity (see *DBWE* 11, 231). Second, the 'formal-analytic' school of sociology is deficient (according to Bonhoeffer) because its concern to study phenomenologically socially constitutive social forces and 'kinds of relation' (a concern which in principle Bonhoeffer approves of) posits, in terms of material content, 'only relations [*Beziehungen*] and interactions [*Wechselwirkungen*]' between individual human beings (see *DBWE* 1, 26–7), and thus treats human beings as 'fixed, isolated objects' that stand external to the socially constitutive and interpersonal process into which the human being is never drawn (see *DBWE* 1, 24). Here, 'the personal center' of each individual human being 'remains unaffected' and fundamentally asocial, with relations between individual human beings being enabled and created only by a person's 'particular social "dispositions"' (see *DBWE* 1, 27). It is this underlying concept of personhood, built on the foundations of 'an atomistic social philosophy' (*DBWE* 1, 24) or anthropology, which, for Bonhoeffer (and despite his in principle approval of the 'formal-analytical' school per se), ultimately renders the school likewise unfit to understand the theological categories of 'church' and 'person', and precisely for the self-same reason as per the 'historical-philosophical' school.

[12] See *DBWE* 1, 80–96; cf., Ferdinand Tönnies, *Community and Society (Gemeinschaft und Gesellschaft)*, trans. Charles P. Loomis (East Lansing: The Michigan State University Press, 1957).
[13] See *DBWE* 1, 62 and 81.
[14] In the course of his analysis Bonhoeffer refers to a fourth construction – the mass (*Masse*) – which he considers outwith the constructed typology. The mass is considered thus in consequence of there being in it no existent form of genuinely social or relational bonding between human wills, but only individual wills (bonding accidentally by) reacting mechanically to external stimuli. See *DBWE* 1, 93–4.
[15] See *DBWE* 1, 86 and 88.
[16] Ibid., 83.
[17] See *DBW* 1, 56.
[18] That is, 'community'. See *DBWE* 1, 88 and 89; cf., Tönnies, *Community and Society (Gemeinschaft und Gesellschaft)*, 37–64 and 103–59. For Tönnies, *Gemeinschaft* and *Gesellschaft* are conceptual constructs or 'types' used to differentiate distinctive sociological entities which arise, respectively, through the natural will (*Wesenwille*) and rational will (*Kürville*) of individuals to associate. Significantly, the types are not mutually exclusive. Tönnies states: 'The essence of both Gemeinschaft and Gesellschaft is found in all kinds of associations' (Tönnies, *Community and Society*, 249). In other words, the types are *ideal* types and as such do not exist empirically in pure form – an

'parallel'[19] – that is, if persons will and intend not each other, but instead a particular goal or purpose beyond the persons themselves – then being-with (but significantly not for) one another is said to be willed as a *means to an end*.[20] Here, human willing (a 'rational purposive will') gives rise not to a 'structure of meaning' but to a 'structure of purpose', or, again, following Tönnies's terminology, the *second* type of empirical social formation – *Gesellschaft*.[21] Thus, in consequence of the directional relation (or determination) of human willing, empirical social formation is constituted either 'by the will to meaning that recognizes the value of community as such'[22] and is constituted *as* 'community' in the first typological sense or 'to serve as a means for the rational will that is strictly directed toward a purpose'[23] and is constituted *as* 'society' in the second typological sense. While the 'unity' of what is willed in the former 'structure of meaning' is itself, therefore, represented in the directional relation (or determination) of human willing, in the latter 'structure of purpose' the directional relation (or determination) of human wills is itself established by the 'unity' of what is willed.[24] Such is the difference between *Gemeinschaft* and *Gesellschaft* as sociological types – a difference which Bonhoeffer proceeds to locate more acutely as operative on a threefold psychological, temporal and personal level.[25]

First, and on the *psychological* level, while the existent form of relational or social bond between human wills that constitutes *Gemeinschaft* is said to be characterized by a '*closeness of connection*', its *Gesellschaft* counterpart is characterized by a '*looseness of connection*'.[26] This is not to say, however, that *Gemeinschaft* and *Gesellschaft* are established constitutively as sociological types by psychological differences, only that the distinct directional acts of human willing – that is, 'reciprocal' and 'parallel' – result in diverse psychological consequences.[27] With respect to reciprocal acts of human willing, such consequences are expressed by Bonhoeffer primarily in terms of shared culture or tradition, such that as a sociological type, *Gemeinschaft*, willed as it is as an end in itself, is marked by forces of 'common feeling, common willing, and co-responsibility' – that is, of 'inmost cohesion' – and thus by a basic psychological attitude of 'mutual inner interest'.[28] Accordingly, human beings can 'live' in the *Gemeinschaft* type,[29] not on utilitarian or purposive relational grounds but on the basis that such communities and their constitutive relational or social bonds are meaningful in-and-of-themselves.

---

understanding that Bonhoeffer, in his own typological construction, follows. Bonhoeffer writes: 'It must be emphasized that no pure type exists in concrete form. There is no community without the connection of wills that exist in a society; but even more certainly, there is no society without the connection of wills existing in a community, because society [*Gesellschaft*] is essentially rooted in community [*Gemeinschaft*].' See *DBWE* 1, 91.

[19] *DBWE* 1, 83.
[20] See *DBW* 1, 56.
[21] That is 'society'. See *DBWE* 1, 88 and 89; cf., Tönnies, *Community and Society*, 64–102.
[22] *DBWE* 1, 88.
[23] Ibid.
[24] See ibid.
[25] The categorization is my own, not Bonhoeffer's.
[26] See *DBWE* 1, 91.
[27] See ibid., 89–90.
[28] See ibid., 90.
[29] See ibid.

In this sense, Bonhoeffer describes the *Gemeinschaft* type (following Max Scheler) as a 'life-community' (*Lebensgemeinschaft*).[30] With respect to parallel acts of human willing, however, such psychological consequences are expressed by Bonhoeffer primarily in terms of that which is precisely and entirely absent in the *Gemeinschaft* type. Thus, as a sociological type, *Gesellschaft*, willed as it is as a means to an end, has (in principle) no shared culture or tradition, no commonality of feeling or willing, and only in their own interest do human beings accept responsibility for it.[31] Here, the basic psychological attitude is one of 'mutual inner indifference',[32] such that each individual member acts only 'in strictest caution toward one another, and thus in simultaneous reserve and personal self-assurance – and finally, insofar as it suits one's purpose, in conventional amiability'.[33] In this sense, human beings cannot 'live' in the *Gesellschaft* type as they do in the *Gemeinschaft* type, for as Bonhoeffer puts it, *Gesellschaft* is but 'an association of rational action'.[34]

Second, and on the *temporal* level, Bonhoeffer sees the difference between *Gemeinschaft* and *Gesellschaft* as operative in the way that both are said to relate variously to time. Willed as it is as an end in itself, *Gemeinschaft*, by its very nature, points to no goal or purpose beyond itself. *Gemeinschaft*, as such, is thus characterized solely by 'meaning' or 'value' (*Wert*), and as 'value-bearing' (*werthaft*) 'stands beyond inner historical limitations' and so 'finds its telos at the boundary of history'[35] – that is, at the limit of time (*grenzzeitlich*),[36] or, in other words, 'in God'.[37] Indeed, as Bonhoeffer goes on to state: 'The nature of community [*Gemeinschaft*] originates in and is willed by God',[38] such that 'the innermost meaning'[39] of genuine community can be said to be located in its orientation to the eschatological telos, existing as it does (by definition) in its coming from God and in its going to God, 'who, as its telos is found only at the limits of history'.[40] In this sense, *Gemeinschaft* is said by Bonhoeffer to also contain – conceptually speaking – 'the *idea of infinite time*, whose only limit is the boundary of time'.[41] Bonhoeffer states: 'The "duration" of community [*Gemeinschaft*] is identical with the duration of history'.[42] As such, the sociological type *Gemeinschaft* (or at least the idea of it) is indissoluble and timeless, being (to one extent or another) analogous to, or a representation of, the eternal life of God in space and time. This 'fundamental indissolubility' constitutes the essential 'holiness' of *Gemeinschaft*.[43] In

---

[30] *DBW* 1, p. 58; cf., Max Scheler, *Formalism in Ethics and Non-Formal Ethics of Values: A New Attempt Toward the Foundation of an Ethical Personalism*, trans. Manfred S. Frings and Roger L. Funk, 5th rev. edn (Evanston: Northwestern University Press, 1973), 526.
[31] See *DBWE* 1, 91.
[32] Ibid.
[33] Ibid.
[34] Ibid., 90.
[35] See *DBW* 1, 235.
[36] See ibid., 64.
[37] Ibid., 235.
[38] Ibid.
[39] Ibid., 64.
[40] Ibid., 235.
[41] Ibid.
[42] Ibid.
[43] See ibid., 64.

contrast, the 'duration' of *Gesellschaft*, willed as it is as a 'means to an end', is relative to the point of realization of its particular and constitutive goal or purpose.[44] In other words, *Gesellschaft* does 'not extend beyond the idea of its constitutive purpose', but instead (and by definition) exists 'necessarily within history', and as such is 'temporally conditioned'.[45] Bonhoeffer writes: 'Here the end of history is actually an end, not a boundary.'[46] As a sociological type, *Gesellschaft* (or again, at least the idea of it), unlike the *Gemeinschaft* type, can thus be said to be dissoluble and 'time-limited', or 'time-bound' (*zeitbegrenzt*).[47]

Third, and most profoundly, Bonhoeffer locates the difference between *Gemeinschaft* and *Gesellschaft* on a *personal* level.[48] This level is understood by Bonhoeffer in reference to the way in which the 'directional' relation (or determination) of human willing gives rise to the sociological (and at root Hegelian) phenomenon of objective spirit (*objektive Geist*).[49] While Bonhoeffer explicitly rejects Hegel's subordination of the individual person to the collective or social process, he nevertheless seeks to build positively upon Hegel's concept. Bonhoeffer writes: 'The tragedy of all idealist philosophy was that it never ultimately broke through to personal spirit. However, its monumental perception, especially in Hegel, was that the principle of spirit is something objective, extending beyond everything individual – that there is an objective spirit, the spirit of sociality, which is distinct in itself from all individual spirit.'[50] Bonhoeffer's task in *Sanctorum Communio* (and specifically, therefore, in relation to the being of the church itself) is thus to 'affirm the latter without denying the former'[51] – something which idealist philosophy is unable to achieve precisely because of its apersonal absorption of individual spirit into corporate or social spirit.[52]

For Bonhoeffer, then, objective (or social) spirit – which here stands in contrastive relation to subjective (or individual) spirit – is said to be the consequence of individual human wills, willing together and with one another in sociality. Where acts of the willing human spirit unite, a third autonomous entity or structure is generated,[53] what today one might describe synonymously as the mentality, mood or culture of a given social group.[54] Furthermore, that structure, which itself is objective spirit, not only 'lives its own life'[55] – in the sense that it stands between and rises above and beyond

---

[44] See ibid., 235 and 64.
[45] See ibid., 235.
[46] Ibid., 235 and 64.
[47] See ibid., 64.
[48] See *DBWE* 1, 102.
[49] See *DBW* 1, 62–8; cf., Georg Wilhelm Friedrich Hegel, 'The Philosophy of Spirit', in Georg Wilhelm Friedrich Hegel, *Encyclopaedia of the Philosophical Sciences in Outline*, ed. Ernst Behler and trans. Steven A. Taubeneck (New York: Continuum, 1990), 483ff.
[50] *DBWE* 1, 74.
[51] Ibid.
[52] See ibid., 193–8, and Bonhoeffer's survey (therein) of the relation between individual and corporate or social spirit in the thought of Schleiermacher, Kant, Fichte and Hegel, and in all of whom he finds the same basic and problematic picture: 'The spirit is one, eternally identical, transpersonal, immanent in humanity; it destroys the concrete person, and thus prevents any concrete concept of community, instead replacing it with the immanent unity of spirit' (*DBWE* 1, 194–6).
[53] See *DBWE* 1, 98.
[54] See Green, *Bonhoeffer*, 39.
[55] *DBWE* 1, 103.

the sum total of individual human wills which constitute and participate in it – but also, moreover, does so, and takes form in such a way, so as to exert its own active will *effectively* upon the groups' individual willing members, ordering and guiding them thereby, and enabling them to experience sociality in a manner external to themselves as something objectively real.[56] Bonhoeffer puts it thus: 'Individuals are confronted [here] by their objectified selves. Their own lives have flowed into the community, and now daily it stands before them as a content and form that they experience, as the regulative principle for their conduct.'[57] Objective spirit operates as the nexus of a community's historical and social, or temporal and spatial dimensions:[58] not only does objective spirit bear a community's historical tradition, but it also acts repeatedly and reciprocally to incorporate both that tradition and new (and existing) individual members into its own corporate or social life, and critically without those individuals ever being absorbed into that life.[59]

Properly understood, therefore, the contrastive relation between 'objective' and 'subjective' spirit is conceived by Bonhoeffer dialectically, as one of metaphysical autonomy and genetic dependence. Indeed, that objective spirit, genetically speaking, arises from, and is given its content and character by, individual human wills willing together and with one another in sociality – with those wills themselves being effected by objective spirit – means that subjective (or individual) spirit in fact lives *in* objective spirit. Here, Bonhoeffer sees the triumph of subjective spirit – precisely *in* its dialectical relation with objective spirit – in the very fact that the objective structure that subjective spirit in sociality creates out of itself is never in reality totally free of itself.[60] However, that objective structure, metaphysically speaking, exists above and beyond that which it arises out of, so as to act effectively – and with its own equal social weight – over and between, or alongside, its individual (or subjective) willing members.[61] Objective spirit thus 'leads an individual life beyond the individual persons, and yet is real only through them'.[62] Prima facie, objective spirit thereby assumes, for Bonhoeffer, *personal* liveliness, because it can be said to lead an individual life beyond the individual human wills willing together and with one another in sociality out of which it arises.[63] Objective spirit *does* assume personal liveliness, however, *only* as it corresponds with the sociological type *Gemeinschaft*, in the sense, that is, that as an end in itself, and thus as value-bearing, the objective spirit of *Gemeinschaft* is timeless and so lives continuously above and beyond the wills of its individual willing members.[64] In distinction, the objective spirit of *Gesellschaft* (again in correspondence with the sociological type itself) is affirmed by Bonhoeffer not as a value or end in itself but only as a means to an end and thus as an objective structure of purpose which is time-limited (*zeitbegrenzt*),

[56] See *DBWE* 1, 98–100 and 209.
[57] Ibid., 99.
[58] See ibid.
[59] See ibid., 209 and 103.
[60] See ibid., 103; cf., Hans Freyer, *Theory of Objective Mind: An Introduction to the Philosophy of Culture*, trans. Steven Grosby (Athens: Ohio University Press, 1998), 82.
[61] See *DBWE* 1, 103.
[62] *DBW* 1, 63.
[63] See ibid.
[64] See ibid., 64.

and which, therefore, ceases (along with *Gesellschaft*) at the point in time at which that purpose is realized.[65] Thus, for Bonhoeffer, the objective spirit of *Gemeinschaft* as a value or end in itself can be said to attain '*personal* character',[66] but the same cannot be said of its *Gesellschaft* counterpart in its being only ever a means to an end. The reason Bonhoeffer gives for this judgement being precisely that 'a *person* can never be only a means to an end'.[67]

It is Bonhoeffer's concept of person, then, that ultimately determines the difference between the two typological forms of objective spirit in terms of how he sees these forms relating to the category of *person*hood. To consider why this is so, and what is at stake in Bonhoeffer's thought here (especially as he comes to relate it, subsequently, to his understanding of *Gemeinschaft* and *Gesellschaft* as sociological types, and thus, ultimately, to his ecclesial thought and its 'both/and' ecclesiological methodology), one must engage, therefore, Bonhoeffer's prior ontological construction of the concept of person (*Personbegriff*), to which (derivatively) 'every concept of community [*Gemeinschaftsbegriff*] stands in essential relation'.[68]

a. *Bonhoeffer's theological ontology of human personhood*

As set out in *Santorum Communio*, Bonhoeffer develops his concept of person in critical dialogue with the wider philosophical tradition, and in particular with the (post-Kantian) German idealism of Fichte, and more specifically Hegel.[69] For Bonhoeffer, human personhood arises not from the category of the epistemological and its immanent resolution of the subject–object relation into the knowing 'I', but rather from the social and ethical encounter between persons in relation:[70] personhood arises only when the 'I' (or cognitive self) (*Ich*) is encountered by the 'You' (*Du*) of another who constitutes a barrier or limit-point to that 'I',[71] beyond which it cannot go. In other words, in socio-ethical encounter, the other, as 'You', transcends or stands over against the 'I' in confrontational or conflictual posture,[72] and as such places

---

[65] See ibid.
[66] Ibid., 65 (emphasis added).
[67] Ibid., 104 (emphasis altered).
[68] Ibid., 19.
[69] See *DBWE* 1, 34–57.
[70] This does not mean, however, as Woelfel supposes, that Bonhoeffer thus rejects the epistemological (or metaphysical) 'completely for the social and ethical in his understanding of the I-Thou relation' (see Woelfel, *Bonhoeffer's Theology*, 121). Instead, as Floyd articulates, Bonhoeffer's '"personalist" restatement of the problematic status of otherness entails no more – *but no less* – than to speak of the object-as-*limit* or "barrier" to the subjective pretension of idealism' (Floyd, *Theology and the Dialectics of Otherness*, 125). For Bonhoeffer, 'What is important is not the nature of the barrier, but that the barrier as such is experienced and accepted as real' (*DBW* 1, 26). Significantly, this experience and acceptance can occur according to Bonhoeffer in the intellectual sphere – in the conflict of knowledge, for example – but not in the epistemological-transcendental sphere of idealism, for the idealist's object is ultimately no barrier at all. See *DBW* 1, 26.
[71] *DBW* 1, 30.
[72] The point is emphasized appropriately by Floyd *contra* Moltmann: 'Rather than being a moment of benign mutuality ... the *relation*, the encounter between distinct *wills*, is initially a moment not just of un-likeness but of *opposition*. And it is not just any opposition, but the opposition engendered by the priority of the Other in the world of an I which would rather establish its own egocentric perspective.' See Floyd, *Theology and the Dialectics of Otherness*, 130; cf., Jürgen Moltmann, 'The Lordship of Christ and Human Society', in Jürgen Moltmann and Jürgen Weissbach, *Two Studies*

before it a socio-ethical decision (*Entscheidung*) or demand (*Forderung*) in response to which arises a burden of responsibility (*Verantwortung*);[73] 'the responsibility first off', as Wayne Whitson Floyd notes, 'to let the Other "be"'[74] – something which the knowing 'I' in idealism, with its boundless epistemic claims, is simply unable to do. Thus, in 'I'–'You' relations, persons are said by Bonhoeffer to be genuinely objective to one another: the 'You' confronts the 'I' with its own integrity – as different, as an 'I' – and consequently 'sets the limit for the subject and by its own accord activates a will that impinges upon the other in such a way that this other will becomes a You for the I'.[75] Indeed, on a purely anthropological level, the reason that another person's subjectivity is self-transcendent is straightforwardly that one's subjective experience of self and the world (the 'You') is not something the cognitive self of another (the 'I') can objectify, precisely because it is *self*-understanding. In Bonhoeffer's 'I'–'You' schematic it follows, therefore, that every human 'You' is an image of the divine 'You', for as the One who subjectively surpasses objectivity as *the* limit-point, God remains always unobjectifiable.

For Bonhoeffer, then, human personhood arises only in the oppositional and dynamic encounter of 'I' and 'You' in socio-ethical relation. The activity of the 'You', as limit-point and demand, is thus person-forming, and human personhood is always constituted by what Floyd describes as a 'dialectics of otherness'.[76] As Bonhoeffer writes, 'Human beings do not exist "unmediated" qua spirit in and of themselves.'[77] Rather, human beings exist in the relational space between one another.[78] Only and always in responsible relation to an*other* – ultimately to God himself – does human personhood arise, and postlapsarian human relations are analogous to, or an altered form of, this most basic God-human relation. Fundamentally, human personhood arises for Bonhoeffer not, then, from relationality per se but rather from a *theological* relationality,[79] and more precisely from a theological relationality indexed by Bonhoeffer *pneumatologically*: one's conscious state of socio-ethical responsibility in relation to another as 'You' arises only as the Holy Spirit of God '"*enters into*" *the person as I*', and works actively to join the human 'You' of the other so that that other becomes a 'You' from whom one's own 'I' arises.[80] In other words, the other is a 'You' only as God the Holy Spirit constitutes it thus. In this sense, human social community is

---

 in the *Theology of Dietrich Bonhoeffer*, trans. Reginald H. Fuller and Ilse Fuller (New York: Charles Scribner's Sons, 1967), 36.
[73] See *DBW* 1, 28 and 32.
[74] Floyd, *Theology and the Dialectics of Otherness*, 141.
[75] *DBWE* 1, 51.
[76] Floyd, *Theology and the Dialectics of Otherness*, xi.
[77] *DBWE* 1, 50.
[78] See Marsh, *Reclaiming Dietrich Bonhoeffer*, 69.
[79] Cf., Green, *Bonhoeffer*, 48; and see Mawson, *Christ Existing as Community*, 56–76.
[80] See *DBWE* 1, 54–6 [56]. This pneumatological indexation of the relational space between human beings thus challenges Marsh's reading of that self-same space as a 'christological between', such that (according to Marsh) 'relation to others [is] mediated and opened up through the person of Jesus Christ alone'. See Marsh, *Reclaiming Dietrich Bonhoeffer*, 76 and 94. On the person-forming action of God the Holy Spirit in Bonhoeffer's theological anthropology and its relation to the 'both/and' ecclesiological methodology of his ecclesial thought, see Section III.ii of this chapter.

established (according to Bonhoeffer) in and through community with God.[81] Indeed, for Bonhoeffer, '*the concepts of person, community, and God* are inseparably and essentially interrelated'.[82] These concepts are interrelated not in the sense that human social community is *subsequent* to community with God, but rather that neither exists without the other.[83]

The rationale for this interdependence between human social community and community with God Bonhoeffer locates in his understanding of the form of God's own personhood. This divine form of personhood, Bonhoeffer argues, exists both internally in the eternal Trinity,[84] and externally in the economy of grace, in *relation*: 'God only "is" as the creator, reconciler, and redeemer, and that being as such is personal being.'[85] Bonhoeffer famously puts it elsewhere in his postdoctoral dissertation: 'There is no God who "is there"; God "is" in relation to persons'.[86] As Greggs states: 'There is no independent divine metaphysics for Bonhoeffer without the relationship of God to humanity: or else, we might say, there is (at least for humanity) no immanent trinity independent of God's divine economy'.[87] Indeed, the only God there is is the God who is in relation (to creation, and climactically to humankind) such that human personhood (and creation) can be understood fully only in that relation[88] – a point which Bonhoeffer explicates most fully in his theological exposition of Genesis chs 1–3, and in particular by his radical reinterpretation therein of the human *imago Dei*.[89]

Prior to Bonhoeffer's lectures *Creation and Fall*, what unites the vast majority of admittedly divergent expositions within classical theology of Gen. 1.26-27 is their individualistic nature.[90] The human *imago Dei* is read primarily either as an immanent capacity or faculty which is possessed by human beings *in se* and per se[91] or as a representative function which is to be carried out or 'mirrored' by them as God's vice-regents on earth.[92] For Bonhoeffer, however, the likeness (or image) of God in

---

[81] See *DBWE* 1, 63.
[82] Ibid., 34.
[83] See ibid., 63.
[84] See *DBW* 3, 28: 'The one who was in the beginning, [is] God himself, Christ, the Holy Spirit.'
[85] *DBWE* 2, 153.
[86] *DBW* 2, 112.
[87] Greggs, 'Bearing Sin in the Church', 87.
[88] See *DBWE* 3, 30: it is 'not that first God was and then God created, but that in the beginning God created'.
[89] See ibid., esp. 60–7.
[90] For a helpful overview of such expositions, see Stanley Grenz, *The Social God and the Relational Self: A Trinitarian Theology of the Imago Dei* (Louisville: Westminster John Knox Press, 2001), 141–203.
[91] Typically, reason, personality, language, intellect and volition. Augustine, for example, develops psychological analogies of the triune God based on the interior life of human personality – the most significant of which (memory, understanding and will) is confined to the mind alone (see Saint Augustine, 'On the Trinity', trans. Arthur West Haddan, in Philip Schaff, ed. *A Select Library of the Nicene and Post-Nicene Fathers of the Christian Church*, vol. 3 (Grand Rapids: Eerdmans, 1956), 10.11.17 – 12.12.19 (3:142–62)). Similarly, Aquinas insists that 'since it is because of his intellectual nature that man is said to be made to the image of God, it follows that he is made to God's image to the highest degree that his intellectual nature is able to imitate God to the highest degree'. See Aquinas, *Summa Theologica*, 1.93.4.
[92] The conception of the *imago Dei* in terms of a mirror (and human beings as the 'brightest mirror' in which God's glory is reflected) is the central metaphor of Calvin, albeit one which Augustine had previously alluded to, and from which Calvin excludes any such notion of '[locating] God's likeness in the dominion given to man, as if in this mark alone he resembled God'. See John Calvin,

humankind consists neither in a general ontological quality or substantive property that human beings inherently have nor in (what might be seen as) obedient ethical action, but only in a *relation* which human beings have with God and (derivatively) with each other. Human beings inherently 'have' the likeness (or image) of God not in the sense of an inherent human capacity or possession, 'something locatably "there" or present at hand', which as such is humankind's to dispose of or realize at its own behest.[93] Bonhoeffer asserts this is only 'very strictly in the sense that that which is like has its likeness *alone* from the archetype, so that that which is like always points or directs us only to the archetype, and in this pointedness or directedness *alone* is it "like"'.[94] The relation, which is the likeness (or image) of God in humankind, 'is not a human capacity, possibility, or a structure of human existence; rather it is the given relation which comes as a gift, a justitia passiva!'[95] For Bonhoeffer, 'It is in this relation into which human beings are set that freedom is given.'[96] Thus, the likeness (or image) – or better, analogy (*analogia*) – which is proper to the human *imago Dei* is not (according to Bonhoeffer) an *analogia entis* but an *analogia relationis*,[97] and that *analogia* is 'the relation given by God and only in this given relation is it analogia'.[98] Bonhoeffer defines this as follows: 'The relation of creature with creature is a God-given relation.'[99] Indeed, that the *analogia* be *given*, and given by *God*, is for Bonhoeffer necessitated in that, in fact, 'there is no such analogia [of being] between God and humankind'.[100]

The reason for this differentiation (in the order of being) between the being of God and human (or created) being, Bonhoeffer proceeds to locate in an affirmation of divine aseity: it is God 'who alone has self-sufficient being in aseity',[101] such that,

---

Commentary on the Book of Psalms, vol. 1, trans. James Anderson (Edinburgh: The Edinburgh Printing Company, 1845), 93–4; Calvin, *Institutes*, I.xv.4 (1:189–90); cf., Augustine, 'On the Trinity', 15.8.14 (3:206–7). On the motif of representation (linked to dominion), see Gerhard von Rad, *Genesis: A Commentary*, trans. John H. Marks (London: SCM Press, 1961), 57–8; and D. J. A. Clines, 'The Image of God in Man', *Tyndale Bulletin* 19 (1968), 87–90 and 95–9.

[93] See *DBW* 3, 61 and 60.
[94] Ibid., 61.
[95] Ibid.
[96] Ibid.
[97] See ibid.
[98] Ibid.
[99] Ibid.
[100] Ibid., 60. Bonhoeffer's rejection of the *analogia entis* recapitulates the point on which he had taken issue (in his postdoctoral dissertation) with the 'being' theology of Erich Przywara, and in particular Przywara's ontology of the *analogia entis* which rendered God and human beings as neither wholly different nor wholly identical to one another. Przywara's stance is one which Bonhoeffer sees as denying the 'act' dynamic (of grace and sin) to the God-human relation, and consequently assimilating this relation into the 'I' (or cognitive self) as its own possibility (see *DBWE* 2, 73–6). On Bonhoeffer's rejection of the philosophical category of 'possibility', see Paul D. Janz, *God, the Mind's Desire: Reference, Reason and Christian Thinking* (New York: Cambridge University Press, 2004), 198–213.
[101] *DBWE* 3, 65. While Bonhoeffer never actually discusses the *ad intra* life of God specifically in terms of Trinitarian persons in relation, Marsh's proposal that 'Bonhoeffer pursues the inquiry of the secondary objectivity of [God in his] revelation within the presupposition of Barth's narration of God's primary trinitarian self-identity' is ultimately persuasive (see Marsh, *Reclaiming Dietrich Bonhoeffer*, viii). Not least, because Bonhoeffer's understanding of human personhood as arising from a theological relationality, on a *non*-Trinitarian reading of God's aseity, would suggest that God's own personhood is itself dependent on his relation to that which is not God – a suggestion which (seemingly) would run counter to Bonhoeffer's own sensibility towards (and varied

(even) in the act of creating, 'God remains completely free over-against that which he creates'.[102] God's act of creation is thus entirely gratuitous and unconditioned. As Ann Nickson puts it: 'Creation is not the actualisation of some already existing possibility, but God's impossible act in creating *ex nihilo*.'[103] In other words, between creator and creation there is only *das Nichts*,[104] but that which the free (uncreated) God creates is itself (after the likeness (or image) of God) created 'free' – derivative and dependent, that is, but with its own essential integrity. In this way is the aseity of God affirmed by Bonhoeffer to establish the non-necessity of creation and creation's ontological ground in God and in God's operative and gracious acts as an 'absolutely unrepeatable, unique, and free event'.[105] While God alone, therefore, exists *in se* and is *un*conditioned – conditioned, that is, by nothing except freedom – and is thus in no way bound to what is created, the freedom of God nevertheless establishes itself precisely as that which binds (simultaneously) God's immanent divine life to that which is not God in creation, and that which is not God in creation to God's immanent divine life.[106] In other words, the divine form of God's own personhood is such that God as creator, reconciler and redeemer 'is the one who has being *for* God's creature [and indeed his creation], binding his freedom to human beings, and giving himself to them'.[107] God, therefore, 'must be thought of not as one who has being *alone*', as God is the one who, in his own free self-offering of himself to humanity in Christ, attests to his own being as a 'being *for* human beings'[108] and substantially so. As Bonhoeffer writes, famously, in his postdoctoral dissertation:

> It is not so much a question of the freedom of God – eternally remaining within the divine self, aseity – on the other side of revelation, as it is of God's coming out of God's own self in revelation. It is a matter of God's *given* word, the covenant in which God is bound by God's own action. It is a question of the freedom of God,

---

affirmation) of God's Trinitarian *in se* being (see, for example, *DBWE* 2, 153; *DBWE* 3, 29; *DBWE* 4, 252 and 303; *DBWE* 5, 29, 33, 49, 65, 72, 78 and 118; *DBWE* 8, 194–6; *DBWE* 9, 367–68; and *DBWE* 14, 795–6), even if that sensibility (and affirmation) nevertheless is, as Holmes notes, absent of any metaphysically satisfying content as to how immanent Trinitarian self-relations are to be understood (see Holmes, 'The Holy Spirit', 168–9 and 176–7). It should be noted that the situation and interpretation of Bonhoeffer's theology within a presupposed framework of Barth's distinction between the primary and secondary objectivity of *God*, and in particular the way in which Marsh restates Barth's distinction (improperly) as between the primary objectivity of God and the secondary objectivity of *revelation* – this restatement being tautological since, as George Hunsinger states, '(by definition) revelation *is* God's secondary objectivity' (hence the alteration to Marsh's words above) – is challenged by George Hunsinger, 'Review: *Reclaiming Dietrich Bonhoeffer: The Promise of His Theology*', *Modern Theology* 12.1 (1996), 121–3, and DeJonge, *Bonhoeffer's Theological Formation*, 104–5. For an apposite but qualified defence of Marsh's proposal, see Clifford J. Green, 'Trinity and Christology in Bonhoeffer and Barth', *Union Seminary Quarterly Review* 60.1–2 (2006), 1–22.

[102] *DBW* 3, 38.
[103] Nickson, *Bonhoeffer on Freedom*, 53.
[104] *DBW* 3, 32.
[105] Ibid., 31.
[106] See ibid., 41: 'God is not bound to creation, but God binds his creation to himself'; and *DBW* 2, 109: 'God's freedom [is] that God binds Godself to human beings.'
[107] *DBW* 3, 60 (emphasis added).
[108] Ibid. (emphasis added).

which finds its strongest evidence precisely in that God freely chose to be bound to historical human beings and to be placed at the disposal of human beings. God is free not from human beings but for them.[109]

In other words, the 'being' of God is said by Bonhoeffer to exist in the 'act' of God becoming *for* us, paradigmatically in Christ by the agency of God the Holy Spirit. For Bonhoeffer, the aseity of God, then, is to be parsed exclusively in reference to God's promeity,[110] such that the freedom of God is to be understood neither abstractly nor formally as God's freedom in Godself *from* human beings, but rather substantially as God's freedom in Godself *for* human beings in the divine economy of grace.[111] Because God's own freedom is thus conceived by Bonhoeffer as existing in relationality, the likeness or analogy of God in humankind is derivatively to be conceived most properly in *free* relational terms analogous to God's own *in se* Trinitarian personhood and his own *a se* self-relation in creation, reconciliation and redemption. Thus, '[to say] that God creates in human beings his image on earth, means, that human being is like the creator in that it is free'.[112] Free, however, not in the sense of being free in-and-of-oneself *from* relation and therefore *self*-constituting but free in the conditioned or created sense of being free *for* relation. Indeed, freedom itself can be thought 'only as a

---

[109] *DBWE* 2, 90–1.
[110] See Marsh, *Reclaiming Dietrich Bonhoeffer*, 127: 'God relinquishes total aseity for the sake of the world, but in relinquishing aseity for the sake of the world God demonstrates the aseity proper to his being: his being is always a being-for.' This 'divine relinquishment' is not, however, 'divine self-negation', but (most properly) divine overflow – 'God's overabounding of himself in love', which 'expresses the very essence of God' (see Marsh, *Reclaiming Dietrich Bonhoeffer*, 127–8). Eberhard Jüngel puts it thus: 'From all eternity, God *is in and of himself* in such a way that he is *for* man. As the Eternal he is for perishable man, whose perishability has its ground in this Pro-Being of God' – that is, in the '*overflowing being*' that God is and by which God goes 'with himself beyond himself'. See Eberhard Jüngel, *God as the Mystery of the World: On the Foundation of the Theology of the Crucified One in the Dispute between Theism and Atheism*, trans. Darrell L. Guder (Edinburgh: T&T Clark, 1983), 221 and 222.
[111] Bonhoeffer's 'substantial' interpretation of God's freedom is developed in critique of the early Barth, and in particular against (what Bonhoeffer sees as) the actualism of (what Bonhoeffer calls) Barth's 'act' theology and its 'formal' understanding of that self-same freedom (see *DBWE* 2, 82–91). To state the position somewhat crudely and from Bonhoeffer's perspective: while the early Barth was rightly concerned to protect God's transcendent freedom, in order to do so he problematically manoeuvred God into the non-objective and thus effectively remote and inaccessible sphere, in which God eternally remains within Godself as the one who, 'from time to time' or 'ever again', impinges or comes upon (*betrifft*) spatio-temporality in discontinuous or momentary but always free and non-objective 'act' (see *DBWE* 11, 241–2; and *DBW* 2, 110). God, as such, 'remains always the Lord, always subject, so that whoever claims to have God as an object no longer has *God*; God is always the God who "comes" and never the God who "is there" (Barth)' (*DBWE* 2, 85). Thus, for Bonhoeffer, the actualism of Barth's 'act' theology utterly precludes any kind of continuous or persistent 'being' of divine revelation when in *actuality* – in the 'act' of God becoming for us in Christ by the agency of the Holy Spirit – God has freely given and bound Godself to that which is not God, such that the 'being' of divine revelation 'is', and concretely so (see *DBWE* 2, 75). In this way does Bonhoeffer see himself as manoeuvring God out of Barth's remote and inaccessible sphere and into 'being' in immediate proximity, and thus as countering the actualism of Barth's 'act' theology as Bonhoeffer perceives it. On Bonhoeffer's understanding of the characteristic nature of 'act' and 'being', see DeJonge, *Bonhoeffer's Theological Formation*, 16–19.
[112] *DBW* 3, 58.

"being-free-for ...", precisely because 'God does not keep God's freedom to God's self' but instead freely binds himself – in relation – to creation.[113] It follows that freedom

> is not something that human being has for itself, but something that it has for others. No human being is free 'in itself' ... Freedom is not a quality of human beings ... a capacity, an ability, or an aspect of being ... it is not a possession, something 'there' to hand, an object; nor is it a form of something 'there' to hand; rather freedom is a relation and nothing else. In fact, it is a relation between two persons. Being free means 'being-free-for-the-other' because I have been bound to the other. Only in relation to the other am I free.[114]

That the human being is free only in relation, moreover, is axiomatic for Bonhoeffer given humankind exists in relational (and created) duality.[115] Furthermore, the fact that Eve is created from the rib of Adam underscores Bonhoeffer's point: 'Adam knows that he is bound in a wholly new way to this Eve who is derived from him.'[116] Bonhoeffer continues, 'This bond is best described in the expression: he now belongs to her, because she belongs to him. They are no longer without each other; they are one and yet two.'[117] One, that is, not in the sense that their subjectivity as individual creatures is obliterated, but rather that the utmost expression of their 'oneness' is in fact realized in their alterity. Thus does Eve as 'the other' who is created as God's creature out of Adam's own life constitute a *God*-given 'limit' (*Grenze*) to Adam in bodily form, which as such a limit is loved by Adam, and by which Adam himself is loved.[118] This mutual love is, however, mediated – and for Bonhoeffer's understanding of *created* freedom in the likeness (or image) of God critically so – by the Holy Spirit of God. Bonhoeffer writes:

> This is what the older dogmatic theologians meant when they spoke of the indwelling of the Trinity in Adam. In the free creature the Holy Spirit worships the creator; uncreated freedom glorifies itself in view of created freedom. The creature loves the creator [and so also the creator's creation] because the creator loves the creature [and His creation]. Created *freedom* is freedom in the Holy Spirit, but as *created* freedom, it is humankind's own freedom.[119]

In other words, the Holy Spirit of God is operative to enable humankind to relate in freedom to the creator and thus to image the freedom of God as God's free creatures in relation. It is precisely in this created and pneumatologically mediated loving relation as male *and* female 'over-against-each-other, with-each-other, and in-dependence-upon-each-other'[120] that creaturely or created freedom consists.[121]

---

[113] See *DBWE* 3, 63.
[114] *DBW* 3, 58–9.
[115] See Gen. 1.27.
[116] *DBWE* 3, 97.
[117] Ibid.
[118] See ibid., 99.
[119] Ibid., 64.
[120] *DBW* 3, 60.
[121] See *DBWE* 3, 64.

To be free as a creature in the freedom that is proper to the *analogia relationis*, and which comes from or through an*other* – ultimately from or through God the Holy Spirit – is, in other words, to be free *from* one*self*: free 'from the lie that I am the only one there, that I am the center of the world … free from oneself for others'.[122] It is for this reason that Bonhoeffer conceives sin as confinement in the *self*:[123] as a grasping after, and claiming for oneself, *un*created freedom, which is witnessed to most originally in Adam's desire to be free *from* the God-given limit to human knowledge,[124] the consequence of which is that Adam himself becomes 'creator, source of life, fountainhead of the knowledge of good and evil'.[125] Such Adamic 'autonomy' is, however, theologically speaking, illusory. For Adam is now 'alone by [himself], he lives out of [his] own resources, he no longer needs any others, he is lord of his own world',[126] and out of his self-sufficiency and self-understanding – and precisely in *in*dependence of God and others – seeks to create his own life. Indeed, in his rejection of the limit imposed upon him by God, Adam destroys his own 'creatureliness' (*Geschöpflichkeit*), and in doing so becomes 'limit*less*' (*grenzenlose*).[127] He rejects the limit that God is, and in the knowledge of good and evil now knows himself not (as a creature) in the reality of his *given* creatureliness, but only – and in opposition to God – out of his own possibility (of being good or evil) and thus as being 'torn-apart' (*Zerrissen*) from God.[128] This rejection of the limit that God is is, however, at once a rejection of the limit that is the relational duality in which Adam has been created as a creature by God. In other words, the destruction of Adam's 'creatureliness' occurs not just on a 'vertical' (divine-human) plane, but concomitantly on a 'horizontal' (human-human) one. In seeking to create his *own* life, Adam as such 'tears' himself apart from Eve. Indeed, the God-given 'limit' that Eve is to Adam in bodily form and which as such Adam loved, Adam now no longer accepts: 'Instead he hates it as God begrudging him something as creator … [Adam] no longer sees the limit that the other person constitutes as grace but as God's wrath. … The limit is no longer the grace that holds the human being in the unity of creaturely, free love; instead the limit is now the mark of dividedness.'[129] In other words, with Adam's fall, 'a third power, sin, has stepped between human beings and God, as between human beings themselves'.[130] The result of this is to reorient human beings away from relationship (on the 'vertical' plane) with God, and (on the 'horizontal' plane) with each other, and towards oneself. Thus, sin *is* individualism. Or as Bonhoeffer puts it in his postdoctoral dissertation: 'Sin is the inversion of the human will (of human essence) into itself.'[131] Postlapsarian humanity is defined by Bonhoeffer as follows: 'Culpable perversion of the will, that is, of human essence. It means to be turned inward into one's self, *cor curvum in se*. Human beings

---

[122] *DBWE* 11, 471 (emphasis added).
[123] See *DBWE* 3, 103–20.
[124] See ibid., 103–10 and 116–17.
[125] Ibid., 121 and 142.
[126] Ibid., 142.
[127] See *DBW* 3, 107 (emphasis added).
[128] See ibid., 115.
[129] *DBWE* 3, 122.
[130] *DBWE* 1, 63.
[131] *DBWE* 2, 144.

have torn themselves loose from community with God and, therefore, also from that with other human beings.'[132]

Thus, the fall of Adam (according to Bonhoeffer) infinitely alters human ontology. The human moves from being created as a creature in the *imago Dei* to being fallen as a creator *sicut deus*.[133] In this sense, the ontology of postlapsarian humanity is such that in its being *sicut deus* human being wills to live a life *in se*, which as such is a sinful perversion of God's own *ad intra* life. In God's own self-sufficient being in aseity 'God wills not to be free for *God's* self'[134] but only (one might say) *from* God's self, and thus free *for* that which is not God. Put alternatively, the life that human being, being *sicut deus*, is tempted to live *in se* is one which in its 'false replication of divine aseity … fails to understand that the freedom of the divine life *a se* is not something which God has grasped and claimed for Godself, but something which only establishes the full graciousness of God who, although He is free from creation, chooses in creation to be free for creation in the divine economy of salvation.'[135] It is precisely to *this* God that the postlapsarian human being (despite its perverted ontology) is related: human 'being is always in relation to Being'.[136] As such, human being is 'being-in-relation-to'[137] – either, and most properly, in eccentric relation to God and each other in *created* freedom or, and most perversely, in interior relation to oneself in *uncreated* freedom. In *both* instances, however, the category of human personhood is prescribed theologically by the freedom of God's own relational ontology – that is, his being free *for* creation and climactically for humankind. Thus, in consequence of God's own divine form of personhood in the likeness (or image) of which human personhood is created, the category of human personhood is a genuinely theological and so relational one. It is for this reason why, for Bonhoeffer, a person cannot ever be a means to an end.

Before proceeding to articulate how this relational ontology of human personhood – to which every concept of human community necessarily stands in derivative relation – is subsequently related by Bonhoeffer to his understanding of the two sociological types *Gemeinschaft* and *Gesellschaft*, it may be helpful to recapitulate two aspects of the foregoing discussion that will be seen to function, critically, in Bonhoeffer's ecclesial thought and its 'both/and' ecclesiological methodology as he proceeds to construct it in dialogue with those types. The first is Bonhoeffer's articulation of the person-forming action of God the Holy Spirit. It is the Holy Spirit of God who is operative in Bonhoeffer's theological anthropology to enable human beings to relate in freedom to the creator, and to thus image the freedom of God as God's free creatures in loving relation with and for one another. It is this pneumatologically mediated loving relation between God and human being, and indeed between human being and human being, that essentially constitutes (as will be seen) the first and second actualizing work of God the Holy Spirit that, for

---

[132] DBWE 2, 137.
[133] See DBWE 3, 113.
[134] Ibid., 63.
[135] Greggs, 'Bearing Sin in the Church', 88.
[136] DBWE 12, 219.
[137] Ibid., 218.

Bonhoeffer, renders the ontic-social relations of the church's pneumatological and eschatological being in space and time unique, such that *God's* church-community combines and surmounts simultaneously all three 'types' of socio-historical human community. The second aspect of the foregoing discussion that will be seen to have a critical function in the construction of the 'both/and' ecclesiological methodology of Bonhoeffer's ecclesial thought is his parsing of the aseity of God exclusively in reference to God's promeity, or more precisely to God's pronobisity in the church.[138] Not only does this establish in Bonhoeffer's theological thought the non-necessity of creation and creation's ontological ground (including the ground of the church) in God and in God's operative and gracious acts, but because those acts (including the operative and gracious act of God the Holy Spirit that creates the particular and contingent socio-historical human community that the church is in its orientation to the eschatological telos) cannot be understood as taking place other than *in* space and time, Bonhoeffer's 'both/and' ecclesiological methodology (as will be seen) neither 'forgets God' like 'ethnographic' ecclesiology nor marginalizes the church's lived socio-historical existence like 'dogmatic' ecclesiology.

That said, how, then, does Bonhoeffer proceed to deploy his theological ontology of human personhood to further specify his understanding of *Gemeinschaft* and *Gesellschaft* as sociological types and the difference between their typological forms of objective spirit in their relation to human personhood? This difference (as demonstrated above) is that objective spirit attains personal character not in correspondence with the sociological type *Gesellschaft* as a means to an end but only with the sociological type *Gemeinschaft* as an end in itself. While *Gemeinschaft* can be interpreted socially or corporately as a unified *individual* collective person (*Kollektivperson*) that is metaphysically autonomous to but genetically dependent upon its individual members,[139] *Gesellschaft*, as a plethora of atomistic wills,[140] cannot. On the basis of this *Kollektivperson* concept,[141] Bonhoeffer argues that *Gemeinschaft* – as a sociological type, and no matter the extent of the basic social unit therein (marriage, family, nation, or humanity per se) – can be understood to exist as a *Kollektivperson* in the *self-same* socio-ethical and theological schematic as an individual person.[142] Consequently, the *Kollektivperson* is capable of being addressed

---

[138] See *DBWE* 2, 90–1: 'God is free not from human beings but for them. ... God is present, that is, not in eternal nonobjectivity but – to put it quite provisionally for now – "haveable", graspable in the Word within the church.'

[139] See *DBW* 1, 48.

[140] See *DBWE* 1, 253.

[141] See ibid., 79; cf., Scheler, *Formalism in Ethics*, 519–61.

[142] It is critical for Bonhoeffer's understanding of the church as he proceeds to develop it in *Sanctorum Communio* – and for his entire ecclesiological (and theological) endeavour – that the *Kollektivperson* of humanity (*Menschheitsperson*) is conceived ontologically and theologically in duality (see, for example, *DBWE* 1, 107–21; *DBWE* 2, 108–9 and 136–61; *DBWE* 14, 350–2 and 374–6; and *DBWE* 15, 344–5). On the one hand – and in consequence of Bonhoeffer's hamartiology – Adam is the *Kollektivperson* of 'old' or sinful humanity. Adam is such because of the notion of reciprocity: the sinful act of the individual being understood as cooperating with and participating in the first sin of Adam, such that the deed of the individual sinner is at once the deed of sinful humanity. Consequently, 'all humanity falls with each sin, and not one of us is in principle different from Adam; that is, everyone is also the "first" sinner' (*DBWE* 1, 115). The *Kollektivperson* of 'old' or sinful humanity-in-Adam (*Adamsmenschheit*) is thus *one*, yet consists of nothing but *individual* sinners.

as an 'I' by a 'You',[143] and thus of being placed, as an 'I', into a position of socio-ethical responsibility in relation to that 'You'. For Bonhoeffer, the *Kollektivperson* is capable, therefore, of relating in freedom to God and of imaging God's freedom as a free creature of God in loving relation to another. By implication, the *Kollektivperson* is also capable of seeking to create its own life in interior relation to itself – that is, of living a life *cor curvum in se*.[144] This argument then enables Bonhoeffer to further

---

Bonhoeffer writes: '*It is Adam, since all individuals are themselves and Adam*' (*DBW* 1, 76). On the other hand – and in consequence of both Bonhoeffer's Christology taking root in an apocalyptically eschatologically indexed pneumatology and his theological concept of *Stellvertretung* – Jesus Christ (as the eschatological person par excellence, and by the agency of God the Holy Spirit the invasive and apocalyptic presence of new creation in space and time) is the *Kollektivperson* of 'new' or redeemed humanity-in-Christ (*neuen Menschheit in Christus*) (see *DBW* 1, 76). For Bonhoeffer, there exists no neutral metaphysics of humanity independent of this theological and more specifically apocalyptically eschatological ontology of being in Adam or in Christ. The separation between those who are lost (*Verlorene*) because of the effect of sin and death and those who are saved (*Geretete*) because of the effect of grace and life is all-embracing (*allumfassende*) (see *DBW* 14, 357). Bonhoeffer states: 'Humanity *is* cut in two' (*DBW* 14, 331). The human being is *either* in Adam in sin *or* in Christ (in the church) (see *DBWE* 2, 153). Outside or apart from these two *Kollektivpersonen* – the community of Adam or of Christ (which is the community of the church) – there is no humanity. Bonhoeffer writes: 'In the Christian doctrine of being, all metaphysical ideas of eternity and time, being and becoming, living and dying, essence and appearance must be measured against the concepts of the being of sin and the being of grace or else must be developed anew in light of them' (*DBWE* 2, 151). That there is no neutral metaphysics of humanity independent of this theological ontology of being in Adam or in Christ is, moreover, the reason why for Bonhoeffer it is necessary to render the sociological categories of social philosophy and sociology subservient to the category of the theological (see Chapter 2, Section IV, of this book). For discussion of Bonhoeffer's concept of *Stellvertretung*, see Section III.ii of this chapter.

[143] See *DBWE* 1, 118–20.

[144] The accuracy and appropriateness of Bonhoeffer's argument here has been questioned from the perspective of contemporary sociology, notably by Berger, 'Sociology and Ecclesiology', esp. 61–4 and 76–9. Indeed, following Berger, one might well ask how a twenty-first-century nation is a community in Bonhoeffer's *Kollektivperson* sense? Or if a marriage always is a community as Bonhoeffer here defines it? Or why is it appropriate to speak of community as a *Kollektivperson* while maintaining that such a position remains empirical? However, Berger's critique and the questions it might pose fails to read aright Bonhoeffer's understanding of *Gemeinschaft* as an *ideal* sociological type, and thus seems to misinterpret his use of it precisely *as* an exploratory device in a *dogmatic* inquiry into the nature and structure of the church that as such is intended *not* to belong to the discipline of sociology (see n.18 in this chapter; and Chapter 2, Section IV of this book). The critique also (when the concepts of *Kollektivperson* and objective spirit are subsequently taken up by Bonhoeffer and reworked *theologically* in relation to the church) seems to misread Bonhoeffer's understanding of the church as *God's* church-community, which as a sociological structure sui generis is irreducible to empirical sociological thought (see Section III of this chapter). Moreover, as Harasta notes, 'not every community [for Bonhoeffer] allows for the *true* realization of [individual or corporate] personhood' (Harasta, 'Bonhoeffer's Lutheran Ecclesiology and Inter-Religious Dialogue', 241). Only the church-community allows for this true realization, and so not *all* communities *will be* a community as Bonhoeffer here defines it. Thus,

> there is but one remedy for our age ... back to the church. ... Our world should become part of the people of God; it should become church ... *that is the goal and meaning of all our communities*. ... Only when a marriage [or 'family', 'nation', or 'state'] is church, where each person sacrifices for the other, where each intercedes on behalf of the other, where each forgives the other's sins, where two live one life, there marriage has attained and fulfilled its deepest meaning [as a *Kollektivperson*]' (*DBWE* 10, 510, emphasis added).

Such attainment and fulfilment is possible, however, only through the work of God the Holy Spirit. See Section III.ii of this chapter.

define the eschatological telos of *Gemeinschaft* (understood as a *Kollektivperson*) in its *temporal* relation. Bonhoeffer writes:

> The community that is from God to God, that bears the limit of time's meaning in itself, stands before God's sight and does not dissolve into the fate of the many. It is willed, created, and has become *responsible*; it must seek repentance, believe in and experience justification and sanctification, and suffer judgment and grace at the limits of time. Clearly, this can happen only 'in' individuals ... and yet it is not individuals, but the whole community that in the individuals, hears, repents, and believes.[145]

As a sociological type, *Gemeinschaft* is thus envisaged by Bonhoeffer as existing at the *eschaton* and eternal judgement (and grace thereby) operative both individually and corporately. Indeed, that an individual belongs at once to several communities and ipso facto to several *Kollektivpersonen* means that the individual is judged both in isolation and as a member of those collective persons.[146] Moreover, existing as it does at the 'limit of time' (*grenzzeitlich*), the sociological type *Gemeinschaft* as a *Kollektivperson* can expect eternal life in the passing of judgement, but its *Gesellschaft* counterpart, precisely because of its apersonal nature and by its being time-limited (*zeitbegrenzt*), cannot. For Bonhoeffer, what is decisive here is that while eternal judgement is passed on both a community and a society, 'it is passed only on the former as collective persons [*Kollektivpersonen*], and only on the latter as entities consisting of individual persons [*Einzelpersonen*]'.[147] In this way, the difference that is operative on the *personal* level between *Gemeinschaft* and *Gesellschaft* as sociological types is coordinated by Bonhoeffer with the difference that is operative on the *temporal* level.

Thus does Bonhoeffer explicate, in this threefold psychological, temporal and personal way, the difference between the first two sociological types of socio-historical human community that arise in consequence of a directional relation (or determination) of human willing. To these two sociological types of *Gemeinschaft* and *Gesellschaft* Bonhoeffer then proceeds to add (briefly) a third: *Herrschaftsverband*.[148] In contrast to the first two types, this third type arises not in consequence of a directional relation (or determination) of human willing but by a *strength* relation.[149] This strength relation, more specifically, is 'a *relation of rule [Herrschaftverhältnis]*' which arises where a weaker will obeys a stronger will from a position of understanding the meaning of what the stronger will commands.[150] Here, empirical social formation is effectively realized (according to Bonhoeffer) as the sociological type *Herrschaftsverband*, and realized *as* *Herrschaftsverband* in the sociological type either of *Gemeinschaft* or *Gesellschaft*.[151]

---

[145] *DBW* 1, 74–5.
[146] See *DBWE* 1, 284.
[147] Ibid.
[148] That is, 'association of (authentic) rule'. See *DBWE* 1, 92.
[149] See *DBWE* 1, 91.
[150] See ibid., 91–2.
[151] See ibid., 92.

Thus far this chapter has articulated Bonhoeffer's constructed threefold typology of socio-historical human community with substantive and necessary reference to his theological ontology of human personhood. It has done so because it is in dialogue with this typology that Bonhoeffer proceeds to build his pneumatologically and apocalyptically eschatologically founded 'both/and' ecclesiological methodology in which the being of the church is conceived as established by God the Holy Spirit as the particular and contingent socio-historical human community that the church is in its orientation to the eschatological telos, and thus (derivatively) as a sociological structure sui generis that combines and surmounts simultaneously the sociological 'types' *Gemeinschaft*, *Gesellschaft* and *Herrschaftsverband*. How Bonhoeffer does this is the concern of the chapter's next section. However, as it will be seen, critical for Bonhoeffer's argument is the difference (as demonstrated earlier) between the way in which *Gemeinschaft* and *Gesellschaft* relate to time. This difference facilitates Bonhoeffer's articulation of an inherent eschatological tension within the being of God's church-community. This eschatological tension, in turn, provides the basis upon which Bonhoeffer argues that *God's* church-community combines and surmounts simultaneously all three sociological types of socio-historical *human* community, but nevertheless *as* a sociological structure. Here, not only the actualizing work of God the Holy Spirit but also, critically, the relation between the Holy Spirit of God and the objective spirit of the church (understood as a *Kollektivperson* in the terms articulated earlier) is key. Indeed, it will be seen that this relation is essentially constitutive of the third actualizing work of God the Holy Spirit by which Bonhoeffer's account of the church gives voice to the asymmetrical yet interconnected relation of divine and human togetherness in the church's being, and holds together and affords appropriate space in that account to *both* God's own being *and* the being of the church's socio-historical human form, such that God's church-community is adequately demarcated as a sociological structure sui generis.

III. *God's* church-community: A sociological structure sui generis

Given the foregoing discussion of Bonhoeffer's constructed threefold typology of socio-historical human community, it is now possible to proceed to demonstrate how, in dialogue with this typology, Bonhoeffer builds the 'both/and' ecclesiological methodology of his ecclesial thought on the pneumatological and apocalyptically eschatological foundations laid in Chapter 2. To do this, this section of the chapter will argue that, for Bonhoeffer, there exists in the being of the church an inherent eschatological tension upon the basis of which, and in consequence of a threefold actualizing work of God the Holy Spirit, *God's* church-community *as* a particular and contingent socio-historical *human* community combines and surmounts simultaneously the sociological 'types' *Gemeinschaft*, *Gesellschaft* and *Herrschaftsverband*.

i. The eschatological tension of God's church-community

In his analysis of the sociological structure of the church's being, Bonhoeffer's starting point is that the church qua church is *both* an 'essential' *and* an 'empirical' reality,[152] which as such (and in the language of this book and its designated ecclesiological 'types') requires the theologian to speak of the being of the church – if she is to speak of it in a genuinely theological manner – from *both* a 'dogmatic' *and* an 'ethnographic' perspective simultaneously. Indeed, that the church is established ('essentially') by God *as* a socio-historical ('empirical') human community is the fundamental basis upon which Bonhoeffer moves to establish the distinctive sociological structure of God's church-community.[153] It is precisely this asymmetrical yet interconnected relation of divine and human togetherness in the church's being that constitutes its twofold relation to Jesus Christ as Christ's body. On the one hand, the church is said by Bonhoeffer to be chosen or realized in Christ from and for all eternity.[154] Being thus, the church is really and wholly established by God in Christ as an ontological reality, and is – eschatologically speaking – 'already completed'.[155] As such, the church is consummated and fulfilled, eternally and at all times. In this 'essential' sense, the church (as *Gemeinschaft*) is perfectly pure and timeless.[156] On the other hand, and also at all times, the church (according to Bonhoeffer) is actualized in the world as Christ's presence.[157] Just as Christ entered spatio-temporality as the presence or 'body' of God, so the church now is the presence or 'body' of Christ in that self-same reality.[158] Bonhoeffer writes: '*The church is "Christ existing as community"*'.[159] As such – and

---

[152] See *DBWE* 1, 125.
[153] See ibid., 122–282.
[154] See *DBW* 1, 85 and 100.
[155] Ibid., 86.
[156] See ibid., 97.
[157] See ibid., 86.
[158] See ibid., 87.
[159] See ibid., 133. The co-inherence between Christ and the church as Christ's body suggested by this leitmotif of Bonhoeffer's ecclesial thought is, however, qualified by Bonhoeffer by reference to the doctrine of the ascension. Bonhoeffer writes: 'Christ has ascended into heaven and is now with God, and we still await Christ's coming' (*DBWE* 1, 140). Thus, 'a *complete* identification between Christ and the church-community cannot be made' (*DBWE* 1, 140). In Bonhoeffer's thought, 'Christ existing as community' suggests *not*, then, that Christ is *only* in the church – in the sense of his being absorbed into it without remainder – but rather that the church as Christ's body is the form or mode of being in which the risen Christ is in spatio-temporality after his ascension (see Tietz, 'The Role of Jesus Christ for Christian Theology', 13; and Christiane Tietz, 'Bonhoeffer on the Ontological Structure of the Church', in Clark and Mawson, ed. *Ontology and Ethics*, 40–1). For Bonhoeffer, the events of Christ's ascension and (future) *parousia*, 'categorically rule out any idea of a mystical fusion between church-community and Christ.' Bonhoeffer continues: 'The same Christ who is present in his church-community will return from heaven' (see *DBWE* 4, 220). With respect to this persistent tension that exists in Bonhoeffer's thought between the heavenly session of Christ and Christ's presence in space and time as the church, Höhne's critique that Bonhoeffer 'does not mention how he sees this as being possible' (Höhne, *Spirit and Sonship*, 149) simply will not do, for it blatantly disregards Bonhoeffer's explicit reference to the work of God the Holy Spirit in his understanding Christ as being 'wholly in the church-community and yet the one who is to come again' (*DBW* 14, 439). Indeed, in the context of discussing the church as Christ's body, Bonhoeffer draws specific attention to 'the pneumatic character' of this tensed relation: 'The church-community of Christ is the present Christ *in the Holy Spirit*' (*DBW* 14, 438). Or as Bonhoeffer writes elsewhere, '*through the Holy Spirit*, the crucified and risen Christ exists as

again eschatologically speaking – the church is 'in the process of growing' towards perfection.[160] In this 'empirical' sense, the church (as *Gesellschaft*) is *im*perfectly *im*pure and time-bound.[161] Thus, for Bonhoeffer, and precisely in consequence of the church's twofold relation to Jesus Christ as Christ's body – a relation which itself is the result of the asymmetrical yet interconnected relation of divine and human togetherness in the church's being – the church can be said to relate to time in accordance with both the *Gemeinschaft* and *Gesellschaft* sociological types. There exists, therefore, in the being of the church an inherent eschatological tension: the church *is* and is at once, perfect and imperfect, pure and impure, timeless and time-bound, *'already completed in Christ'* and *'in him [having] its beginning ... established'*.[162]

In its own ecclesial way, this tension is but an expression of the Lutheran concept *iustus peccator*.[163] The justified one is 'dead to sin and alive to God',[164] transposed from 'old' (or sinful) humanity-in-Adam to 'new' humanity-in-Christ; but 'old' (or sinful) humanity-in-Adam, even if overcome and renewed in reality, is nevertheless still present and remains in the 'new' humanity-in-Christ in actuality.[165] As Bonhoeffer puts it in his postdoctoral dissertation, 'This is the new creation of the new human being of the future that is coming, which *here* is an event already occurring by faith, and *there* is completed for sight.'[166] In other words, 'Adam' is replaced by Christ only in hope, that is, eschatologically, and justification itself is but 'an eschatological prolepsis' – only the 'beginnings' of new life.[167] Thus, the justified one is both saint and sinner, and the church both *sanctorum communio* and *peccatorum communio*, with the latter coexisting in the former.[168] Bonhoeffer writes: 'As a sinful community the church is nevertheless still holy, or rather that in this world it is never holy without also being sinful.'[169] This eschatological tension, or, to use Harasta's terminology, *'ambiguity'*, which exists in the being of 'the sinful-yet-true church',[170] might thus be said to be built by Bonhoeffer on his understanding of spatio-temporality (and life in this reality) as having been 're-made' by the apocalypse of God's gospel, such that space and time, and the being of

---

the church-community' (*DBWE* 4, 220). In and through the Holy Spirit of God, Christ, therefore, is in heaven even as he exists in space and time as the church. Holmes's words are appropriate: 'Jesus' existence as such is pneumatological (spiritual) in nature, meaning his ascended existence is not exhausted in the church' (Holmes, 'The Holy Spirit', 173). While Christ *is* wholly present in the church – it is *his* (earthly) body – he remains its (heavenly) head, and as such stands over against it (see *DBWE* 15, 422). There is, then, according to Bonhoeffer, 'identity and non-identity of the subject with the church-community' (*DBW* 14, 439): or else, one might say, there is a pneumatologically mediated and thus eschatological unity-in-distinction by which the risen and ascended Christ exists as church-community.

[160] See *DBWE* 1, 86 and 211.
[161] *DBW* 1, 97.
[162] Ibid., 88 (emphasis in original).
[163] See Harasta, 'Bonhoeffer's Lutheran Ecclesiology and Inter-Religious Dialogue', 243–9.
[164] Rom. 6.11.
[165] See *DBWE* 1, 213; cf., *DBWE* 1, 107: 'It is not as if Adam were completely overcome; rather, the humanity of Adam lives on in the humanity of Christ.' For a discussion of the actuality of sin in the 'new' humanity-in-Christ, see Eva Harasta, 'Adam in Christ? The Place of Sin in Christ-Reality', in Mawson and Ziegler, ed. *Christ, Church, and World*, 61–75.
[166] *DBW* 2, 161 (emphasis added).
[167] See *DBWE* 1, 124, 213 and *DBW* 1, 144.
[168] See *DBWE* 1, 213.
[169] Ibid., 214.
[170] Harasta, 'The Responsibility of Doctrine', 17.

the church as a particular and contingent socio-historical human community *in* space and time is marked by an active warfare between the 'old' or present (fallen) world and the world of new creation.[171] Furthermore, this eschatological tension proves significant for Bonhoeffer in a threefold way, not least for his understanding of the being of the church as a being which is oriented to the eschatological telos.

First, as Harasta observes, and precisely in consequence of his dogmatic inquiry into the sociology of the church,[172] the tension permits Bonhoeffer to develop his understanding of the Protestant distinction between the visible and invisible church, such that he refuses to separate the latter from the former: 'We do not believe in an invisible church, nor in the realm of God within the church as *coetus electorum*. ... Instead we believe that God has made the concrete, empirical church. ... We believe in the church not as an ideal that is unattainable or yet to be fulfilled, but as a present reality.'[173] Indeed, for Bonhoeffer, 'the "essential" church becomes literally visible in the empirical church.'[174] It is thus 'proper only to speak of the empirical form corresponding to a greater or lesser degree to the essence'.[175] The visible and invisible church are one church.[176] Second, this single empirical church never (according to Bonhoeffer) attains its 'essential' holy nature *fully*, precisely because it is sinful.[177] Third, the inherent eschatological tension in the church's being not only, therefore, affirms the being of the church as sinful and oriented to the eschatological telos but also necessarily suggests an eschatological resolution. This resolution is the bringing of what exists in the church's

---

[171] On this, see Chapter 2, Section II of this book.
[172] On this, see Chapter 2, Section IV of this book.
[173] DBWE 1, 280. Cf., McBride, *The Church for the World*, 119 and 121–2, wherein she refers to Bonhoeffer '[splitting] apart the church's visible and hidden aspects' in consequence of his failure to 'address adequately how the church can be at once the revelation of the new humanity in time *and* a congregation of sinful, and continually sinning human beings'. This inadequacy McBride locates more acutely 'in the fact that [*Sanctorum Communio*] is more ecclesiology – a sociology of the church – than christology', which alone (according to McBride) can account for how the church is 'at once worldly and revelatory'. McBride's reading of Bonhoeffer here not only (seemingly) fails to understand Bonhoeffer's ecclesiology as a dogmatic inquiry into the sociology of the church but seems to misread his understanding of the distinction between the invisible and visible church. McBride's reading, moreover, would also seem to miss the importance of the concept of the church's objective spirit in Bonhoeffer's account of ecclesial sin, and indeed the relation between that spirit and the Holy Spirit. On the relation between the Holy Spirit and the church's objective spirit, see Section III.ii of this chapter.
[174] DBWE 1, 221.
[175] Ibid.
[176] See ibid. In Nielsen's words, this one church is the 'visible-invisible' church (Kirsten Busch Nielsen, 'Community Turned Inside Out: Dietrich Bonhoeffer's Concept of the Church and of Humanity Reconsidered', in Zimmermann and Gregor, ed. *Being Human, Becoming Human*, 94), or perhaps better (and in more Lutheran terms) the hidden church. As Bernd Wannenwetsch observes: 'Hidden means neither visible nor invisible. What is hidden is visible only to the eyes of faith; yet, it is a reality that can be experienced in the flesh. The true Church does not exist behind or beyond the visible Church but is *hidden* within it' (Bernd Wannenwetsch, 'Ecclesiology and Ethics', in Gilbert Meilaender and William Werpehowski, ed. *The Oxford Handbook of Theological Ethics* (Oxford: Oxford University Press, 2005), 66). One might speak, therefore, of the church's 'trans-visibility' (Wannenwetsch, 'Ecclesiology and Ethics', 65). Indeed, for Bonhoeffer, it is only through the eyes of faith that the invisibility of the church is in fact visible. See *DBWE* 1, 220–21. On faith as the prerequisite for seeing and understanding the nature and structure of the church, see Chapter 2, Section IV of this book.
[177] See *DBWE* 1, 212.

being as a present reality only in hope into a state of actual fulfilment at the *eschaton*. At the eschaton, that which in history is brought into being only 'in the beginnings' is fulfilled truly and eternally.¹⁷⁸ Thus, the church, Bonhoeffer argues, 'will remain impure as long as there is history, and yet in this concrete form it is nevertheless *God's church-community*'.¹⁷⁹

It is precisely upon the basis of this eschatological tension in the church's being that Bonhoeffer proceeds to argue, in consequence of a threefold actualizing work of God the Holy Spirit, that God's church-community combines and surmounts simultaneously the three 'types' of socio-historical human community, *Gemeinschaft*, *Gesellschaft* and *Herrschaftsverband*. As the being of the church (as an ontological reality) is realized in Christ from and for all eternity and actualized as Christ's body (to grow) in spatio-temporality, it is, as such, '*to be built within time* upon Christ as its firm foundation'.¹⁸⁰ For Bonhoeffer, it is the work of God the Holy Spirit that builds the church in space and time. This is perhaps somewhat surprising given the backdrop of the Lutheran theological traditions at play in shaping Bonhoeffer's theology. It is, however, critical for the construction of the 'both/and' ecclesiological methodology of his ecclesial thought and the ecclesiological description that flows from it. Bonhoeffer writes: 'In order to build the church as the community-of-God [*Gemeinde Gottes*] in time, God reveals God's own self as *Holy Spirit*. The Holy Spirit is the will of God that gathers individuals together to be the church-community, maintains it, and is at work only within it.'¹⁸¹ For Bonhoeffer, the church is created by the Holy Spirit at Pentecost: out of the gathered assembly the Holy Spirit creates the church,¹⁸² actualizing in space and time that which is realized in Christ.¹⁸³ As such, the church *is* Christ's body *only* as it is created and sustained in the time between the ascension of Christ and the *eschaton* by the work of God the Holy Spirit. Holmes echoes this insight thus: 'The Spirit actualizes the new humanity accomplished in Christ and does so in the church, the church being the social and temporal co-ordinate of the Spirit's activity. ... Put differently, the new humanity whose ontological reality is Christ becomes socially and historically real in the community of the church by the work of the Holy Spirit.'¹⁸⁴ Only as the church is founded on, and brought about by, the event of the Holy Spirit of God, is the church continually made manifest (according to Bonhoeffer) as God's church-community.¹⁸⁵ Indeed, the church 'is only *in* the [Holy] Spirit'.¹⁸⁶ Moreover, for Bonhoeffer, the church

---

¹⁷⁸ See *DBW* 1, 197.
¹⁷⁹ *DBWE* 1, 281 (emphasis added).
¹⁸⁰ Ibid., 153 (emphasis altered).
¹⁸¹ Ibid., 143.
¹⁸² See *DBW* 14, 425–6. On Bonhoeffer's understanding of the founding of the church at Pentecost, see Chapter 4, Section II of this book.
¹⁸³ See *DBW* 11, 275.
¹⁸⁴ Holmes, 'The Holy Spirit', 169.
¹⁸⁵ See *DBWE* 1, 260.
¹⁸⁶ Ibid., 144 (emphasis added). It is important to note the corollary to Bonhoeffer's thought here: 'The Spirit is *only* in the church-community' (*DBWE* 1, 144, emphasis added) – a delimitation of the person and work of God the Holy Spirit that one would wish to contest. While the church might be said to be the most intense (but significantly not yet complete) expression of the Holy Spirit (or else of pneumatological filled-ness in space and time), it is not the *only* expression. Cf., Chapter 1, Section III.iii of this book.

is only as the result of what can be seen as a threefold actualizing work *of* the Holy Spirit.[187] As it will be seen, this threefold work of God the Holy Spirit actualizes and animates the being of *God's* church-community as the particular and contingent socio-historical *human* community that the church in space and time is in its orientation to the eschatological telos, and its unique ontic-social relations as a 'community of [the] Spirit [*Geistgemeinschaft*]'.[188] In articulating this threefold actualizing work of the Holy Spirit of God, Bonhoeffer's account of the church will be seen, moreover, to hold together *both* divine *and* human agency, and to articulate, derivatively, the sui generis sociological structure of *God's* church-community in distinction to *all* other socio-historical forms of human community, such that Bonhoeffer's pneumatologically and apocalyptically eschatologically founded 'both/and' ecclesiological methodology can be said to break through the endemic 'either/or' problematic present in approaches to contemporary ecclesiological discourse. Thus, it is to the task of explicating this threefold actualizing work of God the Holy Spirit to which the chapter now turns.

ii. The pneumatological actualization of God's church-community

For Bonhoeffer, a threefold actualizing work of the Holy Spirit of God is determinative of the being of God's church-community in space and time and its unique ontic-social relations as a sociological structure sui generis. To demonstrate this, it will be argued in what follows that critical to this threefold actualizing work, by which the church's being is established by *God* the Holy Spirit as the particular and contingent socio-historical (and sinful) *human* community that the church in space and time is, is Bonhoeffer's articulation of the person-forming action of God the Holy Spirit, and his understanding of the sociological phenomenon of objective spirit and in particular the relation between the objective spirit of the church and God the Holy Spirit. Indeed, for Bonhoeffer, it is the Holy Spirit of God who creates human personhood in justification

---

[187] See *DBWE* 1, 161–216. Marsh's assertion that 'the Spirit does not make the church actual' and his concomitant statement that 'the Holy Spirit dwelling in the church is actualized solely by revelation in Christ' is thus curious and problematic (see Marsh, *Reclaiming Dietrich Bonhoeffer*, 73). According to Marsh: 'Pneumatology [for Bonhoeffer] is based strictly on Christology: "[The] Holy Spirit has no other content than the fact of Christ"' (Marsh, *Reclaiming Dietrich Bonhoeffer*, 74). While Bonhoeffer does indeed see the Holy Spirit and Jesus Christ as inseparably and essentially interrelated (not least in the work of actualizing the church in space and time), it is not Christology that grounds pneumatology, however, but rather pneumatology that grounds Christology: 'Christ [is] the gift of the Holy Spirit' (*DBWE* 14, 456; cf., Greggs, 'Ecclesiology', 233–4). Marsh is right, therefore, to assert that for Bonhoeffer 'the Holy Spirit has no other content than the fact of Christ'. Indeed, as Bonhoeffer writes: 'Christ is the criterion and the aim of the work of the Holy Spirit, and to this extent Christ himself also participates in building the church in time' (*DBWE* 1, 161). But Christ does so, critically, 'only through the work of the Holy Spirit' (*DBWE* 1, 161). Helpfully, Bonhoeffer gives voice here to the principle of *opera ad extra sunt indivisa* (cf., *DBWE* 14, 482). However, in his analysis that follows he proceeds to conflate (seemingly) the Spirit of Christ with the Holy Spirit (*see* DBWE 1, 210 and 215), and problematically runs the risk, therefore, of failing to differentiate *sufficiently* between the then-and-thereness of the historical person Jesus of Nazareth and the here-and-nowness of Christ's person, and thereby the socio-historical human community that the church is as Christ's body by the work of the Holy Spirit. This conflation (seemingly) thus works against Bonhoeffer's own construction of pneumatology as the foundational dogmatic *res* of ecclesiology.

[188] See *DBWE* 1, 264.

and sanctification. This is the *first* actualizing work of God the Holy Spirit who enables human being to relate in freedom to God and to thus image the freedom of God as God's free creatures in loving relation with and for one another and with and for the world. The creation and mediation of this loving relation with and for one another and with and for the world is the *second* actualizing work of God the Holy Spirit who thus generates and subsequently uses the church's objective spirit as a means to build God's church-community in space and time. This building up of God's church-community in space and time by means of the church's objective spirit is the *third* actualizing work of God the Holy Spirit. In consequence of this threefold pneumatological actualization in space and time of God's church-community the 'both/and' ecclesiological methodology of Bonhoeffer's ecclesial thought, and, derivatively, the sui generis sociological structure of God's church-community, will be brought into view.

As the first actualizing work of God the Holy Spirit, the Holy Spirit is said by Bonhoeffer to create (in justification and sanctification) human personhood in the transposition of human being from being in Adam to being in Christ. In other words, and in what is a truly extraordinary confession of Bonhoeffer's pneumatologically indexed theological anthropology, it is through the Holy Spirit of God that Jesus Christ comes 'into' individual human hearts.[189] In mediating the presence of Christ with*in* human being, the Holy Spirit creates faith, and thereby (in faith) a *new* human being who desires what the Spirit desires and so acknowledges and embraces God's rule.[190] In other words, the Holy Spirit of God creates an eschatologically new, or else, one might say, an *ecclesial* human being, by bringing 'Christ into the hearts of believers such that he then dwells within them.'[191]

In doing so, and as the second actualizing work of God the Holy Spirit, the Holy Spirit renders the ontic-social relations of God's church-community unique – and precisely in consequence of the Holy Spirit transposing the individual human being in Adam into community with God and other human beings in Christ: 'The Holy Spirit establishes the relationship between God and human being and between human being and human being.'[192] Thus, for Bonhoeffer, 'the concept of the individual simply is an

---

[189] See *DBW* 1, 106; cf., *DBWE* 14, 456. It is important to note that this Christological 'coming' is itself ecclesiological. Because the being of the church (as an ontological reality) is said by Bonhoeffer to be realized in Christ from and for all eternity, by Jesus Christ coming 'into' individual human being the being of the church also comes thereby. Bonhoeffer writes: 'When Christ comes "into" us through the Holy Spirit, the church comes "into" us' (*DBWE* 1, 165). Thus, 'the "new human being" is … at the same time Christ and the church' (*DBWE* 4, 219), and '*there is no relation to Christ in which the relation to the church is not necessarily established as well*' (*DBWE* 1, 127). It is for this reason that, for Bonhoeffer, being in Christ is being in the church, and why, subsequently, he affirms the Cyprianic-Augustinian concept of *extra ecclesiam nulla salus*. See *DBWE* 14, 675–8.

[190] See *DBWE* 1, 165; cf., *DBWE* 9, 341–2. The dialectic of faith and church in Bonhoeffer's thought, in which being in the church necessitates the *act* of faith, and the act of faith necessitates *being* in the church, is thus a pneumatologically mediated synthesis of act and being. See *DBWE* 2, 114 and 117–20.

[191] *DBWE* 14, 456. The indwelling of which Bonhoeffer speaks here is an indwelling not just of God the Son but also of God the Father (through the Spirit) and of God the Holy Spirit. See *DBWE* 14, 454–7.

[192] *DBWE* 14, 456. In this sense, the Holy Spirit actualizes in the here-and-now the once-for-allness of Christ's redemptive history with respect to the punishment and overcoming of humankind's disorientation or state of inverted isolation and solitude that for Bonhoeffer is sin – sin that is

unworkable abstraction'.[193] He later puts it thus: 'One can never ask individualistically. We *are* only in the church.'[194] Indeed, being in Christ (in the church) is being which soteriologically is pneumatologically and thus eschatologically oriented and ordered *towards* God and other human beings, such that that being is 'bound into sociality',[195] and, in intent, has a particular goal or purpose: the realization of God's rule and will, by one's love of God and neighbour. In other words, in faith and by the work of the Holy Spirit, God's *church*-community is constituted (according to Bonhoeffer) as a means to an end or purposive society – as *Gesellschaft*, that is – in that that which the church seeks to realize (*God's* rule and will) lies *beyond* its individual willing members. But since God's will is intended *towards* the church itself, *God's* church-community, created as it is as a purposive society or means to an end, is at once constituted as an end in itself or meaningful community – that is, as *Gemeinschaft*. Precisely because one's own love of God and neighbour is derivative of the work of God the Holy Spirit, one is assured that the end towards which one organizes one's relation to another is itself that very relation.[196] In other words, wanting to establish his *own* will, God gives Godself to human beings through the gift of God the Holy Spirit.[197] Being in Christ (in the church) thereby, and thus in loving relation to God and other human beings, the ecclesial human being is given by the Holy Spirit of God both the will to obey and the ability to understand what God commands.[198] As such, 'God establishes God's self as the means to God's own end'.[199]

---

not only existent as an individual and corporate reality but constitutive of postlapsarian broken community (see *DBWE* 1, 107–9 and 145–57; and *DBWE* 2, 136–47 and 150–5). This perverted ontological state of humankind is, however, punished and overcome by the vicarious representative action (*Stellvertretung*) and being of Jesus Christ in his redemptive history. Here, '*his* death is revealed as (having brought about) the death of death, and with this the limit of history composed by death is abolished, the human body has become the resurrection-body, and the humanity-of-Adam has become the church of Christ' (*DBW* 1, 96). But what is here realized in Christ essentially – that is, the possibility of the reorientation of human being and the concomitant creation of new community in Christ – must yet be actualized empirically by God the Holy Spirit orienting (in faith) the human will away from it*self* and back into community with God and other human beings in Christ (in the church). In consequence of the efficacy of Christ's redemptive history to renew that which was severed in the *corpus peccati*, the ontological disorientation of humanity-in-Adam is resolved in faith and by the work of the Holy Spirit as 'the individualistic striving for dominance of the self-empowered subjectivity is broken' (Hans-Richard Reuter, 'Afterword', *DBWE* 2, 183). In this breaking, the human will *in se conversus* is turned outward – away from itself – and reoriented to God and other human beings in 'the complete self-forgetfulness of love'. Bonhoeffer continues: 'I and You [now] face each other no longer essentially in a demanding, but in a giving way, revealing their hearts that have been conquered by God's will' (see *DBWE* 1, 190–1). In Nowers's words: '*Agapē* is therefore a pneumatic gift that translates into the self-surrendering will of the "I" for the "You"' (Nowers, 'Hegel, Bonhoeffer, and Objective *Geist*', 51). This self-surrendering, as Bonhoeffer concludes in his postdoctoral dissertation, 'is the new creation of the new human being of the future, which here is an event already occurring in faith, and there perfected for view'. See *DBWE* 2, 161.

[193] *DBW* 2, 117.
[194] *DBWE* 12, 222.
[195] *DBW* 2, 117.
[196] See *DBWE* 1, 262.
[197] See *DBW* 1, 181.
[198] See ibid., 116.
[199] Ibid., 181.

As a work of God the Holy Spirit, the church exists, then, as a 'duality and unity of will to community and the will to embrace God's purpose'.[200] Moreover, because the church is constituted thus only in virtue of God's will (to rule in love) ruling in it,[201] the church exists concomitantly as *Herrschaftsverband*. Bonhoeffer writes:

> It is the Spirit's work that, by my seeking nothing but to be obedient to God, that is, by my pursuing an end that as such is something other than the community, I completely surrender my will, so that simultaneously I truly love [God and] my neighbor. The Holy Spirit combines the claim to authority [*Herrschaftsanspruch*] with the will to establish purpose and to establish meaning by drawing the person into the Spirit's own course, thus being at once ruler and servant.[202]

Characteristically, the distinctive sociological structure of the being of the church as a community of the Holy Spirit (*Geistgemeinschaft*) – in which, and by the work *of* the Holy Spirit, the sociological types of *Gemeinschaft*, *Gesellschaft* and *Herrschaftsversband* are at once combined and surmounted – is as a '*community of love [Liebesgemeinschaft]*',[203] which itself 'rests on the fundamental sociological law of vicarious representative action [*Stellvertretung*]'.[204] Indeed, such love, in which God's church-community reveals itself as its *distinctive* sociological self, is constituted for Bonhoeffer by two mutually dependent *social acts*: in the church and its members, first, '*being structurally "with-each-other" [Miteinander]*', and second, in the member's '*active "being-for-each-other" [Füreinander] and in the principle of vicarious representative action [Stellvertretung]*'.[205]

With respect to the first of these two social acts, because being in Christ (in the church) is to be located with*in* the *Kollektivperson* of Christ, the church as Christ's body is understood by Bonhoeffer to possess Christ's 'collective personality [*Gesamptpersönlichkeit*]'[206] and thus to be 'a *single* life to such an extent that none of its members could be imagined apart from it'.[207] Consequently, wherever the church member is, there also the church is said to be. On the one hand (and essentially speaking), being 'with-each-other' means that in every life situation God's church-community as the body of Christ and by the work of God the Holy Spirit is passively present *with* the church member. On the other hand (and empirically speaking) being 'with-each-other' means that each church member – and again by the work of God the Holy Spirit – *is* Christ in relation to her neighbour, and actively so: where *she* is, there also *is* '*Christ* existing as church-community', the body *of* Christ.[208] In this empirical sense, therefore, being 'with-each-other' not only presupposes (essentially speaking) but also necessitates (empirically speaking), the second social act of being '*for*-each-other'. As the church member is in Christ (in the church), Christ himself becomes not

---

[200] *DBWE* 1, 263.
[201] See ibid., 264.
[202] Ibid., 262.
[203] Ibid., 266.
[204] *DBW* 9, 478.
[205] *DBWE* 1, 178 (emphasis in original).
[206] Ibid., 140.
[207] Ibid., 178 (emphasis added).
[208] See ibid., 178–82.

only the measure and standard of *loving* action but also – and precisely because of God the Holy Spirit mediating the presence of Christ with*in* human being – the loving power by which the church member and indeed the church itself as Christ's body 'may and ought to become a Christ to the other'.[209] The social act of being 'for-each-other' is thus comprised (according to Bonhoeffer) of loving neighbourly action after the pattern of Christ himself.[210] This loving action is possible, however, only in consequence of the prior work of God the Holy Spirit ordering and orienting human being in Christ (in the church) towards God and other human beings in love. Moreover, because of its will *for* the concrete other (both internal and external to the church-community), it is loving action which necessarily intends (as an end in itself) to form community as *Gemeinschaft*.[211]

Being 'for-each-other' is thus actualized in the church and its members acting vicariously on their neighbour's behalf, or more precisely in place of their neighbour. It is in this way that Bonhoeffer understands the social act of being 'for-each-other', and by definition the entailing and necessarily dependent social act of being 'with-each-other', as resting on a *theologically* defined sociological law of *Stellvertretung*.[212] It is this law, which, for Bonhoeffer, *is* the life-principle (*Lebensprinzip*) both of being in Christ (in the church) and of the church's own (corporate) relational ontology,[213] and renders, ultimately, the ontic-social relations of God's church-community unique. They are unique precisely because both conceptually and really (with respect to the two social acts which in reality flow from it) the sociological law of *Stellvertretung* rests entirely upon, and is made possible only by, the *pneumatologically* mediated *Stellvertretung* of Christ himself. Indeed, Bonhoeffer states: 'Since the love of God, in Christ's vicarious representative action, restores the community between God and human beings, so the community of human beings *with each other* has also become a reality in love once again.'[214] The vicarious representative action of Jesus Christ makes genuine human community possible, then, as a reality (in Christ) in the church – a reality which is actualized, however, by the Holy Spirit of God working to create *God's* church-community in spatio-temporality in the time between the ascension of Christ and the *eschaton*. As Bonhoeffer later puts it (in the context of a discussion of the church's being as a being which is oriented and ordered to the world): 'The concept

---

[209] See *DBWE* 1, 182–3; cf., Martin Luther, *Luther's Works* [hereafter *LW*], ed. and trans. Jaroslav Pelikan, Helmut Lehman et al., 55 vols (Minneapolis: Fortress Press, 1900–1986), 31, 367–8.

[210] See *DBWE* 8, 501; cf., *DBWE* 12, 314ff., and Bonhoeffer's identification therein of Jesus's being as a 'being-for-others', which is the '*pro-me*' (or *pro nobis*) structure of his personal ontology. In other words, the being of Christ's person *is* relatedness.

[211] See *DBWE* 1, 166–72. For Bonhoeffer, this action takes place through the individual church member's and the church's own active work for the neighbour, intercessory prayer and mutual forgiveness of sins. In one way or another, these acts are 'self-renouncing' because they 'involve giving up the self "for" my neighbor's benefit, with the readiness to do and bear everything in the neighbor's place, indeed, if necessary, to sacrifice myself, standing as a *substitute* for my neighbor'. See *DBWE* 1, 184–90 [184]. On the dynamic of internal and external relationality in Bonhoeffer's account of ecclesial being, see Tom Greggs, 'Ecclesial Priestly Mediation in the Theology of Dietrich Bonhoeffer', *Theology Today* 71.1 (2014), 81–91.

[212] See *DBWE* 1, 156.

[213] See *DBW* 1, 89, 92 and 96.

[214] *DBWE* 1, 157 (emphasis altered).

of vicarious representative action [*Stellvertretung*] defines this … relationship most clearly. The Christian community stands in the place in which the world should stand. In this respect it serves the world as vicarious representative; it is there *for* the world's sake.'[215] In fact, the church *is* the church only when it acts for others.[216] Thus, whenever the church as a *Kollektivperson* fails to perceive or stand in its place of responsibility *for* the world the church is no longer God's church-community.[217] For Bonhoeffer, however, the church can be as such *only* as the sociological law of *Stellvertretung* is *theologically* defined – as it is realized in Christ and actualized in the church by the work of God the Holy Spirit. Brendan Leahy notes:

> All the communitarian life of the church is rooted [by Bonhoeffer] in Christ's vicarious action on our behalf. Each person, who is led by the Spirit into actualized ecclesial existence, is enabled to live for and with one another in Christ. The new social sphere that is the church consists in an existence that is not centred on the individual, but rather one that is shared.[218]

This shared existence is constituted by the pneumatologically mediated reciprocal and symbiotic relation of the church and its members being *with* and *for* one another, and *with* and *for* the world – *miteinander* and *füreinander*.

Indeed, that the social acts of being 'with-each-other' and being 'for-each-other' are conceived by Bonhoeffer theologically, or more precisely pneumatologically,[219] ensures that his account of the distinctive sociological structure of the being of God's church-

---

[215] *DBWE* 6, 404 (emphasis added).
[216] See *DBWE* 8, 503.
[217] See *DBWE* 16, 543. In this sense, Bonhoeffer's vision of the church, as Harasta notes, is 'a vision of a fully *diaconal* church' (Harasta, 'The Responsibility of Doctrine', 26). Or, to perhaps sharpen the point, it is a vision of a fully *priestly* church. Greggs writes: 'Standing [before God] in the place of the people (indeed, the world as such) and mediating on the world's behalf [as the church does or is to do according to Bonhoeffer] is precisely the position of the priest with his people' – not least in his bearing the sins of the people and in his testifying back to the people to the reconciling activity of God. See Greggs, 'Ecclesial Priestly Mediation', 81–91 [88]; cf., Tom Greggs, 'The Priesthood of No Believer: On the Priesthood of Christ and His Church', *International Journal of Systematic Theology* 17 (2015), 374–98. For further discussion of the priestly being of the church in Bonhoeffer's ecclesial thought, see Chapter 4, Section III.ii of this book.
[218] Leahy, 'Christ Existing as Community', 41.
[219] For this reason, Nielsen's assertion that 'the mutual vicarious representative action of the members of the church according to Bonhoeffer *actualizes* the church as a "community of spirit"' must be contested as misreading Bonhoeffer's understanding of the sociological structure of the church's being (see Nielsen, 'Community Turned Inside Out', 99). It is not individual church members *in se* and per se who actualize that which is realized in Christ's vicarious representative action but God the Holy Spirit. Nielsen's argument is derivative (seemingly) of her prior statement that '[Bonhoeffer's] understanding of the church is influenced by his anthropology', which – and despite her (relatively brief) account of the movement 'from Bonhoeffer's ecclesiology to his anthropology' (see Nielsen, 'Community Turned Inside Out', 92–4) – problematically misconstrues, and thus obfuscates, the dogmatic locatedness of Bonhoeffer's ecclesiology, of which the foundational dogmatic *res* is not anthropology (or Christology) but an apocalyptically eschatologically indexed pneumatology. Tietz, similarly, makes no space for the agency of God the Holy Spirit in her account of *how* the church and its members are 'with-each-other' and 'for-each-other'. Rather, the agency at work is ascribed by Tietz exclusively to Jesus Christ, and derivatively thereby to individual members of the church as 'the community qualified by Christ'. See Tietz, 'Bonhoeffer on the Ontological Structure of the Church', 41ff. [42].

community as *Liebesgemeinschaft* not only is guarded against a reductive collapsing in ecclesiological description of divine agency into human subjectivity (in a fashion after the 'hard' ethnographic ecclesiologist) but also gives voice to the asymmetrical yet interconnected relation of divine and human togetherness in the church's being. This togetherness affords appropriate space in that account to *both* the operative and gracious (or 'essential') acts of *God and* the being and form of the socio-historical (or 'empirical') *human* community that the church in space and time is in its orientation to the eschatological telos. For what Bonhoeffer's pneumatological and eschatological construction denies *tout court* is precisely any rendering of God's church-community as a community of individual pious persons,[220] or of religiously or ethically motivated 'kindred spirits',[221] such that the church might be regarded as something secondary to the loving social acts of its individual willing members.[222]

To those members and to those acts the church is 'fundamentally "prior"'.[223] The church is not produced or something derived.[224] Instead, it is *'willed by God "prior" to any human will for community'* and in God's sight is thus complete. However, Bonhoeffer simultaneously states of the church (*contra* 'hard' dogmatic ecclesiology) that the church is *'real only as human will for community'*.[225] He continues: *'This antimony is overcome only by the human will being subjected by God to God's own will'*.[226] This overcoming is through the work of God the Holy Spirit. On this Bonhoeffer is clear: 'It is the Holy Spirit who brings Christ to the individuals. ... It is the Spirit who builds up the church by gathering the individuals, even though in Christ the whole building is already complete. ... The Holy Spirit creates the community ... of the members of the body'.[227] For Bonhoeffer, the social acts of the individual willing human spirit unite in the church to generate its objective spirit,[228] and the church's objective spirit, in the sociological forms and functions in which it exists empirically, at once bears 'the historical impact of Jesus Christ' and 'the social impact of the Holy Spirit'.[229] Nevertheless, the unity of human spirit that generates the church's objective spirit does not result from any consensus of human thought, or from any similarity in human conduct, or from any common human intent, but only from a divine unity. This divine unity is that of being in Christ (in the church) and thus of being oriented and ordered towards God and other human beings in love in consequence of the (first

---

[220] See *DBW* 11, 276.
[221] See *DBW* 1, 181.
[222] See *DBW* 11, 276.
[223] *DBWE* 1, 277.
[224] See ibid., and *DBW* 11, 276.
[225] *DBWE* 1, 278.
[226] Ibid.
[227] *DBWE* 4, 221.
[228] That the objective spirit of the church is generated by the social acts of its individual willing members means that it remains as such part of history, and (like its individual members) is therefore particular, contingent and fallible, and thus itself (can be seen to be) oriented to the eschatological telos. See *DBWE* 1, 214–15; cf., *DBWE* 1, 226–50, wherein Bonhoeffer identifies the sociological forms and functions of the church's objective spirit as assembling for worship, preaching, the sacraments of baptism and Eucharist, the priestly office and pastoral care. For further discussion of these sociological forms and functions, see Chapter 4, Section III of this book.
[229] *DBWE* 1, 210.

and second) actualizing work(s) of God the Holy Spirit. Bonhoeffer writes: 'It is not about "agreement in spirit", but about the "unity of the Spirit".'[230] He further argues that the 'church is formed not by [people] meeting together (genetic sociology), rather the church *exists* by the Spirit who is actually in the church-community and consequently it is not derived out of individual wills'.[231] There can, then, be 'no individualization of the church!'[232] The condition of this actualized non-individualism is God the Holy Spirit.[233] Thus, Bonhoeffer is clear that the Holy Spirit of God (*contra* 'hard' ethnographic ecclesiology) establishes the unity of the objective spirit in God's church-community, uniting from above (*"before"* any knowing and willing of the [individual human] members' from below),[234] 'the multitude of persons into a single corporate person, and without dissolving thereby either the particularity or the community of [those] persons'.[235]

The depth of Bonhoeffer's pneumatological insight here is remarkable.[236] To use Yves Congar's words, 'Nothing less than the Spirit *of God* is needed to bring all these different elements [of personal individuality] to unity, and to do so by respecting and even stimulating their diversity.'[237] The Holy Spirit, who is both one and transcendent as 'God *in us*', according to Congar, is alone 'able to penetrate all things without violating or doing violence to them'.[238] Indeed, for Bonhoeffer, the sociological forms and functions of the life of the church's objective spirit, as they exist empirically, are themselves generated and *planted within* the church's objective spirit by God the Holy Spirit,[239] such that those forms and functions must be accounted for in ecclesiological description (*contra* 'soft' dogmatic ecclesiology) with full reference to their spatio-temporal reality.[240] In this sense, the Holy Spirit of God is said by Bonhoeffer to stand as 'guarantor of the efficacy of these forms [and functions]',[241] and does so, not only in virtue of its generative and sustaining relation thereto but also, more specifically, as 'the Holy Spirit *uses* the objective spirit [of the church] as a vehicle for its gathering and sustaining social activity'.[242]

---

[230] *DBW* 1, 129.
[231] Ibid., 102.
[232] *DBW* 11, 288.
[233] See ibid., 289.
[234] See *DBWE* 1, 199 (emphasis added); and *contra* Mawson, *Christ Existing as Community*, 157: '[Bonhoeffer] claims that the interactions of individual Christians ... generate the objective spirit of the church. The objective spirit of the church as a community (*Gemeinde*) is generated from below.' Mawson's reading of Bonhoeffer on this point would thus seem to run counter to Bonhoeffer's own understanding of the generative and efficacious relationship that exists between the Holy Spirit of God and the church's objective spirit.
[235] *DBW* 1, 129.
[236] *Contra* Marsh, *Reclaiming Dietrich Bonhoeffer*, 73: 'Bonhoeffer's sustained response in [*Sanctorum Communio*] to the quandary of the *separateness* of persons and their life together in *inseparable* community is Christological in character.'
[237] Congar, *I Believe in the Holy Spirit*, vol. 2, 17.
[238] Ibid.
[239] See *DBWE* 1, 216.
[240] For further discussion of this accounting, see Chapter 4, esp. Section III of this book.
[241] *DBWE* 1, 216.
[242] Ibid., 215 (emphasis added).

In other words, and in what can be seen as the third actualizing work of God the Holy Spirit, the Holy Spirit, in order to actualize God's church-community as Christ's body in space and time, 'makes use' of the church's objective spirit as both 'object' and 'means' of its actualizing work.[243] Significantly, however, the Holy Spirit does this precisely as the objective spirit of the church-community exists empirically in its 'historically given forms',[244] and thus in spite of its contingent, fallible and sinful aspect, which, as Bonhoeffer notes, belongs both to individual church members and to the objective spirit of the church as a whole.[245] Thus, it is possible for God's *church-community* to be 'subject to the historical ambiguity of all profane communities'[246] and to be sinful in its objective spirit thereby, but without that sinful reality ultimately hindering the actualizing and sanctifying work of the Holy Spirit of God to build *God's* church-community as the socio-historical *human* community that the church in space and time is in its orientation to the eschatological telos.[247] Indeed, Bonhoeffer asserts: 'We have, on the one hand, the ever-changing, imperfect, sinful, objective human spirit; on the other hand we have the Holy Spirit who bears [and in doing so sanctifies] this human spirit, and is eternally one and perfect.'[248] In other words, while the Holy Spirit of God and the church's objective spirit are related, they cannot and must not be equated.[249] The Holy Spirit is, after all, the *Holy* Spirit – 'the Lord and giver of Life' – as the creed makes clear. In Bonhoeffer's words, the Holy Spirit 'is equal in glory and power to God the Father and God the Son'.[250] To conflate or identify in ecclesiological description the completely Holy Spirit of God with the human (and sinful (objective)) spirit of God's church-community – or for that matter with any given form of or culture or practice within that community – is thus wholly inappropriate.[251] It is only as God the Holy Spirit makes use of the church's objective spirit – which itself *is*, however (as demonstrated above), only *because* of the first and

---

[243] See *DBW* 1, 146 and 147. Here, 'object' in the sense that the objective spirit of the church is an expression (*Darstellung*) of God's church-*community* which is actualized by the Holy Spirit of God, and which 'itself is a will towards community, precisely because it subjects itself to God's will to rule'; and 'means' in the sense that the objective spirit of the church – being actuated (*angetrieben*) by that self-same rule – is at once 'a will aiming towards a goal, striving to subject individual spirits ever anew and ever more widely to itself and so to God's ruling will'. See *DBW* 1, 185.

[244] *DBW* 1, 146.

[245] See *DBWE* 1, 215.

[246] Ibid., 216.

[247] Bonhoeffer's claim here, as Mawson observes helpfully, is 'different from claiming the church as such is holy, but that there are still sinful individuals within it'. See Mawson, *Christ Existing as Community*, 160.

[248] *DBWE* 1, 215; cf. *DBW* 1, 147 (emphases altered): 'The objective spirit does not bear these [historically given forms] as one would carry a sack bound to one's back. Rather *it is itself made holy through the load*; it bears it in its heart. That is of course only insofar as the Holy Spirit itself bears [the load] within it.'

[249] *DBWE* 1, 216: 'The objective spirit is not the Holy Spirit.'

[250] *DBW* 14, 800.

[251] *Contra* Hütter, Moltmann and Jenson: see Chapter 1, Section III.iii and III.iv of this book. Cf., Küng, *The Church*, 173: 'The Spirit *is not* the church.' Küng continues: 'It would be dangerous to identify the Church and the Holy Spirit; for the Holy Spirit is the Spirit of God, not of the Church; hence the fundamental *freedom* of the Holy Spirit'. Küng's point (which echoes Bonhoeffer's) is echoed by Tom Greggs, *Theology against Religion: Constructive Dialogues with Bonhoeffer and Barth* (London: T&T Clark, 2011), 127: 'The presence of the Spirit is the *sine qua non* of the church, but the church is not the *sine qua non* of the presence of the Spirit, who in His freedom blows wherever he wills.'

second actualizing works of God the Holy Spirit – that the particular and contingent socio-historical human community that the church is as Christ's body is created, built, sustained and will ultimately be perfected as *God's* church-community in sociological distinction from all other forms of human empirical community. Bonhoeffer is clear: the church is 'the church of God';[252] and it *is* (as such) *only* by the work of God the Holy Spirit. Irrespective of its sinful aspect, God's church-community is, therefore (*contra* 'hard' ethnographic ecclesiology), irreducible *absolutely* to the category of the human empirical or sociological.[253] Indeed, only when 'one takes the claim of the church to be the church of God *seriously*'[254] (*contra* 'soft' ethnographic ecclesiology) does the church's pneumatologically constituted and eschatologically oriented sui generis sociological structure become manifest in distinction from all other socio-historical forms of human community.

IV. Conclusion

This chapter has sought to explicate how Bonhoeffer builds the structure of his 'both/and' ecclesiological methodology on the pneumatological and apocalyptically eschatological foundations of his ecclesial thought laid in Chapter 2. The chapter has done this by explicating, firstly, Bonhoeffer's constructed threefold typology of socio-historical human community with substantive and necessary reference to his theological ontology of human personhood. This was done because of the derivative relation that exists between human community and human personhood, but more critically because in dialogue with this typology of *Gemeinschaft*, *Gesellschaft* and *Herrschaftsverband* Bonhoeffer proceeds to build the pneumatologically and apocalyptically eschatologically founded 'both/and' ecclesiological methodology of his ecclesial thought. The chapter demonstrated how Bonhoeffer does this by articulating, secondly, the inherent eschatological tension that exists in the being of God's church-community, upon the basis of which Bonhoeffer identifies the being of the church as

---

[252] *DBW* 1, 80.

[253] It is for this reason that Mawson's assertion – as a corollary to Bonhoeffer's understanding of the church as sinful, and (seemingly) to Mawson's own applied threefold theological 'dialectic' to human being and social reality per se (see chapter 2, section IV of this book) – that 'there is no *final* basis for distinguishing the Christian community from other human polities' is problematic (see Mawson, 'The Spirit and Community', 468). For Bonhoeffer, there *is* a final basis for distinguishing God's church-community from all other socio-historical forms of human community, and this final basis is the work of the Holy Spirit of God. For a possible mitigation of Mawson's position, see Mawson, *Christ Existing as Community*, 170–5, where he briefly attends to the church as 'a unique or distinct sociological type' which 'displays defining attributes of both the society- and community-types' in consequence of God, in Christ and through Holy the Spirit, making use of, and being actively present and at work in, the church's objective spirit (see Mawson, *Christ Existing as Community*, 172–4 [172 and 173]). *How* this is so for Mawson, or put otherwise, *what* the actual content of this divine activity and work which constitutes the church as a unique sociological structure is, nonetheless remains somewhat unspecified in Mawson's account, not least in relation to the Holy Spirit of God. In light of the analysis offered in this chapter, therefore, Mawson may wish to deepen his account of Bonhoeffer's understanding of the person and work of God the Holy Spirit to unpack more fully the way in which the church for Bonhoeffer *is* a unique sociological type.

[254] *DBW* 1, 80.

a being which is actualized by the Holy Spirit of God as the particular and contingent socio-historical (and sinful) human community that the church in space and time is in its orientation to the eschatological telos, and thus, derivatively, as a sociological structure sui generis that combines and surmounts simultaneously all three 'types' of socio-historical human community. In articulating this eschatological tension and subsequent pneumatological actualization of God's church-community, it was seen that critical to Bonhoeffer's thought not only is his deployment (and understanding) of *Gemeinschaft*, *Gesellschaft* and *Herrschaftsverband* as sociological types, and in particular the way in which *Gemeinschaft* and *Gesellschaft* are said to relate (differently) to time, but also, and most decisively, the specific nature of the Holy Spirit's actualizing work by which the church's pneumatological and eschatological being in space and time and its unique ontic-social relations are said to be actualized.

This work was seen to be threefold: (1) the Holy Spirit of God transposes human being from being in Adam to being in Christ (in the church), thereby creating the ecclesial human being (a human being which is oriented and ordered towards God and other human beings in love); (2) the Holy Spirit mediates the reciprocal and symbiotic relation of the church and its members being with and for one another and with and for the world, such that the ontic-social relations of God's church-community are rendered unique and the realization of God's rule and will in the world is the quintessential ecclesial characteristic; and (3) the Holy Spirit generates the sociological forms and functions of the church's objective spirit which are subsequently used by the Holy Spirit to build the church in space and time. It is God's person and work as *Holy* Spirit, in and upon and outwith the church and its members as God's creatures, that animates, and ultimately perfects, *God's* church-community and its unique ontic-social relations. Moreover, this the Holy Spirit does without negating the integrity of either those relations and the social acts of being with and for one another and with and for the world that are constitutive of them or the particularity and contingency of the church's socio-historical human form, as fallible and sinful as they are. Indeed, for Bonhoeffer, the church *is* and accordingly has being in space and time as *Liebesgemeinschaft* only *as* the operative and gracious act of God the Holy Spirit creates it thus. In the time between the ascension of Christ and the *eschaton* the church exists as the event of the divine act of *convocatio* which takes place in and through the Holy Spirit of God to create in spatio-temporality the particular and contingent socio-historical human community that the church as *congregatio* is in its orientation to the eschatological telos: to *both* God *and* to the world as *Geistgemeinschaft*.

By building his ecclesiological description on pneumatological and apocalyptically eschatological foundations, Bonhoeffer's ecclesial thought thus treats the church as *both* an 'essential' *and* an 'empirical' reality, or (in the language of this book and its designated ecclesiological 'types') from *both* a 'dogmatic' *and* an 'ethnographic' perspective simultaneously. Bonhoeffer's ecclesial thought does this, however, and is enabled to do so only because of the pneumatological and apocalyptically eschatological foundations upon which it is built, and by Bonhoeffer's concomitant understanding of the Holy Spirit of God as he who holds together in the church's being *both* divine *and* human agency. To recall from Chapter 1, therefore, the asymmetrical yet interconnected relation of divine and human togetherness in the church's being expressed *in nuce* in 2 Cor. 6.16, one might say that for Bonhoeffer the Pauline καὶ must be parsed in reference to the Holy Spirit of God. By attending to the work of God the Holy Spirit Bonhoeffer's ecclesiological description can be said to be appropriately dogmatically ordered with due proportion, such that it breaks through the endemic problematic present in approaches to contemporary ecclesiological discourse and offers a therapeutic methodological response to the binarized tendency therein of describing in an account of the church either the *ad intra* or *ad extra* life of God 'dogmatically', or the particular and contingent socio-historical church-community 'ethnographically'.

Indeed, in speaking of the church (as Christ's body) *first* as existing as the event of the divine act of *convocatio* which takes place in and through the Holy Spirit of God, Bonhoeffer affirms emphatically the 'no' of 'hard' dogmatic ecclesiology. He thereby ensures that his account of the church has not 'forgotten God', but safeguarded adequately – by a theology of divine aseity and *contra* 'soft' dogmatic ecclesiology – the non-necessity of the creation and the sheer gratuitous nature of the church's created existence in space and time. In doing so, Bonhoeffer resists, therefore: the collapsing by 'hard' ethnographic ecclesiology of divine agency into human subjectivity without remainder and concomitantly the rending of ecclesiology independent as a doctrinal locus from the doctrine of God; the over-identification by 'soft' dogmatic ecclesiology of the church's being with the being of God; the folding by 'hard' and 'soft' ethnographic ecclesiology of speech about divine action into language about lived ecclesial life and church practice; and the failure to remember in 'hard' and 'soft' ethnographic ecclesiology that the church qua church is uniquely constituted in spatio-temporality by divine agency. While Bonhoeffer's ecclesiological speech appropriately relativizes, therefore, human agency, critically it does not minimalize it. Indeed, because the aseity of God is understood by Bonhoeffer in reference to God's pronobity in the church, the operative and gracious act of God the Holy Spirit that animates *God's* church-community takes place *in* space and time to create the particular and contingent socio-historical *human* community that the church as *congregatio* is in its orientation to the eschatological telos.

At once, therefore, Bonhoeffer's account of the church says an appropriately proportionate 'yes' to the actual being of the (fallible and sinful) church as it is constituted in spatio-temporality by divine agency particularly and contingently. Critically, this particular and contingent being of God's church-community is construed in Bonhoeffer's ecclesial thought (in critique of 'soft' dogmatic ecclesiology) with full reference to its spatio-temporal reality. That reality is neither dissolved actualistically into the eventful act of God (in critique of 'hard' dogmatic ecclesiology) nor treated by Bonhoeffer (in critique of 'hard' and 'soft' ethnographic ecclesiology) either as reducible absolutely to the category of the human empirical or as one variance of the genus of created sociality among others. Rather, God's church-community is articulated as a distinct sui generis sociological structure whose being is *in* the Holy Spirit of God. Thus, Bonhoeffer's account of the church gives voice to the asymmetrical yet interconnected relation of divine and human togetherness in the church's being, and holds together and affords appropriate space in that account to both divine and human agency with due concern for appropriate dogmatic ordering and proportionality. In this, Bonhoeffer's pneumatological and eschatological 'both/and' ecclesiological methodology can thus be said to proffer a 'third way' in ecclesiological description between the Scylla of 'dogmatic' ecclesiology and the Charybdis of 'ethnographic' ecclesiology. Seeking to identify how this 'both/and' ecclesiological methodology of Bonhoeffer's ecclesial thought further functions in his ecclesiological description, and in particular the way in which it enables him to account for the particular and contingent socio-historical human community that the church is in space and time in a genuinely theological way, is the task to which this book now turns.

4

The pneumatological space of God's church-community

I. Introduction

The previous chapter established how Bonhoeffer builds the structure of his 'both/and' ecclesiological methodology on pneumatological and apocalyptically eschatological foundations in dialogue with a threefold typology of socio-historical human community. It was demonstrated that Bonhoeffer's pneumatological and eschatological 'both/and' ecclesiological methodology proffers a 'third way' in ecclesiological description between the Scylla of 'ethnographic' ecclesiology and the Charybdis of 'dogmatic' ecclesiology by articulating the sui generis sociological structure of the being of God's church-community as a particular and contingent socio-historical human community that is *in* the Holy Spirit. In the Holy Spirit *both* divine *and* human agency are held together in Bonhoeffer's ecclesial thought with due concern for appropriate dogmatic ordering and proportionality in ecclesiological description. Indeed, that the church *is* only because of the operative and gracious act of God the Holy Spirit, and thus before any and all human action, means at once that the church has actual being in space and time *as* the socio-historical human community that the church is.[1] For Bonhoeffer, as noted in Chapter 3, the church as *congregatio*, in consequence of the divine act of *convocatio* with*in* space and time, occupies a certain physical space in spatio-temporality. This space, actualized in the time between the ascension of Christ and the *eschaton* by God the Holy Spirit and thus oriented to the eschatological telos as *Geistgemeinschaft*, and concomitantly (and derivatively) as *Liebesgemeinschaft*, might best be identified and understood in Bonhoeffer's ecclesial thought as *pneumatological*.

It is this pneumatological *space* of the church as *congregatio* in its orientation to the eschatological telos that this chapter seeks to outline in its consideration of Bonhoeffer's ecclesiological description, and in particular the way in which his pneumatological and eschatological 'both/and' ecclesiological methodology further

---

[1] Cf., Schwöbel, 'The Creature of the Word', 116–26, wherein Schwöbel observes: *opus Dei* is 'always the condition of the possibility' [119] of *opus hominum* as its 'creative ground' [119], and 'what constitutes something cannot be separated from what is constituted, what is made possible cannot be divorced from what makes it possible' [130]. To not maintain 'the distinction and relation of *opus Dei* and *opus hominum*' [118] is, then, to deny the condition of the church's possibility *qua* church.

enables him to account for the particular and contingent socio-historical human community that the church in space and time is (*contra* 'dogmatic' ecclesiology), in a genuinely theological way (*contra* 'ethnographic' ecclesiology). Put otherwise, the concern of the chapter (and also Chapter 5) is Bonhoeffer's theological, or, more precisely, pneumatological and apocalyptically eschatological conceptualization of spatio-temporality as grounded *extra se* in God and God's operative and gracious acts applied ecclesiologically. Bonhoeffer speaks in relation to the being of the church in space and time *theologically* about empirical phenomenology. This speech is itself the exemplified showing of the very logic of Bonhoeffer's 'both/and' ecclesiological methodology. Moreover, the critical importance of such speech for the wider ecclesiological task cannot be overstated. Bonhoeffer takes spatio-temporality seriously as a theological category and thus as the primary medium of God's ongoing gracious and redemptive economic activity which takes place not only *in* creation but in the most fundamental categories *of* creation: space and time. For Bonhoeffer, space and time are creaturely realities created by God *ex nihilo*. As such, space and time must be said to be *in* creation; creation cannot be said to be *in* space and time.[2] Ontologically speaking, space and time, therefore, and indeed the phenomenal forms and structures which arise therein, including God's church-community, exist only in and with creation, such that they have their ground in the creative and redemptive activity of God. To account for the being of God's church-community in space and time, it is thus necessary to speak theologically about empirical phenomenology, in accordance with, and as a further exemplification of, Bonhoeffer's pneumatological and eschatological 'both/and' ecclesiological methodology.

With the discussion in this chapter being limited to outlining the pneumatological *space* which God's church-community occupies in spatio-temporality, an attempt to outline the eschatological *time* of God's church-community in that self-same reality will be made in Chapter 5. However, to outline in this chapter the *pneumatological* space of God's church-community, and indeed to specify that space further as a *confessional* space,[3] which itself shapes definitively the human empirical form and function(s) of the being of God's church-community as set apart and against the space of the world within the world so as to be with and for the world, the chapter will begin by examining Bonhoeffer's proffered account of the founding of the church at Pentecost in the event of the coming of God the Holy Spirit. In this event, Bonhoeffer suggests, one finds the genesis of the church's own human empirical form and associated vocational function(s). It is this form and its associated vocational

---

[2] See Thomas F. Torrance, *Space, Time and Incarnation* (London: Oxford University Press, 1969), 11. Torrance might be seen to draw out the full import of Bonhoeffer's thought here: the relation between God (as creator) and spatio-temporality (as created) is not a spatial or a temporal relation but a creative (and transcendent) one. God can be neither spatialized nor temporalized because in his own eternal being he is absolutely prior to, and Lord of, the creaturely media of space and time. While God is not limited then by space and time, his active presence *in* space and time – in creation, incarnation and resurrection – nevertheless 'asserts the reality of space and time for God in His relations with us and binds us to space and time in all our relations with Him' (Torrance, *Space, Time and Incarnation*, 24). In other words, God makes himself present and known *in* the medium of space-time.

[3] The specification is my own, not Bonhoeffer's.

function(s), given its pneumatological and eschatological foundation, which leads to the further specification of the pneumatological space of God's church-community as a confessional space. Accordingly, the chapter proceeds, in its second section, to consider certain confessional aspects of this confessional space, looking particularly at the space of proclamation and the space of spiritual care, which Bonhoeffer takes to be definitive of – or, one might say, which fill – the pneumatological and confessional space that the being of God's church-community occupies in space and time. Each confessional space, moreover, is, it will be argued, understood by Bonhoeffer as being *in* the Holy Spirit, in the sense that each space not only is formed in the event of the church's foundation at Pentecost by the coming of God the Holy Spirit but is also operative – functionally speaking – only through the Holy Spirit. In this way, the space of proclamation and the space of spiritual care can be seen to hold together *both* divine *and* human agency in consequence of Bonhoeffer's pneumatological and eschatological 'both/and' ecclesiological methodology. In arguing thus, it will be suggested that in his account of the founding of the church at Pentecost – and indeed in his subsequent understanding of the spaces of proclamation and spiritual care – Bonhoeffer recapitulates in vivid spatial language his argument from *Sanctorum Commmunio* (as explicated in Chapter 3) that the being of God's church-community is actualized in space and time as a sui generis sociological structure by a threefold actualizing work of God the Holy Spirit. Moreover, it will also be suggested that Bonhoeffer is able to conceive of the pneumatological and confessional space of God's church-community as set apart and against the space of the world within the world so as to be with and for the world only because of his pneumatological and apocalyptically eschatological conceptualization of spatio-temporality (as explicated in Chapter 2) in which God's church-community has its being as a particular and contingent socio-historical human community.

II. Pentecost: The event of the foundation of God's church-community

In Part II of Bonhoeffer's *Discipleship*, Bonhoeffer writes that the church as 'the body of Jesus Christ takes up a space on earth', and 'that [which] takes up a space is visible'.[4] Furthermore, the church as Christ's body is visible because of the event of the coming of the Holy Spirit of God at Pentecost. God the Holy Spirit, who, as an 'historic reality', and precisely 'in his visibility', creates God's church-community in space and time and out of the gathered assembly.[5] Bonhoeffer writes: 'The coming of the Spirit and the founding of the church is a visible event, not a matter of invisible inwardness. The Spirit creates for itself space in the world, with visible signs accompanying its own coming.'[6] With the coming of God the Holy Spirit at Pentecost, therefore, 'a bit of world

---

[4] *DBW* 4, 241.
[5] See *DBW* 14, 426 and 427; cf., Chapter 3, Section III.ii of this book.
[6] See *DBW* 14, 426. The church thus becomes visible and is visible only through the work of God the Holy Spirit. The '*kind* of visibility' that 'is to be predicated of the church' is, as Webster puts it,

is created anew', and 'this new creation from the Spirit'[7] is the pneumatological space of God's church-community, and thus the founding of the church's being in space and time. Moreover, in the event of its foundation at Pentecost, and more specifically in the concomitant articulation of the vocation of this new ecclesial creation in Acts 2.42-47, Bonhoeffer sees 'the beginnings and indications' of the church's human empirical form and associated vocational function(s):[8] the apostle's teaching is announced; fellowship is created; the breaking of bread and prayers are enabled; wonders and signs are performed; and possessions and goods are shared – and all in and through the person and work of God the Holy Spirit as the establishing subject of the church-community and its ministry.[9]

As such, the pneumatological space that God's church-community occupies in space and time is, for Bonhoeffer, 'not unequivocal in the world'.[10] The church's founding in the event of the coming of God the Holy Spirit at Pentecost 'is not a matter hidden in a corner, but a visible marking of all who are called' to the church as the city that lies on the hill.[11] As Holmes states, for Bonhoeffer, 'The Spirit's visibility is an ecclesiastical visibility'.[12] Holmes continues: 'The concrete work to which the Spirit gives rise is the church, the visible form of the Spirit's presence in the world'.[13] The Holy Spirit is thus said by Bonhoeffer to expose the church-community (as *Geistgemeinschaft*) 'before the world', and being so exposed the church is subjected immediately – by its own pneumatological visibility – 'to the judgment of the world'.[14] This immediate judgement Bonhoeffer sees being evidenced precisely in the response of some of those gathered in Jerusalem to celebrate the day of Pentecost, and who each had heard the apostles speaking (through the Holy Spirit) in their own native tongue, but nevertheless scorned the reality of the Spirit by deriding the apostles for supposedly speaking intoxicated nonsense.[15] Such 'derision of the world',[16] which arises in consequence of the person and work of God the Holy Spirit in and upon the church-community in the midst of the world, is, for Bonhoeffer, a sure sign that 'the space of the church-community stands out [*abgehoben*] against the space of the world',[17] and is separated or 'definitively set apart'[18] from that latter space as 'a territory with its own authority'[19] or a different form.[20] On the clear demarcation of

---

a '"spiritual" visibility' created by the Spirit's agency, and 'the "phenomenal" form of the church is therefore the phenomenal form of the *church* only in reference to the Spirit's self-gift'. Only by the work of God the Holy Spirit does the church have and engage in the visible phenomena of church life. See Webster, 'On Evangelical Ecclesiology', 25 and 26.

[7] *DBWE* 14, 442.
[8] See *DBW* 14, 431.
[9] See *DBWE* 14, 331, 443–6, 455–7 and 465–6.
[10] *DBW* 14, 427.
[11] Ibid., 426–7.
[12] Holmes, 'The Holy Spirit', 174.
[13] Ibid.
[14] See *DBW* 14, 426 and 427.
[15] See ibid., 427; cf., Acts 2.1-13.
[16] *DBW* 14, 427.
[17] *DBWE* 14, 471.
[18] *DBW* 6, 48.
[19] *DBW* 4, 269.
[20] Ibid., 263.

the pneumatological space of God's church-community from the space of the world, Bonhoeffer is clear:

> The community of the called-out, the ecclesia, the body of Christ on earth ... is the holy church ... the church-community of saints ... and its members are the saints called by God ... sanctified in Jesus Christ ... chosen and set apart before the foundation of the world ... [the church is] God's holy place. God has chosen it. He has made it the [reconciled and purified] church-community of his covenant. ... Now this holy place is the Temple and the Temple is the body of Christ. In the body of Christ the will of God to establish a holy community is thus fulfilled. Set apart from world and sin to be God's possession, the body of Christ is God's holy place in the world. In this holy place God dwells with the Holy Spirit.[21]

Furthermore, the fulfilment of which Bonhoeffer speaks here is itself brought about by the Holy Spirit of God.[22] In and through God the Holy Spirit – the seal (*Siegel*) with which the Christian faithful are locked (*abgeschlossen*) in Christ (in the church) as God's possession – the church-community and its members become God's own indissolubly.[23] The seal cannot be broken because it is secured by God: 'God himself has sealed it and holds the key in his hand.'[24] Thus, being sealed with the unbreakable seal of God the Holy Spirit, God's church-community travels through the world 'like a sealed-up train travelling through a foreign country'.[25] Moreover, this train is assured of reaching its final (salvific) destination for which it awaits and towards which it travels, precisely because the seal with which it is sealed is the Holy Spirit of God who is the pledge of our inheritance towards salvation as God's own people.[26] Consequently, for Bonhoeffer, God's church-community exists in spatio-temporality as 'the living space [*Lebensraum*] of a colony of foreigners'[27] that lives its own life

---

[21] Ibid., 268, 269 and 270.
[22] See ibid., 276.
[23] See ibid.
[24] Ibid.
[25] Ibid. It is interesting to note the trope of Barthian actualism pervading emphatically Bonhoeffer's description here of the 'sealing' of the church and its members in the event of God's *action* – a feature of Barth's theology which Bonhoeffer is often read as having rejected (at least partially) in *Act and Being*, such that Bonhoeffer is positioned, as DeJonge, for example, argues, as 'a theological alternative to Barth' (DeJonge, *Bonhoeffer's Theological Formation*, 39). While DeJonge's exposition of *Act and Being* is without doubt masterful, his over-emphatic reading of both the 'momentary, sheer act' character of Barth's theology, and the 'continuous or historical [being] aspects' of Bonhoeffer's theology (see DeJonge, *Bonhoeffer's Theological Formation*, 39), not only risks misrepresentation of Barth's theology, which might, more properly, be characterized as an 'actualistic *ontology*' (to recall Nimmo's terminology from Chapter 1) but also obscures the deep and abiding affinity between Bonhoeffer and Barth, notwithstanding the critique of Barth present in *Act and Being*. On this deep and abiding affinity, see Andreas Pangritz, *Karl Barth in the Theology of Dietrich Bonhoeffer*, trans. Barbara and Martin Rumscheidt (Grand Rapids: Eerdmans, 1999); and Tom Greggs, 'The Influence of Dietrich Bonhoeffer on Karl Barth', in Matthew D. Kirkpatrick, ed. *Engaging Bonhoeffer: The Impact and Influence of Bonhoeffer's Life and Thought* (Minneapolis: Fortress Press, 2016), 45–63.
[26] See *DBW* 4, 276–7; cf., Eph. 1.13-14.
[27] *DBW* 14, 461.

subject to a foreign power and foreign law as it waits on the One who will come again to come from heaven.[28]

Bonhoeffer thus articulates the space which God's church-community occupies in spatio-temporality as a *pneumatological* space which is (conceived variously as) 'sealed' (*verschlossen*), 'locked-up' (*abgeschlossen*) or (even) 'closed' (*geschlossen*) by God the Holy Spirit in the midst of the world, and so is made to stand out from the space of the world as visibly distinct or set apart in virtue of its pneumatological and eschatological form and associated vocational function(s). In doing so, Bonhoeffer (might be seen) to recapitulate in his account of the founding of the church at Pentecost – perhaps in somewhat surprising and certainly vivid spatial language[29] – the specifically pneumatological and eschatological argument of his doctoral dissertation that God's church-community is actualized in space and time by a threefold actualizing work of God the Holy Spirit. As demonstrated in Chapter 3,[30] that work, firstly, transposes human being (in justification and sanctification) from being in Adam to being in Christ (in the church), thereby creating the *ecclesial* human being (a human being which is oriented and ordered towards God and other human beings in love). That work was seen to be comprised, secondly, by God the Holy Spirit mediating the reciprocal and symbiotic relation of the church and its members being with and for one another and with and for the world, such that the ontic-social relations of God's church-community are rendered unique, and the realization of God's rule and will in the world is the quintessential ecclesial characteristic. Thirdly, and finally, it was seen that God the Holy Spirit generates the sociological forms and functions of the church's objective spirit which are used subsequently by the Holy Spirit of God to build the church in space and time. It is this threefold actualizing work of God the Holy Spirit that Bonhoeffer can be seen now to recapitulate in his account of the founding of the church at Pentecost (and indeed in his subsequent understanding of the spaces of proclamation and spiritual care) in vivid spatial terms.

In recapitulating the first actualizing work of God the Holy Spirit, Bonhoeffer writes that the justified one – the 'total *space*' (*Gesamtraum*)[31] of whose existence the Holy Spirit lays claim to in justification – is taken out of the world into God's holy place, and thereby 'live[s] in a new space of their own [which is God's holy place, the church-community] in the midst of the world'.[32] In the space of this newly created community,[33] the justified one – as the one in whom space itself has now been claimed by God the Holy Spirit – is no longer under the rule of the world, but, being in Christ (in the church), is now under the rule of Christ.[34] Being in Christ (in the church) the

---

[28] See *DBW* 14, 266–7.
[29] On the preponderance of spatial metaphors and descriptors in Bonhoeffer's ecclesial thought, see Donald M. Fergus, 'Dietrich Bonhoeffer's Spatially Structured Ecclesiology: Reconfiguring the Confession of Christ's Presence' (PhD diss., The University of Otago, 2011).
[30] See Chapter 3, Section III.ii of this book.
[31] *DBW* 14, 443.
[32] *DBW* 4, 274.
[33] See ibid., 252.
[34] See ibid. It is important to recall from Chapter 3 that in justification Bonhoeffer understands Jesus Christ (and the church) coming 'into' the individual believer by the work of God the Holy Spirit, such that the Holy Spirit claims the total space of the believer's existence through her being indwelt

justified one is thus no longer in Adam. Moreover, the justified one is preserved in the space of God's church-community into which she has been transposed by God the Holy Spirit in the sanctifying work *of* the Holy Spirit. Bonhoeffer puts it thus:

> The sanctification of the church-community is this: that through God [the Holy Spirit] the church-community is separated from that which is unholy, from sin. Its sanctification is this: that in this [pneumatological] act of sealing-off, the church-community has become God's own chosen possession, God's dwelling place on earth, the place from which judgment and reconciliation go out to all the world. Sanctification is this: that Christians henceforth become completely oriented towards and preserved unto Christ's future that is coming, and towards which they travel.[35]

Bonhoeffer conceives of justification, sanctification and even consummation, then, in spatial terms. Each concept is indexed pneumatologically and eschatologically to the pneumatological space of God's church-community. The human being is transposed into this pneumatological space and thereby (re-) created as an ecclesial human being (justification); the justified one abides in this pneumatological space (sanctification); and the sanctified one is preserved in this pneumatological space until the day of Jesus Christ upon which the train on which she travels reaches its final destination (consummation). Indeed, for Bonhoeffer, 'the aim of the [pneumatological] act of sealing-off [God's church-community from the space of the world] is σωτηρία. Everything is preserved towards that end, so that "at the end" we will be preserved'.[36] Believers, therefore, are justified; the justified, therefore, are sanctified; and the sanctified, therefore (on the day of Christ's future *parousia*), are saved. All this (according to Bonhoeffer) is only in and through the act of God the Holy Spirit, by which Jesus Christ is made our righteousness, sanctification and redemption.[37] In the act of 'sealing-off' God's church-community, the seal of God the Holy Spirit draws, therefore, a clear dividing line between the pneumatological space of God's church-

---

by the Spirit, and through the Spirit by both God the Son and God the Father (see Chapter 3, Section III.ii, n.189 and n.191 of this book). By the work of the Holy Spirit, the one who is justified is, on the one hand, transposed into Christ, such that Christ, in the words of C. F. D. Moule, is 'the "place", the *locus*, where believers are found' (C. F. D. Moule, *The Origin of Christology* (Cambridge: Cambridge University Press, 1977), 56). Believers are thus *in* Christ *through* the Holy Spirit, and Christ, not the world, is the space of their new present existence. It is the action of God the Holy Spirit – as the agent of new creation – on and within persons that brings those persons to life *extra se* in Christ. In doing so, the Holy Spirit is (as the creed affirms) the giver of life, for persons can only have life in Christ (in the church). However, on the other hand, as the Holy Spirit transposes the justified one into life in Christ (in the church), Christ himself (and along with Christ, God the Father) comes by the work of the Holy Spirit 'into' the believer, being 'in' her as she is in Christ. It is through the Holy Spirit that Christ, conversely, to use Mehrdad Fatehi's words, 'is present and active in and among his people exercising his new covenant lordship over and among them' (Mehrdad Fatehi, *The Spirit's Relation to the Risen Lord in Paul: An Examination of Its Christological Implications* (Tübingen: Mohr Siebeck, 2000), 269). It is in virtue of being indwelt by Christ *through* the Holy Spirit of God that the believer is in Christ under his lordship and power.

[35] *DBW* 4, 277.
[36] *DBW* 14, 727.
[37] See *DBW* 4, 296.

community in the world (in which justification and sanctification is (only) thereby possible, and in relation to which consummation will take place), and the space of the world 'against' which God's church-community stands.[38]

Moreover, since the church-community as such is the *polis* set on a hill, the 'political' nature of the church in being established by God the Holy Spirit as God's own possession in *distinction* to the world is an inherent aspect of the church's own sanctification.[39] Critically, however, in conceiving God's church-community as a clearly demarcated pneumatological space of its own in the midst of the world, and thus as a space which is separated from and set with its own internal 'politics' against the space of the world, Bonhoeffer does not think of the church as pursuing its vocation established in the event of its foundation at Pentecost concerned only with its *own* self-preservation. Yes, with the coming of God the Holy Spirit at Pentecost 'a bit of world is created anew' and 'sealed-off' from the world as 'a new act of creation on God's part'.[40] However, as this newly created 'bit of world', God's church-community, because it is created of God's Spirit, is concerned with the Holy Spirit of God and his Word, and thus with '*implementing* this new creation from the Spirit' *in* the world.[41] The very point of God's church-community being sealed-off from the space of the world as a visibly distinct pneumatological space by the Holy Spirit of God is precisely that 'world *be* world and church-community *be* church-community, and that, nevertheless, God's Word goes out from the church-community all over the world, as the message that the earth and that which is in it is the Lord's'.[42]

In making this point, Bonhoeffer can be seen to recapitulate in his account of the founding of the church at Pentecost – and again in vivid spatial terms – what was demonstrated in Chapter 3 to be the second actualizing work of God the Holy Spirit by which God's church-community is actualized (according to Bonhoeffer) in space and time.[43] That work was said to be the mediation by the Holy Spirit of God of the reciprocal and symbiotic relation of the church and its members being with and for one another and with and for the world, such that the ontic-social relations of God's church-community are rendered unique and the rule and will of God is realized in the world by one's own love of God and neighbour through the Holy Spirit. Indeed, being transposed into the pneumatological space of God's church-community by God the Holy Spirit in justification, and being preserved in that space by the Holy Spirit of God in sanctification, the human being as such is recreated as an ecclesial human being: the human being that is oriented and ordered towards God and other human beings in love.[44]

In consequence of this pneumatological transposition and preservation (or recreation) of the human being, the church and its members are said by Bonhoeffer

---

[38] See *DBW* 4, 277.
[39] See ibid.
[40] *DBWE* 14, 442.
[41] See *DBW* 14, 430.
[42] *DBW* 4, 277–8 (emphasis added).
[43] See Chapter 3, Section III.ii of this book.
[44] In this way, the work of God the Holy Spirit is to actualize in space and time that for which redemption is effected – fellowship with God and with one another. See Webster, 'On Evangelical Ecclesiology', 25–6.

to *be* both with and for one another and with and for the world, such that the pnuematological space which the being of God's church-community occupies in space and time exists structurally and actively *out*side of itself: the church and its members *are*, and can only *be* God's church-community, as they are *with* and *for* others. This eccentric existence (to borrow Kelsey's terminology)[45] of God's church-community Bonhoeffer sees as having its genesis in the event of the church's foundation at Pentecost, for the coming of God the Holy Spirit constitutes the church as a new act of creation precisely because 'the Holy Spirit leads the church-community *into community*'.[46] The Holy Spirit comes upon the community of disciples 'in words comprehensible to *everyone*'; Peter proclaims through the Spirit 'the full and free grace of God, which summons *the people* to action, to repentance, and to new life'; and through the Spirit 'the church-community engages in *missionary* activity'.[47] With the coming of God the Holy Spirit and in the concomitant (and pneumatologically mediated) concern for the implementation of the Spirit's act of new creation *in* the world, the community of disciples is turned *out*wards: *out* of the house in which they are staying and devoting themselves constantly to building-up a community oriented and ordered towards God and *itself*, and *to*wards the crowd gathered around it.[48] In this 'turning outward' the community of disciples 'break into the world' as a missionary *church*-community.[49] But by its very nature as a *missionary* church-community this community moves to summon those outside the church, who by the *cor curvum in se* are *self*-possessed, into being in the church – that is, into an ecclesial way of being human, being oriented and ordered by God the Holy Spirit *out* towards God and other human beings in love. It is for this reason why the church is said by Bonhoeffer to 'scorn' the reality of the Holy Spirit when it 'draws back (into it*self*)' in 'invisible *inward*ness'.[50]

With the coming of God the Holy Spirit at Pentecost, 'individual hearts are turned out toward others by the Spirit within the church'.[51] At once, however, as Greggs goes on to state, 'the corporate heart of the church community is turned out toward the world' in its propulsion by the Spirit beyond its own communitarian bounds.[52] As Bonhoeffer writes, and according to its own eccentric identity and vocation established in the event of the church's foundation at Pentecost, the pneumatological space of God's church-community 'does not, therefore, exist just for *itself*, instead

> *its existence is* already always something that reaches *far beyond it*. This is because it is not the space of a cult that would have to fight for its own existence in the world. Rather, the space of the church is the place in which *witness* is given to the foundation of all reality in Jesus Christ. The church is the place where it is *testified*

---

[45] See Kelsey, *Eccentric Existence*.
[46] *DBW* 14, 429.
[47] See respectively, *DBWE* 14, 439, 441 (amended; cf., *DBW* 14, 429) and 721.
[48] See Acts 1.12-14; and 2.1-2, 6 and 14ff.
[49] See *DBW* 14, 724.
[50] See ibid., 427.
[51] Tom Greggs, '*Communio* Ecclesiology: The Spirit's Work of Salvation in the Life of the Church', in Myk Habets, ed. *Third Article Theology: A Pneumatological Dogmatics* (Minneapolis: Fortress Press, 2016), 363.
[52] See ibid., and Greggs, *Theology against Religion*, 143, respectively; cf., *CD*, IV/3, 764.

and taken seriously that God has reconciled the world to himself in Christ, that God so loved the world that God gave his Son for it. The space of the church is not there to fight with the world for a piece of its territory, but precisely to *testify* to the world that it remains the world, namely, the world that is loved and reconciled by God.[53]

It is in its witness and testimony – its *confession* – through the person and work of God the Holy Spirit to the gospel of God that the pneumatological space of God's church-community exists as God's *church*-community with and for others: for the *world's* sake and not for the sake of itself. In this its orientation and order *to*wards God and the world, Bonhoeffer, moreover, locates (and in doing so can be seen to recapitulate his doctoral dissertation's argument of) 'the essential difference between the church and a "religious community"'.[54] Whereas the latter as *Gemeinschaft* 'has its end in itself, in the "religious" as the highest – one might even say: God-given – value',[55] the former, as God's *church*-community, actualized in space and time by God the Holy Spirit and existing as a sociological structure sui generis, is concerned with the realization of 'God's will towards the new creation'.[56] As such, the 'end' of God's church-community is not in itself but in God's will to rule in love. The church, then, is not an end in itself (*Gemeinschaft*) but a means to an end (*Gesellschaft*) – that end being God's will to rule in love and thus far beyond the church and its members. However, God's will towards the new creation is at once God's will towards the church itself, for the church *is* the new creation of the Spirit and 'the *goal* of God's ways on earth'.[57] The church, then, *is* an end in itself (*Gemeinschaft*), but it is as such only *as* a means to an end (*Gesellschaft*) in which God's will to rule in love is realized in the church's being oriented and ordered (as *Herrschaftsverband*) *to*wards God and the world by God the Holy Spirit.[58] Bonhoeffer writes: 'The reality of the church as an end in itself ... consists precisely in its being for the world.'[59] Put otherwise, the pneumatological space of God's church-community as a distinct polity (*Gemeinwesen*) exists in the world subject to 'a double divine purpose', to which it must do justice: to be 'oriented [as a means to an end] towards the world, and precisely in that orientation [being] oriented [as an end in itself] towards itself as the place where Jesus Christ is present'.[60] Therefore, Bonhoeffer continues: 'It is the particular characteristic of the church as a distinct polity that within the de*limited*ness of its own spiritual and material domain it gives expression to the *un*limitedness of the message of Christ, and it is precisely the unlimitedness of the message of Christ that calls the world back into the limitedness of the church-community.'[61]

[53] *DBW* 6, 49 (emphasis added).
[54] *DBW* 14, 430.
[55] Ibid.
[56] Ibid. Cf., Chapter 3, Section III.ii of this book.
[57] See *DBW* 14, 430; and *DBWE* 6, 405 (emphasis added).
[58] On Bonhoeffer's understanding of God's church-community as a pneumatologically constituted *Liebesgemeinschaft* that exists as a sociological structure sui generis by its combining and surmounting (at once) the three types of socio-historical human community *Gemeinschaft*, *Gesellschaft* and *Herrschaftsverband*, see Chapter 3, Section II and III of this book.
[59] *DBW* 6, 411.
[60] Ibid., 409.
[61] Ibid.

For Bonhoeffer, then, the pneumatological space that God's church-community occupies in spatio-temporality is there, ultimately, *for* the world's sake: for the world to find in it, by its confession of the gospel of God through God the Holy Spirit, the world's own fulfilment, standing as the church-community does as the goal of, and the axis around which rotate, God's actions in-and-for the world.[62] To this end, therefore, *God's* church-community *must be* God's *church*-community – as a clearly demarcated pneumatological and confessional space of its own in the midst of the space of the world – in order for the world to be *truly* the world.[63] This is precisely why, for Bonhoeffer, the church, as a visibly distinct space in the world with its own pneumatological and eschatological form and associated vocational function(s), is not to fight with the world for space in the world, but rather is to *confess* to the world that it remains the world – the object, that is, of God's reconciling, redeeming and judging love. Indeed, 'the church can defend its *own* space [in the world] only by fighting, not *for space*, but *for* the salvation of the world.'[64] In fact, for the church to fight otherwise would be for the church to cease to be God's *church*-community and to become instead 'a "religious society"' fighting only for its own sake, and not for the sake of the world by its confession of God's gospel.[65] Bonhoeffer writes: 'The church *is there* only *as a confessing* church, that is as a church which confesses to its Lord and against his enemies. A confessionless or confession-free church is not the church.'[66] Ziegler is right, therefore, to observe that, while Bonhoeffer's conception of God's church-community as the church *for others* necessitates that God's *church*-community exist in the midst of the world *for* these concrete others in the world, that it is *the church* for others necessitates that *God's* church-community can exist in the midst of the world *for* the world only as a *distinctive* community in and *from* the world.[67] The fact of Christian difference,[68] then, or, in Bonhoeffer's terms, the visible reality of the pneumatological space of *God's* church-community set apart and against the space of the world by the seal of God the Holy Spirit, is the sine qua non of God's *church*-community being (with and) *for* the world (and its members being (with and) *for* one another). Indeed, God's

---

[62] See ibid., 408; cf., Wolfhart Pannenberg, *Theology and the Kingdom of God*, ed. Richard John Neuhaus (Philadelphia: The Westminster Press, 1977), 92, wherein (echoing Bonhoeffer) Pannenberg writes: 'The Church forfeits her right to existence when she regards her existence as an end in itself. Secular society needs the Church. Secular society cannot remain secular – aware of its own preliminary character – without the Church as a separate institution to remind the present order of its provisionality.' For discussion of the preliminary character of the world, see Chapter 5, esp. Section II of this book.

[63] The force of Bonhoeffer's point has, most notably, been recapitulated emphatically by Hauerwas in his tireless insistence on the necessity of the church to be first of all the church so that the world can be the world. See, for example, Hauerwas, *A Community of Character*, 50; Hauerwas, *After Christendom? How the Church Is to Behave If Freedom, Justice, and a Christian Nation Are Bad Ideas* (Nashville: Abingdon Press, 1991), 35; Hauerwas, *A Better Hope: Resources for a Church Confronting Capitalism, Democracy, and Postmodernity* (Grand Rapids: Brazos Press, 2000), 157; Hauerwas, *Approaching the End: Eschatological Reflections on Church, Politics, and Life* (Grand Rapids: Eerdmans, 2013), *xi*; and Hauerwas, *The Work of Theology*, 50.

[64] *DBW* 6, 49 (emphasis added).

[65] See ibid., 49–50.

[66] *DBW* 14, 389 (emphasis added).

[67] See Philip G. Ziegler, 'God, Christ, and Church in the DDR – Wolf Krötke as an Interpreter of Bonhoeffer's Theology', in Kirkpatrick, ed. *Engaging Bonhoeffer*, 207.

[68] See ibid., 208.

church-community can exist only as the church *for others* because, as Ziegler notes, it does not exist in space and time *as* those others.[69] In the words of Ernst Lange: 'It is – to put it in exaggerated terms – "church *for* the world" in that the church dares in the obedience of faith to be uncompromisingly a church *against* the world.'[70]

Bonhoeffer's conception of the pneumatological and confessional space that God's church-community occupies in spatio-temporality is thus fundamentally tensile and dynamic: or else, one might say, is eschatological and properly apocalyptic, being derived as it is from his pneumatological and apocalyptically eschatological conceptualization of spatio-temporality,[71] or, in the words of Barry Harvey, from Bonhoeffer's 'apocalyptic imagination' which 'traverses the eschatological interval between the contingency of the present under divine judgment … and the uniting of all things in Christ', and thus at once is *for* and *against* the space of the world.[72] Indeed, the church and its members are 'to abide *in* the world', writes Bonhoeffer, 'for the sake of mounting a frontal assault [*Angriff*] against the world', such that the church's necessary contradiction of the world, in order to be entirely visible to the world, can be 'carried out in [nothing but] the world'.[73] It follows that God's church-community precisely as the pneumatological and confessional space set apart and against the space of the world must neither withdraw schismatically *from* the space of the world nor participate unqualifiedly *in* the space of the world. In fact, to do so would be for the church to abstract itself from the radical ontological, epistemological and moral consequences of God's gospel as an apocalypse, in accordance with which space and time is now 'stretched out' (*ausgespannt*) or 'suspended' (*eingespannt*) between God's 'Yes' and 'No'[74] – that is, between God's being *for* and *against* the world. Thus, if the church withdraws schismatically from the world, the church, in J. Christiaan Beker's words, 'betrays the death and resurrection of Christ as God's redemptive plan *for* the world' that is effected *in* the world and 'threatens to become a purely sectarian apocalyptic movement'.[75] However, if the church participates unqualifiedly in the world, the church 'threatens to become another "worldly" phenomenon, accommodating itself to whatever the world will buy and so becoming a *part* of the ["old" or present (fallen)] world'[76] *against* which the death and resurrection of Christ stands decisively.[77] Moreover, in both a sectarian withdrawal from the world and an accommodationist participation in the world, and from the vantage point of the eschatological and properly apocalyptic register of Bonhoeffer's ecclesial thought, the church advocates (problematically) a false understanding of spatiality itself – one which divides reality as a whole into 'two parts' (*zwei Teile*): a 'sacred' or 'Christian

---

[69] See Ziegler, 'God, Christ, and Church in the DDR', 208.
[70] Ernst Lange, *Kirche für die Welt: Aufsätze zur Theorie kirchlichen Handelns*, ed. Rüdiger Schloz (München: Chr. Kaiser Verlag, 1981), 38 (emphasis added).
[71] See Chapter 2, Section II of this book.
[72] See Harvey, *Taking Hold of the Real*, 34–46 [44] and 254–6.
[73] See *DBW* 4, 260.
[74] See *DBW* 6, 50 and 251.
[75] Beker, *Paul's Apocalyptic Gospel*, 41 (emphasis added).
[76] Ibid. (emphasis added).
[77] For discussion of Bonhoeffer's own construction of these two possible movements as the way of radicalism and the way of compromise, respectively, see Chapter 5, Section II.i of this book.

sphere' (the *regnum gratiae*), and a 'profane' or 'worldly sphere' (the *regnum naturae*), which critically are perceived not in tensile and dynamic terms but in rigid and static terms, and thus as two parts of reality that bump-up or push against one another (*Aneinanderstoßen*) with each battling the other for a piece of its territory.[78] In other words, by either a sectarian withdrawal from the world or an accommodationist participation in the world, the spatiality of reality is conceived by the church dualistically, with two separate spheres ('one divine, holy, supernatural, and Christian; the other worldly, profane, natural, and unchristian')[79] being positioned alongside and (set) opposite each other as conflictual spaces which together exist within 'a unitary space'[80] of reality.[81]

Such thinking is problematic for Bonhoeffer because as he states it 'fails to appreciate the original unity of these opposites in the reality of Christ [*Christuswirklichkeit*], and, as an afterthought, erects in its place a forced unity of opposites by a sacred or profane system that overreaches them'.[82] This system then maintains the static opposition of two separate spheres, which, in reality – given the apocalypse of God's gospel by which spatio-temporality has been remade as eschatological reality – comprise one tensile and dynamic sphere.[83] Indeed, in the reality of Christ as the eschatological person par excellence, 'God and the reality of the world are united together', such that there is only *one* reality – the eschatological reality of God in Jesus Christ through the Holy Spirit.[84] Not only then does the space of the world have no reality independent of this eschatological reality, precisely because in *this* reality the reality of the world has both '*been* accepted' by God and is 'in the movement' of '*becoming* accepted by God',[85] but the space of God's church-community has no reality independent of the space of the world. Bonhoeffer writes: 'What is Christian does not exist otherwise than *in* what is of the world, the "supernatural" only *in* the natural, the holy only *in* the profane, the revelational only *in* the rational.'[86] This is not to say, however, that Bonhoeffer thus merges two separate spheres into one simple sphere. Despite there being only one eschatological *Christuswirklichkeit* in which God and the reality of the world are united, it is critical for Bonhoeffer (*contra* 'hard' ethnographic ecclesiology) that what is Christian is not *identical* with what is of the world, that the natural is not *equivalent* to the supernatural, and that the revelational is not the *precise coordinate* of the rational.[87] Bonhoeffer writes: 'This belonging together of God and world established in Christ does not allow a *static*-spatial distinction, *nor does it abolish the difference between church-*

---

[78] See *DBW* 6, 42 and 41. For a comprehensive and helpful account of Bonhoeffer's engagement with what traditionally has been known as Lutheran two-kingdoms thinking, see DeJonge, *Bonhoeffer's Reception of Luther*, 77–141. For a discussion of two-kingdoms thinking in Luther's own theology (and its two-cities precedent in Augustine), see Heinrich Bornkamm, *Luther's Doctrine of the Two Kingdoms in the Context of His Theology*, trans. Karl H. Hertz (Philadelphia: Fortress Press, 1966).
[79] *DBW* 6, 41.
[80] Harvey, *Taking Hold of the Real*, 255.
[81] See *DBWE* 6, 58 and 59.
[82] *DBW* 6, 44.
[83] See Chapter 2, Section II of this book.
[84] See *DBW* 6, 43–4.
[85] See *DBWE* 6, 59 (emphasis added).
[86] *DBW* 6, 44 (emphasis added).
[87] See ibid., 45.

community and world.⁸⁸ As Bonhoeffer continues, the question arises of 'how to think about this difference without falling back into [static] spatial images.'⁸⁹ The answer, he posits, lies in the type of unity which can be seen (and must be said) to exist between these non-identical aspects of the one *Christuswirklichkeit*. It is a 'polemical' unity which is given only *in* 'this *last things* reality',⁹⁰ and as such is necessarily tensile and dynamic in accordance with the eschatological reality in which it is given: a reality *in* the *movement between* 'the world's both *having been accepted* and *becoming accepted* by God in Christ' through God the Holy Spirit.⁹¹ Moreover, it is precisely this dynamic tension of the polemical unity of the one sphere of spatio-temporality that the church must preserve – against any false thinking of two separate spheres – if God's *church*-community is to exist *in* the world as the pneumatological and confessional space *for* the world by its being *against* the world. Indeed, to collapse this polemically unified dynamic tension of the world's affirmation through its negation, either by a sectarian withdrawal of the church *from* the world or by an accommodationist participation of the church *in* the

---

⁸⁸ *DBW* 6, 54 (emphasis added).
⁸⁹ Ibid.
⁹⁰ See ibid., 45 (emphasis added).
⁹¹ See *DBWE* 6, 59 (emphasis added). McBride's assertion that 'Bonhoeffer's theology in *Ethics* supplements [and progresses] the argument in *Act and Being* [in which human beings are always either in Adam or in Christ] by re-establishing being-in-Christ with Christ-reality [*Christuswirklichkeit*], *within which the whole world dwells*' is, therefore, problematic (see McBride, *The Church for the World*, 128 (emphasis added)). The assertion is problematic because it fails to appreciate the fundamental significance of apocalyptic eschatology in Bonhoeffer's understanding of *Christuswirklichkeit* and the concomitant sense of motion which thereby pertains inherently to spatio-temporality as eschatological reality, and which as such has its being in its being suspended between having been accepted and becoming accepted by God. This tension also pertains inherently to Bonhoeffer's theological ontology of human personhood and his concomitant understanding of human being as being in Adam or in Christ (in the church). The dualism that McBride sees Bonhoeffer constructing by this ontology of human 'being in' is not, therefore, 'too rigid to square with [Bonhoeffer's] later understanding that all reality is Christ-reality' (McBride, *The Church for the World*, 127), precisely because the common and tensile denominator of both concepts as Bonhoeffer conceives them is that they are pneumatologically determined and thus set in a strictly eschatological and properly apocalyptic register. As such, both human being and spatio-temporality are in movement between having been accepted and becoming accepted by God. Moreover, that they are in movement would seem to question the validity of McBride's (related) argument that the *whole* world already dwells with*in* the reality of Christ – an argument which (seemingly) is derivative of her prior (problematic) claim that '*all* of humanity is accepted, judged, *and reconciled* to Christ' (McBride, *The Church for the World*, 127). That the world has been accepted (and judged) and is now in the movement of being and becoming accepted by God in Jesus Christ does indeed mean that the whole world and all of humanity within it is *accepted* by God, but this acceptance does not mean – nor can it mean in light of Christ's (future) *parousia* – that the *whole* world and *all* of humanity is now reconciled to Christ, such that their being is *in* Christ (in the church). Bonhoeffer writes: 'The church-community is separated from the world by nothing other than this, that it believes in the reality of being accepted by God, which belongs to all the world, and precisely in accepting this to be valid for itself it testifies to it being valid for all the world' (*DBW* 6, 54). In other words, the church and its members believe (by faith and in hope) that they are accepted (and judged) by God and so *are* reconciled to Christ having been transposed from being in Adam to being in Christ. However, the world – and critically so – does not believe that it is so accepted (and judged) and so despite *being* accepted (and judged) by God it is *not* yet reconciled to Christ. To this extent the world remains ontologically in Adam. With respect to Bonhoeffer's theological ontology of human personhood, see Chapter 3, Section II.i.a of this book, and on Bonhoeffer's pneumatological and apocalyptically eschatological determination of spatio-temporality and human being, see respectively, Chapter 2, Section II and Chapter 3, Section II and III.

world, is for God's *church*-community to negate the sine qua non by which it actually exists as *God's* church-community *for* the sake of the fulfilment of the world – that is, the church's being sealed-off from the space of the world by the seal of God the Holy Spirit as a visibly distinct pneumatological and confessional space in the world. Thus, Bonhoeffer writes: 'In the name of a better worldliness what is Christian must be used polemically against what is of the world.'[92] But, he continues: 'This polemical use must not be allowed to result … in a self-serving and static sacred-sphere [*Sakralität*].'[93] The church ensures this precisely by its own *confession* of the apocalyptic gospel of God. As it has been demonstrated, this confession is derivative of the event of the church's foundation at Pentecost as a visible reality set apart and *against* the space of the world by God the Holy Spirit. Furthermore, the church's confession is brought about *in* the world by the Holy Spirit of God *for* the world, and through this confession the world is enabled by God the Holy Spirit to come to its own fulfilment. The end and goal of the pneumatological space that God's church-community occupies in spatio-temporality is, then, not to be there for its own sake, but for the sake of the world through its confessing as God's church-community to the gospel of God in the world.

III. God's church-community: Confessional aspects

Given the preceding discussion of Bonhoeffer's account of the foundation of God's church-community at Pentecost, and the derivative delineation of the space that the being of God's church-community occupies in spatio-temporality as pneumatological and confessional, it is now apposite that this chapter proceeds to consider certain aspects of this confessional space. These aspects might be seen as confessional (and functional) spaces that together fill the pneumatological and confessional space that God's church-community is in space and time as a socio-historical human community; the chapter will look at the 'spaces' of proclamation and spiritual care. Furthermore, because these spaces are formed (according to Bonhoeffer) in the event of the church's foundation at Pentecost by the coming of God the Holy Spirit, and operate functionally only through the Holy Spirit, Bonhoeffer articulates each space as being *in* the Holy Spirit. This pneumatological and eschatological construction of the spaces of proclamation and spiritual care proceeds, therefore, to exemplify (as we shall see) Bonhoeffer's pneumatological and eschatological 'both/and' ecclesiological methodology, in that *both* divine *and* human agency are said to be held together in each space in and through the Holy Spirit of God. Moreover, in articulating each space thus, Bonhoeffer can be seen to recapitulate – and again in vivid spatial terms – what was demonstrated in Chapter 3 to be the third actualizing work of God the Holy Spirit by which God's church-community is actualized: the Holy Spirit's actual generation and subsequent use of the sociological forms and functions of the church's objective spirit to build God's church-community in space and time.[94]

---

[92] *DBW* 6, 45.
[93] Ibid.
[94] See Chapter 3, Section III.ii of this book.

i. The 'space' of proclamation

The first (and perhaps most substantial) aspect of the pneumatological and confessional space that God's church-community occupies in spatio-temporality, and which Bonhoeffer articulates as being *in* the Holy Spirit, is the 'space' of proclamation. As the new ecclesial creation *of* the Holy Spirit, God's church-community is the pneumatological and confessional space in which witness is given *through* the Holy Spirit of God. This witness is, in a manner following Peter's at Pentecost, witness to Jesus Christ as Lord and Messiah. Bonhoeffer writes: 'The church ... does not abandon the world to itself but calls it to come under the rule of Christ.'[95] The 'goal' of this calling is not the 'Christianizing' (*Verchristlichung*) or 'churching' (*Verkirchlichung*) of the world, but rather – and through repentance and baptism, and thus through receipt of the gift of God the Holy Spirit – to 'liberate the world for true worldliness', which itself is established in Christ (in the church).[96] Furthermore, this call (according to Bonhoeffer) goes forth from the church to the world pre-eminently in the word preached.[97] Indeed, the office or ministry of proclamation (*das Amt der Verkündigung*) is the mandate given to the church.[98] Bonhoeffer writes: 'God wants a place in which, up to the time of the end of the world, God's word again and again will be spoken, pronounced, passed-on, expounded, and spread. The word that in Jesus Christ came from heaven wants to come again in the form of human speech.'[99] In other words, while the content of what the church is to proclaim is utterly fixed or objectively determined as *God's* word,[100] that it is the *church's* to proclaim is for that content to be necessarily transmitted subjectively through human speech. Moreover, the *divine* content or constant of this *human* speech,[101] notwithstanding the divine intention that such speech go forth from the church 'again and again' and thus in a contemporized form

---

[95] *DBW* 16, 556–7.
[96] Ibid., 560.
[97] On Bonhoeffer and preaching, see Clyde E. Fant, *Bonhoeffer: Worldly Preaching* (Nashville: Thomas Nelson, 1975); Michael Pasquarello III, *Dietrich Bonhoeffer and the Theology of a Preaching Life* (Waco: Baylor University Press, 2017); and Keir Shreeves, 'Bonhoeffer's Homiletics: The Spirit-Impelled Word of the Church for the Church' (PhD diss., University of Aberdeen, 2019).
[98] See *DBW* 6, 399–400.
[99] Ibid., 399. It is important to note that, for Bonhoeffer, the offices of *God's* church-community, as an aspect of its vocational order established in the event of its foundation at Pentecost, are of divine origin and nature – they are given to the church by *God* – and as such are there to serve the church. The offices, Bonhoeffer writes, are '"ministries" (διακονία) (1 Cor. 12:4)'. He continues: 'They are established by God (1 Cor. 12:28), by Christ (Eph. 4:11), by the Holy Spirit (Acts 20:28) *within* the church-community, not *by* the church-community' (*DBW* 4, 245–6). Furthermore, for Bonhoeffer, it is the Spirit who gives the gifts (χαρίσματα) that are necessary for the performance of the offices within the church-community (see *DBW* 14, 454). However, the fact that the offices are established and performed within God's *church*-community means at once that Bonhoeffer conceives them as being in no way independent of the socio-historical *human* community that the church in space and time is – the offices are *given* to the church by God (see *DBWE* 6, 397; and *DBWE* 14, 462–71). Indeed, the offices, notwithstanding their divine origin and nature, are a product, Bonhoeffer argues, of the church's objective spirit as 'the *bearer of the social activity of the Holy Spirit*' (see *DBWE* 1, 233). Thus, by the work of God the Holy Spirit *both* divine *and* human agency can be seen to exist in the offices together, and the offices thereby to exemplify Bonhoeffer's 'both/and' pneumatological and eschatological ecclesiological methodology.
[100] See *DBWE* 14, 443; and *DBWE* 4, 226.
[101] See *DBWE* 14, 444.

subject to change,[102] is guaranteed precisely because *this* human speech, witnessing as it does to the eschatological and apocalyptic reality of Jesus Christ, is itself the work of God the Holy Spirit. In this sense, this human speech (the word preached within God's church-community) is *didache*, and in this the Holy Spirit speaks. The Holy Spirit is, for Bonhoeffer, the reality of this *didache*, and accordingly this *didache* carries within it the promise of the Holy Spirit.[103]

For Bonhoeffer, then, the preached word of the office of proclamation is thus 'truly *God's* word in *human* words'.[104] The preached word is this because God the Holy Spirit speaks in those human words and speaks in such a way to summon those outside the church-community *in*to the church by receiving for themselves the gift of the Holy Spirit through repentance and baptism.[105] Accordingly, the preached word carries within it 'an inherent motion towards church-community'.[106] The preached word seeks to accept 'old' or sinful humanity-in-Adam and to transpose that humanity into 'new' or justified humanity-in-Christ (in the church) as humanity which is oriented and ordered towards God and other human beings in love – something which the preached word is enabled to do precisely because God the Holy Spirit works into the hearers of the word the faith that Christ *has* accepted them and *will* accept them again today.[107] The preached word of grace is thus, as Holmes observes, 'not a word that the church can summon on its own accord'.[108] The Spirit brings this word.[109] Indeed, for Bonhoeffer, 'the *concretissimum* [of the gospel of God] can be spoken only by the Holy Spirit' and 'every *concretum* of human words remains an *abstractum* when the Holy Spirit himself has not said them'.[110] The Holy Spirit alone enables the word preached as a *human* word to go forth from the church to the world as a *divine* word. This word has the power to effect in space and time the building-up of God's *church*-community by its calling those outside the church to let themselves be summoned to the church. The purpose of the preached word is that through it the Holy Spirit of God brings individual spirits under the rule of God and thereby makes them members of the church-community.[111] In this way, the word preached is by the Spirit a divine word which bears 'the social activity of the Holy Spirit', notwithstanding the 'contingency, imperfection, and sin' with which the preached word as a human word is necessarily fraught.[112] The Holy Spirit of God thus actualizes God's church-community in space and time by its use of the preached word of the office of proclamation as one of the constitutive sociological forms and functions of the church's objective spirit, the

---

[102] *DBW* 14, 479; cf., *DBWE* 1, 233.
[103] See *DBW* 14, 432.
[104] *DBWE* 4, 227.
[105] See *DBWE* 14, 441; cf., *DBW* 14, 539: '"being" … comes from the outside, it is bestowed upon you through the word of God, through baptism.' For discussion of Bonhoeffer's account of baptism as an aspect of the space of proclamation, see the paragraphs that follow.
[106] *DBW* 4, 243.
[107] See ibid., 244.
[108] Holmes, 'The Holy Spirit', 170.
[109] See *DBWE* 6, 290.
[110] *DBW* 12, 228.
[111] See *DBWE* 1, 234.
[112] See ibid., 233.

existence and efficacy of which is itself derivative of, and guaranteed by, God the Holy Spirit.[113]

The logic inherent to Bonhoeffer's articulation of the office of proclamation in the word preached as one of the constitutive sociological forms and functions of the church's objective spirit is mirrored in his treatment of the sacraments of baptism and Eucharist as confessional (and functional) acts of that self-same office, and which, by their witness to Jesus Christ as Lord and Messiah, further delineate the space of proclamation within the pneumatological and confessional space that God's church-community occupies in spatio-temporality. Bonhoeffer writes: 'Sacraments are acts of the church-community and, like preaching, they unite within themselves the objective spirit of the church-community and the Holy Spirit who is operating through it.'[114] Sacraments are at once *both* the gracious gift of *God and* the *human* act of the church-community and its members: essentially, and paradoxically, sacraments are a 'passive action'[115] in virtue of the person and work of God the Holy Spirit. Baptism is thus according to Bonhoeffer: 'not something that human beings offer to God, but instead is the *offer of Jesus Christ*' to human beings *through the Spirit*, and as such 'requires a passive role on our human part'.[116] The offer or 'gift of baptism', writes Bonhoeffer

> is the Holy Spirit. The Holy Spirit is Christ himself dwelling in the hearts of the believers. ... The baptized are the house in which the Holy Spirit has made his dwelling (οἰκεῖ). The Holy Spirit guarantees that Jesus Christ remains present with us and his community. ... By the sending of the Holy Spirit into the hearts of the baptized, the certainty of knowing Jesus is not only received, but will be built up and strengthened through the closeness of the community.[117]

Through the gift of the Holy Spirit, then, the baptized receives Christ into her heart. She is baptized *into* Jesus Christ,[118] being transposed from being in Adam to being in Christ (in the church) and being oriented and ordered thereby towards God and other human beings as one who has been 'rescued from the rule of the world' and '[delivered] from the last judgment'.[119] This is to say, baptism, by reception of (Christ through) God the Holy Spirit, is 'the actual consummated transposition of human being' into the church as Christ's body, the 'act of sealing-off' the baptized 'in the [pneumatological and] eschatological church-community for the day of judgment'.[120] The gift received (passively) in baptism is the bestowal of ecclesial 'being', which itself might be seen to constitute 'the eschatological character of baptism'.[121] Notwithstanding that human beings are, in this sense, the 'purely passive' subject of baptism,[122] baptism

---

[113] See Chapter 3, Section III.ii of this book.
[114] *DBWE* 1, 240.
[115] *DBWE* 4, 207.
[116] *DBW* 4, 221 and *DBWE* 4, 209; cf., *DBWE* 16, 558–9.
[117] *DBW* 4, 223–4.
[118] See *DBWE* 4, 207.
[119] See *DBW* 4, 221; and *DBW* 16, 566.
[120] *DBW* 16, 569.
[121] *DBWE* 16, 554.
[122] Ibid., 558.

'must never be understood as a mechanical process' or 'automatic event' (*mechanischer Vorgang*), for it demands (of the passive subject) a visible and public act of (ongoing) ecclesial obedience.[123] For Bonhoeffer, the 'break [*Bruch*] with the world'[124] that is effected internally in the life of the baptized through the gift of God the Holy Spirit given in baptism 'must become externally visible' by the baptized 'being a part of the worship and life of the church-community'.[125] The baptized *live* – and must do so, according to Bonhoeffer, *actively* – *in* 'the *living-space* [*Lebensraum*] of the visible church-community'.[126] The sacrament of baptism thus '*demands* faith'.[127] This is not only a confession of faith in which (through God the Holy Spirit) the death of Christ for us is proclaimed but also the decision of faith by which the baptized daily live out of the once-and-for-all-ness of Christ's death and (by the Holy Spirit of God) are 'active' in maintaining their belonging to the church-community.[128] Moreover, both the confession of faith and the ongoing decision of faith are necessary expressions or forms of the gift of faith,[129] which is given (in justification consummated in baptism) and preserved (in sanctification enacted in the Eucharist) by the gracious act of God the Holy Spirit.

As a 'passive action', therefore, baptism, on the one hand, is '*God's* effective act in the gift of grace'[130] through the work of God the Holy Spirit, according to which the baptized (by faith and in hope) are transposed into being in Christ (in the church), and, on the other hand, is the mandate to the baptized that they remain within God's church-community through *human* acts of (Spirit-inspired) faithful obedience.[131] This

---

[123] See *DBW* 4, 223; and *DBWE* 4, 210.
[124] *DBWE* 4, 208.
[125] *DBW* 4, 224.
[126] *DBWE* 4, 210 and 232.
[127] *DBWE* 1, 241 (emphasis added).
[128] See ibid., 247; *DBWE* 4, 210; and *DBWE* 16, 559. With respect to the emphasis on the work of the Holy Spirit here, Bonhoeffer writes: 'The Holy Spirit gives us a true understanding of Christ's nature (1 Cor. 2:10) and of his will; the Holy Spirit teaches and reminds us of all that Christ has said to us (John 14:26); the Holy Spirit guides us into all truth (John 16:13), so that we may not be lacking in the knowledge of Christ, and may understand the gifts bestowed on us by God.' See *DBWE* 4, 209–10.
[129] See *DBW* 16, 572 and 574.
[130] *DBWE* 1, 241 (emphasis added).
[131] See ibid. This holds true for Bonhoeffer whether the baptism in question is that of a believing adult or an infant. 'Baptism', writes Bonhoeffer, 'takes place only where there is faith' (*DBWE* 16, 560). In the case of adult baptism 'this means the conscious confession of faith' by the believing adult (*actus reflexus*), and her concomitant 'pure reception' of faith as the gift of God (see *DBWE* 16, 560). Through this gift, Bonhoeffer argues, 'the self [*das Ich*] is entirely superseded' (*actus directus*) – that is, in faith the baptized receives faith as 'a share in an event in which God alone and wholly is the one acting, as Father, Son, and Holy Spirit' (see *DBWE* 16, 558). Moreover, this faith, received by the believing adult in faith through God the Holy Spirit, is at once the faith of the church-community, which as such always precedes the faith of the individual (see *DBWE* 16, 563). This prevenient nature of the church's faith vis-à-vis the individual's faith is critical for Bonhoeffer in the case of infant baptism, for while the child *might* be said to have faith as *actus directus* (see *DBWE* 1, 241; *DBWE* 2, 159; *DBWE* 14, 736; and *DBWE* 16, 560) the child cannot be said to have the confession of faith as *actus reflexus* (see *DBWE* 14, 736). However, precisely because of the prevenient nature of its faith, the church-community, by virtue of its objective spirit, is able to provide the conscious confession of faith vicariously on behalf of the child who is baptized. Thus, the church-community, Bonhoeffer writes, 'receives baptism in a faith that intercedes for the child to be baptized' (*DBWE* 16, 563). Or as he puts it in *Sanctorum Communio*, 'the only subject absorbing the sacrament in

self-same 'both/and' baptismal logic, which exemplifies the logic of Bonhoeffer's 'both/and' ecclesiological methodology, is further replicated in his treatment of the Eucharist, and in particular his insistence therein that the Eucharist can be understood only as both the given gift of *God* to God's people and a *human* act before God.[132] In this latter sense, the Eucharist is the free gathering together of God's *church*-community to confess its faith before God.[133] However, this free confessional gathering, paradoxically, is not free (in the sense of being *self*-chosen),[134] but rather is 'an obedient symbolic act visible for everyone', which expresses the fact that this freely willing church-community is *God's* church-community and 'that God visibly recognizes it as such'.[135] The Eucharist is thus *given* to God's church-community as 'a symbolic action of *God's* effective will for community'.[136] This community is one that God summons, as God the Holy Spirit speaks in the word preached; constitutes, as God the Holy Spirit transposes human being in Adam into community with God and other human beings in Christ (in the church) in baptism; and now preserves, as God the Holy Spirit assures the baptized of both the gift and mandate given in baptism in the Eucharist.[137] In the Eucharist the spiritual presence of Christ is not given symbolically, but actually.[138] For Bonhoeffer, Christ becomes alive in the believers as the church-community as

faith remains as such the objective spirit of the church-community' (*DBW* 1, 164). This is to say that God uses the objective spirit of the church-community as a means to God's own end: to bestow grace on the child (see *DBW* 1, 164). Baptism is thus an 'objective act of the church-community upon the child' that is effective because the Holy Spirit of God is present and actively uses the objective spirit of the church-community (see *DBW* 1, 282). At once, however, and again on behalf of the child who is baptized, the whole church-community also receives the mandate of baptism, such that the church-community is to carry the child within its own (corporate) life and worship (see *DBW* 1, 165). The meaning of infant baptism is thus limited for Bonhoeffer 'where it is certain that baptism will be the first and last time that the child has contact with the church-community' (*DBW* 1, 165). On the distinction between *actus directus* and *actus reflexus* and its relation to faith, see Chapter 2, Section II n.18 of this book.

[132] See *DBW* 1, 166.
[133] See *DBWE* 1, 244.
[134] See ibid.
[135] *DBW* 1, 167. As Mawson observes, helpfully, this 'twofold nature' of the Eucharist in Bonhoeffer's thought requires the ecclesiologist to attend – if the Eucharist is to be spoken of in a genuinely theological manner – to both 'the embodied practices and social interactions' of the Eucharist at the human or sociological level, and 'God's presence and work' in the Eucharist. Mawson writes: 'The significance of this concrete practice is not available via sociological methods directly. An approach that neglects God's presence and work is unable to account for what the Eucharist empirically and concretely is.' See Mawson, *Christ Existing as Community*, 167–9 [167 and 168].
[136] *DBW* 1, 166 (emphasis added).
[137] See *DBWE* 1, 243. The way this assurance comes to the individual according to Bonhoeffer should also be noted. This way is that of through the tactile or sensory (embodied) nature of the elements themselves, such that the individual is assured of the gift of God's grace in both body and spirit (see *DBWE* 1, 243). Although Bonhoeffer makes no further application of his point here, the trajectory of his thought is indicative not only of his 'both/and' ecclesiological methodology but also of his contention that the pneumatological and confessional space of God's church-community is set apart and against the space of the world *in* the world so as to be *with* and *for* the world. The elements of bread, wine and water, by which the church-community in its sacramental order is preserved and constituted, embody in their very materiality the solidarity of the church with the world. Cf., Greggs, *Theology against Religion*, 136–7.
[138] On the 'givenness' of Bonhoeffer's sacramental theology, see Christopher Dodson, 'The God Who Is Given: Bonhoeffer's Sacramental Theology and His Critique of Religion' (PhD diss., University of Aberdeen, 2016).

the Holy Spirit of God works in and through the eucharistic elements to assure the believer of two things.[139] First, the believer is assured that Christ's vicarious suffering and death are for her benefit to the extent that Christ gives community with himself as *gift*.[140] Second, the believer is assured that Christ enables the church-community to become new such that Christ gives the church-community to itself as *mandate*.[141] This mandate is the obligation for the church and its members to love the *other*, bearing and being borne by each other as those who are enabled by God the Holy Spirit within the worshipping life of the church to live with and for one another and with and for the world. This obligation, moreover, Bonhoeffer sees fulfilled, pre-eminently, in what might be seen as the 'space' of spiritual care: the second confessional aspect which fills the pneumatological and confessional space that God's church-community occupies in spatio-temporality.

ii. The 'space' of spiritual care

For Bonhoeffer, the service of love one to another (*Dienst der Liebe aneinander*), or fraternal love (*Bruderliebe*), is an office or ministry (*Amt*) of God's church-community established in the event of its foundation at Pentecost.[142] As such, the office of spiritual care (*Seelsorge*) – as with the office of proclamation – is an 'actual ministry of the Holy Spirit'[143] *given* to the church by God to be *performed* by the church. In the function of spiritual care, therefore, *both* divine *and* human agency is said by Bonhoeffer to be held together in and through God the Holy Spirit. Bonhoeffer writes that the performance of spiritual care by one church member to another as διακονία 'is not left to the whims and capabilities of the individual'.[144] The following is true instead for Bonhoeffer: 'The Spirit gives the necessary gifts – the χαρίσματα. The *charisma is the subjective presupposition for objective service to the church-community as enabled by the Holy Spirit*.'[145] Διακονία is thus not the result of a Christian's willingness to help and serve, but rather is established by God as the ordering law through which the church as Christ's body lives, and by which the visibility of the Holy Spirit is manifest as being with and for another.[146] Indeed, through διακονία, according to Bonhoeffer, the law of vicarious representative action is actualized. This actualization happens in God's church-community as one church member becomes the burden-bearer of another after the pattern of, and through, Christ's own being and action.[147] This becoming is possible, however – to recall the argument of Chapter 3 – only by the *a priori* soteriological work of God the Holy Spirit recreating human being as an ecclesial human being, which as such is oriented and ordered towards God and other human

---

[139] See *DBW* 1, 166.
[140] See ibid.
[141] See ibid.
[142] See *DBW* 14, 445 and 454.
[143] See ibid., 556 and 445, respectively.
[144] Ibid., 454.
[145] Ibid.
[146] See ibid., 453 and 455.
[147] See *DBWE* 14, 474–6; cf., *DBWE* 5, 100-103; and *DBWE* 4, 88: 'As Christ bears our burdens, so we are to bear the burden of our sisters and brothers.'

beings in love.[148] For Bonhoeffer, this burden-bearing love is known and experienced in God's church-community concretely and pre-eminently in the service or ministry of listening.[149] Bonhoeffer further describes this (pointedly) as *Brüderliche Seelsorge*.[150]

As fraternal spiritual care, the function or goal of the ministry of listening is to expose or uncover sin and to educate into the hearing of God's word.[151] Uncovering sin and educating into hearing God's word, as Muers observes, 'are of course recognizable as traditionally appropriated to the Holy Spirit'.[152] Indeed, *opus elenchticum, didacticum, paedagogicum* and *paracleticum* comprise for Bonhoeffer the fourfold office of God the Holy Spirit: the Spirit is the One who refutes a false understanding of sin and convicts the world of sin; who teaches and guides into all truth; who educates into the *ordo salutis*; and who comforts with the word of the God of all consolation.[153] Each work of this fourfold office of the Holy Spirit of God is operative, therefore, *necessarily* in and through the ministry of listening, in order for that ministry to function as fraternal spiritual care through which one church member serves another by bearing the burden of that other. For Bonhoeffer, the greatest service of the ministry of listening, which thus operates as fraternal spiritual care only in and through God the Holy Spirit, is hearing the confession of another.[154] The fundamental reason for this is that in the practice of confession of sins by one church member to another – itself a work of the first aspect of the fourfold office of God the Holy Spirit, for the 'holy self-recognition'[155] of one's sinful standing before God can come only from the Spirit – not only is sin *exposed*, and concomitantly borne as a burden by the one who acts as *Stellvertreter* for the sake of another,[156] but God's word of forgiveness is *heard* as the one acting as *Stellvertreter* speaks that word to the one for the sake of whom they act.[157] In confession, Bonhoeffer

---

[148] See Chapter 3, Section III.ii of this book.
[149] See *DBWE* 5, 98–9. For a discussion of the ministry of listening, see Muers, *Keeping God's Silence*, 154–79.
[150] See *DBW* 5, 83. As set out by Bonhoeffer, *Seelsorge* encompasses not only the ministry or service of listening but also the ministry or service of active or practical helpfulness; bearing with the dispositions and sins of others; forgiveness, in the form of intercessory prayer for one another; and speaking God's Word of comfort and admonition one to another. See *DBWE* 5, 98–107.
[151] *DBW* 14, 559.
[152] Muers, *Keeping God's Silence*, 156.
[153] See *DBWE* 14, 483–4; Jn 14.16-17, 26-27, 15.26, 16.7-8, 13; and 2 Cor. 5.4.
[154] See *DBWE* 5, 99.
[155] *DBW* 10, 490.
[156] On Bonhoeffer's notion of taking on and bearing the sins (or guilt) of another as an aspect of what it means to act as *Stellvertreter*, see Schließer, *Everyone Who Acts Responsibly Becomes Guilty*; and McBride, *The Church for the World*, esp. 129–32. It should be noted that both Schließer and McBride read Bonhoeffer's account of confessing sin and accepting guilt as founded exclusively on his Christology (see Schließer, *Everyone Who Acts Responsibly Becomes Guilty*, 47; and McBride, *The Church for the World*, 57). However, the suggestion herein is that as an aspect of the pneumatological and confessional space of God's church-community, the most foundational dogmatic *res* of confession is, for Bonhoeffer, not Christology but an ecclesiologically indexed pneumatology. Cf., Greggs, 'Bearing Sin in the Church', 90–1.
[157] The way in which Bonhoeffer's thought here holds together *both* divine *and* human agency should be noted. The word of forgiveness as *God's* word is as such outside of us (*extra nos*), but this *divine* word has nevertheless been 'put [by God] ... into the mouth of *human* beings so that it may be passed on to others' (*DBWE* 5, 32). However, only as God the Holy Spirit speaks in those human words are those human words enabled to go forth and be heard as a divine word. See Section III.i of this chapter.

writes: 'The brother stands before us as a sign of the truth and grace of God. He is given to us to help us. He hears our confession of sin and forgives us of our sins in Christ's stead.'[158] In confessing sins one to another, sin is thus exposed to one's fellow believer and taken away by her, such that in confession 'one becomes a Christ to another'.[159] In this way, each Christian, as a member of God's church-community, is there *for the other* 'as a priest by virtue of Christ's own priesthood'.[160] However, because the church and its individual members are understood by Bonhoeffer to be structurally 'with-each-other' such that wherever the church member is there also the entire church is,[161] in the practice of confession and forgiveness of sins one to another, sin is not just borne and forgiven by an *individual* believer but by the church-*community* as well. Bonhoeffer writes: 'In the one brother to whom I confess my sins and by whom my sins are declared forgiven, I meet the whole church-community.'[162] In this sense, it is the community that bears the sin of the individual believer and speaks to that individual (both in word and sacrament) the word of forgiveness which the church-community has at its disposal.[163] Critically – and for the self-same reason – it is not just the *individual* believer who has her sins taken away and who hears God's word of forgiveness in the practice of confession and forgiveness of sins one to another, but the *church*-community itself.

Indeed, for Bonhoeffer, just as the individual believer in Christ (in the church) is oriented and ordered towards God and other human beings in love, such that they are enabled by God the Holy Spirit to become a 'burden-bearer' of another and especially of another's sin, so also is God's church-community oriented and ordered to the world and its sin. In fact, and in accordance with its vocation established in the event of its foundation at Pentecost,[164] one might say that, as the pneumatological and confessional space of spiritual care, the church's mode of being in the world, to use McBride's construction, 'is confession of sin unto repentance.'[165] Put otherwise, one might say that the church's mode of being in the world is *priestly*. Bonhoeffer writes: 'The Christian church-community stands in the place in which the whole world should stand. In this respect it serves the world as its vicarious representative; it is there for the world's sake.'[166] He further states: 'From its beginning and by virtue of its very nature, the church-community stands in a place of responsibility for the world that God in Christ has loved.'[167] Bonhoeffer presents this responsibility not only in terms of God's church-community being the space of proclamation but also, and provocatively, in terms of the church being the space of spiritual care, and as this (latter) space becoming

---

[158] *DBW* 5, 94.
[159] *DBW* 14, 750.
[160] See *DBW* 1, 170 and 171. Thus, it is not the individual or the church per se who forgives sins. Only Christ is able to take on and forgive human sin in judgement and justification. But in confessing and forgiving sins one to another in Christ's name, the individual is drawn into and participates in being in Christ (in the church), and thereby in the community of confession that God's church-community is as the space of spiritual care. See *DBWE* 6, 142; cf., *DBWE* 1, 248; and *DBWE* 10, 509.
[161] See Chapter 3, Section III.ii of this book.
[162] *DBW* 5, 95.
[163] See ibid., 110 and *DBWE* 2, 112–13.
[164] Cf., Acts 2.38.
[165] McBride, *The Church for the World*, 6.
[166] *DBW* 6, 408.
[167] *DBWE* 16, 543.

the vicarious burden-bearer of the sins and guilt of the whole world before God.[168] Bonhoeffer writes: 'The church is today the community of people who, grasped by the power of Christ's grace, recognize, confess, and take upon themselves their personal sins as well as the Western world's falling away from Jesus Christ as guilt towards Jesus Christ.'[169] Bonhoeffer continues:

> With this confession [*mea culpa, mea culpa, mea maximus culpa*] the whole guilt of the world falls on the church ... and because here it is confessed and not denied, the possibility of forgiveness is opened ... here there are people who take all – really all – guilt upon themselves, not in some heroic decision of self-sacrifice, but simply overwhelmed by their own guilt towards Christ.[170]

In individuals confessing and forgiving sins one to another, the church in its priestliness, then, both takes on and confesses the sins and guilt of the rest of the world to which it contributes and in which it participates, and in consequence of which hears and receives the word of God's forgiveness along with the individual believer in its midst.[171] In and through many individuals, God's *church*-community confesses and acknowledges before God its sin and guilt in relation to the world.[172] Thus in the practice of confession of sins by one church member to another, the pneumatological and confessional space that God's church-community occupies in spatio-temporality is identified most properly as the space that is set apart from and against the space of the world, in its being truly in and for the world. Where there is *no* confession of sin God's *church*-community, accordingly, fails to perceive and actualize its priestly responsibility in and for the world, and thereby ceases to be *God's* church-community.[173]

---

[168] Typically, the disposition of the priest before God vis-à-vis her people.
[169] *DBW* 6, 126.
[170] Ibid., 127.
[171] Here, Bonhoeffer is indebted to, but moves beyond Martin Luther's understanding of priesthood (in relation to the priesthood of Christ and that of all believers). Luther relates the priesthood of Christ to individual believers, in relation first to prayer and intercession, and second to teaching the Word of God (see *LW* 31, 353–5; cf., *LW* 44, 127–9). This, then, determines the individual priesthood of *each* believer. Luther writes: 'Now just as Christ by his birthright obtained these two prerogatives, so he imparts them to and shares them with everyone who believes in him. ... Hence all of us who believe in Christ are priests ... in Christ' (*LW* 31, 354), and as such 'are worthy to appear before God to pray for others and to teach one another divine things' (*LW* 31, 355). While Bonhoeffer assents doctrinally to this Lutheran approach (see *DBWE* 1, 206, 236 and 266), he moves beyond it, however, with his suggestion that priesthood as an identity in fact belongs to the church and not to each individual believer (or to the total sum of individual believers in the church) independent so-to-speak of the church as Christ's (priestly) body, in which the believer participates and by which the believer's priesthood is established and sustained. On the priestly identity of the church in Bonhoeffer's thought, see Greggs, 'Ecclesial Priestly Mediation', 81–91; and Greggs, 'The Priesthood of No Believer', esp. 386–7.
[172] Bonhoeffer's hamartiology, in which the sin of the individual believer is understood at once to be the sin of Adam (and thus of the world) for which one is, therefore, personally culpable, is clearly at work here. Because the being of the church is 'in' the individual believer through God the Holy Spirit mediating the presence of Jesus Christ (in whom the church's being as an ontological reality is realized) with*in* the believer, the church corporately – as a 'collective I' (*Gesamtich*) formed by the actualizing work of God the Holy Spirit – must also acknowledge personal culpability for the sins of the world. Cf., Chapter 3, Section II and III.ii of this book; and see *DBWE* 6, 137.
[173] See *DBWE* 11, 326; and *DBWE* 16, 543.

In the practice of confession, then, in which both the individual believer and the church-community stand as burden-bearer of the sins and guilt of another in order to speak the word of forgiveness to that other, Bonhoeffer's 'both/and' ecclesiological methodology is decisively at work. Indeed, as the quintessential service of the office of spiritual care, the *human* practice of confession is given to God's church-community to perform by *God* the Holy Spirit in the event of the church's foundation at Pentecost. Moreover, the actual practice of confession of sins by one church member to another and by the church-community itself can be performed (according to Bonhoeffer) only in and through the Holy Spirit of God. As the foregoing discussion has demonstrated, it is God the Holy Spirit who is operative in confession to uncover sin and educate into hearing the word of forgiveness, and it is the Holy Spirit who ensures that that word which is spoken as a *human* word is truly *God's* word such that it goes forth and is heard as a *divine* word. Thus, in the practice of confession (and in the wider service of spiritual care) *both* divine *and* human agency are said by Bonhoeffer to be held together in and through the Holy Spirit of God.

IV. Conclusion

This chapter has argued that the space occupied by the socio-historical human community that God's church-community is in spatio-temporality is, for Bonhoeffer, founded in the event of the coming of God the Holy Spirit at Pentecost, and thus is best identified and understood as a *pneumatological* space. This pneumatological space, as it has been outlined in this chapter, is to be further specified most properly, in virtue of the human empirical form and associated vocational function(s) given to God's church-community by the Holy Spirit of God in the event of the church's foundation at Pentecost, as a *confessional* space – a space which itself can be said, moreover, to be filled by the spaces of proclamation and spiritual care. In articulating his ecclesiological description in this pneumatologically spatialized way, it has been seen that Bonhoeffer both recapitulates, in vivid spatial terms, the prior argument of *Sanctorum Communio* in relation to the actualization of the church in space and time by the threefold work of God the Holy Spirit and identifies, critically – in consequence of his pneumatological and apocalyptically eschatological conceptualization of spatio-temporality – the being of God's church-community as the pneumatological space set apart and against the space of the world *in* the world in order to be *with* and *for* the world. God's church-community exists in spatio-temporality in the time between the ascension of Christ and the *eschaton*, and has being therein as *God's* church-community only in and by the Holy Spirit of God and *as* God's *church*-community confesses through God the Holy Spirit the gospel of God to the world in the particular and contingent events of proclamation and spiritual care. In this way Bonhoeffer's account of the socio-historical human community that the church in space and time is as a pneumatological and confessional space treats with all seriousness spatio-temporality as a theological category – commensurate, that is, with its creaturely and eschatological nature, space and time having been pneumatologically and apocalyptically determined.

Moreover, it is an account that further displays Bonhoeffer's pneumatological and eschatological 'both/and' ecclesiological methodology, in critique of both 'dogmatic' and 'ethnographic' ecclesiology. In accordance with the event of its foundation at Pentecost (and *contra* 'hard' ethnographic ecclesiology), the pnuematological and confessional space that the socio-historical human community that God's church-community is in spatio-temporality comes into being only because of the operative and gracious act of *God* the Holy Spirit. However, this pneumatological and confessional space that God's church-community occupies in spatio-temporality is said by Bonhoeffer (*contra* 'soft' ethnographic ecclesiology) to have a sui generis nature as a new act of creation in *distinction* to the space of the world. Furthermore, as a new act of creation this pneumatological and confessional space that God's church-community occupies in spatio-temporality is said by Bonhoeffer (*contra* 'hard' and 'soft' dogmatic ecclesiology) to have the sui generis nature of its being as *God's* church-community only *as* that socio-historical human community engages in the church practice of confessing (in and through the Holy Spirit of God) the gospel of God to the world in the particular and contingent events of proclamation and spiritual care. Moreover, these spaces themselves have been demonstrated to display Bonhoeffer's pneumatological and eschatological 'both/and' ecclesiological methodology: the spaces of proclamation and spiritual care have their *divine* being and content *in* the Holy Spirit of God, and *through* the Holy Spirit they operate functionally and effectively as particular and contingent *human* events of the pneumatological and confessional space of God's church-community. It is the Holy Spirit of God who enables the word preached to be *God's* word in *human* words; who mediates the gift of *God's* grace in the *human* acts (and material elements) of the sacraments of baptism and Eucharist; and who makes the word of forgiveness spoken in confession as a *human* word go forth and be heard as a *divine* word. By the work of God the Holy Spirit *both* divine *and* human agency can thus be seen to be held together in the spaces of proclamation and spiritual care as an exemplified showing of the very logic of Bonhoeffer's 'both/and' ecclesiological methodology. Having now outlined in its consideration of Bonhoeffer's ecclesial description the *space* that God's church-community occupies in spatio-temporality as a socio-historical human community, the book turns, in its final chapter, to the being of God's church-community in *time*.

5

The eschatological time of God's church-community

I. Introduction

Having identified and outlined in Chapter 4 the space which God's church-community occupies in spatio-temporality in the time between the ascension of Christ and the *eschaton* as pneumatological, the concern of this chapter – in view of Bonhoeffer's pneumatological and eschatological conceptualization of spatio-temporality as grounded *extra se* in God and God's operative and gracious acts – is the being of God's church-community in time. This time is the 'time' within which the church as *congregatio* exists as a particular and contingent socio-historical human community in consequence of its actualization *in* space and time as the event of the divine act of *convocatio* of the Holy Spirit of God. As demonstrated in Chapter 2 and recapitulated in Chapter 4, spatio-temporality (according to Bonhoeffer) has been apocalypsed by the advent in space and time of God in Christ by the Holy Spirit, such that spatio-temporality is located, properly, only in relation to God, being 'stretched out' (*ausgespannt*) or 'suspended' (*eingespannt*) between God's 'Yes' and 'No'.[1]

That space-time is suspended thus means that the creaturely media of space and time are fundamentally dynamic, having their being determined by an eschatological and teleological movement of God the Holy Spirit which is operative *in* space and time, travels *through* space and time, and *fulfils* space and time by drawing space-time to its consummation in new creation.[2] This eschatological and teleological movement, being as it is definitive of space and time, in turn means that, for Bonhoeffer, space-time – including the phenomenal forms and structures (ecclesial or otherwise) arising in space and time – is understood first and foremost not as an anthropological or sociological category but as a theological and, indeed, an eschatological one, standing under the promise of new heavens and a new earth. To account for the being of God's church-community in time, therefore, it is necessary (according to Bonhoeffer) to speak *theologically* about empirical phenomenology, in accordance with and as a further exemplification of the logic inherent to Bonhoeffer's own 'both/and' ecclesiological methodology in which the sui generis sociological structure of *God's*

---

[1] See Chapter 2, Section II and Chapter 4, Section II of this book.
[2] See Torrance, *Space, Time and Incarnation*, 11–12 and 72.

church-community as a particular and contingent socio-historical *human* community is said (in therapeutic response to the endemic 'either/or' problematic) to be *in* the operative and gracious act of God the Holy Spirit.[3]

This operative and gracious act of God the Holy Spirit, and the Holy Spirit's associated eschatological and teleological movement in time, through time and outwith time, is initiated by God's apocalypse of space and time and continued with the coming of God the Holy Spirit at Pentecost into space-time as the proleptic manifestation of new creation and the agency by which the church's being as a new act of creation is actualized. Most critically for the concern of this chapter, this work of the Holy Spirit of God invests the *eschata* with decisive temporal-historical significance. Bonhoeffer writes: 'An awareness of temporality … is only possible where thought is determined … by the entrance of God into history at a definite place and point in time.'[4] In the event of God's eschatological and apocalyptic incursion into space and time in Christ by the Holy Spirit of God, Bonhoeffer argues that 'history becomes serious, without being sanctified', such that 'God's "Yes" and God's "No" to history … bring into every historical moment an unending and irremovable tension'.[5] In fact, here, in this tension between God's 'Yes' and God's 'No', history 'first becomes *genuinely* temporal', and in its *genuine* temporality 'it is history to which God has said Yes'.[6] The reason that history *first* becomes genuinely temporal in the event of God's apocalypse of space and time is, as John Macquarrie observes, that 'what closes a [temporal] series' is what 'gives to [that series] any meaning or character it may have'.[7] In other words, the only way that time is measured *qua* time is by it being measured against its final end; and precisely because the final (future) end of time has moved decisively into space and time in Christ by the Holy Spirit of God, and continues in the person and work of God the Holy Spirit to do so in (present) space and time, time (according to Bonhoeffer) is now measured against its final (future) end, and history thereby acquires a temporal *genuineness*, such that history is to be taken seriously as *history*. One might say, that the temporal-historical coordinate of space-time is conceived properly, therefore, only in relation to the work of the end-time gift of God the Holy Spirit in it, through it and outwith it, and by which time itself is oriented and ordered by God to the eschatological telos. This time, which is thus *God's* time as the time between apocalypse and (future) *parousia* and in which God's church-community has its being, might therefore best be identified and understood in Bonhoeffer's thought as *eschatological*.

It is this eschatological *time*, and in particular the dynamic relationality that exists between God and temporal-historical reality as (perhaps) the defining aspect of this time, which this chapter seeks to outline in order to then consider the critical significance of this time for Bonhoeffer's theological account of the being of God's church-community as a particular and contingent socio-historical human community *in* eschatological time. Indeed, only when one understands the dynamic relationality that exists in Bonhoeffer's thought between God and temporal-historical reality in

---

[3] See Chapter 1, Section III; Chapter 3, Section III; and Chapter 4, esp. Section I of this book.
[4] *DBW* 6, 93–4.
[5] Ibid., 94.
[6] See ibid (emphasis added).
[7] John Macquarrie, *Christian Hope* (Oxford: Mowbrays, 1978), 32.

eschatological time, can one understand the ecclesiological significance for Bonhoeffer of this time. To this end, the first substantive section of the chapter engages Bonhoeffer's *Ethics* fragment, *Die letzten und die vorletzten Dinge*,[8] in which he articulates most clearly, in terms of his categories of 'last things' and 'things before the last',[9] the dynamic relation in which God and temporal-historical reality stand in eschatological time. As will be seen, this relation is one which not only upholds the decisive significance of the final reality of God (or 'last things') *over against* temporal-historical reality but concomitantly (and derivatively) also invests temporal-historical reality (or 'things before the last') with decisive significance *for* the final reality of God. Given that temporal-historical reality is therefore seen by Bonhoeffer as both *conditioned by* and *preserved for* the final reality of God, it is suggested that the dynamic (and polemical) relationality which exists in Bonhoeffer's thought between God and temporal-historical reality is best accounted for by reference to the category of divine *patience*.

Having engaged Bonhoeffer's *Ethics* fragment and outlined the dynamic relationality which exists in his thought between God and temporal-historical reality in eschatological time, and come subsequently – in virtue of indexing this relation to the category of divine patience – to further specify eschatological time as the time of God's patience, the chapter then turns, in its second substantive section, to consider the ecclesiological significance of this time. In seeking to establish the significance of eschatological time as the time of God's patience for a theological account of the being of God's church-community, Bonhoeffer's motif of 'preparing the way' (*Wegbereitung*)[10] will be deployed to articulate a specific ecclesial *commission* which Bonhoeffer sees as definitive of the being of *God's* church-community as a particular and contingent sociohistorical *human* community in eschatological time. This commission necessitates that God's church-community, in light of the dynamic relationality which exists between God and temporal-historical reality in eschatological time as a consequence of God's patience, engages in responsible ecclesial *action* – action which is possible, however, only from within the pneumatological space of God's church-community and which, in and through the Holy Spirit of God, works towards establishing two empirical conditions in the world. These two conditions are 'being human' (*Menschseins*) and 'being good' (*Gutseins*).[11]

It is in working towards the establishment of these two conditions by engaging in responsible ecclesial action that the church and its members are said by Bonhoeffer

---

[8] See *DBW* 6, 137–62.
[9] The more customary translation of *letzten* and *vorletzten* as 'ultimate' and 'penultimate' is jettisoned in an attempt not only to preserve the different senses (and variety of ways) in which Bonhoeffer uses the terms but also to emphasize the temporal-historical coordinate of the doctrine of last things as Bonhoeffer understood it, and which the English terms 'ultimate' and 'penultimate' may obscure. As Macquarrie notes: 'The "last things" may be the things that come along at the end of a series, and here "last" has primarily a temporal significance. Yet … the "last things" may also be understood as what is final and ultimate, what is of most importance; and in some modern theologians … the eschatological is virtually voided of any temporal reference and is understood as the ultimate or decisive moment' (Macquarrie, *Christian Hope*, 32; cf., Harvey, *Taking Hold of the Real*, 36). It is this latter concern which leads, therefore, to the less customary translation (at least in English language commentary on Bonhoeffer) of *letzten* and *vorletzten*.
[10] *DBW* 6, 153.
[11] See ibid., 157–62, 163–217 and 218–99.

to 'prepare the way' (*Bereitet den Weg*) for last things to come into and upon the things before the last in fulfilment of their specific ecclesial commission. In fulfilling the commission thus, the church and its members are thereby said to ensure that the human empirical form and associated vocational function(s) of the being of God's church-community in eschatological time is in fact commensurate with and upholds the dynamic relationality which exists between God and temporal-historical reality in this time as the time of God's patience. In this way, the specific ecclesial commission of God's church-community fulfilled in responsible ecclesial action will be seen to hold together, in and through the Holy Spirit of God, *both* divine *and* human agency in accordance with and as a further exemplification of Bonhoeffer's pneumatological and eschatological 'both/and' ecclesiological methodology.

II. The last things and things before the last

Bonhoeffer begins his discussion of *Die letzten und die vorletzten Dinge* by presenting justification as 'a last thing'[12] – as an eschatological event in which past and future are conjoined in the present of 'God's last word',[13] and which as the word of 'forgiveness' embraces and overcomes past sin, and as the word of 'preservation' bears and upholds future life.[14] Thus, the whole of life, including the life of the future that is yet to come, is concentrated in this one present moment – in the eschatological event of 'God's last word' 'when Christ [himself] enters into the human being' by God the Holy Spirit.[15] Indeed, it is precisely because of the *content* of God's last word that it is God's *last* word, for this content itself *is* eschatological. Jesus Christ is the eschatological person par excellence. His own pneumatological filled-ness and raising from the dead announces and begins the world of new creation in space and time, and the ἀρραβών and ἀπαρχή of his (future) *parousia*. This ἀρραβών and ἀπαρχή is the Holy Spirit whose own movement in, through and outwith space and time ensures that the world of new creation already resides in, and continues to unfold itself within, present space and time in the time between apocalypse and (future) *parousia*. The content of God's last word, then, is the pneumatologically mediated eschatological and teleological movement of the dynamic (future) being of Godself,[16] *and* it should be noted – to recall the argument of Chapter 3 and 4 – the pneumatological and eschatological being of God's church-community which is realized (as an ontological reality) *in* Christ from and for all eternity.[17]

This eschatological content of God's last word, moreover, means that it is God's *last* word for Bonhoeffer in two senses. First, it is such in a *qualitative* sense: 'It implies the complete severance of everything that precedes it. ... It is never the natural or necessary end of the way pursued thus far, but rather is the complete condemnation

---

[12] *DBW* 6, 137.
[13] Ibid., 141.
[14] See ibid., 137; cf., Lindsay, 'Eschatology', 264: 'The ultimacy of this justification is, by definition, thoroughly eschatological.'
[15] See *DBW* 6, 138.
[16] On the futurity of God's being, see Chapter 2, Section II, n.18 of this book.
[17] See Chapter 3, Section III.ii, n.189 and n.191, and Chapter 4, Section II, n.34 of this book.

and devaluation of that way because it is God's own free word compelled by nothing. Therefore, it is the irreversible last word, the last reality.'[18] God's last word is the judgement on everything that stands before it.[19] Second, however, God's last word is God's *last* word in a *temporal* sense: 'It is always preceded by something ... that is, quite genuinely, by a span of time, at the end of which it stands.'[20] As God's *last* word, therefore, God's last *word* is the entirely gratuitous, non-necessary and unconditioned free act of Godself, which negates all that precedes it and every existing notion of continuous and self-consistent temporal-historical sequencing, and which also establishes the genuineness of all that which does precede it, giving to that span of time and everything within it both its meaning and its character *as* things before the last.[21] Because God's last word establishes the genuineness of things before the last in its negation of them, things before the last cannot be thought to have any value in-and-of-themselves.[22] Bonhoeffer writes: 'There is nothing before the last as such, such that anything could be justified as before the last in itself.'[23] Rather, the next-to-lastness of what is before the last is established

> only through the last thing, which is to say [it becomes a thing before the last only] in the moment [of eschatological justification] in which what is before the last has become repudiated or has lost its force as a thing in itself. It is not then a condition of the last thing, but rather the last thing conditions the thing before the last. Consequently, the thing before the last is not a state of being in itself, but rather a judgment which the last thing passes on that which [qualitatively and temporally] has preceded it.[24]

As he puts it elsewhere: 'This finding [of "a wholly other final reality, namely, the reality of God the creator, reconciler, and redeemer"] is the turning point and pivot of any and all knowledge of reality.'[25] By definition, therefore, things before the last, despite their complete repudiation by the last things, nevertheless remain in existence, albeit in an existence which, generatively speaking, *is* only in its relation to the last things. As Paul Janz argues, 'The penultimate ... as pen-*ultimate* can never claim any independent

---

[18] DBW 6, 140. The echo of Barth's voice here is unmistakable: 'The last thing, the ἔσχατον ... is never the continuation ... but on the contrary always the radical severance of everything before the last.' See Karl Barth, *Das Wort Gottes und die Theologie: Gesammelte Vorträge* (München: Chr. Kaiser, 1929), 67.
[19] DBW 6, 140.
[20] Ibid., 141.
[21] Things before the last is, then, everything standing before (in a qualitative sense) and all that precedes (in a temporal sense) God's last word as a last thing. In the context of Bonhoeffer's presentation of justification as a last thing, it should be noted, however, that for the one who *is* justified in the event of God's last word, things before the last at once include (*because* the last things have actually been found by the justified one in *present* space and time in the event of their justification) 'all that *follows* the last thing [here that event of justification itself] in order again to precede the last thing [here (presumably) the last thing which is still to come in the event of Christ's (future) *parousia*]' (*DBW* 6, 151).
[22] See *DBW* 6, 142.
[23] Ibid., 151.
[24] Ibid.
[25] Ibid., 33 and 32.

status apart from the ultimate.'[26] One would wish to add, however, that as *pen*-ultimate the penultimate, in its properly conceived relation to the ultimate, must always claim its own derived value, and thus the generative relationship in which last things and things before the last stand is one of '*unidirectional* dependency'.[27] This relationship, Bonhoeffer observes, can, however, be resolved (problematically) in one of two extreme forms – by either a radical resolution or a resolution of compromise.[28]

i. The way of radicalism or compromise?

On the one hand, the radical resolution attends only to last things and 'in it sees only the complete severance with things before the last'.[29] In other words, in the radical resolution priority is given to last things over against the things before the last from which one seeks to break-off entirely out of a hatred (*Haß*) for what exists.[30] Bonhoeffer writes: 'Facing the coming end there is for ["radical"] Christians only the last word and last behaviour. What will befall the world as a result [of that end] is of no consequence anymore; the ["radical"] Christian bears no responsibility for that. The world must burn after all.'[31] On the other hand, the resolution of compromise attends only to things before the last and thus severs the last things from all that is before it in principle out of a hatred (*Haß*) for the last things.[32] In the resolution of compromise, then, it must be stated: 'Things before the last retain their rights as such, but are not threatened or endangered by the last thing. The world still stands; the end is yet to come … the last thing remains wholly beyond everyday life and in the end serves simply as the eternal justification for every existent thing.'[33] Everyday life, moreover, must, for the compromise Christian, be actively protected against the in-breaking (*Einbruch*) of last things into the sphere or domain (*Bereich*) of things before the last:[34] 'One must manage the world only by means of the world. The last thing is to have no say in the formation of life in the world.'[35] For Bonhoeffer, both resolutions are therefore likewise extreme: both set last things and the things before the last in mutually exclusive opposition, and in doing so wrongly absolutize, respectively, the end of all things and that which now exists.[36] Thinking from the end of all things and making this end absolute, the radical resolution destroys the things before the last by way of last things, while the resolution of compromise (thinking from that which now exists and making this existence absolute) expels the last things from things before the last.[37] In the former case, the last things cannot tolerate things before the last, and in the latter case, the things before the

---

[26] Janz, *God, the Mind's Desire*, 194.
[27] Ibid.
[28] See *DBW* 6, 144–8.
[29] Ibid., 144.
[30] See ibid., 146.
[31] Ibid., 144–5.
[32] See ibid., 145 and 147.
[33] Ibid., 145.
[34] See ibid., 147.
[35] Ibid., 147–8.
[36] See ibid., 146.
[37] See ibid., 145–6.

last cannot tolerate last things.³⁸ In both cases ideas that are right and necessary per se are brought into inextricable conflict.³⁹

For Bonhoeffer, however, Christian life is not a matter of radicalism or compromise.⁴⁰ The reason for this is that what in the radical resolution and the resolution of compromise is set against each other – ultimately, God and temporal-historical reality, and thereby the relation in which the last things and things before the last stand – is in fact one in the eschatological reality of God in Christ by the Holy Spirit.⁴¹ In the pneumatologically mediated life, death and resurrection of Jesus Christ, Bonhoeffer recognizes both God's 'Yes' and God's 'No' to temporal-historical reality: one sees God's love towards God's creation in the incarnation; God's judgement of fallen creation in the crucifixion; and God's will for a new world in the resurrection (and in the coming of God the Holy Spirit at Pentecost).⁴² In this way, the eschatological reality of God in Christ by the Holy Spirit provides both 'the ultimate foundation and the ultimate negation of every existent thing'.⁴³ Indeed, here (in this eschatological reality), 'affirmation and contradiction are bound together', such that the justified one 'must continue to reckon with the worldliness of the world, but at the same time also with the rule of God over it'.⁴⁴ In the terms of the categories of *letzten* and *vorletzten*, the last thing is 'the judgment on all that is before the last, but at the same time [is] grace for the things before the last'.⁴⁵ For Bonhoeffer, then, to split apart (*auseinanderzureißen*) the last things and things before the last in the way that both the radical resolution and the resolution of compromise do could not be more perverted given their original unity – and hence *actual* resolution – in the eschatological reality of God in Christ by the Holy Spirit.⁴⁶ Furthermore, it is not just the *fact* of this original unity which causes Bonhoeffer to refute the resolution of the relation between the last things and things before the last in the approach of radicalism and compromise, but more specifically the *type* of unity that this original unity is, and critically the *effect* that this unity has on temporal-historical reality itself.

To recall the argument of Chapter 4,⁴⁷ God and the reality of the world, as non-identical aspects of the one eschatological *Christuswirklichkeit*, exist in a *polemical* unity. They exist in a tensive simultaneity which accords not only with the being of Christ's own person but also with the being of space and time being in the movement between the reconciliation and judgement of God. The being of space and time has been effected by God's apocalypse of spatio-temporality in Christ through the agency of God the Holy Spirit. This eschatological and apocalyptic incursion of the final reality of God into space and time – or, one might say, the 'in-breaking' of the future end of time and the life of new creation into the 'old' or present time of fallen creation – is the

---

³⁸ See ibid., 145–6.
³⁹ Ibid., 146.
⁴⁰ See ibid.
⁴¹ See ibid.
⁴² See *DBWE* 6, 157–9 and 223–4.
⁴³ *DBW* 6, 222.
⁴⁴ Ibid., 223.
⁴⁵ Ibid., 150.
⁴⁶ See ibid., 148–9.
⁴⁷ See Chapter 4, Section II of this book.

effective transformation of temporal-historical reality into eschatological and properly apocalyptic reality, such that time is now 'stretched out' (*ausgespannt*) or 'suspended' (*eingespannt*) between the 'Yes' and 'No' of God.[48] With this 'unending and irremovable tension'[49] inherent within time, time can thus be thought only as tensile and dynamic – that is, as *eschatological* time between apocalypse and (future) *parousia*, which as such contains within itself simultaneously, by the person and work of God the Holy Spirit, the dynamic relationality of *both* the final reality of God (or last things) *and* temporal-historical reality (or things before the last).

For Bonhoeffer, the relation between last things and things before the last in eschatological time must, therefore, be parsed and understood only in reference to this dynamic tension. After all, given this tension, time *is* redeemed but is still in the movement *towards* redemption. The justified one has *found* the 'last thing' and in Christ (in the church) through God the Holy Spirit is human in 'a *new* resurrected way', but 'old' or sinful humanity-in-Adam continues to live on wit*hin* her as she remains and lives out her life unto death *in* the world of things before the last.[50] Indeed, the resurrection itself, and the coming of God the Holy Spirit at Pentecost, *is* the end of this 'old' or present time of fallen creation, but things before the last are *not* abolished thereby.[51] Rather, in the resurrection and by the coming of God the Holy Spirit, the last things break *into* things before the last as the proleptic manifestation of *new* creation.[52]

---

[48] See *DBW* 6, 32–3. By this idea of temporal 'in-breaking', Bonhoeffer conceives the event of God's eschatological and apocalyptic incursion into space and time in Christ by the Holy Spirit as that which 'explodes the form of time' (*DBW* 1, 89). Or as Kristopher Norris puts it, as that which 'effects a deconstructing [of time] and simultaneously [a] reconstructing, renewing, and transforming [of] time' (Kristopher Norris, 'The Incarnational Church: Bonhoeffer's Political Ecclesiology of Transformation in *Discipleship* and *Sanctorum Communio*', in Kirsten Busch Nielsen, Ralf K. Wüstenberg and Jens Zimmermann, ed. *In Dem Rad in die Speichen fallen: Das Politische in der Theologie Dietrich Bonhoeffers* (München: Gütersloher Verlagshaus, 2013), 331). Time, as such, is 'apocalyptically charged' (Douglas Harink, *SCM Theological Commentary on the Bible: 1 & 2 Peter* (London: SCM Press, 2009), 180). For this reason, Manoussakis's suggestion that the emphasis in Bonhoeffer's eschatology 'lies not on some beyond-this-world, end-of-times utopia but on the quiet and unnoticeable unfolding of the eschaton through the ephemeral and the everyday' is problematic (see John Panteleimon Manoussakis, 'On the Phenomenology of Creation: Between Dietrich Bonhoeffer's and Jean-Yves Lacoste's Eschatology', in Kirkpatrick, ed. *Engaging Bonhoeffer*, 287). Yes, Bonhoeffer's eschatology is concerned primarily and uncompromisingly with *this* world, but it is so only because of the apocalyptic 'in-breaking' of the eschaton into the world, which, for Bonhoeffer, given the cosmic ontological, epistemological and moral effects of God's gospel *as* an apocalypse, is an event far from 'quiet', 'unnoticeable', or for that matter bound to the 'ephemeral'. Rather, the emphasis in Bonhoeffer's apocalyptic eschatology is perhaps better seen as being on a loud, visible and, in the words of Sergius Bulgakov, 'catastrophic *transcensus*' of the world, which takes place *in* the world and by which the very being of the world is transfigured. See Sergius Bulgakov, *The Bride of the Lamb*, trans. Boris Jakim (Grand Rapids: Eerdmans, 2002), 417.

[49] *DBW* 6, 94.

[50] See ibid., 150.

[51] See ibid.

[52] See ibid. The dynamic relationality of last things and things before the last thus expresses and preserves the inherent tension that Bonhoeffer sees (and is witnessed to in scripture) between the 'already' and 'not yet' of God's kingdom: the last things have already come into the things before the last such that the latter is now charged with the former, but the former (as that which is last, temporally speaking) is yet to come. Cf., Mk 1.15; Jn 4.23 and 5.25. For a helpful exegetical discussion of the tension as witnessed to in scripture, see Chrys C. Caragounis, 'Kingdom of God, Son of Man and Jesus' Self Understanding', *Tyndale Bulletin* 40 (1) (1989), 2–23.

The things before the last must not, then, be considered – as they are in the radical resolution – as irrelevant to the last things and thus open to destruction, for things before the last in fact are the outer-covering (*Hülle*) of the last things.[53] At once, however, last things must not be considered – as they are in the resolution of compromise – as beyond things before the last and thus as intolerable to this life, for 'God is beyond in the midst of our life'.[54] As Bonhoeffer later writes, neatly emphasizing the necessary unity of that which in the radical resolution and the resolution of compromise is split apart, '*redemption* [is] within *history*'.[55] For Bonhoeffer, redemption (conceived as a 'last thing') does not mean 'redemption [*out* of "things before the last" – that is], *out* of sorrows, hardships, anxieties, and longings, out of sin and death, into a better life beyond'.[56] Indeed, in consequence of the Christian hope of resurrection, the justified one 'does not have, like the believers of redemption-myths, a final escape *out* of earthly tasks and difficulties, but rather, like Christ ... the Christian must taste the whole of earthly life to the full'.[57] Bonhoeffer continues: 'This this-worldliness [*Das Diesseits*] must not be allowed to be abolished before its time'.[58] In short, the relation between the last things and things before the last, because of the eschatological time in which they exist simultaneously and tensively, is such that (from the perspective of the apocalypse of God's gospel) last things neither destroy nor sanction things before the last as such.[59] Rather, Bonhoeffer writes, the 'last things keep open [*offengehalten*] a certain space [*Raum*] for the things before the last'.[60] What is kept open is a space *in* time, in which the things before the last exist not only in dependence upon the last things but also to 'be *preserved* for the sake of the last things'.[61] In their respective destruction and sanctioning of things before the last as such, the radical resolution and the resolution of compromise both, therefore, advocate a false understanding of temporality itself – temporality, inherent to which (precisely because it is *eschatological* time) is the dynamic relationality between the final reality of God and temporal-historical reality, but which both the radical resolution and the resolution of compromise fail to take seriously. As Bonhoeffer puts it, the relation between the last things and things before the last is thus defined (most properly) in reference to 'an encounter beyond all radicalism and all compromise'[62] – that is, an encounter between God and temporal-historical reality which, in consequence of God's apocalyptically eschatological and teleological movement in Christ by God the Holy Spirit into, within and beyond space and time, might best be accounted for in Bonhoeffer's thought by reference to the category of divine patience.[63]

---

[53] See *DBW* 6, 149.
[54] *DBW* 8, 408.
[55] *DBWE* 8, 447 (emphasis altered).
[56] *DBW* 8, 500 (emphasis added).
[57] Ibid., 501 (emphasis added).
[58] Ibid.
[59] See *DBW* 6, 151.
[60] Ibid.
[61] Ibid., 152 (emphasis added).
[62] Ibid., 151.
[63] The category of divine patience, notwithstanding Bonhoeffer's certain awareness of it, is not an obvious concern within Bonhoeffer's theological oeuvre. The suggestion that the dynamic relationality that exists in his thought between last things and things before the last might best

ii. The patience of God: A motif for eschatological time

In the context of his discussion of the relation between last things and things before the last, it is, as Bonhoeffer notes, of decisive importance that (in eschatological time) things before the last be preserved for the sake of the last things.[64] Why this should in fact be so is addressed only obliquely in *Die letzten und die vorletzten Dinge*.[65] However, in *Ethics* working note No. 61, Bonhoeffer writes (under the heading *Die vorletzten Dinge*): 'Belief in Creation: God of time and of patience, not only of severance, of judgment.'[66] Working note No. 50 also records: 'Time – another expression for the patience of God, with the goal that humanity becomes God's own possession.'[67] In other words, for Bonhoeffer, the eschatological time in which the last things and things before the last exist in dynamic relationality is the time of God's patience. As the time of God's patience eschatological time is *derivative* time. Time, that is, whose character and meaning, in fact whose very existence, is wholly dependent upon God's *gift* of time to his creation and his creatures such that he is *patient* with them unto redemption in and through time. One might say, therefore, that (according to Bonhoeffer) the patience of God is God's giving of time to things before the last in accordance with God's will to allow graciously that which he has created – most fundamentally the media of space and time – continued creaturely existence for the sake of its own fulfilment.[68] In this way, God's giving of time to things before the last is, moreover, the gift of *intentioned* time. Time is directed towards and thereby intends the specific end of things before

---

be accounted for by reference to this category is thus mine and not (explicitly) Bonhoeffer's. In what follows, the category of divine patience is proposed as the most appropriate way to index Bonhoeffer's thick theological description of the dynamic relationality in which last things and things before the last exist in eschatological time. The category is so proposed because that relation – in consequence of the movement of God the Holy Spirit with respect to space and time – is understood by Bonhoeffer only in reference to the conditionality and eschatological horizon which things before the last are invested with by last things in the time between apocalypse and (future) *parousia*. This divine investment, moreover, necessitates that things before the last be preserved for the last things precisely because the things before the last now exist – to echo the language of scripture's key affirmation of God's gracious patience (2 Pet. 3.8ff.) – in the mode of promise. In this promissory mode, things before the last are subject to an existence which *is* only because of God's 'Yes', and which awaits its own future fulfilment because of God's 'No'. It is for these reasons that the category of divine patience is thus deployed in what follows to account for the dynamic relationality that exists in Bonhoeffer's thought between the last things and things before the last in eschatological time.

[64] See *DBW* 6, 152.
[65] See ibid., 152 and 154.
[66] *ZE*, 54.
[67] Ibid., 55.
[68] The proximity to Barth of Bonhoeffer's understanding of the concept of God's patience should be noted here. For Barth, the patience of God is God's 'purposeful concession of space and time' to his creation and his creatures, such that he accepts their existence as a reality 'distinct from', but 'side by side with', the reality of his own existence. This acceptance thus ensures that '[God] does not suspend and destroy … this other [reality] but accompanies and sustains it and allows it to develop in freedom.' Moreover, because God in Christ by the Holy Spirit intervenes with*in* and *for* this other reality, God in fact takes up the cause of the creature and creation to the effect that space and time is kept for them by God, in order that God can have space and time for them in the form of their faith in his Word. God thereby fulfils God's will towards his creation and his creatures by the gift of spatio-temporality that is 'given with a definite intention'. In other words, space and time (and freedom therein) is given (and allowed) by God in expectation of a response in faith to the One who is the gift-giver. See *CD* II/1, 407–22 [408, 411, 410 and 408].

the last when God, in and through Christ's own self in his (future) *parousia*, is all in all.[69] It is this intentioned gift of time to things before the last and God's concomitant acceptance *of* time such that time is maintained as eschatological time for the purpose of the fulfilment of God's creation and his creatures, that, for Bonhoeffer, is the patience of God. As things before the last await their fulfilment in new creation in the event of Christ's (future) *parousia*, things before the last are thus necessarily caught up in consequence of the economy of God's patience in the eschatological and teleological movement of God the Holy Spirit towards their own redemptive and salvific 'end', in, through and outwith space and time.

Indeed, as Bonhoeffer notes in the context of his seminar on the New Testament concept of patience (ὑπομονή), '*the goal of* ὑπομονή *is* σωτηρία'.[70] Accordingly, the patience of God is then linked by Bonhoeffer to both God's ἀνοχή and God's μακροθυμία. The patience of God is his 'holding back' and 'long-suffering' in relation, primarily, to the (continuing) presence of sin in this 'old' or present (fallen) world in the time between apocalypse and (future) *parousia*, and thus (temporally speaking) the gracious delay of the final exercise of his passion in the event of the resurrection of the dead and the last judgement. This time is a delay which in 'God's kindness is meant to lead ... to repentance',[71] or, as Bonhoeffer conceives it, has as its object, by the eschatological and teleological movement of God the Holy Spirit, the (future) salvation of all creatures and the drawing of creation to its consummation in the world of new creation.[72] The fact of this withholding by God of God's last word, or else, one might say, God's restraint of Godself unto redemption, Bonhoeffer sees evidenced paradigmatically in the raising of Jesus Christ from the dead by God the Holy Spirit: 'What takes place [in the resurrection] is not the destruction of life in the body but its new creation. ... In the resurrection we recognize that God has not given up on the earth, but has himself won it back. God has given it a new future, a new promise.' The resurrection, he continues,

> is the grace of Jesus Christ, that he does not yet reveal himself to the world openly; because in the same moment in which that were to happen, the end and with it the judgment on unbelief would be here. Thus, the Risen One withholds any visible self-vindication before the world. In his hidden glory he is with his church-community and allows himself to be witnessed to, to all the world, through the word, until he comes again on Judgment Day, visible for all people.[73]

For Bonhoeffer, then – and precisely until the risen and ascended Christ comes from heaven to exercise, finally, God's passion on earth – it is impossible not to think of the patience of God also in relation to the New Testament concept of hope (ἐλπίς).[74]

---

[69] See Rachel Muers, 'Silence and the Patience of God', *Modern Theology* 17.1 (2001), 86–7.
[70] *DBWE* 15, 354.
[71] Rom. 2.4b.
[72] See *DBWE* 15, 354–5; cf., *ZE*, 55.
[73] *DBW* 16, 472 and 474.
[74] See *DBWE* 15, 353.

Bonhoeffer speaks of this in 'After Ten Years' as 'optimism'.[75] 'Optimism', he writes, is 'the will for the future that is coming', and more specifically 'to hope for a better future that is coming onto the earth and to prepare for it'.[76] Bonhoeffer continues: 'It may be that Judgment Day will dawn tomorrow; then we will gladly lay down the work of our hands for [this] better future that is coming, but not before.'[77] To live, therefore, either by the way of radical Christianity and 'dream longingly of a more beautiful future that is coming and thereby try to forget the present',[78] or by the way of compromise Christianity and 'collapse [life] into the present'[79] without remainder, are for the Christian in the time of God's patience two equally impossible positions. Instead, the only possible position is 'the very narrow and sometimes barely discoverable way of taking each day as if it were the last, and yet, in faith and responsibility, living as if there is still a great future that is to come'.[80] This narrow or optimistic way or better still *patient* way in which life is lived actively in eschatological time between 'the tension of the salvific future that is coming and the empirical present'[81] is thus grounded by Bonhoeffer in God's *own* patience towards redemption.

Indeed, one can live patiently, hoping actively, in other words, for the coming of *God's* future – which itself is the *world's own* future for the future of God comes to *this* world – only because God in Christ by the Holy Spirit *has* come, *is* coming and in his own (future) *parousia will* come again. For Bonhoeffer, the one who is patient and who thus watches and waits for God's coming future is enabled to be patient and so watch and wait only because she has been made (in justification) eschatologically new in Christ (in the church) by God the Holy Spirit, and thereby knows that God is the God who comes.[82] Bonhoeffer states:

> The God who will *come* is the One who has *already* come. ... The same God, who entered into the midst of history ... is the First and will be the Last. God has come. For this reason alone can we wait for him to come again and yet again, and for him one day to come for the last time, no longer veiled in history's clothing of suffering and of death, but visible to all the world as Judge and Redeemer at the end of time.[83]

Thus, the justified one, as the eschatologically new human being of God's future, *is* and can be the patient one only because of God's eschatological and apocalyptic incursion into spatio-temporality and the concomitant economy of God's patience, which concedes to this (created) reality a reality of its own in the time between apocalypse and (future) *parousia*. The patient way in which the justified one is to live in

---

[75] *DBW* 8, 36.
[76] Ibid.
[77] Ibid.
[78] Ibid., 35; cf., *ZE*, 54.
[79] *DBW* 8, 35; cf., *ZE*, 54.
[80] *DBW* 8, 35.
[81] *DBW* 15, 340; cf., *DBW* 8, 226: 'We live in the time of things before the last and believe in the last things, is that not so?'
[82] See *DBW* 11, 388, 389 and 394; cf., Chapter 2, Section II and Chapter 3, Section III of this book.
[83] *DBW* 11, 393 (emphasis added).

eschatological time as the time of God's patience is possible, then, *humanly* speaking, only in consequence of the *divine* patience towards that which God has created. Furthermore, in God's restraint of Godself to hold back the final exercise of God's passion on earth for the sake of the earth's own (future) fulfilment in new creation, things before the last are *preserved* dependently and intentionally in relation to the last things. It is precisely this dependent and intentioned relation derivative of God's patience in which things before the last exist, which, moreover, renders for Bonhoeffer the patience of God ultimately as a 'patience arising out of love'.[84] Until the redemption of creation, patience arising out of love 'bears all things, believes all things, hopes all things, [and] endures all things',[85] and, as Muers notes, 'specifies God's love as the will to give *time* to the beloved, and, in that giving of time, to continue in love'.[86] This is such that, in the time between apocalypse and (future) *parousia*, the object of God's patient love – the things before the last – is not only preserved, but *is* preserved because the things before the last *are* (and are intended to be) caught up in the redemptive and salvific movement of God the Holy Spirit in, through and outwith this eschatological time. Put differently and helpfully by Muers: 'To affirm that God's love is patient love is to affirm that God's love is the answer to the question "Why is there time?"'[87] In God's gracious gift of (intentioned) time to his creation and his creatures, the patient love of God preserves the things before the last (and the time in which they exist as eschatological time), and in that preservation wills those things (and that time) to their own fullness in redemption and salvation in advance of their end in the event of Christ's (future) *parousia*.

For Bonhoeffer, things before the last *must* then be 'preserved for the sake of the last things'[88] *because* of the economy of God's patience. For in its holding back of the final exercise of God's passion on earth, the patience of God in fact intends that in eschatological time as the time of God's patience last things come into and upon the things before the last, such that the latter is prepared for the (final) coming of the former (and thereby the latter's own future end) according to God's own purpose. Thus, the economy of God's patience is God's act of being-loving in accordance with God's will that the eschatological time in which things before the last exist is not 'a time of empty waiting',[89] as if the time between apocalypse and (future) *parousia* was 'sheer temporariness'.[90] Rather, eschatological time is, as Harink states, 'time pregnant with the *patience* of God', such that 'we live in the *fullness* of time of God's gracious patience

---

[84] *DBW* 15, 342.
[85] 1 Cor. 13.7.
[86] Muers, *Keeping God's Silence*, 93 (emphasis added); cf., Eberhard Jüngel, 'Gottes Geduld – Geduld der Liebe', in *Wertlose Wahrheit: Zur Identität und Relevanz des christlichen Glaubens, Theologische Erörterungen III*, 2. Auflage (Tübingen: Mohr Siebeck, 2003), 190–1: 'In his patience God again demonstrates that he is love ... since in his patience God proves himself as the One who is for his creature, as the One who is for the existence of another. God is patient in that he takes time into himself in order to grant time and space to another. In this respect, the purity of love is tested in patience.' For Jüngel, patience 'says "yes" to the being other of the beloved other with the result that it bestows upon the other space and time'.
[87] Muers, 'Silence and the Patience of God', 86.
[88] *DBW* 6, 152.
[89] Harink, *1 & 2 Peter*, 180.
[90] Ziegler, 'Voices in the Night', 139.

– a time given to us in which to repent'.⁹¹ In Bonhoeffer's language, this time is a time given to us in which to 'prepare the way' for last things to come into and upon the things before the last.⁹² Moreover, we are given this task of preparing the way precisely because the time in which we are given graciously by God to live is, as eschatological time, time fulfilled (*erfüllt*).⁹³ Time, in other words, has been brought into *proper* or *genuine* being – that is, intentioned being – by God's eschatological and apocalyptic incursion into it in Christ, who, through the agency of the Holy Spirit of God, is 'the fullness of time'.⁹⁴ Time, subsequently, is now 'kept' by the economy of God's patience as eschatological time for the task of preparing the way. To this extent, Bonhoeffer's understanding of the patience of God echoes the central Judeo-Christian affirmation that God is patient that one finds summarized in 2 Peter 3:

> With the Lord one day is as a thousand years and a thousand years are as one day. The Lord is not late to fulfil his promise … but is patient towards you, not willing that any should perish, but that all should come to repentance … [as] … we await new heavens and a new earth. … Therefore, beloved, while you are awaiting [and hastening] these things, strive to be without spot or blemish in his sight, at peace, and regard the patience of our Lord as salvation.⁹⁵

For Peter, the patient way of God's people waiting for the arrival of new creation is thus an *active* waiting. In other words, this waiting, to use Peter's language, is a 'hastening'

---

⁹¹ Harink, *1 & 2 Peter*, 180.
⁹² See *DBW* 6, 153ff.
⁹³ See *ZE*, 55. That time is fulfilled and brought into proper being in Bonhoeffer's thought only in the event of the apocalypse of God's gospel may in part be what drives his later assertion that the 'world has come of age [*mündig*] *through* Jesus Christ' (*DBW* 8, 504), such that 'the world that *has* come of age [*Mündigkeit*] … is now actually better understood than it understands itself, namely, from the gospel and from Christ' (*DBW* 8, 482). The world does not – and cannot – come of age by itself because things before the last exist only in a generative and dependent relation to the last things. Things before the last thus have no value in-and-of-themselves. Only in the event of the apocalypse of God's gospel is the next-to-lastness of what is before the last genuinely established – fulfilled or brought to adulthood (*Mündigkeit*), that is – in consequence of things before the last being thereby intentioned towards the last things in the redemption and salvation of creation. For Bonhoeffer, spatio-temporality *is* a theological category and one must speak, therefore, *theologically* about empirical phenomenology, not least in relation to the socio-historical or human empirical reality of a world whose being *has been* fulfilled in the apocalypse of God's gospel, and *will be* fulfilled in a final transfiguration of worldly being in the event of Christ's (future) *parousia*. There is thus a need to query the appropriateness of Green's reading of *Mündigkeit* as being *first* a general anthropological category, which Bonhoeffer interprets, *subsequently*, theologically (see Green, *Bonhoeffer*, 248–58). The case instead is rather more nuanced with the theological and anthropological categories existing in a dynamic relationality dependent – through the event of the apocalypse of God's gospel – on the category of the theological. For a *theological* specification of *Mündigkeit* and its cognate category of 'religionlessness', see Tom Greggs, 'Religionless Christianity in a Complexly Religious and Secular World: Thinking Through and Beyond Bonhoeffer', in Stephen Plant and Ralf K. Wüstenberg, ed. *Religion, Religionlessness and Contemporary Western Culture: Explorations in Dietrich Bonhoeffer's Theology* (Frankfurt am Main: Peter Lang, 2008), 111–25; cf., Greggs, *Theology against Religion*, 39–73. On Bonhoeffer's category of 'religionlessness', see Wüstenberg, *A Theology of Life*.
⁹⁴ *ZE*, 55.
⁹⁵ 2 Pet. 3.8-9, 13, 12 and 14–15 (amended). For a helpful discussion of 2 Peter 3, notably in parallel with treatments of eschatological delay in Jewish apocalyptic tradition, see Richard J. Bauckham, 'The Delay of the Parousia', *Tyndale Bulletin* 31 (1980), 3–36.

(σπεύδοντας) within eschatological time of the arrival of new creation in consequence of the repentance and 'godly acts' (εὐσεβείας) of the eschatologically new people of God in Christ (in the church).[96] Or as Bonhoeffer might put it, the patient way of God's people waiting for the arrival of new creation is a 'working' for the future that is coming onto the earth in consequence of the church and its members preparing the way for last things to come into and upon the things before the last in advance of the event of Christ's (future) *parousia*. The waiting which Bonhoeffer envisages, and which, in one sense, is definitive of the patient way of God's people, consists, then, not in a passive doing nothing but rather in an active doing something.[97] As Christoph Friedrich Blumhardt defines it, that 'something' is the church's 'eagerness to smooth the way' for the coming of God through the church's own practical and tangible action in the world – action that is to work for the good of the world and thereby is intended towards putting the world right.[98] Moreover, such action is necessary precisely because 'everything ... that is and comes from God's kingdom must first be *prepared* on earth'.[99] Thus, when the church acts – when it '"hasten[s]" and "wait[s]" towards God like this, the consummation is prepared'.[100]

This preparation does not mean, however, that the arrival of new creation in the event of Christ's (future) *parousia* is (in any way) *conditional* upon the church's action, either on its repentance and godly acts or on its preparing the way (effectively) for last things to come into and upon the things before the last. The event of Christ's (future) *parousia* in which new heavens and a new earth will arrive onto the earth is conditioned only by *God* – by God's sovereignty over space and time as created realities. Yes, the patient way of God's people waiting for the arrival of new creation is an active or *working* waiting, but in eschatological time as the time of God's patience it remains nonetheless an active or working *waiting*: 'About that day and hour no one knows, neither the angels in heaven nor the Son, but only the Father.'[101] At the same time, because things before the last exist only (according to Bonhoeffer) in a generative and dependent relation to the last things, things before the last have 'no capacity to "make" or to "find" a way'[102] to the last things such that they might condition their arrival in any event. Bonhoeffer argues that there is in fact no method, no way to the last things from things before the last: 'Method is the path *from* things before the last *to* the last things. Preparing the way is the path *from* the last things *to* things before the last.'[103] In the time between apocalypse and (future) *parousia*, and, temporally speaking, at the

---

[96] See 2 Pet. 3. 11-12.
[97] See Christoph Friedrich Blumhardt, *Waiting in Action* (Farmington: The Plough Publishing House, 1998), 28; cf., DBWE 8, 49: 'Inactive waiting and dully looking on are not Christian responses. Christians are called to action.'
[98] Blumhardt, *Action in Waiting*, 77.
[99] Ibid., 78.
[100] Karl Barth, 'Afterword', in Blumhardt, *Action in Waiting*, 222.
[101] Mk. 13.32. The patient way of God's people waiting for the arrival of new creation is to be seen, therefore, in what Barth describes (commenting on the ideas of Blumhardt) as 'a double movement in heaven and on earth' (Barth, 'Afterword', in Blumhardt, *Action in Waiting*, 220-1). The patient way of God's people is both a waiting for the coming of new creation from God in heaven and a working on earth towards that coming.
[102] Janz, *God, the Mind's Desire*, 195.
[103] DBW 6, 159 (emphasis added).

end of this eschatological time, it is for the last things – and for the last things alone – to make their *own* way into and upon things before the last.[104]

For Bonhoeffer, the church's task of working actively for the future that is coming onto the earth by its preparing the way for last things to come into and upon the things before the last cannot – and must not – therefore be equated simply with the creation or realization of 'certain desirable and conducive [*Zweckmäßig*] conditions' on the earth.[105] Indeed, it is not *human* agency – not even 'religious', 'godly' or 'Christian' agency, and certainly not the agency of the church's orthodoxy or orthopraxy – that conditions the arrival of new creation, but *divine* agency. This divine agency is the economy of God's patience which is *un*conditioned. More precisely, the agency is conditioned only by Godself being patient, and the goal of God's patience *is* the salvation and redemption of creation and creaturely being in new creation. The patience of God does not end, so-to-speak, sometime or somewhere, in the sense of it being either exhaustible or constrained by human action,[106] but instead is *patiens quia aeternus*,[107] and thereby is free from *im*patience. To make the divine patience – and derivatively the arrival of new creation – conditional in any way, therefore, would be to render the divine patience *impatient*, and to suggest, concomitantly, a point at which it might be exhausted or come to an end, which itself would be to negate, problematically, the divine patience as *God's* patience.

Notwithstanding that the arrival of new creation is conditioned in Bonhoeffer's thought by the patience of God alone, this conditioning should not be understood to detract from the church's task of working *actively* for the future that is coming onto the earth by preparing the way for last things to come into and upon the things before the last through its own repentance and godly acts. Indeed, the foregoing discussion has demonstrated that the economy of God's patience keeps eschatological time as the time of God's patience precisely for this task – a task, then, which, while *not conditioning* either the coming of last things into and upon the things before the last in eschatological time, or the final coming of last things at the end of this time in the event of Christ's (future) *parousia*, nevertheless *does hasten* their coming. Bonhoeffer writes:

> Preparing the way is a matter of actual intervention in the visible world. … Nevertheless, everything depends on this action being a spiritual reality. … Only a spiritual preparing the way will be followed by the gracious coming of the Lord. But this means that visible deeds … must be deeds of humility before the coming Lord, and that means deeds of repentance. Preparing the way means repentance … but … repentance demands deeds. So preparing the way certainly has very definite conditions in view that are to be produced.[108]

---

[104] See Janz, *God, the Mind's Desire*, 195.
[105] See *DBWE* 6, 164. Here, 'conducive' in the sense that in their purposed intent towards the arrival of new creation those conditions might (somehow) be considered to condition that arrival.
[106] See Jüngel, 'Gottes Geduld – Geduld der Liebe', 192.
[107] The saying is Augustine's and is taken from Bauckham, 'The Delay of the Parousia', 26.
[108] *DBWE* 6, 164–5 (amended); cf., *DBW* 6, 156–7.

What, then, are these conditions that Bonhoeffer has in view, and which the active working of the church and its members to prepare the way for last things to come into and upon the things before the last is to produce in eschatological time? And how, specifically, are the visible deeds or action from which these conditions result rendered spiritual by Bonhoeffer such that the way that is prepared is itself spiritual, and is thus one which is followed by and does hasten the gracious coming of God? It is to these concerns, and to the implications of Bonhoeffer's thought here for the being of God's church-community as a particular and contingent socio-historical human community in eschatological time, that this chapter now turns to in seeking to establish the ecclesiological significance of this time as the time of God's patience.

III. Preparing the way: Ecclesiological implications

At the outset of the following discussion it is important to note that the point of identification between the being of the church and the categories of last things and things before the last is not lost on Bonhoeffer himself, notwithstanding the ethical context out of which the categories arise.[109] Following the trajectory of Bonhoeffer's own thought, therefore, it is apposite that the chapter now seeks to establish the ecclesiological significance of these categories, not least in relation to Bonhoeffer's motif of preparing the way, by which he envisages the church and its members working actively in eschatological time as the time of God's patience to hasten the coming of last things into and upon the things before the last. As Bonhoeffer imagined it would, and as it will be seen, Bonhoeffer's thought here offers fertile ground in which to root a theological account of the being of God's church-community in space and time and serves, therefore, to bear fruit for the task of further exemplifying his pneumatological and eschatological 'both/and' ecclesiological methodology. This exemplification can be seen most clearly in relation to a specific ecclesial *commission*, and concomitant responsible ecclesial *action* (derivative of this commission), that Bonhoeffer sees as definitive of the being of God's church-community as a particular and contingent socio-historical human community in eschatological time. In fulfilling this commission in responsible ecclesial action, the church and its members, in and through the Holy Spirit of God, not only prepare the way for last things to come into and upon the things before the last but also uphold the dynamic relationality which exists in eschatological time as a consequence of God's patience between God and temporal-historical reality. Indeed, because responsible ecclesial action is possible for Bonhoeffer only from within the pneumatological space of God's church-community, and thus is operative – functionally speaking – only by the Holy Spirit of God, it is action which can be seen to hold together *both* divine *and* human agency as a consequence of Bonhoeffer's pneumatological and eschatological 'both/and' ecclesiological methodology.

As Bonhoeffer proceeds to articulate it in *Die letzten und die vorletzten Dinge*, the work of the church and its members preparing the way for last things to come into

---

[109] See *DBWE* 8, 365.

and upon the things before the last in eschatological time, is directed, empirically speaking, towards the production of two concrete 'conditions': 'being human' (*Menschseins*) and 'being good' (*Gutseins*)'[110] – the first of which is understood as the condition of the possibility of the second.[111] These two conditions as things before the last are identifiable, moreover, only from the perspective of last things and thus only in their generative and dependent relation to the last things.[112] Consequently, being human is 'conditioned and constituted by being justified'[113] in one's encounter with the eschatological content of God's last word. For Bonhoeffer, 'Only the one who is justified becomes a "human being."'[114] In other words, only the one who is in Christ (in the church) has *true* – ecclesial – being as an eschatologically new *human* being. This true being is the consequence of Jesus Christ (and the church) coming by God the Holy Spirit 'into' the heart of the individual in justification, and the individual human being in Adam being transposed thereby into community with God and other human beings in Christ (in the church).[115] For Bonhoeffer, *what being* human is cannot be separated from *who human* being is. Being human, Bonhoeffer writes, 'is not a thing, an essence, or a concept, but a person – more specifically, a particular and unique person',[116] the eschatological person of Jesus Christ, 'the human being *par excellence*'.[117] To *be human*, therefore, is to respond to or to answer the life of Jesus Christ with one's own life, such that the 'Yes' and 'No' of God in Christ by the Holy Spirit to temporal-historical reality is incorporated and united in one's own life.[118] This is what *to be good* means for Bonhoeffer. Bonhoeffer writes: 'Good is life as it is in reality, that is, in its origin, its essence, and goal, life as understood by the statement: Christ is my life. Good is not a quality of life but "life" itself. Being good [*Gutsein*] means "to live".'[119] One lives only as one is human in answering or responding to Jesus Christ. One *is* human *and* good, therefore, only as one is oriented and ordered by God the Holy Spirit towards God and other human beings in Christ (in the church) in love. In this sense, the pneumatological space that God's church-community is in spatio-temporality thus bears the form of both being human and being good that in reality is meant to be borne by all people.[120]

To recall the argument of Chapter 3, being human and being good is, one might say, the temporal-historical form of the church and its members being – both ontologically and sociologically (in consequence of the social acts which constitute the relational ontology of God's church-community) – with and for one another and with and for the world. This way of being is possible, however, only with*in* the pneumatological space of God's church-community, resting as it does, fundamentally,

---

[110] *DBW* 6, 157.
[111] See Janz, *God, the Mind's Desire*, 195.
[112] See *DBW* 6, 151 and 152.
[113] Ibid., 152.
[114] *DBWE* 6, 160.
[115] See Chapter 3, Section III.ii and Chapter 4, Section II of this book.
[116] *DBWE* 6, 249–50.
[117] Ibid., 232.
[118] See *DBW* 6, 254.
[119] *DBWE* 6, 253.
[120] See ibid., 97.

on a pneumatologically defined sociological law of *Stellvertretung*.[121] For Bonhoeffer, the conditions of being human and being good that are to be produced by the work of the church and its members preparing the way for last things to come into and upon the things before the last in eschatological time, cannot be conceived, therefore, otherwise than in reference to God's *church*-community living a 'responsible life' (*verantwortlichen Lebens*) in 'responsible action' (*verantwortlichen Handelns*).[122] This action, in and through the Holy Spirit of God, walks towards, takes hold of and overcomes the presence and power of 'lovelessness' in the world,[123] in accordance with and after the pattern of the reality of Christ's own vicarious representative action.[124] Thus, for Bonhoeffer, what it means for the church and its members to *be* and to reveal itself *as* 'human' and 'good' is: to act on behalf and for the good of one's neighbour; to devote one's life completely to the life of another;[125] to bear witness to Jesus Christ as Lord and Messiah in the word preached and celebrated in the sacraments of baptism and Eucharist;[126] to practice *Brüderlich Seelsorge*; or to hear confession and actively take on the sins and guilt of another before God, including the sins and guilt of the whole world.[127] It follows, therefore, that such responsible ecclesial action, by which the church and its members, in and through the Holy Spirit of God, *are* human *and* good, and through which the conditions of being human and being good are produced – empirically speaking – both in the pneumatological space of God's church-community and in the space of the world, is what comprises the visible deeds of repentance by which the church and its members are said by Bonhoeffer to work actively, in fulfilment of their specific ecclesial commission, to prepare the way for last things to come into and upon the things before the last in eschatological time.

Indeed, for Bonhoeffer, being human and being good, in the form of responsible ecclesial action, is definitive of the being of God's church-community as it waits actively for the coming of new creation in eschatological time because it *is* action that prepares the way for last things to come into and upon the things before the last. It is action that *does* prepare the way for last things to come into and upon the things before the last, or action which *is* 'a spiritual reality'[128] that hastens the event of Christ's (future) *parousia*, precisely because it is *responsible* ecclesial action: ecclesial action is taken in '"accordance with reality" [*das Wirklichkeitsgemäßen*]'[129] – the reality, that is, of the apocalypse of God's gospel *in* space and time and by which spatio-temporality is 'stretched out' (*ausgespannt*) or 'suspended' (*eingespannt*) between God's judgement of fallen creation and his concomitant calling into existence, out of love for this creation: new creation. Ecclesial action is responsible, therefore, when in accordance with the reality of the apocalypse of God's gospel it takes place *concretely* not in abstraction

---

[121] See Chapter 3, Section III.ii and Chapter 4, Section II and III of this book.
[122] See *DBW* 6, 218–44 and 254–89 [256 and 269].
[123] See *DBWE* 8, 49; and Jüngel, 'Gottes Geduld – Geduld der Liebe', 192.
[124] See *DBWE* 6, 231–5.
[125] See ibid., 257–60.
[126] See ibid., 132, 256 and 352–62; and Chapter 4, Section III.i of this book.
[127] See *DBWE* 6, 275–83; and Chapter 4, Section III.ii of this book.
[128] *DBWE* 6, 164.
[129] Ibid., 222.

from the world but through the church and its members entering *in*to the world; when it works actively for the promised renewal of the world, in virtue of the church and its members being oriented and ordered by God the Holy Spirit towards God and other human beings in love; and, ultimately, when in humble recognition that the renewal of the world is promised or else conditioned only by the economy of God's patience, it surrenders itself as *human* action to the loving, judging and reconciling action of *God*, which alone draws the world to the world's own fulfilment in new creation.[130]

In other words, responsible ecclesial action can be said to be action which holds together *both* divine *and* human agency in consequence of Bonhoeffer's pneumatological and eschatological 'both/and' ecclesiological methodology: it is action that, in and through God the Holy Spirit, is both 'worldly through and through'[131] (in that it concentrates on the next-to-lastness of what is before the last – that is, on the actual empirical situation in which the world exists – reckoning, as Bonhoeffer puts it, with 'the worldliness of the world'), and that, in and through God the Holy Spirit, is the proleptic manifestation in the world of the world of new creation, reckoning with the coming of last things into and upon the things before the last (or as Bonhoeffer puts it, with 'the rule of God over the world').[132] Moreover, in being action that, in and through the Holy Spirit of God, reckons with the in-breaking (*Anbruch*) of last things into and upon the things before the last, it is action which also always takes place *in* the things before the last, waiting on the coming of last things.[133] Responsible ecclesial action thus according to Bonhoeffer prepares the way for last things to come into and upon the things before the last. Such action, then, commensurate as it is with the task of the church and its members preparing the way in eschatological time for last things to come into and upon the things before the last, is, as Bonhoeffer puts it, 'a commission of immeasurable responsibility given to all who know about the [first and final] coming of Jesus Christ'.[134] For Bonhoeffer, this responsibility given to God's church-community is immeasurable, because, as he continues:

> The hungry need bread, the homeless need a home, the person deprived of rights needs justice, the lonely need community, the undisciplined need order, and the slave needs freedom. [To which one could – and indeed should – add: those outside the church need summoning to the church, the sin of the church and its members needs bearing and forgiving, and the sins and guilt of the world need taking on by the church and confessing]. It would be a blasphemy against God

---

[130] See *DBW* 6, 245, 226 and 227. Bonhoeffer continues: 'To what extent a human action serves the divine goal of history … is something that is beyond what any person can know with ultimate certainty. It is left to the hidden counsel of God' (*DBW* 6, 226). For Bonhoeffer, God's action is always the condition of the efficacy and possibility of human action. Therefore, human action – if it *is* to be a spiritual reality – must always be an action (or deed) of humility, precisely because of its divine ground and the agency of God the Holy Spirit which alone is able to draw it into God's own action.

[131] *DBW* 6, 227.
[132] See ibid., 223.
[133] See ibid., 160.
[134] *DBWE* 6, 163.

and neighbour to leave the hungry hungry, precisely because God is closest to those in deepest need. For the sake of Christ's love which belongs to the hungry just as it does to me, we break bread with the hungry and share our home with them. If the hungry do not come to faith, the guilt thus falls on those who refused them bread. To bring bread to the hungry is preparing the way for the coming of grace. What happens here is something before the last. To give bread to the hungry is not yet to proclaim to them God's grace and justification, and to have received bread does not yet mean to stand in faith. But for the one who does it [give bread to the hungry] for the sake of the last things, this before the last thing [giving bread to the hungry] stands in relation to the last things. It is a thing before *the last*.[135]

What is clear from this extended quotation is that, for Bonhoeffer, the active work of responsible ecclesial action (be it giving bread to the hungry, confessing sins one to another, summoning those outside the church to the church or securing justice for the disenfranchised) requires God's church-community to attend *above all* – out of concern *for* the last things and in its waiting *on* the last things – to that which is *before* the last. Bonhoeffer writes: 'The church, while waiting for Judgment Day, has an obligation to the *historical* future that is coming. The church's perspective on the end of all things must not paralyse its *historical* responsibility.'[136] God's church-community avoids such paralysis in the active work of responsible ecclesial action, which fulfils the commission to prepare the way for last things to come into and upon the things before the last in eschatological time, and by which the concrete conditions of being human and being good are produced in order to hasten both that coming and the final coming of last things at the end of this time.

To recall the argument of Section II.i, because the last things and things before the last exist in eschatological time in dynamic relationality, and because God's church-community (accordingly) is commissioned to prepare the way for last things to come into and upon the things before the last in responsible ecclesial action, God's church-community can neither understand itself nor succumb to acting in eschatological time as either a radicalized community set apart and against the worldliness of the world or a community of compromise absorbed so absolutely in the world that it cannot tolerate God's rule over the world. Indeed, for Bonhoeffer, a radical resolution by the church and its members of the relation between the last things and things before the last is 'pharisaical'.[137] It renders God's church-community (problematically) as 'some kind of would-be proto-Christian ideal church-community' that dismisses the world out of hatred of the world.[138] However, *God's* church-community, if it is to engage in responsible ecclesial action in light of its commission to prepare the way for the coming of last things into and upon the things before the last in eschatological time, must instead serve the world in all of its historical worldliness 'up to the end [of this

---

[135] *DBW* 6, 155.
[136] Ibid., 123–4 (emphasis added).
[137] See *DBWE* 6, 155–6.
[138] See *DBW* 6, 147; cf., *DBW* 1, 258.

time]' in love.¹³⁹ This commission and the love of the world it necessitates is why, for Bonhoeffer, and before God,

> it makes a difference ... whether, in the midst of a fallen, lost world, people preserve or shatter the order of marriage, whether they practise justice or despotism. Of course, those who preserve marriage and protect justice are still sinners, but it makes a difference whether or not the things before the last are respected and taken seriously. Part of preparing the way is to value highly and empower the things before the last for the sake of the last things that are approaching.¹⁴⁰

Furthermore, this love of the world which respects and takes seriously the things of the world is why the deprivation of the 'conditions that are a part of being human' in the world – the things before the last, that is – in fact hinders the efficacy of or impedes the actual coming of last things into and upon the things before the last.¹⁴¹ The things before the last must, therefore, be preserved in eschatological time by God's church-community for the sake of the last things. Indeed, given the dynamic relationality that exists between the last things and things before the last in eschatological time, the present fallen world (*as* a thing before the last) is understandable *only* as 'the world *preserved* and *kept* by God for the coming of Christ'.¹⁴² One might say (to recall the argument of Section II.ii), the world is understandable only in the time of God's patience – a time which is kept (as eschatological time) by the economy of God's patience for the task of preparing the way, and thus for God's church-community to live as human beings 'a "*good*" life'¹⁴³ in responsible ecclesial action that attends to the actual empirical situation in which the world exists. Such action thereby seeks the world's own preservation and preparation for the event of Christ's (future) *parousia* by helping the world to *become* human and good. This task demands, therefore, that God's church-community resists the radical resolution of the relation between last things and things before the last which would dismiss the very (before the last) things *of* the world. It is these (before the last) things that the church and its members are in fact commissioned in eschatological time to preserve for the sake of the world's own future fulfilment.

It is crucial, however, that the church and its members, in engaging that commission in eschatological time, also resist any movement towards becoming in that time a community of compromise. In other words, in their attention to the next-to-lastness of what is before the last – indeed, in their active love of the worldliness of the world, necessary so as to avoid the danger of acting as a radicalized community in the world – the church and its members must not accommodate or acculturate (*Anpassung*) themselves to the world,¹⁴⁴ such that God's rule *over* the world is relinquished by them in the world. In carrying out the commission to prepare the way for last things to

---

¹³⁹ See *DBW* 6, 147.
¹⁴⁰ *DBWE* 6, 166 (amended); cf., *DBW* 6, 158.
¹⁴¹ See *DBW* 6, 152 and 154.
¹⁴² Ibid., 158.
¹⁴³ Ibid., 158.
¹⁴⁴ See ibid., 148.

come into and upon the things before the last, the church and its members, yes, are *in* the world, and with and for the world out of genuine Christian love, but such love cannot – and must not – tolerate the world absolutely. The world itself is after all a thing *before* the last. For the world to reach its own future fulfilment, therefore, or, to use Jüngel's language, 'for the victory of love to reach over the power of lovelessness' in the world,[145] the last things have to come into and upon the things before the last and accordingly must be attended to by the church and its members with the utmost seriousness.

Given its commission to prepare the way for last things to come into and upon the things before the last, God's *church*-community must, then, resist becoming in eschatological time either a radicalized community or a community of compromise. Bonhoeffer writes: 'The task is to strengthen the things before the last through an emphatic proclamation of the last things, and to protect the last things by preserving the things before the last.'[146] *God's* church-community does this in fulfilment of its specific ecclesial commission in responsible ecclesial action – action by which, in and through the Holy Spirit of God, the two concrete conditions of being human and being good which prepare the way for the coming of last things into and upon the things before the last are produced. In consequence of this, the church and its members uphold, against the dangers of either radicalism or compromise – and in exemplification of Bonhoeffer's pneumatological and eschatological 'both/and' ecclesiological methodology – *both* the last things *and* the things before the last in accordance with the dynamic relationality in which they exist in eschatological time.

In responsible ecclesial action God's *church*-community can be seen to ensure, therefore, that its temporal-historical form is commensurate with the purposed intent of eschatological time in which it has its being as *God's* church-community. Indeed, to collapse the polemically unified dynamic tension of *both* last things *and* things before the last in eschatological time, *either* by a radical dismissal of the world *or* by a compromised tolerance of the world, would be for God's church-community to misunderstand itself *as* God's church-community. The reason being that, on the one – radical – hand, the church and its members negate the next-to-lastness of the being of God's *church*-community as itself a thing *before* the last, that is, as a temporal-historical *human* community intentioned by God the Holy Spirit towards the coming of last things into and upon the things before the last both in eschatological time and in the redemption and salvation of creation at the end of this time. On the other – compromised – hand, however, the church and its members negate the lastness of the being of *God's* church-community as itself a *last* thing, that is, as the temporal-historical human community whose being in eschatological time is *in* the operative and gracious act of God the Holy Spirit. Put otherwise, in responsible ecclesial action, God's church-community shows itself to be *both* recipient *and* goal of God's patience.[147] As a thing *before* the last, God's *church*-community *receives* eschatological time as the time of God's patience such that in its waiting for the coming of new

---

[145] Jüngel, 'Gottes Geduld – Geduld der Liebe', 192.
[146] *DBW* 6, 161.
[147] See Muers, 'Silence and the Patience of God', 87 and 96.

creation it works actively to prepare the way for last things to come into and upon the things before the last in accordance with its own intentioned being towards God and the world. As a *last* thing, however, *God's* church-community *is* the proleptic manifestation in eschatological time of that which eschatological time as the time of God's patience is in fact intentioned: new creation. In this sense, the time of God's patience, most properly, can be said to be the eschatological time of God's church-community.

IV. Conclusion

On the basis of Bonhoeffer's pneumatological and apocalyptically eschatological conceptualization of spatio-temporality as grounded *extra se* in God and God's operative and gracious acts, this chapter has argued that the time within which God's church-community has its being is best identified and understood as *eschatological* time. As outlined in the above discussion, this time is defined most properly – because of the economy of God's patience – by an existent dynamic relationality between God and temporal-historical reality in which temporal-historical reality is conditioned by and preserved for the final reality of God in new creation. This dynamic relationality that exists in Bonhoeffer's thought between God and temporal-historical reality has been explicated in terms of his categories of last things and things before the last, with respect, in particular, to his related motif of preparing the way. The chapter has done so to establish the critical significance of eschatological time as the time of God's patience for Bonhoeffer's theological account of the particular and contingent socio-historical human community that the church in space and time is. The chapter has suggested that this significance lies in the specific ecclesial commission that God's church-community is given in eschatological time, and the concomitant responsible ecclesial action to which God's church-community is summoned in fulfilment of this commission, in consequence of the dynamic relationality that exists between God and temporal-historical reality in this time as the time of God's patience.

Moreover, because responsible ecclesial action is particular and contingent human action possible only from within the pneumatological space of God's church-community, in and through the Holy Spirit of God this action prepares the way effectively for the coming of last things into and upon the things before the last. This action works towards establishing in the church and in the world the concrete conditions of being human and being good. As such, responsible ecclesial action is action which in the time of God's patience upholds the existent dynamic relationality between God and temporal-historical reality in this time. Responsible ecclesial action does so because in accordance with this dynamic relationality of the final reality of God and temporal-historical reality in the time of God's patience, it is action which at once is (1) *human* action that, in and through the Holy Spirit of God, is concentrated on the actual empirical situation in which the world exists as a thing before the last; and (2) *divine* action because, in and through God the Holy Spirit, it is action which reckons with the in-breaking of last things into and upon the things before the last and as such is the proleptic manifestation in the world of the world of new creation. Responsible ecclesial action resists, therefore, the resolution of the relationality between last things and things before the last in the way of either radicalism or compromise. By its upholding of the polemically unified dynamic tension of *both* last things *and* things before the last in the time of God's patience, responsible ecclesial action can thus be said to hold together, in and through the Holy Spirit of God, *both* divine *and* human agency as a further exemplification of Bonhoeffer's pneumatological and eschatological 'both/and' ecclesiological methodology.

Conclusion

This book has been concerned with the asymmetrical yet interconnected relation of divine and human togetherness in the church's being as described by Dietrich Bonhoeffer. The book has also been concerned derivatively with a necessary and genuinely theological articulation in ecclesiological description of *both* divine *and* human agency in accordance with which, and out of due concern for appropriate dogmatic ordering and proportionality therein, the ecclesiologist satisfies the most basic ecclesiological task. This task has been said to be that of holding together in an account of the church *both* the being of God and God's operative and gracious acts *and* the being of the church's socio-historical human form which is derivative of and dependent upon those divine acts.

In Chapter 1, it was demonstrated that in approaches to contemporary ecclesiological discourse, and with disregard for the most basic ecclesiological task, there exists an endemic 'either/or' problematic of attending in ecclesiological description *either* to the church's socio-historical human form 'ethnographically' *or* to God's *ad intra* or *ad extra* life 'dogmatically'. Moreover, it was established that in both 'hard' and 'soft' approaches to 'dogmatic' and 'ethnographic' ecclesiology, ecclesiological speech tends towards disorder and disproportion both in terms of its material dogmatic content and formal presentation, such that the ability of the ecclesiologist to prosecute the most basic ecclesiological task successfully is limited.

In light of this endemic problematic present in approaches to contemporary ecclesiological discourse, the book has argued, with reference to Bonhoeffer's own historic construction of the endemic problematic, that Bonhoeffer's ecclesial thought, because of its 'both/and' ecclesiological methodology, proffers both material content by which to analyse critically and constructively the endemic 'either/or' problematic, and, over against other ecclesiological contributions to the field of ecclesiology per se, a unique methodological approach to ecclesiological description which treats therapeutically the endemic problematic. To argue thus, Chapter 2 identified the strictly theological, and more specifically pneumatological and apocalyptically eschatological foundations of Bonhoeffer's ecclesial thought that serve to fund his 'both/and' ecclesiological methodology in which the being of the church is conceived from both a 'dogmatic' and an 'ethnographic' perspective simultaneously. In laying these theological foundations, the chapter demonstrated (as a corrective to extant material on Bonhoeffer's ecclesiology) that in terms of 'relational' systematicity the foundational dogmatic *res* of Bonhoeffer's ecclesiology is not Christology or theological anthropology, but, most properly, an apocalyptically eschatologically indexed pneumatology. On this basis, it was argued that any engagement with Bonhoeffer's ecclesial thought must be theologically founded on his understanding of the being of the church in space and time being oriented to the eschatological telos in virtue of the person and work of God the Holy Spirit.

Having laid the theological foundations of Bonhoeffer's ecclesial thought in Chapter 2, Chapter 3 articulated, in dialogue with Bonhoeffer's constructed threefold typology of socio-historical human community, how the structure of Bonhoeffer's 'both/and' ecclesiological methodology is built, subsequently, on those pneumatological and apocalyptically eschatological foundations. Critically, it was seen that Bonhoeffer's pneumatological and eschatological 'both/and' ecclesiological methodology enables him to conceive and speak of the church's being as established and sustained by God the Holy Spirit *as* the particular and contingent socio-historical (and sinful) human community that the church in space and time is in its orientation to the eschatological telos. On the basis of this construction, it has been argued that Bonhoeffer thus understands the church as a pneumatological and eschatological community in space and time: in the time between the ascension of Christ and the *eschaton*, the church exists as the event of the divine act of *convocatio* which takes place in and through the Holy Spirit of God to create in spatio-temporality the particular and contingent socio-historical human community that the church as *congregatio* is. It is precisely Bonhoeffer's account of the Holy Spirit of God that holds together in the church's being an account of *both* divine *and* human agency – with the latter (out of due concern for appropriate dogmatic ordering and proportionality in ecclesiological speech) being relativized but not minimalized by the former – and thereby ensures the efficacy of Bonhoeffer's 'both/and' ecclesiological methodology as a therapeutic treatment to the endemic 'either/or' problematic present in approaches to contemporary ecclesiological discourse. Chapter 3 concluded, therefore, that in Bonhoeffer's 'both/and' ecclesiological methodology – in critique and correction of the disordered and disproportionate ecclesiological speech at work in 'dogmatic' and 'ethnographic' ecclesiology – both the non-necessity or sheer gratuitous nature of the church's being in space and time is secured, and the church's socio-historical human form is (derivatively and appropriately) accounted for. This was seen to be the result, however, only of the operative and gracious act of God the Holy Spirit, *in* which the being of *God's* church-community as a particular and contingent socio-historical *human* community is said to *be*, as the Holy Spirit of God works in and upon and outwith the church and its members to animate and ultimately perfect God's church-community and its unique ontic-social relations as *Geistgemeinschaft* in spatio-temporality. This pneumatologically and apocalyptically eschatologically founded 'both/and' ecclesiological methodology thus brought into view the sui generis sociological structure that the church in space and time is, in distinction to all other socio-historical forms of human community, but nevertheless *as* a sociological structure.

Having articulated Bonhoeffer's pneumatological and eschatological 'both/and' ecclesiological methodology, and identified, derivatively, the sui generis sociological structure of God's church-community as *Geistgemeinschaft* and concomitantly *Liebesgemeinschaft*, it was then outlined, in Chapters 4 and 5, how Bonhoeffer's 'both/and' ecclesiological methodology further enables him to account for the particular and contingent socio-historical human community that the church in space and time is, in a genuinely theological way. In both chapters, Bonhoeffer's pneumatological and apocalyptically eschatological conceptualization of spatio-temporality as grounded *extra se* in God and God's operative and gracious acts was engaged to demonstrate how, in a theological account of the church's being, empirical phenomenology must be spoken of theologically, in accordance with, and as a further exemplification of, the logic inherent to Bonhoeffer's own 'both/and' ecclesiological methodology. Accordingly, Chapter 4 demonstrated how the 'space' that God's church-community occupies in spatio-temporality as *congregatio* is understood by Bonhoeffer as a pneumatological space. It was seen that this pneumatological space, in consequence of the event of its foundation in the coming of God the Holy Spirit at Pentecost by which the church receives from the Holy Spirit of God its own human empirical form and associated vocational function(s), is set apart and against the space of the world *in* the world in order to be *with* and *for* the world. Significantly, then, God's *church-community* exists in spatio-temporality and has being as *God's* church-community therein, only in and by the Holy Spirit of God *and* as the church and its members confess – through God the Holy Spirit – the gospel of God to the world in the events of proclamation and spiritual care. More acutely, the pneumatological space of God's church-community was, therefore, specified as a confessional space, which itself was understood to be filled by the 'spaces' of proclamation and spiritual care. These 'spaces' were said to have their genesis in the event of the church's foundation at Pentecost and thus to have *both* their *divine* being and content, *and* their operative and effective functionality as particular and contingent *human* events of the pneumatological space of God's church-community in and through the Holy Spirit of God. It was argued, therefore, that both the space of proclamation and the space of spiritual care, being *in* the Holy Spirit in this way, consequently hold together both divine and human agency in exemplification of Bonhoeffer's pneumatological and eschatological 'both/and' ecclesiological methodology.

The 'both/and' ecclesiological methodology of Bonhoeffer's ecclesial thought and the concomitant seriousness with which he treats spatio-temporality theologically as a pneumatological and apocalyptically eschatological category was then further explicated in Chapter 5. Here, Bonhoeffer's categories of last things and things before the last were engaged to establish that the 'time' within which God's church-community has its being is understood by Bonhoeffer as eschatological time. Definitive of this time is a dynamic relationality between God and temporal-historical reality. It was suggested that this relationality is best accounted for in Bonhoeffer's thought by reference to the category of divine patience, and in consequence of which God's church-community is given in eschatological time as the time of God's patience a specific ecclesial commission which is fulfilled in responsible ecclesial action. This action was seen to be particular and contingent human action that is possible only from within the pneumatological space of God's church-community. This action is possible in and through God the Holy Spirit and works towards establishing in the church and the world the concrete conditions of being human and being good. This action thereby prepares the way in the time of God's patience for the coming of last things into and upon the things before the last in accordance with, and as a buttress of, the dynamic relationality that exists in this time between God and temporal-historical reality. Moreover, because responsible ecclesial action can be seen in eschatological time as the time of God's patience to uphold – in and through the Holy Spirit of God – *both* the final reality of *God and* temporal-*historical* reality, it was concluded that it is action which serves to exemplify Bonhoeffer's pneumatological and eschatological 'both/and' ecclesiological methodology, in which both divine and human agency are held together in the being of God's church-community by an account of God the Holy Spirit.

In light of the argument of this book, the book stands primarily as a contribution to the field of Bonhoeffer scholarship dedicated to pursuing evermore responsible interpretations of Bonhoeffer's theology and especially his ecclesiology on the basis of his complete theological oeuvre. In its identification of the pneumatological and apocalyptically eschatological foundations of Bonhoeffer's ecclesial thought, and in its derivative establishment of his pneumatological and eschatological 'both/and' ecclesiological methodology, in which an account of God the Holy Spirit serves to hold together in the being of God's church-community an account of both divine and human agency with appropriate dogmatic ordering and proportionality, the book has proffered, over against extant Bonhoeffer scholarship, a more deeply theological reading of Bonhoeffer's understanding of the church as a pneumatological and eschatological community in space and time. In doing so, the book has established, over against extant Bonhoeffer scholarship, that the foundational dogmatic *res* of Bonhoeffer's ecclesiology is most properly an apocalyptically eschatologically indexed pneumatology. Indeed, Bonhoeffer's ecclesial thought cannot be understood without the strictly pneumatological and apocalyptically eschatological foundations upon which it is built. Derivatively, therefore, the book has developed constructively, within the context of Bonhoeffer's ecclesiology, what is a vital but understudied theme in his theology – his pneumatology and concomitant apocalyptic eschatology – and issued, critically, a significant corrective to the well-trodden path in extant Bonhoeffer scholarship of indexing his ecclesiology to Christology, or (less commonly) to a theological anthropology. Finally, and in consequence of its argument that Bonhoeffer's pneumatological and eschatological 'both/and' ecclesiological methodology offers both material content by which to analyse constructively and critically an endemic 'either/or' problematic in approaches to contemporary ecclesiological discourse, and most vitally a therapeutic methodological response in relation thereto, the book has hopefully contributed something to the craft of ecclesiology per se, not least by its illumination of the fundamental importance of Bonhoeffer's ecclesial thought for all those who would wish to account theologically for the 'glory and greatness' of the word 'church'.[1]

As a contribution to both the ongoing task of interpreting Bonhoeffer's theological and ecclesiological legacy and the wider ecclesiological discussion concerning the church's self-understanding, this book is but a beginning. However, if the argument and claims made herein withstand critical review then they pose several possible lines of enquiry that necessitate (and hopefully stimulate) further dialogue and debate. First, for extant Bonhoeffer scholarship, the claim that Bonhoeffer's ecclesiology and ecclesiological methodology is indexed (and so must be read) pneumatologically and apocalyptically eschatologically is evocative. Indeed, given the

---

[1] See *DBWE* 10, 505.

weight of argumentation within such scholarship which not only indexes Bonhoeffer's ecclesiology Christologically but also treats his pneumatology and eschatology either somewhat dismissively or crudely, it is a claim that invites a response.

Second, for the wider ecclesiological endeavour, the identification of an endemic 'either/or' problematic present in approaches to contemporary ecclesiological discourse, together with the derivative claim that Bonhoeffer's 'both/and' ecclesiological methodology (as a unique methodological approach to ecclesiological description) is therapeutic to this problematic such that it sets a programmatic theological grammar for ecclesiology per se, is again evocative, and the implications of this are arguably profound. If the claim holds good – as the book purports it does – then the ecclesiologist who wishes to speak about the being of the church in a genuinely theological manner must ensure, in accordance with Bonhoeffer's pneumatological and eschatological 'both/and' ecclesiological methodology, that her account of the church (both in terms of its material dogmatic content and formal presentation) holds together *both* divine *and* human agency, such that both *God's* own being and the being of the church's socio-historical *human* form are spoken of appropriately with due concern for appropriate dogmatic ordering and proportionality in ecclesiological description. The ecclesiologist will do this only by attending to the work of the Holy Spirit of God and treating spatio-temporality seriously as a pneumatological and apocalyptically eschatological category. How this programmatic theological grammar for the ecclesiological endeavour might sit, however, with proponents of the so-called 'Ecclesiology and Ethnography' movement,² or for that matter with any one of the individual theologians read in Chapter 1 as being illustrative of either 'dogmatic' or 'ethnographic' ecclesiology and thus of the endemic 'either/or' problematic, is an open question. In this regard, further reflection, therefore, is needed, and a detailed comparative study of Bonhoeffer's pneumatological and eschatological 'both/and' ecclesiological methodology with any one of the theologians identified in Chapter 1 may prove illuminating, perhaps affording the opportunity to sharpen some of the signal insights proffered herein. But what is certain is that to speak of the church without due attention to the work of the Holy Spirit of God who brings the church about as an event is, as Greggs avers, 'ecclesiological Nietzscheanism'.³

Third, and finally, the socio-historical human church-community, if it understands itself as *God's* church-community that has its being only in and by the operative and gracious act of God the Holy Spirit, will, as Bonhoeffer urges, be a church that lives not for one single hour without thinking and praying the age-old prayer of Pentecost: '*Come, O Holy Spirit!*'⁴ Unpacking what this might mean for church practitioners today who seek to nurture the church's being by their own leadership of or participation in the church, is a task to which Bonhoeffer's ecclesial thought thus summons one to, and which on the basis of this book could be considered critical if those who participate in

---

² See Ward, ed. *Perspectives*, together with Scharen, ed. *Explorations*.
³ See Greggs, *Dogmatic Ecclesiology Volume One*, 14. Indeed, the account of the church that Greggs offers in the first volume of his *Dogmatic Ecclesiology* is precisely the type of account that (despite its title) sits well within the programmatic theological grammar for ecclesiology per se which Bonhoeffer's 'both/and' ecclesiological methodology sets.
⁴ See *DBWE* 14, 180.

and lead the church are to do so as people who understand what the church is and what constitutes the church as the church. Whatever this means in the time between the ascension of Christ and the *eschaton* for the church to be a church of *epiclesis*, however, one thing can be affirmed from the consideration of Bonhoeffer's ecclesiological description herein: the church is the church of God the Holy Spirit and its renewal will come from the Holy Spirit of God alone.

Bibliography

Adams, Nicholas and Elliot, Charles. 'Ethnography Is Dogmatics: Making Description Central to Systematic Theology'. *Scottish Journal of Theology* 53 (2000): 339-64.
Aquinas, Thomas. *Summa Theologica*. Translated by Fathers of the English Dominican Province. Westminster: Christian Classics, 1981.
Avis, Paul. *The Church in the Theology of the Reformers*. London: Marshall, Morgan & Scott, 1981.
Avis, Paul. *Ecumenical Theology and the Elusiveness of Doctrine*. London: SPCK, 1986.
Avis, Paul. *Reshaping Ecumenical Theology: The Church Made Whole?* London: T&T Clark, 2010.
Badcock, Gary D. *The House Where God Lives: Renewing the Doctrine of the Church for Today*. Grand Rapids: Eerdmans, 2009.
Barker, H. Gaylon. *The Cross of Reality: Luther's Theologia Crucis and Bonhoeffer's Christology*. Minneapolis: Fortress Press, 2015.
Barth, Karl. *Church Dogmatics*. 4 vols in 13 pts. Edited and translated by G. W. Bromiley, T. F. Torrance et al. Edinburgh: T&T Clark, 1956-1975.
Barth, Karl. *Das Wort Gottes und die Theologie: Gesammelte Vorträge*. München: Chr. Kaiser, 1929.
Barth, Karl. *Dogmatics in Outline*. Translated by G. T. Thomson. London: SCM Press, 1949.
Barth, Karl. *The Epistle to the Romans*. Translated by Edwyn C. Hoskyns. Oxford: Oxford University Press, 1968.
Barth, Karl. *God, Grace and Gospel*, Scottish Journal of Theology Occasional Papers No. 8, trans. James Strathearn McNab. Edinburgh: Oliver and Boyd, 1959.
Barth, Karl. *God Here and Now*. Translated by Paul M. van Buren. London: Routledge and Kegan Paul, 1964.
Barth, Karl. 'The Real Church'. *Scottish Journal of Theology* 3 (1950): 337-51.
Bauckham, Richard J. 'The Delay of the Parousia'. *Tyndale Bulletin* 31 (1980): 3-36.
Beker, J. Christiaan. *Paul's Apocalyptic Gospel: The Coming Triumph of God*. Philadelphia: Fortress Press, 1982.
Bethge, Eberhard. *Dietrich Bonhoeffer, A Biography: Theologian, Christian, Man for His Times*. Revised & edited by Victoria J. Barnett. Minneapolis: Fortress Press, 2000.
Blumhardt, Christoph Friedrich. *Waiting in Action*. Farmington: The Plough Publishing House, 1998.
Boff, Leonardo. *Church: Charism & Power: Liberation Theology and the Institutional Church*. London: SCM Press, 1985.
Boff, Leonardo. *Ecclesiogenesis: The Base Communities Reinvent the Church*. New York: Orbis Books, 1986.
Bonhoeffer, Dietrich. *Dietrich Bonhoeffer Werke*. 17 vols. Edited by Eberhard Bethge et al. Gütersloh: Gütersloher Verlagshaus, 1986-1999.
Bonhoeffer, Dietrich. *Dietrich Bonhoeffer Works*. 17 vols. Edited by Wayne Whitson Floyd Jr. et al. Minneapolis: Fortress Press, 1996-2014.

Bonhoeffer, Dietrich. *Zettelnotizen für eine "Ethik", Ergänzungsband zu DBW 6*. Edited by Ilse Tödt. München: Chr. Kaiser Verlag, 1993.

Borg, Marcus J. *Jesus: A New Vision: Spirit, Culture, and the Life of Discipleship*. San Francisco: Harper & Row, 1987.

Bornkamm, Heinrich. *Luther's Doctrine of the Two Kingdoms in the Context of His Theology*. Translated by Karl H. Hertz. Philadelphia: Fortress Press, 1966.

Brittain, Christopher C. 'Why Ecclesiology Cannot Live By Doctrine Alone: A Reply to John Webster's "In the Society of God"'. *Ecclesial Practices* 1 (2014): 5–30.

Brown, Delwin, Greeve Davaney, Sheila and Tanner, Kathryn, eds. *Converging on Culture: Theologians in Dialogue with Cultural Analysis and Criticism*. Oxford: AAR/Oxford University Press, 2001.

Brunner, Emil. *The Christian Doctrine of the Church, Faith, and the Consummation: Dogmatics Volume III*. Translated by David Cairns. London: Lutterworth Press, 1962.

Brunner, Emil. *The Misunderstanding of the Church*. Translated by Harold Knight. London: Lutterworth Press, 1952.

Buckley, James J. and Yeago, David S., eds. *Knowing the Triune God: The Work of the Spirit in the Practices of the Church*. Grand Rapids: Eerdmans, 2001.

Bulgakov, Sergius. *The Bride of the Lamb*. Translated by Boris Jakim. Grand Rapids: Eerdmans, 2002.

Calvin, John. *Commentary on the Book of Psalms*. Vol. 1. Translated by James Anderson. Edinburgh: The Edinburgh Printing Company, 1845.

Calvin, John. *Institutes of the Christian Religion*. 2 vols. Edited by John T. McNeill, translated by Ford Lewis Battles. Louisville: Westminster John Knox Press, 2011.

Campbell, Douglas A. *The Deliverance of God: An Apocalyptic Reading of Justification in Paul*. Grand Rapids: Eerdmans, 2009.

Caragounis, Chrys C. 'Kingdom of God, Son of Man and Jesus' Self Understanding'. *Tyndale Bulletin* 40, no. 1 (1989): 2–23.

Cavanaugh, William T. *Torture and Eucharist: Theology, Politics, and the Body of Christ*. Oxford: Blackwell, 1998.

Chapman, Mark. 'On Sociological Theology'. *Journal for the History of Modern Theology* 15 (2008): 3–15.

Clark, Adam C. and Mawson, Michael, eds. *Ontology and Ethics: Bonhoeffer and Contemporary Scholarship*. Eugene: Pickwick Publications, 2013.

Clines, David J. A. 'The Image of God in Man'. *Tyndale Bulletin* 19 (1968): 53–103.

Coakley, Sarah. *God, Sexuality, and the Self: An Essay 'On the Trinity'*. Cambridge: Cambridge University Press, 2013.

Congar, Yves. *I Believe in the Holy Spirit*. Translated by David Smith. New York: The Crossroad Publishing Company, 2015.

Crossan, John Dominic. *The Historical Jesus: The Life of a Mediterranean Jewish Peasant*. Edinburgh: T&T Clark, 1991.

de Boer, Martinus C. 'Paul, Theologian of God's Apocalypse'. *Interpretation* 56, no. 1 (2002): 21–33.

de Gruchy, John W., ed. *Bonhoeffer for a New Day: Theology in a Time of Transition*. Grand Rapids: Eerdmans, 1997.

de Gruchy, John W. 'A Concrete Ethic of the Cross: Interpreting Bonhoeffer's Ethics in North America's Backyard'. *Union Seminary Quarterly Review* 58, nos. 1–2 (2004): 33–45.

DeJonge, Michael P. *Bonhoeffer's Reception of Luther*. Oxford: Oxford University Press, 2017.

DeJonge, Michael P. *Bonhoeffer's Theological Formation: Berlin, Barth, and Protestant Theology*. Oxford: Oxford University Press, 2012.
de Lubac, Henri. *The Church: Paradox and Mystery*. Translated by James R. Dunne. Shannon: Ecclesia Press, 1969.
de Lubac, Henri. *The Splendour of the Church*. Translated by Michael Mason. London: Sheen and Ward, 1956.
Dodd, Charles H. *The Parables of the Kingdom*. London: Nisbet & Co., 1935.
Dodson, Christopher. 'The God Who Is Given: Bonhoeffer's Sacramental Theology and His Critique of Religion'. PhD diss., University of Aberdeen, 2016.
Dramm, Sabine. *Dietrich Bonhoeffer: An Introduction to His Thought*. Translated by Thomas Rice. Peabody: Hendrickson Publishers, 2007.
Dramm, Sabine. *Dietrich Bonhoeffer and the Resistance*. Translated by Margaret Kohl. Minneapolis: Fortress Press, 2009.
Dulles, Avery. *Models of the Church*. New York: Image Books, 2002.
Dumas, André. *Dietrich Bonhoeffer: Theologian of Reality*. Translated by Robert McAfee Brown. London: SCM Press, 1971.
Dunn, James D. G. *Christianity in the Making Volume 1: Jesus Remembered*. Grand Rapids: Eerdmans, 2003.
Durham, John I. *Word Biblical Commentary, Volume 3: Exodus*. Mexico City: Thomas Nelson, Inc. 1987.
Fant, Clyde E. *Bonhoeffer: Worldly Preaching*. Nashville: Thomas Nelson, 1975.
Farrow, Douglas. *Ascension & Ecclesia: On the Significance of the Doctrine of the Ascension for Ecclesiology and Christian Cosmology*. Edinburgh: T&T Clark, 1999.
Fatehi, Mehrdad. *The Spirit's Relation to the Risen Lord in Paul: An Examination of Its Christological Implications*. Tübingen: Mohr Siebeck, 2000.
Feil, Ernst. *The Theology of Dietrich Bonhoeffer*. Translated by Martin Rumscheidt. Minneapolis: Fortress Press, 1985.
Fergus, Donald M. 'Dietrich Bonhoeffer's Spatially Structured Ecclesiology: Reconfiguring the Confession of Christ's Presence'. PhD diss., The University of Otago, 2011.
Floyd, Wayne Whitson. *Theology and the Dialectics of Otherness: On Reading Bonhoeffer and Adorno*. Lanham: University Press of America, 1988.
Ford, David F. and Stamps, Dennis, eds. *Essentials of Christian Community: Essays for Daniel W. Hardy*. Edinburgh: T&T Clark, 1996.
Freyer, Hans. *Theory of Objective Mind: An Introduction to the Philosophy of Culture*. Trans. Steven Grosby. Athens: Ohio University Press, 1998.
Fulkerson, Mary McClintock. *Places of Redemption: Theology for a Worldly Church*. Oxford: Oxford University Press, 2007.
Godsey, John D. *The Theology of Dietrich Bonhoeffer*. London: SCM Press, 1960.
Green, Clifford J. *Bonhoeffer: A Theology of Sociality*. Rev. edn. Grand Rapids: Eerdmans, 1999.
Green, Clifford J. 'Trinity and Christology in Bonhoeffer and Barth'. *Union Seminary Quarterly Review* 60, nos. 1–2 (2006): 1–22.
Green, Clifford J. and Carter, Guy, eds. *Interpreting Bonhoeffer: Historical Perspectives, Emerging Issues*. Minneapolis: Fortress Press, 2013.
Greggs, Tom. *Dogmatic Ecclesiology Volume One: The Priestly Catholicity of the Church*. Grand Rapids: Baker Academic, 2019.
Greggs, Tom. 'Ecclesial Priestly Mediation in the Theology of Dietrich Bonhoeffer'. *Theology Today* 71, no. 1 (2014): 81–91.

Greggs, Tom. 'The Priesthood of No Believer: On the Priesthood of Christ and His Church'. *International Journal of Systematic Theology* 17 (2015): 374–98.
Greggs, Tom. *Theology against Religion: Constructive Dialogues with Bonhoeffer and Barth*. London: T&T Clark, 2011.
Gregor, Brian and Zimmermann, Jens, eds. *Bonhoeffer and Continental Philosophy: Cruciform Philosophy*. Bloomington: Indiana University Press, 2009.
Grenz, Stanley. *The Social God and the Relational Self: A Trinitarian Theology of the Imago Dei*. Louisville: Westminster John Knox Press, 2001.
Gunton, Colin E. *The Actuality of Atonement: A Study of Metaphor, Rationality and the Christian Tradition*. Edinburgh: T&T Clark, 1988.
Gunton, Colin E., ed. *The Cambridge Companion to Christian Doctrine*. Cambridge: Cambridge University Press, 1997.
Gunton, Colin E. *The Christian Faith: An Introduction to Christian Doctrine*. Oxford: Blackwell Publishing, 2002.
Gunton, Colin E. *Intellect and Action: Elucidations on Christian Theology and the Life of Faith*. Edinburgh: T&T Clark, 2000.
Gunton, Colin E. *The One, the Three and the Many: God, Creation and the Culture of Modernity*. Cambridge: Cambridge University Press, 1993.
Gunton, Colin E. *Theology Through the Theologians: Selected Essays, 1972–1995*. Edinburgh: T&T Clark, 1996.
Gunton, Colin E. '"Until He Comes": Towards an Eschatology of Church Membership'. *International Journal of Systematic Theology* 3 (2001): 187–200.
Gunton, Colin E. and Hardy, Daniel W., eds. *On Being the Church: Essays on the Christian Community*. Edinburgh: T&T Clark, 1989.
Gustafson, James M. *Treasure in Earthen Vessels: The Church as a Human Community*. New York: Harper & Brothers, 1961.
Habets, Myk, ed. *Third Article Theology: A Pneumatological Dogmatics*. Minneapolis: Fortress Press, 2016.
Haight, Roger. *Christian Community in History*. Vol. 1. New York: Continuum, 2004.
Harasta, Eva. 'Bonhoeffer's Lutheran Ecclesiology and Inter-Religious Dialogue: A Dogmatic Reading of Bonhoeffer'. In *Bonhoeffer and Interpretative Theory: Essays on Methods and Understanding*. Edited by Peter Frick, 239–50. Frankfurt am Main: Peter Lang, 2013.
Harasta, Eva. 'The Responsibility of Doctrine: Bonhoeffer's Ecclesiological Hermeneutics of Dogmatic Theology'. *Theology Today* 71, no. 1 (2014): 14–27.
Hardy, Daniel W. *Finding the Church: The Dynamic Truth of Anglicanism*. London: SCM Press, 2001.
Hardy, Daniel W. *God's Ways with the World: Thinking and Practising Christian Faith*. Edinburgh: T&T Clark, 1996.
Hardy, Daniel W. and Ford, David F. *Praising and Knowing God*. Philadelphia: The Westminster Press, 1985.
Hardy, Daniel W. and Sedgwick, P. H., eds. *The Weight of Glory: A Vision and Practice for Christian Faith: The Future of Liberal Theology*. Edinburgh: T&T Clark, 1991.
Hardy, Daniel W. with Hardy Ford, Deborah, Ochs, Peter and Ford, David F. *Wording a Radiance: Parting Conversations on God and the Church*. London: SCM Press, 2010.
Harink, Douglas. *Paul Among the Postliberals: Pauline Theology beyond Christendom and Modernity*. Grand Rapids: Brazos Press, 2003.
Harink, Douglas. *SCM Theological Commentary on the Bible: 1 & 2 Peter*. London: SCM Press, 2009.

Harvey, Barry. *Taking Hold of the Real: Dietrich Bonhoeffer and the Profound Worldliness of Christianity*. Eugene: Cascade Books, 2015.
Hauerwas, Stanley. *After Christendom? How the Church Is to Behave If Freedom, Justice, and a Christian Nation Are Bad Ideas*. Nashville: Abingdon Press, 1991.
Hauerwas, Stanley. *Approaching the End: Eschatological Reflections on Church, Politics, and Life*. Grand Rapids: Eerdmans, 2013.
Hauerwas, Stanley. *A Better Hope: Resources for a Church Confronting Capitalism, Democracy, and Postmodernity*. Grand Rapids: Brazos Press, 2000.
Hauerwas, Stanley. *A Community of Character: Toward a Constructive Christian Social Ethic*. Notre Dame: University of Notre Dame Press, 1981.
Hauerwas, Stanley. *Christian Existence Today: Essays on Church, World, and Living In Between*. Eugene: Wipf & Stock, 2010.
Hauerwas, Stanley. *Hannah's Child: A Theologian's Memoir*. London: SCM Press, 2010.
Hauerwas, Stanley. *In Good Company: The Church as Polis*. Notre Dame: University of Notre Dame Press, 1995.
Hauerwas, Stanley. *The Peaceable Kingdom: A Primer in Christian Ethics*. Notre Dame: University of Notre Dame Press, 1983.
Hauerwas, Stanley. *Sanctify Them in the Truth: Holiness Exemplified*. Edinburgh: T&T Clark, 1998.
Hauerwas, Stanley. *With the Grain of the Universe: The Church's Witness and Natural Theology*. Grand Rapids: Brazos Press, 2001.
Hauerwas, Stanley. *The Work of Theology*. Grand Rapids: Eerdmans, 2015.
Healy, Nicholas M. *Church, World, and the Christian Life: Practical-Prophetic Ecclesiology*. Cambridge: Cambridge University Press, 2000.
Healy, Nicholas M. *Hauerwas: A (Very) Critical Introduction*. Grand Rapids: Eerdmans, 2014.
Healy, Nicholas M. 'Karl Barth's Ecclesiology Reconsidered'. *Scottish Journal of Theology* 57 (2004): 287–99.
Healy, Nicholas M. 'Practices and the New Ecclesiology: Misplaced Concreteness?' *International Journal of Systematic Theology* 5 (2003): 287–308.
Healy, Nicholas M. 'What Is Systematic Theology?' *International Journal of Systematic Theology* 11 (2009): 24–39.
Hegel, Georg Wilhelm Friedrich. *Encyclopaedia of the Philosophical Sciences in Outline*. Edited by Ernst Behler, translated by Steven A. Taubeneck. New York: Continuum, 1990.
Hegstad, Harald. *The Real Church: An Ecclesiology of the Visible*. Cambridge: James Clarke & Co., 2013.
Höhne, David A. *Spirit and Sonship: Colin Gunton's Theology of Particularity and the Holy Spirit*. Farnham: Routledge, 2016.
Holyer, Robert. 'Toward an Eschatology of the Past'. *Theology* 89 (1986): 209–18.
Honecker, Martin. *Kirche als Gestalt und Ereignis: Die sichtbare Gestalt der Kirche als dogmatisches Problem*. München: Chr. Kaiser Verlag, 1963.
Hopper, David H. *A Dissent on Bonhoeffer*. Philadelphia: Westminster Press, 1975.
Hunsinger, George. 'Review: *Reclaiming Dietrich Bonhoeffer: The Promise of His Theology*'. *Modern Theology* 12, no. 1 (1996): 121–3.
Hütter, Reinhard. *Suffering Divine Things: Theology as Church Practice*. Translated by Douglas Stott. Grand Rapids: Eerdmans, 2000.
Janz, Paul D. *God, the Mind's Desire: Reference, Reason and Christian Thinking*. New York: Cambridge University Press, 2004.

Jenson, Robert W. *Systematic Theology*. 2 vols. New York: Oxford University Press, 1997 and 1999.
Jüngel, Eberhard. *God as the Mystery of the World: On the Foundation of the Theology of the Crucified One in the Dispute between Theism and Atheism*. Translated by Darrell L. Guder. Edinburgh: T&T Clark: 1983.
Jüngel, Eberhard. *Wertlose Wahrheit: Zur Identität und Relevanz des christlichen Glaubens, Theologische Eröterungen III*. 2. Auflage. Tübingen: Mohr Siebeck, 2003.
Kelly, Geffrey B. and Nelson, F. Burton. *The Cost of Moral Leadership: The Spirituality of Dietrich Bonhoeffer*. Grand Rapids: Eerdmans, 2003.
Kelsey, David. *Eccentric Existence: A Theological Anthropology*. 2 vols. Louisville: Westminster John Knox Press, 2009.
Kirkpatrick, Matthew D., ed. *Engaging Bonhoeffer: The Impact and Influence of Bonhoeffer's Life and Thought*. Minneapolis: Fortress Press, 2016.
Komonchak, Joseph A. 'Ecclesiology and Social Theory: A Methodological Essay'. *The Thomist* 45 (1981): 262–83.
Komonchak, Joseph A. *Foundations in Ecclesiology*, Supplementary Issue of the Lonergan Workshop Journal. Vol. 11. Boston: Boston College, 1995.
Kuhns, William. *In Pursuit of Dietrich Bonhoeffer*. Dayton: Pflaum Press, 1967.
Küng, Hans. *The Church*. London: Burns & Oates, 1967.
Küng, Hans. *Structures of the Church*. London: Burns & Oates, 1965.
Lange, Ernst. *Kirche für die Welt: Aufsätze zur Theorie kirchlichen Handelns*. Edited by Rüdiger Schloz. München: Chr. Kaiser Verlag, 1981.
Lawrence, Joel. *Bonhoeffer: A Guide for the Perplexed*. London: T&T Clark, 2010.
Leahy, Brendan. '"Christ Existing as Community": Dietrich Bonhoeffer's Notion of Church'. *Irish Theological Quarterly* 73 (2008): 32–59.
Lindbeck, George A. *The Nature of Doctrine: Religion and Theology in a Postliberal Age*. Louisville: Westminster John Knox Press, 1984.
Lindsay, Mark R. 'Bonhoeffer's Eschatology in a World "Come of Age"'. *Theology Today* 68, no. 3 (2011): 290–302.
Luther, Martin. *Luther's Works*. 55 vols. Edited and translated by Jaroslav Pelikan, Helmut Lehman et al. Minneapolis: Fortress Press, 1900–1986.
Macquarrie, John. *Christian Hope*. Oxford: Mowbrays, 1978.
Manrodt, David H. 'The Role of Eschatology in the Theology of Dietrich Bonhoeffer'. PhD diss., The Ecumenical Institute, St. Mary's Seminary and University, 1978.
Marsh, Charles. *Reclaiming Dietrich Bonhoeffer: The Promise of His Theology*. New York: Oxford University Press, 1994.
Marsh, Charles. *Strange Glory: A Life of Dietrich Bonhoeffer*. London: SPCK, 2014.
Martyn, J. Louis. *Galatians: A New Translation with Introduction and Commentary*. New York: Doubleday, 1997.
Mawson, Michael and Ziegler, Philip G., eds. *Christ, Church and World: New Studies in Bonhoeffer's Theology and Ethics*. London: Bloomsbury T&T Clark, 2016.
Mawson, Michael and Ziegler, Philip G., eds. *The Oxford Handbook of Dietrich Bonhoeffer*. Oxford: Oxford University Press, 2019.
Mawson, Michael. *Christ Existing as Community: Bonhoeffer's Ecclesiology*. New York: Oxford University Press, 2018.
Mawson, Michael. 'The Spirit and the Community: Pneumatology and Ecclesiology in Jenson, Hütter and Bonhoeffer'. *International Journal of Systematic Theology* 15 (2013): 453–68.

Mawson, Michael. 'Theology and Social Theory – Reevaluating Bonhoeffer's Approach'. *Theology Today* 71, no. 1 (2014): 69–80.
Mayer, Rainer. *Christuswirklichkeit: Grundlagen, Entwicklung und Konsequenzen der Theologie Dietrich Bonhoeffers*. Stuttgart: Calwer Verlag, 1969.
McBride, Jennifer M. *The Church for the World: A Theology of Public Witness*. New York: Oxford University Press, 2012.
Meilaender, Gilbert and Werpehowski, William, eds. *The Oxford Handbook of Theological Ethics*. New York: Oxford University Press, 2005.
Metz, Johannes B. *Theology of the World*. Translated by William Glen-Doepel. New York: Herder and Herder, 1969.
Milbank, John. 'Enclaves, Where Is the Church?' *New Blackfriars* 73 (1992): 341–52.
Milbank, John. *Theology and Social Theory: Beyond Secular Reason*. Oxford: Basil Blackwell, 1990.
Moltmann, Jürgen. *The Church in the Power of the Spirit: A Contribution to Messianic Ecclesiology*. Translated by Margaret Kohl. London: SCM Press, 1977.
Moltmann, Jürgen. *The Coming of God: Christian Eschatology*. Translated by Margaret Kohl. Minneapolis: Fortress Press, 1996.
Moltmann, Jürgen. *Theology of Hope: On the Ground and the Implications of a Christian Eschatology*. Translated by James W. Leitch. London: SCM Press, 1967.
Moltmann, Jürgen and Weissbach, Jürgen. *Two Studies in the Theology of Dietrich Bonhoeffer*. Translated by Reginald H. Fuller and Ilse Fuller. New York: Charles Scribner's Sons, 1967.
Moule, Charles F. D. *The Origin of Christology*. Cambridge: Cambridge University Press, 1977.
Muers, Rachel. *Keeping God's Silence: Towards a Theological Ethics of Communication*. Oxford: Blackwell Publishing, 2004.
Muers, Rachel. 'Silence and the Patience of God'. *Modern Theology* 17, no. 1 (2001): 85–98.
Murray, Paul D., ed. *Receptive Ecumenism and the Call to Catholic Learning: Exploring a Way for Contemporary Ecumenism*. Oxford: Oxford University Press, 2008.
Nelson, R. David, Sarisky, Darren and Stratis, Justin, eds. *Theological Theology: Essays in Honour of John B. Webster*. London: Bloomsbury T&T Clark, 2015.
Nickson, Ann L. *Bonhoeffer on Freedom: Courageously Grasping Reality*. Aldershot: Ashgate, 2002.
Niebuhr, H. Richard. *The Purpose of the Church and Its Ministry*. New York: Harper & Brothers, 1956.
Niebuhr, H. Richard. *'The Responsibility of the Church for Society' and Other Essays*. Edited by Kristine A. Culp. Louisville: Westminster John Knox Press, 2008.
Nielsen, Kirsten Busch, Wüstenberg, Ralf K. and Zimmermann, Jens, eds. *In Dem Rad in die Speichen fallen: Das Politische in der Theologie Dietrich Bonhoeffers*. München: Gütersloher Verlagshaus, 2013.
Nimmo, Paul T. *Being in Action: The Theological Shape of Barth's Ethical Vision*. London: T&T Clark, 2007.
Nygren, Anders. *Christ and His Church*. Philadelphia: The Westminster Press, 1956.
Ochs, Peter. *Another Reformation: Postliberal Christianity and the Jews*. Grand Rapids: Baker Academic, 2011.
O'Grady, Colm. 'The Church the Body of Christ in the Theology of Karl Barth and in Catholic Theology'. *Irish Theological Quarterly* 35, no. 1 (1968): 3–21.

Ott, Heinrich. *Reality and Faith: The Theological Legacy of Dietrich Bonhoeffer*. Translated by Alex A. Morrison. Philadelphia: Fortress Press, 1972.

Pangritz, Andreas. *Karl Barth in the Theology of Dietrich Bonhoeffer*. Translated by Barbara and Martin Rumscheidt. Grand Rapids: Eerdmans, 1999.

Pannenberg, Wolfhart. *Systematic Theology*. Vol. 3. Translated by G. W. Bromiley. Grand Rapids: Eerdmans, 1998.

Pannenberg, Wolfhart. *Theology and the Kingdom of God*. Edited by Richard John Neuhaus. Philadelphia: The Westminster Press, 1977.

Pasquarello III, Michael. *Dietrich Bonhoeffer and the Theology of a Preaching Life*. Waco: Baylor University Press, 2017.

Perrin, Norman. *The Kingdom of God in the Teaching of Jesus*. London: SCM Press, 1963.

Phillips, John A. *Christ For Us in the Theology of Dietrich Bonhoeffer*. New York: Harper & Row, 1967.

Plant, Stephen and Wüstenberg, Ralf K., eds. *Religion, Religionless and Contemporary Western Culture: Explorations in Dietrich Bonhoeffer's Theology*. Frankfurt am Main: Peter Lang, 2008.

Quash, Ben. *Found Theology: History, Imagination and the Holy Spirit*. London: Bloomsbury T&T Clark, 2013.

Quash, Ben. *Theology and the Drama of History*. New York: Cambridge University Press, 2005.

Rahner, Karl. *Theological Investigations*. 23 vols. Translated by Karl-H. Kruger, David Bourke et al. London: Darton, Longman & Todd, 1961–1992.

Rasmussen, Larry. *Dietrich Bonhoeffer: His Significance for North Americans*. Minneapolis: Fortress Press, 1990.

Rasmusson, Arne. *The Church as Polis: From Practical Theology to Theological Politics as Exemplified by Jürgen Moltmann and Stanley Hauerwas*. Notre Dame: University of Notre Dame Press, 1995.

Ratzinger, Joseph Cardinal. *Called to Communion: Understanding the Church Today*. Translated by Adrian Walker. San Francisco: Ignatius Press, 1996.

Ratzinger, Joseph Cardinal (Pope Benedict XVI). *Church, Ecumenism, and Politics: New Endeavors in Ecclesiology*. Translated by Michael J. Miller et al. San Francisco: Ignatius Press, 2008.

Ratzinger, Joseph. *Introduction to Christianity*. Translated by J. R. Foster. London: Burns & Oates, 1969.

Sanders, Ed P. *The Historical Figure of Jesus*. London: Allen Lane/The Penguin Press, 1993.

Sauter, Gerhard. 'The Concept and Task of Eschatology – Theological and Philosophical Reflections'. *Scottish Journal of Theology* 41 (1988): 499–515.

Sauter, Gerhard. *Die Theologie des Reiches Gottes beim älteren und jüngeren Blumhardt*. Zürich: Zwingli Verlag, 1962.

Schaff, Philip, ed. *A Select Library of the Nicene and Post-Nicene Fathers of the Christian Church*. Vol. 3. Grand Rapids: Eerdmans, 1956.

Scharen, Christian B., ed. *Explorations in Ecclesiology and Ethnography*. Grand Rapids: Eerdmans, 2012.

Scharen, Christian B. '"Judicious Narratives", or Ethnography as Ecclesiology'. *Scottish Journal of Theology* 58 (2005): 125–42.

Scheler, Max. *Formalism in Ethics and Non-Formal Ethics of Values: A New Attempt toward the Foundation of an Ethical Personalism*. 5th Rev. edn. Translated by Manfred S. Frings and Roger L. Funk. Evanston: Northwestern University Press, 1973.

Schillebeeckx, Edward. *Church: The Human Story of God*. New York: The Crossroad Publishing Company, 1996.

Schillebeeckx, Edward. *The Church with a Human Face: A New and Expanded Theology of Ministry*. New York: The Crossroad Publishing Company, 1988.

Schließer, Christine. *Everyone Who Acts Responsibly Becomes Guilty: The Concept of Accepting Guilt in Dietrich Bonhoeffer: Reconstruction and Assessment*. Neukirchen-Vluyn: Neukirchener Verlag, 2006.

Schlingensiepen, Ferdinand. *Dietrich Bonhoeffer 1906-1945: Martyr, Thinker, Man of Resistance*. Translated by Isabel Best. London: T&T Clark, 2012.

Schlink, Edmund. *The Coming Christ and the Coming Church*. Edinburgh: Oliver & Boyd, 1967.

Schweitzer, Albert. *The Quest of the Historical Jesus*. Translated by W. Montgomery. London: Adam and Charles Black, 1910.

Seeberg, Reinhold. *Christliche Dogmatik*. Erster Bd. Leipzig: A. Deicherticshe Verlagsbuchhandlung, 1924.

Shreeves, Keir. 'Bonhoeffer's Homiletics: The Spirit-Impelled Word of the Church for the Church'. PhD diss., University of Aberdeen, 2019.

Smith, Ronald Gregor, ed. *World Come of Age: A Symposium on Dietrich Bonhoeffer*. London: Collins, 1967.

Sorum, Jonathan D. 'The Eschatological Boundary in Dietrich Bonhoeffer's *Nachfolge*'. PhD diss., Luther Northwestern Theological Seminary, 1994.

Tanner, Kathryn. *Theories of Culture: A New Agenda for Theology*. Minneapolis: Fortress Press, 1997.

Thompson, Marianne Meye. *Colossians and Philemon: The Two Horizons New Testament Commentary*. Grand Rapids: Eerdmans, 2005.

Tönnies, Ferdinand. *Community and Society (Gemeinschaft und Gesellschaft)*. Translated by Charles P. Loomis. East Lansing: The Michigan State University Press, 1957.

Torrance, Thomas F. *Royal Priesthood*, Scottish Journal of Theology Occasional Papers No. 3. Edinburgh: Oliver and Boyd, 1955.

Torrance, Thomas F. *Space, Time and Incarnation*. London: Oxford University Press, 1969.

Torrance, Thomas F. *Theology in Reconstruction*. Eugene: Wipf & Stock, 1996.

Troeltsch, Ernst. *The Social Teaching of the Christian Churches*. 2 vols. Translated by Olive Wyon. London: George Allen & Unwin, 1931.

van der Ven, Johannes A. *Ecclesiology in Context*. Grand Rapids: Eerdmans, 1996.

Volf, Miroslav. *After Our Likeness: The Church as the Image of the Trinity*. Grand Rapids: Eerdmans, 1988.

Volf, Miroslav and Bass, Dorothy C., eds. *Practising Theology: Beliefs and Practices in Christian Life*. Grand Rapids: Eerdmans, 2002.

von Balthasar, Hans Urs. *Theo-Drama: Theological Dramatic Theory*. 5 vols. Translated by Graham Harrison. San Francisco: Ignatius Press, 1988–1998.

von Rad, Gerhard. *Genesis: A Commentary*. Translated by John H. Marks. London: SCM Press, 1961.

von Ranke, Leopold. *The Theory and Practice of History*. Edited by Georg G. Iggers. Abingdon: Routledge, 2011.

Ward, Pete. *Participation and Mediation: A Practical Theology for the Liquid Church*. London: SCM Press, 2008.

Ward, Pete, ed. *Perspectives on Ecclesiology and Ethnography*. Grand Rapids: Eerdmans, 2012.

Webster, John. *Confessing God: Essays on Christian Dogmatics II*. London: T&T Clark, 2005.
Webster, John. *Holiness*. London: SCM Press, 2003.
Webster, John. *Holy Scripture: A Dogmatic Sketch*. Cambridge: Cambridge University Press, 2003.
Webster, John. 'On Evangelical Ecclesiology'. *Ecclesiology* 1, no. 1 (2004): 9–35.
Webster, John. *Word and Church: Essays in Christian Dogmatics*. Edinburgh: T&T Clark, 2001.
Webster, John, Tanner, Kathryn and Torrance, Iain, eds. *The Oxford Handbook of Systematic Theology*. New York: Oxford University Press, 2007.
Weiss, Johannes. *Jesus' Proclamation of the Kingdom of God*. Translated by Richard H. Hiers and David L. Holland. London: SCM Press, 1971.
Welch, Claude. *The Reality of the Church*. New York: Charles Scribner's Sons, 1958.
Welker, Michael. *God the Revealed: Christology*. Translated by Douglas W. Stott. Grand Rapids: Eerdmans, 2014.
Werntz, Myles. *Bodies of Peace: Ecclesiology, Non-Violence, and Witness*. Minneapolis: Fortress Press, 2014.
Williams, Anna N. *The Architecture of Theology: Structure, System, and Ratio*. Oxford: Oxford University Press, 2011.
Wittgenstein, Ludwig. *Philosophical Investigations*. Rev. 4th edn. Translated by G. E. M. Anscombe, P.M.S. Hacker and Joachim Schulte. Oxford: Wiley-Blackwell, 2009.
Woelfel, James W. *Bonhoeffer's Theology: Classical and Revolutionary*. Nashville: Abingdon Press, 1970.
Wright, N. T. *Jesus and the Victory of God*. London: SPCK, 1996.
Wüstenberg, Ralf K. *A Theology of Life: Dietrich Bonhoeffer's Religionless Christianity*. Translated by Doug Stott. Grand Rapids: Eerdmans, 1998.
Ziegler, Philip G. 'Dietrich Bonhoeffer – An Ethics of God's Apocalypse?' *Modern Theology* 23, no. 4 (2007): 579–94.
Ziegler, Philip G. 'Eschatology and Secularity in the Late Writings of Dietrich Bonhoeffer'. In *Dietrich Bonhoeffer's Theology Today: A Way between Fundamentalism and Secularism?* Edited by John W. de Gruchy, Stephen Plant and Christiane Tietz, 124–38. München: Gütersloher Verlagshaus, 2009.
Ziegler, Philip G. '"Voices in the Night": Human Solidarity and Eschatological Hope'. In *Who am I? Bonhoeffer's Theology through His Poetry*. Edited by Bernd Wannenwetsch. London: T&T Clark, 2009.
Zimmermann, Jens and Gregor, Brian, eds. *Being Human, Becoming Human: Dietrich Bonhoeffer and Social Thought*. Cambridge: James Clark & Co., 2010.
Zizioulas, John D. *Being as Communion: Studies in Personhood and the Church*. London: Darton, Longman & Todd, 1985.
Zizioulas, John D. 'Le Mystère de l'Église dans la tradition orthodoxe'. *Irénikon* 60 (1987): 321–35.

Index

Act and Being 58 n.20, 64–5, 85, 86 n.100, 87, 90, 97, 102 n.192, 117 n.25, 126 n.91
actualism 25 n.86, 28, 52, 88 n.111, 117 n.25
actus directus 57 n.18, 131 n.131
actus reflexus 57 n.18, 131 n.131
Adams, Nicholas 3 n.12
analogia entis 86
analogia relationis 86, 90
Anderson, Victor 32
anthropology, theological 8, 63 n.61, 71 n.96, 83–91, 101, 126 n.91, *see also* person (personhood)
  ecclesiology and 8–9, 68–9, 70 n.96, 105 n.219, 165, 168
Aquinas, Thomas 57 n.13, 85 n.91
ascension, the 21 n.46, 96 n.159
aseity, divine 19, 24, 26, 28, 46, 86–9, 91, 92, 111
Augustine, of Hippo 85 n.91, 85 n.92, 125 n.78, 154 n.107
Avis, Paul 40 n.191, 55 n.2

Badcock, Gary D. 63 n.63
baptism 106 n.228, 128, 129, 130–2, 138, 157
  infant 131 n.131
Barker, H. Gaylon 66 n.77
Barth, Karl 2 n.3, 4 n.12, 22 n.59, 24–5, 27, 28 n.106, 28 n.107, 37, 46, 58 n.21, 61 n.49, 76 n.3, 86 n.101, 88 n.111, 117 n.25, 143 n.18, 148 n.68, 153 nn.100, 101
Baukham, Richard J. 152 n.95, 154 n.107
Beker, J. Christiaan 61 n.51, 124
Berger, Peter 69 n.89, 93 n.144
Bethge, Eberhard 56 nn.5, 6, 63 n.63, 66 n.78, 67 n.82
Blumhardt, Christoph Friedrich 153
Boff, Leonardo 32 n.132
Borg, Marcus J. 59 n.33

Bornkamm, Heinrich 125 n.78
Brittain, Christopher C. 30–1, 33 n.146
Brown, Delwin 31 n.122
Brunner, Emil 21–2, 27
Buckley, James J. 38 n.171
Bulgakov, Sergius 146 n.48

Calvin, John 17, 64 n.65, 85 n.92
Campbell, Douglas A. 61 n.51
cantus firmus 66 n.77, 67
Caragounis, Chris C. 146 n.52
Cavanaugh, William T. 4 n.12, 41 n.197
Chan, Simon 48 n.241
Chapman, Mark 32 n.128
Christ existing as community 9, 67 n.82, 96–7, 103
Christuswirklichkeit (Christ-reality) 125–6, 145
church, the
  actualization of 1–3, 6–7, 75, 77, 96–7, 99–109, 133–6
  as body of Christ 21–2, 23–4, 24–5, 27, 28 n.107, 30, 48–9, 50–1, 96–7, 99, 103–4, 108–9, 115, 117
  as *communio* 46–51
  as event 2, 25, 28, 30, 48, 50–1, 73, 76–7, 99–110, 115–22, 166–7, 169
  as invisible 24–5, 98
  realization of 96–7, 99, 101 n.189, 102 n.192, 105, 136 n.172
  space of 113–37
  sui generis sociological nature 2, 6, 9 n.18, 69 n.89, 77, 95–109, 116–24, 127–37, 138, 166
  time of 139–62
  as visible 24–5, 29–31, 98, 115–20, 123–4, 154–62
  witness of 38, 43–4, 57, 119–24, 128–33, 155–62
Clines, David J. A. 86 n.92
Coakley, Sarah 15 n.6

collective person (*Kollecktivperson*) 92–4, 95, 103, 105
compromise 124 n.77, 144–5, 147, 150, 159, 160–1, 163
confession 122–7, 134–7, 157
Congar, Yves 64 n.65, 107
covenant 4–5, 13–14
creation 34 n.154, 43, 85–92, 114, 148
  non-necessity of 2, 19, 24, 26, 51, 64 n.65, 73, 87, 92, 111, 143, 166
Creation and Fall 5, 56–7, 67, 68, 85
creatureliness 87–91
creed
  Apostles 65 n.68
  Nicene-Constantinopolitan 10 n.23, 64–5, 67, 108
Crossan, John Dominic 59 n.33

Davaney, Sheila Greeve 29 n.110, 31 n.125
de Boer, Martinus C. 61 n.51
de Gruchy, John W. 4 n.13
DeJonge, Michael P. 55 n.2, 66 n.77, 87 n.101, 88 n.111, 117 n.25, 125 n.78
de Lange, Fritz 63 n.63
de Lubac, Henry 22–3, 31 n.121, 49 n.247, 51 n.262
Discipleship 7, 56 n.6, 115
docetism, ecclesiological 24
Dodd, C. H. 59 n.33
Dodson, Christopher 132 n.138
dogmatic ecclesiology 3–4, 5, 13, 16–17, 37, 47 n.234, 52, 75–6, 165
  Bonhoeffer and 53–4, 62, 67 n.82, 72–3, 92, 106, 107, 110–12, 114, 138, 165–8
  'hard' 16, 17–29, 30, 31, 33, 37, 38, 41, 45–6, 48, 49 n.249, 51, 52
  'soft' 16, 45–52
Dramm, Sabine 59 n.34, 65 n.68
Dulles, Avery 17 n.8
Dumas, André 60 n.39, 66 n.77, 69 n.89
Dunn, James D. G. 59 n.33
Durham, John I. 57 n.18

ecclesial
  action 8, 11, 103–5, 141–2, 153–4, 155–63, 167–8

commission 8, 141–2, 155–63, 167–8
  human being 101–2, 110, 118, 119, 120–1, 133–4, 156
  responsibility 8, 105, 135–6, 141–2, 155–63, 167–8
ecclesiology
  asymmetry in 2, 4–5, 13–16, 95, 96–7, 105–6, 110–11
  and Christology 8–9, 34, 46, 51 n.262, 54, 64–7, 100 n.187, 101 n.189, 105 n.219, 165, 168–9
  detheologization of 33–35
  naturalization of 19–20, 33–7, 44–5
Elliot, Charles, *see* Adams, Nicholas
eschatology 55–63
  apocalyptic 10, 60–3, 126, 146 n.48, 168
  the church and 1–3, 5–8, 10, 46–51, 56–61, 62–5, 96–100, 124–7, 139–62, 165–6, 167–9
  last things 7, 8, 60 n.45, 64, 126, 141, 142–63, 167
  things before the last 7, 8, 60 n.45, 141, 142–63, 167
  this-worldly 60–1, 145–7
Ethics 7, 56 n.6, 126 n.91, 141, 148
ethnographic ecclesiology 3–4, 5, 13, 16–17, 29–45, 52, 53, 165
  Bonhoeffer and 53–4, 63, 65, 73, 75–7, 92, 96, 106, 107, 109, 110–12, 113–14, 125, 138, 165–8
  hard 16, 29–37, 41, 42, 44, 49 nn.246, 249, 52, 54, 71 n.96
  soft 16, 37–45, 51, 52, 54, 70 n.89
ethnography
  dogmatics and 3 n.12
  ecclesiology and 17 n.8, 27 n.99, 29–37, 38 n.170, 40 n.191, 41, 48 n.240, 169
eucharist 20–4, 49–51, 130, 131–3, 138, 157
extra ecclesiam nulla salus 101 n.189

faith 57 n.18, 69 n.86, 148 n.68, 150, 159
  the church and 24, 25 n.88, 31 n.126, 32–3, 40 n.191, 49 n.246, 71, 98 n.176, 101 n.190, 124
fides directa 57 n.18

fides reflexa 58 n.18
  the Holy Spirit and   101, 101 n.192, 129
  sacraments and   131–2
Fant, Clyde E.   128 n.97
Farrow, Douglas   21 n.46, 22, 63 n.63
Fatehi, Mehrdad   119 n.34
Feil, Ernst   56 nn.5, 6, 66 n.77, 67 n.82
Fergus, Donald M.   118 n.29
Fichte, Johann Gottlieb   81 n.52, 83
Finkenwalde   7, 66
Floyd, Wayne Whitson   66 n.77, 83 n.70, 83 n.72, 84
found theology   42
Freyer, Hans   82 n.60
Fulkerson, Mary McClintock   17 n.8, 32–4, 35

God
  freedom of   47, 87–9, 91, 108 n.251
  futurity of   57 n.18, 142 n.16
  kingdom of   22, 43, 50, 58 n.25, 59, 146 n. 52, 153
  patience of   7–8, 141–2, 148–55, 160, 161–2, 167–8
  as Trinity   46, 85, 86 n.101
Godsey, John D   65 n.77, 67 n.82
grammar, theological   4, 10, 38, 169
Green, Clifford J.   9 n.18, 60 n.46, 66 n.77, 69 n.89, 70 n.96, 81 n.54, 84 n.79, 87 n.101, 152 n.93
Greggs, Tom   3 n.8, 9–10, 15 n.6, 15 n.7, 26, 27 n.105, 64 n.63, 65 n.76, 66 n.77, 67 n.82, 85, 91 n.135, 100 n.187, 104 n.211, 105 n.217, 108 n.251, 117 n.25, 121, 132 n.137, 134 n.156, 136 n.171, 152 n.93, 169
Grenz, Stanley   85 n.90
Gunton, Colin E.   18 n.16, 46–8, 49 n.247, 50
Gustafson, James   31–2, 33, 34 n.150, 36

Haight, Roger   30, 34 n.149, 35
Hamilton, William   56 n.5, 6
Harasta, Eva   59 n.31, 65 n.75, 66 n.77, 67 n.82, 69 n.86, 93 n.144, 97, 98, 105 n.217
Hardy, Daniel W.   41–3, 45 n.225, 47 n.231, 50 n.251

Harink, Douglas   61, 62 n.56, 146 n.48, 151–2
Harvey, Barry   56 nn.6, 7, 60 n.41, 61 n.50, 66 n.77, 67 n.82, 71 n.96, 124, 125 n.80, 141 n.9
Hauerwas, Stanley   4 n.12, 17 n.8, 37–9, 44, 47 n.231, 48 n.240, 123 n.63
Healy, Nicholas M.   17 n.8, 39–41, 43–4
Hegel, Georg Wilhelm Friedrich   81, 83
Hegstad, Harold   30 n.113, 34 n.148, 35, 69 n.89
Höhne, David   63 n.63, 96 n.159
Holmes, Christopher R. J.   10 n.26, 60, 64 n.63, 87 n.101, 97 n.159, 99, 116, 129
Holyer Robert   56 n.6, 58 n.23
Holy Spirit
  the church and   1–3, 5–10, 22, 24–6, 40, 41–3, 46–51, 54–5, 57–68, 76–7, 95, 99–109, 113–37, 139–40, 155–63, 165–8, 169–70
Honecker, Martin   55 n.4, 57 n.14
hope   147, 149–50
  theologians of   61 n.49
Hopper, David H.   66 n.77
humanity   69 n.89, 92–33, 126 n.91, 148
  in Adam (*see* sin, being in Adam)
  in Christ   93 n.142, 97, 99, 100–1, 118–19, 129, 146, 156
  postlapsarian   90–1, 102 n.192
Hunsinger, George   87 n.101
Hütter, Reinhard   17 n.8, 40 n.193, 108 n.251

idealism
  dogmatic   18, 28, 30, 38–9, 40 n.191, 42, 47 n.234, 49 n.249, 52, 62, 73
  (post-Kantian) German   81, 83–4
imago Dei   85–6, 91

Janz, Paul D.   86 n.100, 143–4, 153 n.102, 154 n.104, 156 n.111
Jenson, Robert W.   46 n.226, 48–50, 51 n.262, 108 n.251
Jesus Christ
  as collective person (*Kollektivperson*)   93 n.142, 103

as human for others 93 n.142, 102 n.192, 104–5, 126 n.91, 135, 145, 152 n.93
as καινὸς ἄνθρωπος 47 n.234, 58–9, 72, 93 n.142, 125, 142–3, 149, 156
Jüngel, Eberhard 88 n.110, 151 n.86, 154 n.106, 157 n.123, 161
justification 142–4, 156
Holy Spirit and 97, 100–1, 118–20

Kant, Immanuel 81 n.52
Kelly, Geffrey B. 64 n.63
Kelsey, David 38, 121
Komonchak, Joseph 30, 35–6
Kuhns, William 66 n.77, 67 n.82
Küng, Hans 46 n.227, 47, 49 n.249, 51, 108 n.251

Lange, Ernst 124
Lawrence, Joel 67 n.82
Leahy, Brendan 66 n.77, 67 n.82, 105
Life Together 7
Lindbeck, George 4 nn.12, 14, 29 n.110
Lindsay, Mark 10, 56 nn.6, 7, 8, 142 n.14
love 100–6, 110, 118, 120–4, 133–7, 145, 151, 156–61
Luther, Martin 55 n.2, 66 n.77, 104 n.209, 125 n.78, 136 n.171
Lutheran 55, 97, 98 n.176, 99, 125 n.78, 136 n.171

McBride, Jennifer M. 62 n.59, 63 n.63, 66 n.77, 98 n.173, 126 n.91, 134 n.156, 135
Macquarrie, John 140, 141 n.9
Manoussakis, John Panteleimon 56 n.6, 146 n.48
Manrodt, David H. 10 n.25, 56 n.7, 60
Marsh Charles 60 n.34, 66 n.77, 69 n.89, 84 n.78, 80, 86 n.101, 88 n.110, 100 n.187, 107 n.236
Martyn, J. Louis 61 n.51, 62 nn.54, 55
Mawson, Michael 9 n.18, 64 n.63, 67 n.82, 69 nn.87, 89, 75 n. 2, 76 n.3, 84 n.79, 107 n.234, 108 n.247, 109 n.253, 132 n.135
Mayer, Rainer 55 n.4
Metz, Johannes B. 61 n.49
Milbank, John 20–1, 27 n.99, 41 n.196, 70 n.89

Moltmann, Jürgen 47 n.234, 48 n.240, 58 n.20, 59 n.34, 61 n.49, 83 n.72, 108 n.251
Moule, C. F. D. 119 n.34
Muers, Rachel 58 n.20, 60 n.36, 63 n.63, 66 n.77, 134, 149 n.69, 151, 161 n.147

Nelson, F. Burton, *see* Kelly, Geffrey B.
Nickson, Anne L. 63 n.63, 66 n.77, 87
Niebuhr, H. Richard 30 n.117, 31 n.126, 36 n.167
Nielsen, Kirsten Busch 98 n.176, 105 n.219
Nieman, James 34 n.149
Nimmo, Paul T. 25 n.86, 117 n.25
Norris, Kristopher 146 n.48
Nowers, Jeff 67 n.82, 102 n.192
Nygren, Anders 21 nn.44, 46, 22 n.62, 49 n.247, 51 n.262

objective spirit 81–3, 92, 93 n.144, 98 n.173, 100, 107
of the church 63 n.63, 95, 98 n.173, 100–1, 106–8, 109 n.253, 110, 118, 127, 128 n.99, 129, 130, 131 n.131
relation to Holy Spirit 63 n.63, 95, 98 n.173, 100–1, 106–9, 110, 118, 129–30
Ochs, Peter 42 n.203
O'Grady, Colm 28 n.107
ontology 36, 43, 60 n.39, 62 n.59, 70 n.89, 71 n.96, 83–92, 92 n.142, 104, 126 n.91, 156
order, dogmatic
in ecclesiology 3–4, 5, 13–20, 23–4, 26, 28, 29–30, 35–7, 39–40, 45, 46, 51, 52, 64–5, 69, 72–3, 76, 110–12, 113, 165–6, 169
Ott, Heinrich 55 n.4, 60 n.39, 66 n.77

Pangritz, Andreas 117 n.25
Pannenberg, Wolfhart 61 n.49, 123 n.62
Pasquarello III, Michael 128 n.97
Paul (the apostle) 13–14, 34, 61
Letter to the Colossians 34
Letter to the Corinthians 4, 5, 6, 10 n.10, 13, 14, 16, 57 n.18, 58 n.20, 59 n.26, 111, 128 n.99, 131 n.128, 134 n.153, 151

Letter to the Ephesians   10 n.23, 117 n.26, 128 n.99
Letter to the Romans   10 n.23, 58 n.20, 59 n.26, 97, 149
Pentecost   2, 60, 115, 116, 128, 140, 145, 146
  foundation of the church   7, 59, 99, 114, 115–27, 128 n.99, 133, 135, 137, 138, 167
Perrin, Norman   59 n.33
person (personhood)   63 n.61, 71 n.96, 77 n.11, 83–95, 109, *see also* anthropology, theological; ecclesial, human being
  God's own   85–9, 91
  and the Holy Spirit   84, 89–90, 91–2, 100–1, 120–1, 133–4
  I-You relation   83–5
Peter (the apostle)   121, 128
  Letter to Peter   148 n.63, 152–3
Pfeifer, Hans   64–5
phenomenology   7, 17, 114, 139, 152 n.93, 167
Phillips, John A.   65 n.77, 66 n.77
pneumatology, *see* Holy Spirit
preaching   106 n.228, 128–30
preparing the way   8, 141–2, 152–62, 167–8
priesthood
  of all believers   136 n.171
  of Christ   135, 136 n.171
  of the church   103–5, 135–6
proclamation, space of   7, 115, 118, 127, 128–33, 137–8
promeity   88, 92
pronobisity   92, 111
proportion, dogmatic
  in ecclesiology   2, 3–4, 5, 15–17, 20, 23–4, 26, 27–8, 30, 35–7, 41, 45, 46, 51–2, 53, 69, 72–3, 76, 110–12, 113, 165–6, 169
Przywara, Erich   86 n.100

Quash, Ben   40 n.187, 42 nn.203, 204

radicalism   124 n.77, 144–7, 150, 159–62
Rahner, Karl   40 n.191
Rasmussen, Larry   56 n.4
Rasmusson, Arne   44 n.221

Ratzinger, Joseph   23–4, 26–7, 35, 45
repentance   66 n.77, 94, 121, 129, 135, 149, 152–4, 157
Reuter, Hans-Richard   102 n.192

sacrament, *see* baptism; eucharist
sanctification
  Holy Spirit and   100–1, 118–20, 131
Sanctorum Communio   5, 6, 7, 55, 63 n.63, 65, 68–72, 77, 81, 92 n.142, 98 n.173, 115, 131 n.131, 137
Sanders, E. P.   59 n.33
Sauter, Gerhard   55 n.4, 61 n.49
Scharen, Christian B.   17 n.8, 27 n.99, 29 n.111, 169 n.2
Scheler, Max   80, 92 n.141
Schillebeeckx, Edward   17 n.8, 31
Schleiermacher, Friedrich   81 n.52
Schließer, Christine   66 n.77, 134 n.156
Schlingensiepen, Ferdinand   59 n.34
Schlink, Edmund   55 n.2
Schweitzer, Albert   59 n.33
Schwöbel, Christoph   20 n.34, 55 n.2, 113 n.1
Seeberg, Reinhold   57 n.13
Shreeves, Keir   128 n.97
sicut Deus   91
sin   33 n.143, 41 n.193, 69 n.89, 70 n.89, 90–1, 97 n.165, 101 n.192, 149
  being in Adam   69 n.89, 70 n.89, 92 n.142, 97, 126 n.91
  confession of   134–7, 158
  cor curvum in se   90, 93, 121
  ecclesial   31 n.121, 39, 52, 97–8, 108
  fall, the   90–1, 92 n.142
  forgiveness of   104 n.211, 134–7, 138, 142, 158
  harmartiology   92 n.142, 136 n.172
  individualism   90, 101–2, 107
social philosophy   68–72, 93 n.142
  atomistic   78 n.11
sociological formations
  association of rule (*Herrschaftsverband*)   94
  community (*Gemeinschaft*)   78–83, 92–4
  mass (*Masse*)   78 n.14
  society (*Gesellschaft*)   78–83, 92–4
sociology   68–72, 77 n.11, 93 n.142, 93 n.144, 98

formal-analytic 77–9
historical-philosophical 77 n.11
Sorum, Jonathan D. 56 n.6
space-time
  apocaplyse of 2–3, 61–2, 97–8, 114–15, 124–7, 139–40, 145–6, 150, 152 n.93, 157–8
  church in 1–2, 3, 5–8, 14–15, 21, 26, 28, 30–1, 37, 44–7, 50–1, 58, 72–3, 77, 96 n.159, 104, 110–11, 113, 115–38, 151–62, 166–8
  conditionality of 7, 141, 148–55, 158, 162
  eschatological nature 2, 7, 58–61, 114–15, 124–7, 145–6, 162, 166–7, 169
  preservation of 7, 119, 126, 140–2, 146–52, 159–61
spiritual care 134–7
space of 7, 115, 118, 127, 133–8
Stellvertretung (vicarious representative action) 9 n.20, 93 n.142, 102 n.192, 103–6, 133–6, 156–7
systematicity, theological 1 n.3, 15, 54–5, 65, 165

Tanner, Kathryn 29 n.110, 32
task, ecclesiological 2–4, 5, 9 n.18, 10–11, 14–16, 17, 19–20, 25–6, 29–30, 32–4, 38 n.170, 40 n.191, 41, 48 n.240, 68, 70 n.92, 114, 165, 168–70
theology
  convergence on culture 29
  deregionalization 18–19, 20
Thompson, Marianne Meye 34 n.154
Tietz, Christiane 66 n.77, 96 n.159, 105 n.219
Tönnies, Ferdinand 78–9

Torrance, Thomas F. 21, 22 n.51, 24, 26, 114 n.2, 139 n.2
Trinity, the 85, 86 n.101, 89
  the church and 17–19, 22, 40, 42–3, 45 n.225, 46–9, 50
  social trinitarianism 18, 45–6, 51
Troeltsch, Ernst 75 n. 2, 77 n.11
types, ecclesiological 2, 3 n.12, 13, 16–52, 53, 75–7, 95–112

van der Ven, Johannes A. 17 n.8, 30, 36 n.164
Volf, Miroslav 38 n.171, 50 n.257
von Balthasar, Hans Urs 39–40
von Rad, Gerhard 86 n.92
von Ranke, Leopold 62 n.57

Wannenwetsch, Bernd 98 n.176
Ward, Pete 17 n.8, 29 nn.109, 110, 30 n.112, 34, 169 n.2
Webster, John 3 n.8, 17–20, 21, 24, 25–6, 27, 28, 31 n.121, 35, 45, 51 n.263, 115 n.6, 120 n.44
Weiss, Johannes 59 n.33
Welch, Claude 3 n.9, 28 n.106, 31 n.126, 36
Welker, Michael 63 n.63
Werntz, Myles 64 n.63
Williams, Anna N. 2 n.3, 15 n.5
Wittgenstein, Ludwig 4 n.14
Woelfel, James W. 56 n.5, 66 n.77, 83 n.70
Wright, N. T. 59 n.33
Wüstenberg, Ralf K. 66 n.77, 152 n.93

Yeago, David S., *see* Buckley, James J.

Ziegler, Philip G. 55 n.3, 56 n.6, 60 n.35, 61–2, 123–4, 151 n.90
Zizioulas, John 50–1

www.ingramcontent.com/pod-product-compliance
Lightning Source LLC
Chambersburg PA
CBHW070638300426
44111CB00013B/2163